GNVQ Advanced

Leisure and Tourism

John Ward • Phil Higson •
William Campbell

STANLEY
THORNES

First published in 1994 by:
Stanley Thornes (Publishers) Ltd
Ellenborough House
Wellington Street
CHELTENHAM
Glos. GL50 1YD
United Kingdom

Reprinted 1995 (twice)

A catalogue record for this book is available from The British Library.

ISBN 0 7487 1744 7

Typeset by Columns Design & Production Services Ltd, Reading.
Printed and bound in Great Britain at The Bath Press, Avon

Contents

About this book

Its main purpose

The main purpose of this book is to provide background knowledge for students following GNVQ Leisure and Tourism courses. It will be of particular help in preparing for the unit tests required by these qualifications.

For many students, Leisure and Tourism will be an entirely new subject and the book will help to clarify many important concepts which explain the basis of how the industry operates. Understanding these is an important preparation for students beginning work on their own assignments.

The text includes background information, featuring case study material reflecting current industry practice. Tasks are integrated into the text to enable students to test their understanding and draw their own conclusions about relevant issues. Many of these tasks will also be useful in developing core skills.

The assignments

The assignments in this book are not intended to be detailed and prescriptive guidelines which will see students through an activity from start to finish without support from a tutor. They do, however, provide good starting points from which to develop structured tasks which are appropriate to a specific locality or group of students.

Many GNVQ units place emphasis on research within the school or college locality and so the assignments have been kept sufficiently flexible to accommodate this need. The resources needed for each assignment have not, for the most part, been specified. This will enable students themselves to consider how to identify what resources they need as they develop their individual action plans and negotiate with their tutors how they intend to approach each task. In particular, they will need to plan both what local resources they will need to complete the assignment and also how they might set about gathering these. It is worth bearing in mind that in order to achieve merit or distinction students must show evidence of their ability to plan, seek and handle information.

It is very likely that students will wish to adapt or modify some of the assignments suggested, so that they more accurately reflect their own interests or the resources to which they have access. They may also wish to add tasks to the assignments in order to cover a wider range of GNVQ performance criteria.

Centres wishing for more detailed assignments, covering all the elements of each GNVQ Leisure and Tourism unit, and based on specific examples of working practice in a range of leisure and tourism companies and organizations, would find the following books helpful:

Ward, John, *GNVQ Leisure and Tourism Assignments Book 1* (Stanley Thornes Publishers, 1993)

Ward, John, *GNVQ Leisure and Tourism Assignments Book 2* (Stanley Thornes Publishers, 1993)

Acknowledgements

The authors and publishers would like to thank the following people and organizations for permission to reproduce photographs and other material:

Elise Ward (pages 3, 153, 195, 229); The Mansell Collection (page 10); The Royal Pavilion Art Gallery & Museums (page 15); Bob Holland (pages 20, 45, 66, 111, 114, 124, 202, 214, 223, 244, 277); Thomson Travel Group (pages 32, 34); British Airways (page 40); English Tourist Board (pages 62, 196); The David Lloyd Clubs (page 69); Carl Munn (page 87); British Midland (page 97); Forte plc (page 101); The Tussauds Group (pages 105, 106, 147, 157); Canterbury Cathedral (page 125); Hancock Museum (page 150); American Express (page 181); Montagu Ventures Ltd (page 193); Melcourt Industries (page 207); The Princes Risborough Photographic Society (page 222); Ecotec/Calderdale Borough Council (page 231); Steve Troup (page 235); Imperial War Museum (page 248); Tony Stone Images and the Telegraph Colour Library for the cover photographs. All other photographs were supplied by the author.

Every effort has been made to contact copyright holders and we apologize if any have been overlooked.

1   Key definitions and terminology

What is covered in this chapter

This chapter establishes what is meant by the terms 'leisure' and 'tourism'. It shows how people make use of the greater leisure time now available to them. It considers the basic motives and purposes behind tourism, and provides an introduction to the structure of the industry, stressing the links between leisure and tourism.

- What is leisure?
- Growth of leisure time
- Different uses of leisure time
- What is tourism?
- Types of tourism
- Sectors of the tourism industry
- The growth of tourism
- The links between leisure and tourism

1.1 What is leisure?

Most people consider that during various parts of their daily lives their time is not their own. They may have to go to work, look after young children, study or attend meetings. A certain amount of their time will be taken up with physical needs like eating and sleeping. Whatever time remains beyond these duties and necessities is called **leisure**. People make individual choices about how to use this leisure time. The activities which they participate in during their leisure time are collectively described as **recreation**.

As Figure 1.1 shows leisure time is not evenly distributed among the population as a whole. Retired people have the most free time, while women in full-time employment have the least. This does not necessarily mean that retired people make the most use of leisure facilities since they may also belong to the group with the lowest incomes. This means that many expensive facilities, such as private golf clubs, may prove beyond their means.

Growth of leisure time

The increase in the amount of leisure time available is due to a variety of factors:
- working hours have been reduced;
- holidays with pay have become a legal entitlement for workers;
- life expectancy has increased;
- technological developments, like washing machines and dishwashers, have enabled people to spend much less time on domestic chores.

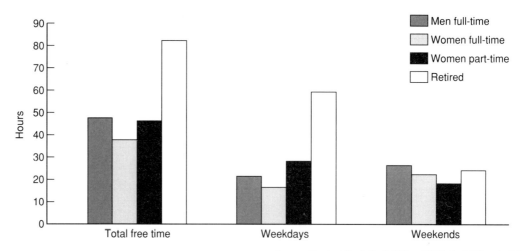

Source: Central Statistical Office 1992, *Social Trends 22*

Figure 1.1   Free time in a typical week, Great Britain 1990

Different uses of leisure time

The use of leisure time can be categorized in a number of ways. It may be active, as in the case of participating in a sport, constructing a model or doing DIY. On the other hand much leisure time is occupied passively, in doing things like watching television or listening to music. Much leisure time is spent in the home, but many people travel to make use of a wide range of available recreational facilities like theatres, sports centres and museums. Leisure activities themselves can be sub-divided into different areas of interest such as:

- sport;
- home entertainment;
- hobbies and pastimes;
- reading;
- public entertainment;
- holiday activities like sightseeing.

There is clearly a direct link between leisure and tourism in that tourists use part of their leisure time to go on holiday.

Activity

1 Draw up a list of selected leisure activities, either based on the one in Table 1.1 below, or drawn from your own interests.
2 Estimate what proportion of the weekly disposable income of your teaching group is spent on each of these activities.
3 Devise a questionnaire that you can use as a group to encourage your parents or older relatives to recall their leisure spending habits when they were your age.
4 What conclusions can be drawn from comparing the results of these two pieces of research?

Table 1.1 Percentage share of consumer spending by selected leisure activities

Activity	1986	1991	% growth 86–91
eating out	4.45	5.54	24
holidays	2.82	2.95	5
sports	1.48	1.89	28
recreational music	0.89	0.98	10
books	0.60	0.67	11
computers	0.25	0.28	12
alcohol	6.80	6.32	−7
gambling	0.81	0.67	−17
newspapers	0.97	0.84	−13

Source: Healey Centre 1992 – 'Planning for social change 1992–3'

1.2 What is tourism?

All forms of tourism involve movement from a place of residence to a destination. Generally tourists stay long enough in the destination to undertake activities and use facilities there. Since the destination is invariably outside the areas where the tourist lives and works, the presence of tourism generates activities which may be distinct from those of the local resident and working populations. Tourists may indulge in sun-bathing, swimming, souvenir shopping or taking photographs. Resident populations may also pursue these activities but not in such a concentrated way.

Tourists generally visit destinations for a fixed period of time, returning home at the end of it. In other words, visitors arriving at a destination in order to seek work or

A day at the seaside

find permanent accommodation are not regarded as tourists. However those arriving for a conference, a local event, a day trip or a business meeting would be included as tourists. This is because they meet most of the criteria applied in defining tourists. They travel to the destination, make a temporary stay, and use some of the services and facilities available there.

Types of tourism

Table 1.2 Why do people choose to travel?

Why do people choose to travel?	In which areas might these needs and desires be met?	What might tourists do to satisfy these needs?
1 To increase their feeling of physical well-being	– rest – relaxation – improved climate – physical activity – attractive/comfortable surroundings	– sleep longer, sit in a deckchair – sunbathe, read, chat – spend more time in the fresh air/ sunshine – walk, swim, exercise – experience picturesque scenery – stay in a luxury hotel
2 To satisfy a personal interest or curiosity	– in a particular foreign country – in the past – in art – in local tradition – in sport	– converse in a foreign language – visit historic sites and buildings – visit museums and galleries – experience music/dance performance – witness arts/crafts manufacture – observe/participate in events, activities or festivals
3 To improve, at least temporarily, the quality of their social life	– broadening circle of friends – improving family relationships – escape – entertainment	– join a club/take a special interest holiday – take an organized tour/cruise – spend more time together: do things together – get away from home/work pressures – forget stress/responsibilities – seek entertainment facilities more easily accessible/affordable than at home
4 To improve their work or social status	– education/learning opportunities – business – new experience	– attend courses/conferences: go on special interest holidays – attend meetings, discuss new projects, establish new contacts – seek less well-known places – buy unusual souvenirs

People become tourists for different reasons and tourism is often analysed on the basis of the main purpose behind individual travel. The most common motivations for tourism are:

- rest and relaxation;
- visiting friends and relatives;
- business.

Many visits combine several purposes. Other common reasons for travel include:
- study;
- medical treatments;
- pilgrimages and attendance at religious festivals;
- attending festivals, exhibitions and conventions;
- attending sporting events.

Other important distinctions are used to distinguish between different types of tourism. Overseas travel, or international tourism, has grown rapidly since the advent of cheaper charter flights, but in many parts of the world, including the United States, the majority of residents take holidays within their own country. This is known as **domestic tourism**.

The length of time visitors stay in a destination is used to distinguish tourists from **excursionists**, those who spend less than 24 hours in the location they are visiting. The length of the journey to the destination provides another criterion for different types of tourism. Destinations which can only be reached by a flight in excess of eight hours are commonly described as **long haul** destinations, while those requiring a shorter journey are referred to as **short haul** destinations.

Sectors of the tourism industry

One of the problems in analysing the tourism industry arises from the difficulty of deciding where its boundaries lie. Many of the sectors which form part of the whole, such as transport and retailing, are also providing services to non-tourists at the same time. The most important sectors of the tourism industry are:
- transport (e.g. air, rail, ferry and road services);
- accommodation and catering (e.g. hotels, restaurants);
- tour operators and travel agents;
- visitor attractions and events;
- services (e.g. financial, guides, tourist information);
- tourist organizations (e.g. regional and national tourist boards, Automobile Association (AA)/Royal Automobile Club (RAC), local government departments).

The growth of tourism

The increased demand for tourism is the product of the same reasons which led to the growth of leisure time generally – shorter working hours and a shorter working life, paid holidays, less time spent on domestic chores and an increasing emphasis on the desirability of developing leisure, as well as work interests and skills. Additional factors include:
- an increase in average disposable income;
- greater mobility;
- improved marketing of holidays and destinations;
- a·reduction in the cost of air fares;
- greater emphasis on the need to escape daily stress.

Demand for tourism and leisure is affected by changes in the economic and political climate. Tourism and leisure both require time and money. In a recession people tend to have more time and less money. Political changes can quickly reduce the appeal of some destinations, for example the recent politically motivated attacks on tourists in Egypt. In countries like Britain, where the population spends a greater amount on

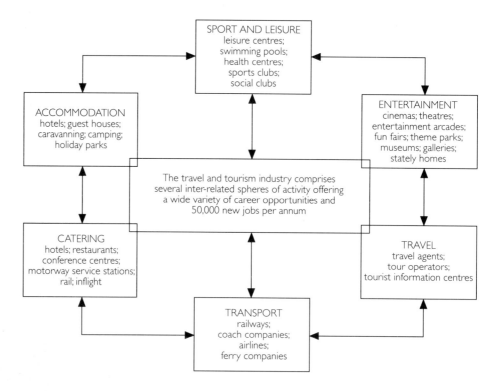

Figure 1.2 The travel and tourism industry

holidays overseas than is received from incoming tourists, the government supports initiatives aimed at increasing the amount of domestic tourism.

Links between leisure and tourism

Tourists create a demand for leisure facilities because, during the period of their stay away from home, little of their time is taken up with work responsibilities. Leisure facility providers attempting to meet this demand face the problem that, while local demand for leisure facilities may remain constant, the demand from tourists is likely to reveal significant seasonal differences.

There are strong economic links between tourism and leisure. A recent report by the Sports Council estimated that domestic tourists and overseas visitors between them spent £1.6 billion a year on sport in the UK. Activities like cycling, walking and golf have become a focus for the development of existing and new tourist resorts. Participation in sports like sailing, cycling and orienteering has increased at the expense of the numbers taking part in team sports. International sporting events, like the Olympic Games, attract a range of national applications not simply because the potential host nations have an interest in athletics. The main appeal lies in the spending power of the large number of foreign visitors who will be attracted by the event. A number of cities around the world, including Birmingham, Glasgow and Sheffield in the UK, have used major leisure developments as a means of regenerating city centres. They worked on the principle that an improved living environment for local people would attract more individuals and businesses with money to invest in the area.

Table 1.3, taken from a joint policy statement by the West Country Tourist Board and the south-west region of the Sports Council, illustrates some of the connections between sporting activities and tourism.

Table 1.3 Main sporting activities undertaken by tourists in the West Country

Activity	Percentage participating
Hiking, hill walking	undertaken by 20% of the holiday visitors to the West Country
Swimming	by far the biggest activity on holiday – 24% of the total holiday market
Angling	undertaken by around 4% of holidaymakers
Motor/sail boating, canoeing, windsurfing	powered boating is undertaken by around 2% of holiday visitors, while sailing and other watersports are pursued by 4%

Activity

1 List the most popular leisure facilities in your area.
2 Devise a method of research to establish what proportion of the users of each of three of these facilities are local and what proportion travel to them from outside the region.
3 Suggest three factors or actions which might increase the number of local users and three factors or actions which might increase the number of users drawn from outside the region.

Assignment 1
The leisure and tourism industry

This assignment develops knowledge and understanding of the following elements:
1.1 Describe the scale and contexts of the leisure and tourism industry
1.2 Investigate UK leisure and tourism products
1.3 Investigate the variety of local services and products

It supports development of the following core skills:
Communication 3.1, 3.2, 3.3

A new television series entitled *Industrial Change in the Twentieth Century* is being planned for students in the 16–19 age group. One episode will focus on the leisure and tourism industry.

Your tasks

1 Describe *ten* one-minute film excerpts that you would include in this episode, to illustrate important moments in the industry's development, as well as highlighting current trends.

2 Write the commentary that would accompany each of these excerpts.

2 Patterns and trends in leisure and tourism

What is covered in this chapter

This chapter outlines the most significant changes in people's use of leisure time over the last two centuries, focusing particularly on factors which changed their travel habits. It reviews current trends in leisure and tourism by examining tourism employment patterns, the activities in which tourists participate and the spending habits of tourists.

- The nineteenth century
- The twentieth century
- The current state of leisure and tourism

2.1 The nineteenth century

Travel and tourism

The growth of leisure travel

Holiday centres existed in England in the eighteenth century and were often associated with medical cures. For those who could afford to travel and spend time waiting for the cures to take effect, places like Bath and Cheltenham, with their spa waters, or Brighton and Bognor Regis, offering the benefits of sea bathing, attracted visitors. As their numbers grew, so did the demand for accommodation and entertainment, though these resorts remained largely the province of the wealthy until the spread of the railway system in the nineteenth century. Travel overseas was similarly an indulgence available only to the rich. During the eighteenth century a 'Grand Tour' of Europe's major cities – in particular Paris, Rome, Florence and Venice – had been regarded as a valuable part of a young aristocrat's education. Since most transport was horse-drawn such journeys could only be undertaken by those with unlimited amounts of time available to them.

Even by the nineteenth century travel was still limited by the speed of the transport available and by the state of the roads. Many roads were subject to a turnpike system which required passengers to stop and pay tolls as they passed. Stage coaches were still a common form of travel between towns, only disappearing in the middle of the century as the railway network spread. Routes were rapidly laid between major towns and cities, and rail proved a much cheaper means of travel than existing road services. Hotels were built close to many of the major railway stations.

Transport developments, especially of steam boats and railways, provided a major boost to British holiday resorts. Places like Margate, Blackpool and Southport grew as a result of direct transport links with major cities. Day trippers stepped off paddle steamers on to the end of newly-erected piers or took rail excursions from industrial cities to the coast. The Industrial Revolution saw a flow of people moving from agricultural occupations to work in mills and factories, considerably swelling the urban populations, as well as increasing their earning potential.

Increases in international travel

The middle of the century saw a rise in the number of overseas travellers, though it still represented only a very small fraction of the population as a whole. After the success of the Great Exhibition at Crystal Palace in 1851, which drew huge numbers of visitors from far and wide, the Paris Exhibition of 1855 prompted Thomas Cook to organize his first overseas tour. He opened a London office in 1865 and organized his first American tour in the following year. Regular ferry services across the Channel and to Ireland were in operation by the 1860s. Though still mainly the preserve of the wealthy, other overseas destinations, such as Italy and Switzerland, were the subject of a growing number of organized tours. India and the Far East became much easier to reach as a result of the opening of the Suez Canal in 1869. In the same year a link between the Union Pacific and Central Pacific railways meant that the USA could be completely crossed by rail. In the 1880s the first skiing holidaymakers departed from Britain to Switzerland.

Shipping

Shipping in particular flourished, boosted by improvements in ship design. Steam power and iron hulls made long voyages quicker and safer, and regular transatlantic services became a reality. Cunard began a regular service to America in 1840, while P & O sailed regularly to India and the Far East. Shipping companies earned valuable income from carrying transatlantic post. Steamship services ran along major English

The Great Exhibition in Hyde Park, London, 1851

rivers like the Thames and the Avon, and there were regular services between London and Margate, and London and Gravesend. Services from Liverpool to New Brighton, Rhyl, Llandudno and the Isle of Man hastened the development of those destinations as holiday centres.

Railways

Railways were probably the single most significant factor in the nineteenth century that affected how people spent their holidays. The Liverpool and Manchester Railway was opened in 1830 and others followed so that, by the middle of the century, there was over 7000 miles of track. Agreements between the different companies eventually meant that passengers could travel uninterrupted across track belonging to different companies. The system created opportunities for excursions such as those arranged by Thomas Cook, whose first organized rail excursion in 1841, from Leicester to Loughborough, cost exactly one shilling!

New uses of leisure time

Expansion of leisure activities

The Bank Holiday Act of 1871 created four public holidays a year and it rapidly became a tradition for workers to take day trips to the coast or the countryside, particularly on August Bank Holiday. Activities such as walking, cycling and skiing formed the basis of organized holidays for the first time, reaffirming the connection between holidays and health.

The choice of leisure activities expanded during the second half of the century. The theatre was popular – with melodrama and music hall having a wide appeal. Sport increased its importance as a spectator activity, evidenced by such movements as the foundation of the Football League in 1888 and the holding of the first modern Olympic Games in 1896.

Activity

Use your local reference library to help you compile a short report about some of the ways in which people living in your area 100 years ago used their leisure time.

Your report might include reference to sport, public performances, fairgrounds and festivals.

2.2 The twentieth century

Travel and tourism

Car ownership

The early years of the twentieth century saw a considerable increase in the private ownership of cars. In 1902 63 motor cars took part in a reliability trial, making the journey from Crystal Palace to Folkestone and back at an average speed of 8 miles per hour! The trial drew the conclusion that cars were almost as reliable as, even if considerably more expensive than, railways, though they were inclined to cause upset to some of the many horse-drawn vehicles still on the road. Descriptions of August Bank Holiday in 1906 suggest that many Londoners took advantage of a heatwave to take trips in horse-drawn trams up to Hampstead Heath, at a cost of two pence. The Ford Motor Company was formed in Detroit in 1903, and in the same year the British Parliament required all private cars to be numbered and registered. Bus and coach services began to appear in the years immediately following the First World War.

Increase in road traffic

Car ownership increased steadily after the First World War, resulting in a decline in the fortunes of bus and coach companies. Previously inaccessible areas were exposed to tourism, resulting in the opening of roadside restaurants, country hotels, and camping and caravan sites. The first Butlins holiday camp was opened in 1937 at Skegness, sparking an enthusiasm for holiday camps, with their on-site facilities and ready-made entertainment, which was well established by the outbreak of war in 1939.

These factors contributed to the increase in the volume of traffic, which in turn necessitated an improvement in the national road system. Stretches of dual carriageway and eventually the development of a motorway system considerably reduced the time required to travel by road between major cities. In more recent times, however, traffic congestion and parking problems in cities, as well as concerns about the atmospheric pollution created by car exhaust emissions, have encouraged a revival in the profitability of some inter-city rail routes. High speed trains have considerably cut journey times between cities and, for business travellers especially, enabled the travelling time to be used profitably. The improvement of road links to Channel ports like Dover encouraged families to take their own cars to the Continent. Holiday companies developed packages offering motorists ferry tickets, overnight *en route* stopping places and holiday accommodation.

Shipping decline

Ships had dominated many of the world's international routes between the wars and it was not until the mid 1950s that a greater number of passengers crossed the Atlantic by air than by sea. The number of passengers opting for sea travel on long distance routes fell sharply from this point. Some shipping lines attempted to adapt passenger liners as cruise ships, but their design was not generally well suited to this change of use. Cross-Channel ferry services did flourish, and the introduction of hovercraft and hydrofoils considerably reduced the time taken on some crossings. A new breed of cruise ships emerged and quickly became successful where a range of ports of call were within easy reach, for example in the Mediterranean and the Caribbean.

Activity

No cruise line runs a regular service which circumnavigates Britain. A shipping company comes up with the idea of a Round Britain Cruise. You are part of a working party whose role is to discuss generally the feasibility of this idea. Discuss the following questions.

1 What sort of market might the idea appeal to and why ?
2 What kind of ship, and what sort of facilities, would be needed to satisfy the needs of the market you have identified?
3 What ports of call would you recommend and why ?
4 What factors might make it very difficult to operate this service at a profit?

Railways

The period between the wars saw a rise in road traffic, mainly at the expense of the railways. Four railway companies – the Great Western Railway, London Midland Scottish, London North Eastern Railway and the Southern Region – were established in 1921. Local rail services suffered from lack of investment in the inter-war years. Railways generally were still dependent on the shipment of industrial requirements, like coal and oil, and manufacturing products, for their profits. The economic decline of the late 1920s and early 1930s considerably reduced the amount of freight which needed transportation. At the same time road haulage companies were setting up in competition with the railway companies. One of the few areas in which railway traffic increased during these years was the Bank Holiday excursions to the coast. It was estimated that 500,000 visitors crowded into Brighton on August Bank Holiday 1935, the majority arriving by train or special coach. In 1936 the first train ferry service between Dover and Dunkirk was launched. Trains leaving Victoria station at 10 p.m. would arrive in Paris at 8.55 the following morning and passengers would not have had to leave their sleeping compartment at any point on the journey.

Air travel

The First World War stimulated an interest in the potential of air travel. The 1920s saw air services develop both in Germany and in America, though initially these were primarily mail services. British companies, such as Imperial Airlines, flew mail to India and the colonies. For a time civil flying was still banned, and so the first air service between London and Paris catered mainly for military passengers. The flight took $3^1/2$ hours at an average speed of 97 miles per hour. In 1924 there was the most serious air crash in Britain suffered up to that time when eight people died as a flight from Croydon to Paris crashed shortly after take-off. Throughout the 1930s air travel remained beyond the means of all but the wealthy and was still not a particularly fast or reliable means of transport. It was not until 1939 that Pan Am's Dixie Clipper made the first transatlantic passenger flight. However, several developments prior to the war were to have a significant impact later. In 1935 Gatwick aerodrome was opened with the intention of relieving some of the congestion at Croydon. It was to have its own railway station on the London–Brighton line and its air traffic control system improved on previous capabilities by handling six aircraft at a time!

Airline development

The existence of large numbers of trained pilots in the years after the war was a factor in rapid airline development. London's main air terminal was moved from Croydon to Heathrow. The pace of change was such that initially passenger reception was carried out in tents. A nationalized company, the British Overseas Airways Corporation (BOAC), operated a number of long range services, few of which were profitable. British European Airways (BEA), specializing in shorter European routes, was financially more successful. The two companies were eventually merged in 1971 when they were jointly administered by the British Airways Board. From the point of view of the passenger the most rapid advance presented by air travel was the time taken to cover long distances. A few days before the outbreak of war the first jet-powered aeroplane, designed by Heinkel, had been tested in Germany. By 1945, the average cruising speed of the larger passenger aircraft, boosted by technological improvements developed during the war, was more than twice what it had been in 1939. However, airliners still carried only a fraction of the passengers they can handle currently. The Lockheed Constellation aeroplane, for example, which carried many Pan Am and TWA passengers in the late 1940s and early 1950s had to be modified to increase its passenger capacity from 44 to 81.

Use of leisure time

Choice of leisure activities

The choice of available leisure activities continued to grow during the twentieth century. The century had begun, in 1901, with the first transatlantic wireless message sent by Marconi from Cornwall in England and picked up in Newfoundland in Canada. By 1910 Edison had demonstrated the first talking pictures and D. W. Griffith had made *In Old California*, the first film from Hollywood. In 1926 John Logie Baird demonstrated the principle of transmitting moving pictures by wireless and in the same year plans were laid for the establishment of a public broadcasting corporation named after a previous company owned by the wireless makers, the BBC. A year later came the first film with live dialogue, *The Jazz Singer*, starring Al Jolson. It was not until 1936, however, that the first talking pictures on television were transmitted from the BBC's Alexandra Palace studios to a showroom at Olympia. Radio remained the major source of home entertainment until the 1950s. The Coronation of Queen Elizabeth II in 1953 prompted a 25 per cent increase in television ownership within a single year.

In Britain greyhound racing was introduced in 1926 at Belle Vue Stadium, Manchester, and its instant popularity saw further tracks developed at Wembley, White City and Haringey. Rambling became established as an organized leisure

West Pier, Brighton, between the wars

activity, though not without some initial difficulties. A mass trespass was staged in the Peak District in 1932, aimed at highlighting the issue of public access to mountains and moors. Five people were arrested in this protest about the proportion of moorland which was privately owned and reserved for activities like grouse shooting. At the time only 1,212 acres of the Peak District's total of 150,000 acres was then open to the public.

In 1937 the government launched a national keep fit campaign. A central feature of this campaign was the provision of more leisure amenities, including gymnasiums, playing fields, swimming baths, camp sites, community centres and a national college of physical training.

The emergence of the tourism industry

Holiday entitlement

In 1938 the government passed the Holidays with Pay Act, and by doing so removed an obstacle to many potential holidaymakers. However the agreements on paid holidays were voluntary and the intervention of the Second World War meant that it was perhaps a decade before the Act began to have any observable impact on people's travel behaviour.

Activity

Read the following extract about the costs of staying in Blackpool in 1937:

> Bed and breakfast cost from 3 shillings to 7 shillings and sixpence. For full board, which meant a room with breakfast, midday meal and high tea at six o'clock, you would pay from 6 shillings to 9 shillings and sixpence in a boarding house. If you wanted to go up the scale and chose a licensed hotel, you paid 15 shillings for full board. Those who had bed and breakfast picked up odd meals in the small cafes along the sea front, and for steak and chips they paid between 1 shilling and sixpence and 2 shillings and sixpence. A cup of coffee was 4 pence.

Source: Looking Back at Holidays by Maggie Angeloglou, EP Publishing, 1975

1 Using the figures given estimate the costs for a party of four adults to take (a) the cheapest, (b) the most expensive 1937 holiday to Blackpool.
2 Given that 2 shillings is the equivalent of 10p, convert these two estimates into modern currency values.
3 Estimate the cost of a week's holiday in a seaside resort now (a) in a boarding house, (b) in a small to medium sized hotel.
4 If the average weekly earnings in 1937 were roughly £6 and they are now approximately £300, what conclusions can you draw about the relative holiday costs then and now?

Package holidays

Travellers in the 1950s were discouraged from going abroad by the imposition of a travel allowance which in 1953 stood at £40. The upper limit on this travel allowance fluctuated according to the prevailing economic conditions and did not finally disappear until 1970.

The beginnings of modern British holiday traditions can perhaps be most clearly seen in the departure of the first de Havilland Comet turbojet from London to Johannesburg in 1952. Though only 36 passengers were carried and the flight required 5 stops during its 24-hour duration, it was a major step towards making air travel accessible to a mass market. The Boeing company in America quickly produced larger, more economical planes, the most influential of which was the Boeing 707. The emergence of these revolutionary jets, most of which were bought by national airlines running scheduled services, left a glut of propeller aircraft which charter airlines were able to purchase at low prices. By 1970 the first jumbo jet, the Boeing 747, had carried 352 passengers on a single transatlantic flight.

Horizon is generally credited with organizing the first package holiday, to Corsica, in 1950, but others quickly followed, targeting especially resorts in the Mediterranean. Low profit margins and the seasonal nature of package tourism led the surviving tour operators to extend their products during the 1970s. This was initially achieved through skiing and winter sun packages, but by 1980 the International Leisure Group was offering cheap holidays to Florida, more distant but with a much longer 'warm' season. The appeal of Disneyworld, as well as favourable dollar exchange rates, meant that during the 1980s Orlando became one of the most popular overseas destinations for British tourists. Self-catering holidays were also developed as a means of appealing to families seeking both flexible and economic holiday arrangements. Table 2.1 gives an indication of the increase in the numbers of UK citizens who have travelled overseas in the last 40 years.

Table 2.1 Total outbound passengers (business and leisure)

1953	3.8
1958	5.8
1963	8.1
1968	12.4
1973	21.8
1978	29.3
1983	36.5
1988	47.9
1990	53.2

(figures in millions)

Source: Central Statistical Office

Problems created by the rapid rise of the travel industry

The rapid growth of the travel industry was not without its problems. In 1974 Court Line, the owners of a major holiday company called Clarksons, went out of business with debts of £50 million. Up to 100,000 holidays were lost and 50,000 tourists were stranded abroad. The company's collapse highlighted issues of how holidays were priced and how existing bonds to protect clients against companies going out of business were totally inadequate. Laker Airways, which had attempted to challenge the major national airlines with cheaper transatlantic tickets, went out of business in 1982 after only five years of operation.

International events in more recent times have also taken a hand in affecting the business of tour operators. The combination of the Gulf War and a recession contributed to the collapse of the International Leisure Group, operators of Intasun and Air Europe, in 1991. High interest rates charged on the purchase of new aircraft coincided with a reluctance of the public to spend money on holidays, both because of their personal reduced spending power and because of the fears of terrorist activity against British aircraft.

Impressions of work in Mackay Brothers travel agency in Aberdeen in 1953
Discounting was completely unknown in 1953. There was a price in the programme and that was the price the client paid. Selling for the summer season began in March and was more leisurely than today. The period from October to March was as quiet as April to September was hectic. Very few people could afford holidays abroad in winter as the foreign currency allowance was £25 per person which had to include the net cost of the hotel. Overseas package holidays were mainly by rail and the distinction between travel agents and tour operators was more blurred in those days, with many agents putting together their own holiday packages. For example Mackay Brothers ran a seven night trip to Kitzbuhel by rail for just over £36 – nearly £44 if you went by air.

Source: quoted in *Travel Trade Gazette*, 40th Anniversary Supplement

The role of tourist boards in the development of tourism

The Development of Tourism Act of 1969 saw the establishment of the British Tourist Authority, and the Scottish and Wales Tourist Boards. The Act showed government recognition of the importance of the tourism industry, both as an employer and as a generator of income. It made provision both for a more co-ordinated marketing effort to attract overseas visitors to Britain, and for an improvement in the facilities and attractions which might appeal to these visitors. Local grants were made available to stimulate the development of hotels, attractions and other tourist facilities. The actual number of foreign visitors to the UK has certainly mushroomed since, with a figure of 5 million recorded in 1969 having more than trebled to 18.5 million by 1992.

The English Tourist Board (ETB) co-ordinates the work of 11 regional tourist boards – covering Cumbria, East Anglia, East Midlands, Heart of England, London, Northumbria, North West, South East, Southern, West Country, and Yorkshire and Humberside. Central funding is devolved to these regional boards which also raise money from the local tourism industry and from commercial activities. Their activities include:

- regional strategy and development (e.g. Local Area Initiatives);
- marketing campaigns (e.g. short breaks to the area);
- classification and grading of accommodation (see ETB leaflet below);
- tourist information centre networking;
- participation in staff training schemes.

Source: ETB Annual Report 1993

Sure signs of where to stay

2.3 The current state of leisure and tourism

Present trends in tourism

The contribution of tourism to the economy

In 1990 spending by overseas visitors to Britain was estimated at £6.88 billion. This figure had risen to £7.9 billion by 1992. Of these visitors 43 per cent are holidaymakers, while 21 per cent are on business trips and 21 per cent are visiting friends or relatives. When added to the spending generated by domestic tourism, the importance of the total turnover of the tourism industry to the national economy is clear. In 1989 it was calculated to represent over 4 per cent of the total UK gross domestic product (GDP).

Tourism spending has continued to grow despite the problems of the worldwide economy. Table 2.2 gives an indication of this steady upward trend.

Table 2.2 Total holiday expenditure (4+ night holidays) 1965–91

Year	Britain £m	Abroad £m	Total £m
1965	460	265	725
1968	570	320	890
1971	810	630	1260
1974	1100	740	1840
1977	1570	1360	2930
1980	2420	3510	5930
1983	2640	5000	7640
1986	3050	6740	9790
1989	3820	10150	13970
1991	4670	11310	15980

Source: British National Travel Survey/British Tourism Survey Yearly

It was not until 1978 that spending by British holidaymakers overseas first exceeded their spending on domestic tourism, but by 1991 70 per cent of the money the British spent on holidays was spent on holidays abroad. The major growth came in the 1970s when, for example, spending on overseas holidays grew almost five-fold between 1974 and 1980. The growth in spending on domestic holidays shows a far more steady increase. In fact, the most recent figures suggest a possible eventual reverse in the trend for the growth in overseas spending to outstrip that on domestic holidays. In the period 1989–91, the increase in domestic spending rose by 22 per cent, as against an 11 per cent rise in overseas spending. A number of factors may account for this – unfavourable exchange rates, the Gulf War, recession, and an increase in spending on second holidays and short breaks.

Cost is a factor in determining whether people choose to holiday abroad or not. Table 2.3 shows the estimated expenditure and average size of the groups travelling on holidays in Great Britain over four nights, and those taken abroad for more than one night. It suggests that on average people spend more on overseas holidays than they do on domestic ones, with the cost of air travel being a major factor accounting for the difference. In the period covered by these statistics it could be argued that the percentage increase in spending on domestic holidays has more than matched that on overseas holidays. The late 1970s saw sharp rises in holiday expenditure, both domestic and overseas, with a much steadier rate of growth since. The average party size suggests that more families with children take holidays within the UK than overseas, though a slight increase in the size of parties going overseas is matched by a slight decrease in the size of parties taking domestic holidays.

Table 2.3 Estimated expenditure incurred on British holidays and holidays abroad, and estimated party sizes

	1974	1976	1978	1980	1982	1984	1986	1988	1990	1991
Average cost of GB holiday per person (£)	27	39	44	67	78	88	98	112	129	137
Average size of GB party	2.6	2.6	2.6	2.6	2.4	2.4	2.5	2.4	2.4	2.5
Average cost of holiday abroad per person (£)	107	162	201	287	327	351	376	443	507	550
Average size of party going abroad	1.9	2.0	2.1	2.0	2.0	2.0	2.0	2.1	2.1	2.1

Source: British National Travel Survey/British Tourism Survey Yearly

Activity

1 Taking into account the average party size, calculate the actual average amount spent by the British on domestic and overseas holidays for the years listed in Table 2.3.
2 Use computer software to represent these data in a format which you think shows the contrasts most clearly.

Advances in technology

Technology has had a major impact on travel arrangements in recent times. Transactions which include booking, confirmation and the issue of tickets can be carried out instantly on a computer screen. Larger travel agency chains are equipping counter staff with personal computers which should eventually enable them to make travel arrangements through all the available computer reservations systems (CRSs). These CRSs provide central banks of information about scheduled airline bookings, car rental, hotel accommodation and the booking of leisure activities such as sport or the theatre. A queuing system is used to manage incoming messages from airlines and hotels so that none are lost. Individual requirements of different clients can be held in the systems and automatically implemented whenever they make a reservation. CRSs make it possible to identify unsold holidays rapidly, enabling tour operators to react with special offers or promotions. The next stage the travel industry will face is the potential for clients to book holidays direct through computer terminals or adapted television sets. Travel agents would have to demonstrate that the advantage of convenience would be more than outweighed by the loss of specialist information and advice.

Air traffic control at Luton Airport

Computers have revolutionized other aspects of leisure and travel. Notable examples would include air traffic control, automated aircraft flying and landing procedures, computerized navigation, automated baggage handling, hotel management and security systems, automated leisure club membership and payment systems, and computerized fitness machines.

> **Features of the Galileo Central System**
> - Serves over 11,000 terminals in 2,250 agencies
> - Guarantees seats with more than 130 airlines
> - Obtains credit card approvals
> - Provides on-screen access to latest information
> - Links with RoomMaster, providing access to and information about 27,000 properties and 184 hotel chains
> - Links with CarMaster, giving access to 44 major worldwide car hire companies at 15,000 locations
> - Links with Product Directory, offering services including entertainment bookings, foreign currency and insurance, and training

However, computers are not the only major technological change of recent times. The development of new materials offering greater flexibility, durability and strength has affected the design of aeroplanes, cars, furnishings, communications systems and sports equipment. Composite materials, made by bonding together two different substances, have proved particularly valuable. For example, thin carbon fibres embedded in plastic have been used to produce stronger, lighter frames for tennis rackets. Similar materials have been used for the casings of jet engines. Optical fibres, made from sand, have replaced copper wires for sending telephone messages. They are cheaper, easier to obtain and suffer from less interference.

Environmental concerns mean that research will continue into alternative fuel sources for transport. For example magnetic levitation (sometimes called maglev) is used on some railway systems and was first introduced on the service between Birmingham airport and the railway station which serves it. The system uses the properties of magnets to attract and repel, both to lift the trains off the track and to move them forwards. Apart from the fact that the system produces no noxious exhaust it also considerably reduces maintenance costs. Similar concerns may lead to a re-examination of the feasibility of using airships on a more regular basis, and of extending the range and capacity of electrically-powered vehicles.

Competition

Competition between the multiples and the small independent companies has dominated the travel agency scene throughout the 1980s and into the 1990s. Table 2.4 shows the increase in the number of branches which the main multiples now operate.

Table 2.4 Increase in travel agency branches (ABTA figures)

Company	1983	1993
Lunn Poly	70	662
Thomas Cook	192	390
Pickfords	207	335
A.T. Mays	75	301
Hogg Robinson	84	254
Co-op Travelcare	36	172

However, a large number of small independent companies continue to operate, often specializing in particular destinations or types of holiday. Their provision of a wider range of products and their ability to create tailor-made travel arrangements should ensure their survival at a time when a significant number of clients seem to be turning away from traditional package deals. The multiples are able to extract very high rates of commission, sometimes as high as 17.5 per cent, from their suppliers, but they will often only deal with a limited number of tour operators. Discounting has commonly been used as a means of increasing market share, while special low deposit offers are also a common means of attracting clients away from competitors.

Vertical integration

Vertical integration, whereby a single company extends its activities into another stage of the distribution process, is the current target of a number of travel companies. They seek to gain a controlling interest in a tour operation, an agency chain and an airline. This enables them to sell their own products without paying commission and gives them priority in purchasing airline seats. It also allows significant economies of scale, lowering costs because of the increased purchasing power of a larger organization. The most obvious examples are the Thomson organization which took over the travel agency chain, Lunn Poly, and the airline, Britannia Airways, and Airtours, a tour operator with its own airline, which purchased the travel agency chains, Pickfords and Hogg Robinson (since renamed 'Going Places'). The issue of whether these alliances give sufficient customer choice has resulted in the matter being referred to the Office of Fair Trading.

Airtours' purchase of travel agencies is a good example of **forward integration**, where a producer acquires another business which operates nearer to the final customer. This represents an attempt to guarantee outlets for sales. An example of **backward integration** is where a tour operator buys into an airline in order to guarantee enough seats for its package holiday travellers. The tendency towards vertical integration is increased when firms are uncertain about trends in their industry, a circumstance which has certainly been true in the travel industry in the 1990s.

The hospitality industry

The recession of the early 1990s has resulted in changes in the hospitality industry. As room rates fell, hotels were forced to review their pricing policies. Customers have come to expect discounted prices at hotels. Hotels were also hit by the dramatic fall in property values. Owners with high mortgages could find the sum borrowed standing at a higher level than the market value of the property. As visitor numbers increased in 1992 and 1993, average UK occupancy rose. Some of that improvement was due to the opening of more chain-owned budget lodges. The sector's difficulties led to a number of cost-cutting exercises, both by making hotel staff redundant, and by cutting the costs of wages, food and beverage. Table 2.5 shows a comparison of average hotel costs and profits for the years 1991/2 and 1992/3.

Table 2.5 Profit and loss account – hotels sector (in £ millions)

	1991/2	1992/3
Turnover	12,587.6	12,303.7
Wage costs	4,262.4	3,953.2
Food and beverage costs	2,819.5	2,586.0
Other purchases	2,844.8	2,717.2
Total bought-in costs	5,664.2	5,303.2
Operating profit	2,661.0	3,047.2

Source: Pannell Kerr Forster Associates/ Caterer & Hotelkeeper

Employment in hotels stands at just below a quarter of a million people, of which 60 per cent are female. A recent hotel catering and training company report suggested that 44 per cent of the total hotel workforce is made up of part-time employees. With payroll costs amounting to almost one-third of turnover, it is easy to see why staff cuts appear to be the easiest way to save money. Hotels will have to face the issue of the extent to which cost-cutting affects levels of service and as a consequence makes the product less attractive to customers.

Activity

The following pie chart in Figure 2.1 shows what proportion of all meals produced by catering companies and organizations are served to different sectors:

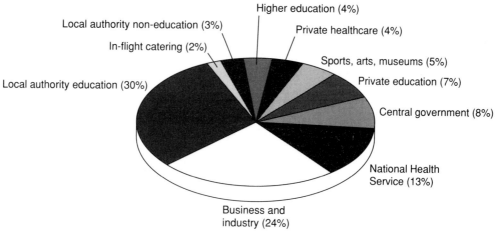

Figure 2.1 Pie chart of meals

1 Identify some factors which might cause these proportions to change over the next few years.
2 Discuss which of these sectors might be the most profitable for a catering organization to operate in. Do you think profitability is likely to be closely related to the number of meals sold? What other factors will affect profit?
3 A rapidly expanding company manufacturing soft drinks is considering diversifying through the purchase of a catering operation. How might they view these figures?

Future priorities for tourism development

Priorities must take current trends into account. The traditional two-week holiday at a single destination has declined in Britain. Other travel markets have in part replaced it, namely:

- short breaks;
- day trips;
- special interest and activity holidays;
- business travel.

The overall effect has been to lengthen the holiday season but to reduce the number of visitors to traditional seaside resorts. Alongside these changes has come a steady increase in the number of overseas visitors coming to Britain. Planning and investment are needed if tourist developments are successfully to meet changing demands.

The English Tourist Board's strategy for tourism for the years 1991 to 1995, entitled 'Planning for Success', identified five issues which the industry would need to tackle:

- balancing the need of visitors, host communities and the environment;
- improving quality and value for money;
- improving transport and communications;
- increasing standards of training and professionalism;
- encouraging tourism growth and development.

In order to achieve these objectives a number of development priorities were suggested as being vital to the continued growth of tourism. They were:

- a new, major, nationally recognized tourist attraction;
- an expansion of the number of purpose-built holiday villages;
- more new accommodation offering good value for money to families;
- more good-quality holiday cottages;
- an expansion of farm holiday schemes;
- more emphasis on design and environmental awareness in all tourist developments.

'Discover the English Seaside'

In 1991 a national marketing campaign, 'Discover the English Seaside', set out to arrest the decline of many traditional British seaside resorts. TV and press advertising were used in an attempt to persuade British holidaymakers that these traditional resorts still had much to offer. The number of resorts participating in the on-going campaign had risen to 41 by early 1993 and the hope is that this will give a boost to domestic tourism. The government is keen to support this kind of initiative since any increase in domestic tourism both brings increased taxation revenue in VAT and also reduces the flow of money taken out of the country by people taking holidays abroad. Seven resort areas have been allocated funds through a scheme of Local Area Initiatives (LAIs). The LAIs are partnerships between the public and private sectors which aim to raise the level of investment in local tourist development.

Present trends in leisure

The contribution of leisure to the economy

Leisure has become a much more prominent industry in financial terms. Success as a performer can bring rapid wealth, while the major spectator sports can generate huge sums through admission charges, sponsorship and television fees. This success in turn creates employment opportunities for actors, performers and players, but, in much greater numbers, for those who supervise and provide tuition for the expanding number of leisure activities now available. It is estimated that there are 210,000 businesses directly involved with leisure and that these employ 13.5 per cent of all UK employees. The rise in leisure employment has been at the expense of employment in more traditional industries as Table 2.6 shows.

Table 2.6 Employment in the UK in selected sectors, 1990 (in thousands)

Mechanical engineering	765
Banking and finance	634
Food, drink and tobacco	557
Paper, printing and publishing	496
Sport-related economic activity[1]	467
Postal services and telecommunications	441
Chemical industry	329
Agriculture, forestry and fishing	305
Footwear and clothing	301
Sport-related economic activity[2]	262
Timber and wooden industries	254
Textiles	214

Notes
1 including commercial non-sport sector
2 excluding commercial non-sport sector

Source: Henley Centre; Department of Employment

Activity

Study Table 2.7 below, relating to sport-related employment in the UK in 1990 and discuss the questions which follow it.

Table 2.7 Sport-related employment

Sector	Male full-time	Male part-time	Female full-time	Female part-time	Total
Commercial sport	46,751	13,059	31,026	42,445	133,281
Voluntary sector	41,821	8,649	14,884	13,631	78,985
Commercial non-sport	100,360	8,637	55,321	41,337	205,655
Central government: transport	1,041	4	83	8	1,136
Local government: sports facilities	4,309	3,498	3,608	9,560	20,975
Local govt: teachers	9,953	400	9,824	3,488	23,665
Local govt: local transport	2,580	145	270	98	3,093
Local govt: police	300		128		428
TOTAL	207,115	34,392	115,144	110,567	467,218

Source: Henley Centre for Forecasting 1992 'The economic aspect of sport in the UK in 1990'

1 What kind of activities might be classified as 'commercial non-sport'?
2 What proportion of those employed in sport-related jobs are part-time? Why do you think this figure is relatively high?
3 What different patterns of employment can you distinguish between male and female employees in sport? What explanations might there be to account for the differences?
4 What do the figures suggest about the relative importance of the public, private and voluntary sectors as providers of sport-related employment?

A healthy lifestyle

The links between good health and an active lifestyle are frequently highlighted in the media. Articles, and radio and television programmes, supported by school health education programmes, constantly reinforce the message that a combination of poor diet and lack of exercise harms physical health, and may also have an impact on people's general feelings of well-being. Evidence that this message is making an impression can be seen through the increase in health and fitness centres, the growth of keep-fit classes and the increased sales of fitness videos, and sports and leisure equipment.

Fitness centre philosophy and practice
Lean Machine and its 'quality of life' philosophy will help you protect yourself against:
- stress and the diseases it can cause
- the side-effects of a sedentary lifestyle
- the damage caused by excessive consumption of food and alcohol
- the risk of sickness or injury.

It will help you conquer:
- smoking • boredom • lethargy • depression

You do it by mixing two main types of exercise.

Cardio-vascular:
This activity works the heart, lungs and circulation. It improves aerobic fitness and stamina, and helps to get rid of stress. It also acts to eliminate toxins from the bloodstream.

Resistance:
This works on specific muscle groups and can improve body tone, shape, suppleness and strength.

Source: The Unipart Group of Companies – Lean Machine

A wider choice of leisure activities and venues

Our choice of leisure activity has expanded very rapidly. Thirty years ago school sports would probably have included football and cricket for boys, hockey and netball for girls, and perhaps some swimming and athletics for those schools with the necessary resources. Many schools now offer tennis, badminton, gymnastics, and a variety of skiing and outdoor activity trips. Access to clubs offering sports like bowling, windsurfing, rowing, golf, horse-riding and orienteering is easier. The belief that this wider choice was diluting the development of skills and expertise in the more traditional British sports has led to the establishment of national training schemes and centres, intended to bring on exceptionally talented individuals. Drama and music remain part of the school curriculum, even though they have come under some pressure in the upper years of many secondary schools. However active participation in amateur dramatic groups, choirs, orchestras, pop groups and clubs catering for a wide spectrum of other arts activities is still widespread.

Theme parks were a major growth area in the 1980s and traditional out-of-home entertainment venues, like pubs, had to increase the range of facilities and services which they offered in order to continue to attract people. Quiz nights, karaoke evenings and live music performances could be found in a great many pubs by the end of the decade. Competition has increased from private, licensed sports clubs which subsidize the upkeep of their sports facilities through bar takings and social events. While visits to pubs, wine bars and theatres seem to have remained fairly constant in the last two years, cinema audiences have grown.

Attendances at visitor attractions suggest that locations benefit from improving their educational value. Museums, in particular, have developed imaginative interpretive exhibitions and interactive learning displays. At their most sophisticated, these can use high technology to produce electronic sounds and movements which simulate reality. The Natural History Museum, for example, has a Dinosaurs Gallery which uses technology to show how dinosaurs looked, lived and moved.

Responsibility for the development of sport and the arts

Much sport is in the hands of sports clubs and is therefore run largely by volunteers. The government is currently being challenged, especially by the Central Council for Physical Recreation, which represents over 200 British sporting bodies and associations, over the comparative lack of tax incentives received by British sporting organizations in relation to their European Community (EC) equivalents. The council is also campaigning to improve standards of sport in schools. It faces the dual challenge, first of the sale of many school sports grounds by local education authorities and second of the declining number of teachers with sufficient time to devote to sporting activities which are often held outside school hours. The council also runs schemes to train community sports leaders and to increase the level of sponsorship for sport.

The Sports Council

This independent organization was established in 1972, mainly funded by central government. Its main objectives are:

- to increase participation in sport;
- to increase the quantity and improve the quality of sports facilities;
- to raise the standards of sports performance;
- to provide information.

It runs five centres of excellence specializing in swimming, tennis, gymnastics, football and athletics, and national centres for water sports and for mountain activities. Its activities also include:

- financing national coaching schemes;
- financing and running a campaign against the use of drugs in sport;
- identifying the need for and advising on the design and development of multi-purpose sports centres;
- providing a range of data and information about sport in the UK.

The arts are equally dependent on the support of local voluntary groups. The Arts Council (described below) supports a variety of such groups and projects, but the arts are now less frequently viewed as part of a generously subsidized service which should be available to the community. Organizations like small local theatres are increasingly having to produce programmes of popular entertainment only, in order to generate sufficient income to survive with lower levels of grant or subsidy. For the same reason orchestras may increase their concentration on very popular composers like Mozart or Beethoven and very rarely perform the work of less well-known or new composers.

The Arts Council of Great Britain

This organization took over the work of the Council for the Encouragement of Music and the Arts, a government-supported national body which began work during the Second World War. The Council was re-formed under its present name in 1964. Its main objectives are:

- to develop and improve the knowledge, understanding and practice of the arts;
- to increase the public accessibility of the arts;
- to advise and co-operate with the government, local authorities and other bodies.

It has separate divisions for dance, drama, film, video and broadcasting, literature, music, touring and visual arts. Its activities, many of them administered by regional arts boards, also include:

- supporting local arts organizations and projects;
- lobbying in support of adequate funding for the arts;
- supporting major city festivals promoting the arts (e.g. 1992 Birmingham City of Music);
- promoting the importance of the arts within the education system.

Future priorities for leisure development

Indoor developments

The nature of the British climate means that outdoor leisure activities can be easily ruined by the weather. This both discourages local participation and inhibits the number of overseas visitors who may be attracted. The development of large indoor leisure complexes can play a major part in making domestic holidays appeal to more British families, thus avoiding some of the flow of cash to destinations overseas, as well as making Britain a more attractive destination for families from abroad. Indoor centres also play a part in the development of sporting prowess, especially in sports like athletics and tennis, where winter outdoor training can be problematic.

Regeneration

The development of canals and ports as leisure facilities is increasingly seen as a means of encouraging wider economic recovery. The presence of water provides both a pleasing visual environment, and leisure facilities for boating and other water sports. More extensive marina developments, such as the one in Brighton in East Sussex, tend to encourage the building of further leisure facilities such as hotels, pubs, restaurants, sports centres, shops and entertainment centres.

Community use or individual excellence?

One major dilemma facing many future leisure developments is that, where limited funds are available, should sport or arts for all the community or the pursuit of excellence be the higher priority? This conflict is evident in developments such as the building of new swimming pools. Traditional rectangular pools were suitable for the training of swimmers for competition, but increasingly families demand more features which are purely for enjoyment, such as water slides or jacuzzis.

Funding

As traditional sources of funding, such as grants and sponsorship, appear to be on the decline, so leisure facilities and organizations are seeking other forms of financial support. Though sponsorship of major arts and sports events or organizations remains, sponsors are becoming more cautious about the image of individual sports, works of art and performances. Environmental and health concerns also mean that some leisure organizations end sponsorship deals themselves on the grounds that the activity of the sponsor appears to conflict with their own interests. Many sports, for example, have ended their sponsorship agreements with cigarette manufacturers.

Sport has traditionally received a considerable income from gambling, particularly through betting on horse races and through the football pools. The future could see sport and the arts benefiting from the proceeds of a national lottery.

Assignment 2
Patterns and trends in leisure and tourism

This assignment develops knowledge and understanding of the following elements:
1.1 Describe the scale and contexts of the leisure and tourism industry
1.2 Investigate UK leisure and tourism products
1.3 Investigate the variety of local services and products
6.2 Select and provide management information

It supports development of the following core skills:
Communication 3.1, 3.2
Application of number 3.3

Your tasks

1 Interview three local industrialists on the subject of the current state of the leisure and tourism industry.
2 Write a report which summarizes their views.
Your report could include comment on some or all of the following:
- current problems in the industry;
- future trends;
- employment and profitability prospects;
- regional and seasonal factors;
- demographic and lifestyle changes;
- skills requirements;
- the role of education.

3 The present provision of leisure and tourism products and services

What is covered in this chapter

This chapter describes the range of products and services which the leisure and tourism industry supplies. It concludes by considering the broad roles of the public, private and voluntary sectors in contributing to this provision.

- Holidays
- Transport
- Visitor attractions
- Accommodation and catering
- Agency, information and financial services

- Sports participation facilities
- Sports spectator facilities
- Entertainment facilities
- Other recreation facilities

3.1 The provision of holidays

Tour operators

Tour operators directly control the range and type of holidays available to the public. They plan and market holiday packages to selected destinations. This involves organizing travel and accommodation, setting a price for each holiday product, producing brochures advertising the holidays arranged and selling the brochures to interested customers. Though some of these products are sold directly to the public, the great majority are purchased through travel agents' offices. These holiday packages, using charter flights, and including accommodation and services such as travel transfers and resort representatives, are known as **inclusive tours by charter** (ITC).

The task of the tour operator is a complex one. Most of the planning, including a commitment to use specific accommodation and means of transport, has to be done well in advance of any customers' commitment to purchase. Brochures advertising the travel and accommodation arrangements have to be printed up to six months before the holidays are actually taken, since many people book early in order to be sure of their preferred choice.

Transport arrangements, in particular, require advanced planning. Accommodation and flights may have to be booked as much as 18 months in advance. Package tours generally use charter flights but flight costs are not easy to calculate. The cost of aviation fuel is notoriously unstable and the flights themselves need to be more than 80 per cent full for the tour operator to cover the costs of chartering the plane. The suitability of accommodation has to be checked in advance. Generally tour operators will guarantee to take an agreed number of rooms in advance. They have to be aware of the temptation for some hotels, expecting there to be some cancellations and some 'no shows', to double book rooms. Brochures will generally feature the specific accommodation within the selected destinations, and so this has to be photographed and text written before the design of the finished product can be completed.

A tour operator begins by choosing which destinations to feature. Bigger companies will have marketing departments which will research current market trends and try to anticipate changes in public holiday preferences. This research will include issues like how much potential travellers are willing to spend, how far they will travel and whether destination loyalty outweighs their desire to visit new places. Exchange rates may be a factor in an operator's choice of which destinations to offer, since rate changes mean previously expensive destinations can suddenly become much cheaper. This was a major factor in the growth of holidays to Florida in the early 1980s. Destinations are generally selected on the basis of five essential criteria:
1 their accessibility;
2 their attractions;
3 the quality of local facilities and services;
4 the availability of excursions;
5 the political stability of the area.

Once destinations have been selected the operator must ensure that the accommodation, facilities and services they offer are of an adequate quality to make customers feel they are good value for money. When accommodation contracts have been drawn up, the operator will calculate prices for each holiday offered. These will usually included a number of variable factors:
• the type of accommodation;
• the number in the party;
• the type of transport used;
• the point of departure;
• the time of year.

What should a brochure tell you about a new or unfamiliar destination?

This information is an extract from a brochure featuring Mauritius

Entry requirements
A valid passport, or an internationally recognized travel document, and a valid return or onward passage ticket are required. Visitors should have adequate funds to cover the duration of their stay.

Health regulations
Yellow fever vaccination certificates are required if you are arriving from an infected area. Cholera vaccination is no longer required, and according to the recent epidemiological situation there is no malaria risk.

Time zone
Local time is four hours ahead of Greenwich Mean Time and three hours ahead of mid European time.

Language
English is the official language and is widely understood. French and Creole predominate in everyday life, while a number of oriental languages are also spoken.

After brochures have been prepared operators have to sell their products. Larger companies will often have a sales team which will visit travel agents and update them on the new range of holidays being offered. The travel agencies sell the tour operators' products and receive a commission, usually a percentage of their sales, in return. Tour operators often invite selected travel agency staff to visit destinations which they wish to promote in order to give them some first-hand knowledge of their products.

Operators taking customers regularly to the same destination will often provide a **resort representative** or rep. The role of the rep is to welcome new arrivals and ensure that travel transfers go smoothly. They are available to organize excursions, provide expert local advice and, if necessary, deal with any emergencies. They are also responsible for the quality control of the product, in that they provide regular reports from the destination which enable the company to monitor accurately what people enjoy about it and what negative comments have been noted.

Larger tour operators tend to concentrate on destinations like the Spanish Costas with a large accommodation supply. The volume of business they generate enables them to negotiate better rates for hotel rooms and airline seats. Smaller operators, unable to compete on price in the larger resorts, often choose to specialize in specific destinations or types of holiday, especially those which appeal more to the independent traveller.

Activity

Read the extract below, taken from the Thomson Travel Group's 1992 Annual Report:

> In contrast to 1991 when the difficulties of the holiday business were mainly caused by external events, most of the problems experienced in 1992 arose from decisions made within the industry. In total, we estimate the number of holidays operated by UK tour operators in the year to have been 15% more than in 1991, despite the continuing recession. The majority of this growth was a direct result of decisions taken by many operators to offer, and maintain, volumes for 1992 well in excess of what circumstances indicated would be sensible. Summer 1992 programmes were planned in the immediate wake of the collapse of the International Leisure Group (ILG), at that time the country's second largest operator, and many operators felt that they could take much of the ILG business and put on speculative capacities to accommodate it. Unfortunately, insufficient sales in the peak booking months of January and February were masked by the forthcoming general election and the anticipated economic recovery thereafter. By the time it was clear that there was excess capacity, the key decision dates for reducing volumes had passed and most of the excess stayed on sale. This severely depressed prices in the late sale market and most operators will have experienced disappointing financial results. A number of small operators ceased trading during the year as a result.

1 What factors does the extract suggest tour operators have to take into account in deciding how many holidays to offer each year?

2 Why were the months of January and February critical to those operators who had increased the number of holidays they were offering in 1992?

3 Why did they fail to reduce the volume they had available and what consequences did this have?

4 How do you think this series of events would affect tour operators' plans for the volume of holidays they would plan to sell in 1994?

Range of holiday products

The range of holiday products available at any given time can be classified in a number of ways. Using the eight criteria which follow would establish most of the distinctive features of each product:

1 the distance travelled from home to destination;
2 the length of the stay;
3 the time of year;
4 whether the holiday is a full package, flight only, accommodation only, or fly-drive;
5 the quality of the accommodation and the travel options;
6 the main features of the destination(s);
7 whether the holiday focus is fixed, two-centre or touring;
8 whether the holiday is mainly active or passive.

Distance

Distance is an important factor in choosing holidays. Long journeys take more time, are generally more expensive and are more tiring. The location of many tourist destinations is often within relatively easy reach of the wealthier countries which generate the majority of tourists. Hence many tourists from Britain holiday in the Mediterranean rather than Hawaii or Bali. Recent trends have shown Europeans to be more willing to travel further afield to '**long haul**' destinations – those over 3000 km from the point of origin or which take more than five hours of flying time to reach. A major reason for this has been a reduction in air fares for these longer distances. Proximity to airports generally increases the popularity of destinations, though more tour operators are developing holidays, using adaptable transport like four-wheel drive vehicles, to less accessible places.

Length of stay

Package holidays dependent on charter flights can often only be booked in weekly blocks. However, many tour operators recognize that customers are increasingly demanding flexibility. There are now far more opportunities to extend stays, to combine destinations and to customize travel arrangements to suit individual travellers. The traditional one- or two-week summer holiday still exists for many people, but it is often supplemented by various excursions and short breaks. Short breaks, often incorporating a weekend, evolved both as a means of lengthening the holiday season of destinations and also of filling rooms in hotels which were much busier during the week.

Time of year

Most tour operators grade their prices according to the time of year their customers are travelling. The most popular, or 'peak', season is the most expensive and the 'low' season is the cheapest. As package holidays developed in the 1960s the peak season coincided with school summer holidays, the period when the Mediterranean resorts were hottest. Once long haul travel became more affordable, those seeking sunshine were able to travel to warmer climates all year round. All the larger tour operators now produce a 'Winter Sun' brochure. Destinations without the luxury of year-round mild climates, including those within Britain, developed a number of counter-attractions to draw visitors outside the main holiday season. One approach was to offer packages including activities, while another was to build covered facilities, like those at Center Parcs, and so eliminate factors like poor weather altogether.

Flexible holiday packages

Many tourists still opt for a destination and spend their whole holiday in the same place. However, the increasing demands for flexibility mean that most tour operators offer different elements of the holiday package separately or in varying combinations. Customers may purchase flight only or accommodation only deals. They may combine different holiday destinations within the same package. Those wishing to tour at their own speed may invest in a **fly-drive** arrangement, whereby they travel around in a hire car, booking their own accommodation as they go. In some countries accommodation vouchers can be issued and cashed in at any hotel belonging to a specified hotel chain.

Quality

Some tour operators operate largely with 'upmarket' customers in mind. They will choose top of the range accommodation, in general five-star hotels, comfortable travel arrangements and the highest level of services and facilities. They avoid destinations which might be perceived as unattractive or overcrowded. These principles are reflected in their prices.

Thomsons 1993 Winter Sun brochure contained the following promise to customers:

The Thomson Promise

We promise that, if we change your accommodation or your flights we will reduce the price of your holiday. The less notice we give you of a change before your holiday, the higher the compensation we will give you.

We guarantee:

- Your named accommodation as booked
- Your UK airport
- Your date of departure from the UK
- The length of your holiday (the number of nights)
- Day flights will not be changed to following night flights

The price of your holiday is fully guaranteed and will not be subject to any surcharges. Once you have made your booking and paid your deposit, then the cost of your holiday cannot be increased.

Other operators look to the mass market, seeking to take large numbers of tourists to popular, accessible destinations. Their prices are accordingly lower, as are their profit margins, and they often seek to maintain their profit levels by increasing their share of the market. As the expectations of consumers have risen, fuelled by wide media coverage of the travel business, so have concerns about quality and all the major operators have had to devote more time to customer service issues.

The features of the destination

The most basic element of choice in holiday products lies in deciding where to go. The features of Blackpool are clearly different from those of Vienna. The appeal to potential holidaymakers of the seaside, the countryside, historic cities or leisure parks will depend on a variety of factors – age, background and temperament among them. Many destinations offer a combination of features. The holiday product needs to offer the customer an escape from the routine or stress of their daily lives, and an increasing number of destinations are developing or exploiting attractions and activities designed to encourage escapism of one sort or another – for example theme parks, fantasy games, themed role-play weekends, historical and heritage museums, and exhibitions.

Fixed, two-centre and touring holidays

Though many holidaymakers still opt for a stay in a single destination, there is an increasing tendency for people to combine two different types of holiday within a single package. They may be seeking to experience two contrasting places or, more commonly, to combine a restful break with a more active one. For example, tourists on a beach holiday in Florida could choose to combine this with a Caribbean cruise. Those recovering from an active week on safari in Kenya could follow it with a restful week in the Maldive Islands. Many tour operators offer touring holidays with pre-arranged accommodation stops, so that tourists can visit a number of destinations along a set itinerary, using either public transport, their own vehicles or hire cars.

Active or passive

British holiday photographs of the 1950s seem to show the great majority of holidaymakers sitting in deckchairs doing very little. While rest and relaxation is still a major priority for many tourists the range of activities available in tourist destinations has widened considerably. Mediterranean seaside resorts offer windsurfing, boating, water-skiing and para-gliding almost as a matter of course. In Spain and Portugal purpose-built tourist developments have evolved around golf courses. In Britain centres offering activities like skiing, climbing, canoeing and orienteering have increased in popularity. Not that all the activities are sporting ones. A number of centres have developed holiday packages incorporating courses to improve skills in arts and crafts.

Activities in Uzbekistan

Uzbektourism, the national tourism company of the republic of Uzbekistan, is keen to attract more visitors for the former Soviet Union republic. The area lies along the Great Silk Road which runs through Bukhara, Samarkand and Tashkent. Believing the area to have much to offer the more adventurous holidaymaker, the following activity holidays have been developed:

- trekking
- rafting and kayaking
- biking tours
- skiing
- desert journeys
- cave exploration
- rock climbing
- mountaineering

3.2 The provision of transport

The last decade has witnessed some gradual changes in the use of different means of transport in Britain. Generally speaking the amount of travelling has increased, though 1991 figures suggest this general growth may have peaked in 1990. Air and rail systems have seen an overall increase in use, though specific parts of the rail system in particular have declined. Less distance is being covered by people using buses and coaches, but there has been a marked increase in the mileage clocked up by people using cars and motor bikes. Table 3.1 compares the relative distances travelled by people using these different forms of transport.

Table 3.1 Passenger transport use (measured in billion passenger km)

	1981	1986	1990	1991
Air	3	4	5	5
Rail	34	37	41	38
Buses and coaches	49	47	46	45
Cars and motor bikes	406	475	597	596
Bicycles	5	5	5	5
TOTAL	497	568	693	689

Source: Department of Transport

Railways

Very few countries in the world are currently adding to their rail systems, generally because it is seen as a more expensive option than road development. Most of those with extensive rail systems rely heavily on government subsidies in order to keep the services going. Environmentalists are probably the strongest supporters of railways now, arguing that they produce less pollution and congestion. The extent of the British railway system has been substantially reduced since the Second World War. Dr Beeching was brought in by the government in the 1960s to head British Railways and institute a programme to cut many unprofitable branch lines. In 1993 British Rail has again cut a sizeable number of trains from its winter timetable and reduced the number of carriages on others, arguing that these are not sufficiently popular to bring in an acceptable level of revenue.

High speed train development is one area of success for modern railways. InterCity routes provide a service which particularly appeals to business travellers. They can move between city centres without the parking problems that road transport brings, and without the need to transfer from airports which are generally some way outside the city and hence the business area. An added attraction is that the travelling time can be used as part of the working day.

Railways are still much in demand by those who commute from the countryside, from the suburbs or from dormitory towns to city jobs. These services are increasingly under pressure since it is difficult to run them economically. They require a high concentration of staff and rolling stock, and yet both of these resources are only fully used during the two rush hour periods. As a result many commuter services lose money and find it difficult to persuade government to invest in new rolling stock, track, stations and operational systems. Attempts to increase the use of rail services at off-peak times include discounted fares, promotions linked with other retail products and special offers combining rail travel with hotel accommodation. Particular markets which would find it easier to use the train in off-peak periods were targeted by rail-cards entitling students and senior citizens to reduced fares. In 1993 a bill to privatize British Rail was introduced, though many observers feel that only the profitable parts of the service will appeal to potential private owners. Major railway stations, with their profitable retailing activities, are likely to be among the first assets to be put up for sale.

Railways have played a part in the revival of tourism in destinations where branch lines have been taken over by steam train enthusiasts. Locomotives, both full size and narrow gauge, have been lovingly restored by voluntary labour and attract visitors to take nostalgic rail journeys in locations like Ffestiniog in Wales, the Severn Valley, and Minehead in Somerset. Steam locomotives are being introduced on popular tourist lines in Scotland. Railway centres, like the one at Didcot, use limited sections of track to exhibit moving locomotives to paying visitors.

The opening of the Channel Tunnel in 1994 should prove a stimulus to some British rail routes. However many passengers will use the service to transport their own vehicles. Therefore the development of the route highlights the need for easy links between different transport systems, at least from the consumer's point of view. Also, for Tunnel rail passengers wishing to reach London, rapid access from the coast to the capital's terminus may prove critical to its success.

Le Shuttle

Eurotunnel actually has three tunnels between England and France – one for rail traffic in each direction and a third which will act as a service tunnel. The 50 km long tunnels will carry trains 40 m under the sea bed between Folkestone and Calais. The service tunnel will provide for maintenance, ventilation and safety.

Passenger and freight trains will use the tunnel 24 hours a day. Le Shuttle is the name given to the drive-on drive-off vehicle transportation system which will carry cars, coaches and motor cycles. Each shuttle will carry 120 vehicles between the two terminals in 35 minutes.

Trains will depart every 15 minutes at peak times, and the terminals will provide easy access to and from motorway systems. There will be no pre-booking system. Passengers will simply arrive and pay by cash, credit card or a ticket purchased through a travel agent. Customs and immigration clearance will be given by both French and British officials before boarding.

Motorists will drive their vehicles directly into double deck carriages and will then stay with their vehicles, although there is room for occupants of vehicles to get out and stretch their legs.

A new type of railway development which has the attraction of reduced construction costs is the light railway, such as the one which services London's Docklands. The system can be constructed to run above the level of existing buildings (the system which runs around Sydney in Australia actually passes through some city centre buildings) and so can give rapid access to city centres. Light railway systems can also save costs as a result of being highly automated. However their passenger-carrying capacity is limited by the size and strength of the rolling stock, and the power of the systems used to drive them. Cities like Manchester have gone back to a previously popular railed passenger system – the tram. These are relatively light and cheap to build, as well as having the advantage of being able to run on track laid on both rail and road systems.

Improving standards on national rail systems

In an attempt to attract more customers, as well as retaining existing ones, British Rail set a number of punctuality standards on its main services and these are closely monitored. These standards required 90 per cent of InterCity and longer Regional services to arrive within ten minutes of their scheduled time. Targets were set for 92 per cent of the trains on the mainly commuter-used Network SouthEast system and 90 per cent of the shorter Regional service to arrive within five minutes of their scheduled time. Table 3.2 indicates how successfully these objectives have been met.

Table 3.2 British Rail – percentage of trains arriving within punctuality targets

	1986–7	1990–1	1991–2
InterCity	85	85	84
Network SouthEast	91	90	91
Regional – express and long rural	91 }	90	92
Regional – urban and short rural		90	90

Source: Department of Transport

Activity

1 Discuss the factors which you think are likely to affect the punctuality rate of a specific rail service.
2 Study Table 3.2 and comment on the relative performances of InterCity, Network SouthEast and Regional services.
3 What do you think might account for their different punctuality success rates?
4 What other criteria, apart from punctuality, do you think people use in deciding whether rail travel is appropriate for a particular journey?

Air transport

Air travel has the advantage of coming up against no natural barriers. The only things which prevent aeroplanes taking the shortest route between two points are adverse weather conditions, air traffic congestion and countries which restrict flights across their territory for political reasons.

The expansion of airline services has had a major effect on tourism. It has enabled people to travel further afield by reducing both the cost and the time involved in long journeys. The development of wide-bodied jets, like the Boeing 747, enabled more passengers to be carried and in doing so reduced the costs per passenger. The development of charter flights further reduced costs since they could be more accurately matched to the demand for seats than scheduled flights which were obliged to run to a set timetable. Charter flights which were not selling well were often **consolidated**, so that passengers from two flights were combined on a single one.

The competition for take-off slots is acute at major airports like Heathrow and Gatwick, and scheduled flights generally take priority. This means charter flights often take off early or late in the day, but it has also led many tour operators to make greater use of regional airports like Luton, Birmingham and Manchester. While this may save time for people travelling from the regions, tour operators generally levy a surcharge on departures from regional airports. Night flights from most British airports are restricted in the interests of residents living nearby, but a proposal to change the sound-based categories which determine the type and number of aircraft permitted to do so is a current concern.

Congestion over major airports like Heathrow has become an increasing problem, especially early in the morning when both commuter flights from domestic airports and overnight transatlantic flights have to circle in a queue, waiting their turn to land. The ability of pilots to keep to tight time schedules is often hindered by the lateness of other aircraft occupying the same air corridors. Computerized air traffic control has raised punctuality levels of domestic flights, but safety demands that aircraft are kept a reasonable distance apart, both in flight and on the runways. Airlines apply for slots for scheduled flights six months in advance. The traffic density permitted in different sectors of UK air space is fixed, limited by the number of flights per hour which local air traffic control can handle. London's air traffic control dealt with approximately 3500 aircraft movements a day in 1992, about 900 of these being transatlantic flights from Britain or other parts of Europe. Transatlantic flights present air traffic control with more problems than domestic flights because their routes are dependent on wind conditions over the Atlantic.

The ability of air transport to compete with other transport systems is very dependent on fuel prices. With much of the world's oil coming from the Middle East, not the most politically stable part of the world over the last two decades, prices worldwide can change very rapidly as changing international relationships threaten shortages. Fluctuations in the price of oil often result in airlines having to pass on surcharges to their customers.

Modern airlines seek cost-efficient aircraft. New aircraft are expensive, but on the other hand they reduce maintenance and engineering costs. Most airlines lease aircraft or borrow money for their purchase so that the repayments can consume a large portion of their income. **Leasing** is often a popular option because it enables airlines to respond quickly to changes in passenger demand, either by terminating leasing arrangements or negotiating additional ones. Larger planes reduce the number of pilots and maintenance staff the airline needs to employ. Supersonic jets like Concorde may be very rapid and cross the Atlantic in little more than three hours, but they are very expensive to run, and in terms of noise and fuel consumption come into frequent conflict with environmental interests. The high costs of air travel means that airlines are under great pressure to fill as many seats on each flight as possible. Prices are often discounted, especially to those booking well in advance and those willing to risk not being able to travel by booking very close to the time of the flight's departure.

The last decade has seen an expansion of frequent departure shuttle air services linking major British cities. Scheduled flights to and from important European business centres like Paris, Amsterdam and Brussels have also become more frequent. This extract from a *Travel Weekly* article published towards the end of 1993 provides an example of the increasing competition on European air routes.

Sabena to launch 'one class' East Midlands service

Belgian carrier Sabena is to launch a one-class service from East Midlands Airport to Brussels. The one-class service is an attempt to wrestle more high-spending passengers from its two UK rivals, British Airways and British Midland. General

Manager Etienne de Nil confirmed Sabena would offer two or three flights a week from April 1994 . . . BA also operates flights from Birmingham to Brussels. De Nil added that Sabena was considering further boosting its network of seven UK departure points in an attempt to become the market leader between the UK and Brussels. The airline has already explored the possibility of launching new services from Cardiff, Southampton, Teesside and Norwich. de Nil claimed Sabena had a 35% share of the market compared with BA's 40%.

Concorde

Short flights are expensive because more fuel is used in take-off and landing than in cruising. Handling charges while the aircraft are on the ground are higher because operating short routes means spending more time on the ground. The popularity of these shuttle services, used primarily by business travellers, has boosted the production of smaller, more fuel-efficient jets. Smaller aircraft also require less runway space and hence can use smaller, more centrally sited airports like the London City airport. In 1992 200,000 passengers took advantage of its services to European cities including Paris, Amsterdam, Brussels, Dublin and Frankfurt.

Airports are usually sited away from city centres, mainly because they require extensive amounts of space, preferably on flat land without natural obstructions in the path of the approaches of the aircraft. Their success, particularly with business travellers, is dependent on the services they can provide – including retailing, car parking and business lounges – as well as the ease of access they can provide to city centres. Heathrow attracted over 45 million passengers in 1992, making it the world's busiest international airport. This success has led to proposals for a fifth terminal building that would enable an increase almost doubling passenger capacity by early next century. There are also proposals to complete a fast railway link between the airport and Paddington railway station.

Table 3.3 Predicted traffic increases at Frankfurt/Main Airport

	1990	1995	2000	2005	2010
Capacity development					
Co-ordinated runway capacity (movements/hour)	64	70	75	77	80
Traffic forecast					
Movements per year in thousands	342.8	367.3	377.9	385.1	392
Passengers per year in millions	29.6	35.2	40.6	46.4	52.7

Source: 1990/95 Master Plan, Flughafen Frankfurt/Main

The Civil Aviation Authority, set up in 1971, plays a major part in the regulation of British airlines. This involves setting standards and guidance for air traffic control services, approving air fares and granting licences to operate to companies providing air travel services. However the regulatory controls over routes, capacity and fares are due to be relaxed within the European Community (EC) in the 1990s. This should allow greater freedom for airlines operating within Europe to determine their own fares on scheduled flights, increase their carrying capacity and investigate the development of regional routes. Regional airports have seen a growth in small airlines like Yorkshire European Airways. This company operates 3 18-seater turbo prop aircraft on routes between Leeds, Southampton, Belfast, Teeside and Aberdeen.

Activity

Study Table 3.4 below showing the method of travelling to France, the Irish Republic and Spain by UK travellers in 1976, 1984 and 1991:

Table 3.4 Methods of travelling from the UK *(Figures represent the number of visits in thousands)*

Country visited	1976 air	1976 sea	1976 all	1984 air	1984 sea	1984 all	1991 air	1991 sea	1991 all
France	500	1643	2143	798	3684	4482	1715	5671	7386
Irish Republic	445	803	1248	440	1112	1552	920	1177	2097
Spain	2078	177	2255	4594	429	5022	4548	340	4887

Source: extracted from International Passenger Survey

1 What trends can you identify from this table?
2 Identify any figures which appear to go against the general trends. What possible explanations might there be for this?
3 How might ferry services to Spain and airline services to the Republic of Ireland seek to increase their share of the total number of passengers?

Road transport

The main attraction of roads is that they can reach the most inaccessible places. Nearly every house, farm, office and factory has access to the national road system in Britain. Once the road is there the public are free to use it. In rural areas where public transport has disappeared, private cars have become a vital link with the amenities that are only available in towns.

Unlike motorway systems in France, Spain and Italy, motorists are not directly charged for using specific sections of road in Britain. Not surprisingly in 1988 the Department of Transport estimated that roads accounted for 92 per cent of passenger transport: 90 per cent of this consisted of cars and vans, and a mere 1 per cent was accounted for by coaches and buses.

Coaches have for years provided a cheap alternative to rail travel. They have the advantage of being able to offer a much greater variety of pick-up points and, with the introduction of on-board toilets and video screens, can undertake much longer non-stop journeys than they used to. The acknowledged safety risks of longer continental coach journeys have led to regulation of drivers' hours and control of maximum coach speeds. Their main disadvantage is that they are subject, like all road traffic, to traffic congestion. Indeed, in popular rural areas where the roads are often narrow, it is argued that they can be a major cause of congestion. However their ability to carry the same number of passengers as 25 or 30 cars makes this debate inconclusive. They tend to be popular with holidaymakers who like touring. Modern design has improved their comfort, while at the same time giving much better all-round viewing of scenery and attractions.

Private car ownership has expanded enormously since the end of the Second World War and it is predicted that the rate of growth will continue into the next century. Fewer than a third of households had the regular use of a car in 1961, but by 1990 this proportion had risen to two-thirds. The car offered people greater freedom in terms of where they went, how long they took to get there, what route they followed, and when and where they stopped on the way. For families in particular, some of the strain was taken out of travelling. Road transport, especially buses and taxis also formed important links between points of arrival and departure, like airports and railway stations, and accommodation facilities.

Table 3.5 shows the main method of transport used to reach the destination on holidays of four nights or more in selected years between 1971 and 1991.

Table 3.5 Main method of transport used to reach the destination on holidays of four plus nights in Great Britain between 1971 and 1991

Method of transport (%)	1971	1976	1981	1986	1991
Car	69	69	69	72	78
Bus/coach	15	13	12	15	12
Train	13	11	13	8	6
Other	3	4	5	4	4

Source: British National Travel Survey/British Tourism Survey Yearly

Alongside the growth in car ownership went an increase in the purchase of camping gear and caravans. Services like roadside catering, car hire and motels have also flourished. The increasing number of travellers who take their vehicles overseas has encouraged the development of a range of support services offering route information and insurance packages. The growth in traffic has led to the introduction of dual carriageways, motorways and bypasses.

Owners of private cars pay a tax to licence their vehicles but generally do not pay directly to use the roads. With the costs of road building increasing and regular concerns being expressed about the environmental harm caused by excessive road traffic, a pilot scheme is currently being tried in Cambridge which monitors electronically, through a system of beacons, the distances motorists in the trial travel within the city boundaries. This could be the first move towards a system of charging motorists who wish to drive in congested areas.

Park and ride schemes

Many cities popular with visitors use park and ride schemes to try to reduce the number of cars coming into the city centre, and to ease parking problems. Parking spaces on the outskirts are made available on major incoming routes and frequent bus services carry visitors to the city centre. The Bath scheme, outlined below, is typical.

In addition to central car parks there are three park and ride sites – at Newbridge Road, Lansdown and Bath University, Claverton Down.

Opening times are:

Newbridge Road	Monday – Saturday	0730 – 1930
Lansdown	Monday – Friday	0730 – 1930
Claverton Down	Saturday only	0830 – 1830

Parking is free and buses run every 15 minutes to and from the city centre. Adults are charged 50 pence return and accompanied children go free.

Researchers are continually seeking means of powering road vehicles without the pollution problems of the petrol or diesel engine. The use of unleaded petrol and the fitting of catalytic converters in new cars has reduced, though not eliminated, the harmful effects of car exhaust fumes. Buildings and statues in cities popular with tourists, such as Athens, suffer more rapid damage as a result of traffic pollution. Much of the research work has focused on attempts to produce an electric car whose batteries do not need constant recharging. Fuel cells producing electricity using oxygen from the air with hydrogen may have a long term future. Flywheels operated by magnets may ultimately prove a valuable source of electricity. Cleaner fuels like natural gas could be used in the future to drive turbine engines. Aerodynamic design can reduce wind resistance and cut the amount of fuel required.

The increasing use of four-wheeled vehicles by tour parties in remote areas poses a threat to some vulnerable landscapes. Such vehicles can cross sand dunes and rugged landscape, but the fact that they are often operating in very dry or very wet conditions, means they can easily contribute to soil erosion and the destruction of vegetation which has taken years to establish itself. In areas like Ayers Rock in Australia it is now illegal to drive such vehicles off the surfaced roads.

Activity

Read the Ministry of Transport's list of suggested ways of reducing road congestion in cities.

> 1 Improve the quality of bus services
> 2 Offer attractive rail services to commuters
> 3 Devise new transport systems
> 4 Make use of natural highways, such as rivers, and constructed ones, such as canals and disused railway lines
> 5 Use new technology to help motorists avoid congested areas
> 6 Take measures to eliminate badly parked vehicles
> 7 Encourage cyclists and pedestrians

1 Choose a town near you where there is evidence of traffic congestion caused at least in part by visitors and discuss each of the above options as a possible or realistic solution.
2 Write a letter to the local newspaper arguing a strong case for the solution which you think would best meet local needs while at the same time appearing practical and affordable.

Water transport

Island nations like Britain naturally tend to have a shipping tradition. Britain has an extensive system of inland waterways consisting of navigable rivers and canals largely constructed in the eighteenth century. Water transport always suffered from the drawback of being slow. The railways reduced its importance in freight-carrying terms and many of the canals fell into disuse. However, in recent years, many have been restored for leisure use, and barges and cabin cruisers have become popular as holiday accommodation. Many old dockland areas have been renovated and are now in use as leisure facilties. They may offer water sports like windsurfing or power boat racing. The Albert Dock in Liverpool has converted old office and warehouse buildings on the dock side into a series of museums and retail outlets.

Despite the imminence of the opening of the Channel Tunnel cross-Channel ferries remain a popular means of holiday travel to continental Europe. The Tunnel will cut down the time the crossing takes but the ferry companies will continue to be an attractive option for those wishing to begin their holiday in Normandy, Brittany, or further afield in Spain or Scandinavia. Their success depends on being able to get cars and passengers on and off ferries rapidly. This again reinforces the need for good transport links, in this case between the port and the road system leading out of it. Demand varies seasonally, peaking in the holiday months of July and August. Day trips to France, often involving shopping in French hypermarkets, have been a recent growth area, boosting low season demand. However all ferries, including services operated by hovercraft and hydrofoils, can be seriously affected by adverse weather conditions. Delays and cancellations are always a risk in winter. Ferry services form a vital link with Ireland, and with smaller islands like the Isle of Wight, the Isle of Man, the Hebrides and the Shetlands.

Canal barges have proved popular as holiday accommodation

Cruises have become a popular holiday option, both along rivers like the Nile in Egypt, and in regions like the Caribbean and the Mediterranean with a warm climate, a range of attractive ports of call and access via a convenient airport. Long haul tour operators increasingly offer cruises further afield in areas noted for spectacular scenery, like Alaska, or interesting wildlife, like the Galapagos Islands off Ecuador. Purpose-built cruise ships offer a range of accommodation, from economy class to luxury suites, and the kind of facilities and entertainments tourists might expect to find at resort destinations.

Activity

Read these extracts, all relating to the Galapagos Islands.

This extract comes from a travel guide to the Islands:

> These famous islands lie more than 500 miles west of Ecuador's coast. These volcanic islands are bleak, rocky and remote. They became famous as a result of the voyage of the 'Beagle' which arrived there with scientist Charles Darwin aboard. Its remarkable wildlife was instrumental in his formulation of the Theory of Evolution.
>
> Today visitors can still see giant tortoises, lizards and iguanas. The Islands are now a national park and in 1978 UNESCO declared them to be 'the universal natural heritage of humanity'. Not surprisingly there is concern about the growing presence of tourism but it is hoped that limited accommodation, the high cost of getting there, and the preservation rules imposed on tourists by the National Park authorities will restrict any negative impact.

This one comes from a tour operator's brochure:

> The islands are perfect for photographers. However, you need to do a lot of walking to get the best out of them and the ground under your feet can be rugged and slippery. Dinghies are used for landing on individual islands and you need to be reasonably athletic to get in and out of these. You should wear rubber-soled shoes at all times and be prepared for the heat. The islands are right on the Equator.

This one describes four types of cruise ships currently touring the Islands:

> (i) deluxe yachts – cabins for 2 persons with private facilities and air conditioning – all meals served – hot water at all times
>
> (ii) standard yachts – shared bathroom facilities – meals taken communally
>
> (iii) tourist motor yachts – air-conditioned double cabins – regular weekly departures
>
> (iv) economic yachts – very basic cabins – crew cook own meals

Work in groups to produce an agreed range of suggestions in answer to each of the following questions.

1 List the number of potential conflicts of interest suggested in these three sources of information.
2 Make a list of rules which you think it would be appropriate for the Islands National Park to insist were observed by all cruise visitors.
3 If a long haul operator was intending to include Galapagos Island cruises in its brochures for the first time, what conclusions do you think they might draw about their potential market?
4 How do you think this would affect the design and text of the brochure entry?

3.3 Visitor attractions

People generally choose where to travel on the basis of what they will do when they get there. They may be seeking entertainment, exercise, or the pursuit of a particular interest or leisure activity. Some of the things they may be attracted to are natural, such as scenery, while others are constructed, such as towns or theme parks. Table 3.6 below illustrates the attractions to be found in four different types of destination.

Table 3.6 Visitor attractions

Seaside resorts	– beach for those who like swimming and sunbathing
	– range of sports, e.g. tennis, golf, windsurfing
	– range of entertainments, e.g. shows, funfairs, casinos
Historic towns and cities	– churches, ancient monuments
	– museums and galleries
	– sites of battles and historic events
Countryside	– views
	– footpaths and nature trails
	– picnic sites
	– outdoor sports, e.g. fishing, climbing, canoeing
Leisure parks	– rides
	– children's shows and entertainments
	– formal gardens, zoos

Scenery

Since the great majority of the population lives in cities, it is not surprising that the attractions of peace, quiet and a change of scenery draw them towards the country-side. The types of landscape which most frequently attract visitors are coastline, hills and mountains, rivers and lakes, and forests and heaths. The most popular **coastal areas** tend to be those with accessible sandy beaches where the tides and sea currents are not strong enough to represent a danger to bathers. Previous residential and industrial development will lessen the resort's attractiveness. The attraction of **hills and mountains** is often their remoteness. They offer both good views and varied activities such as walking and skiing. Above all they represent a strong contrast to the city, and people go there seeking peace and quiet and a chance of uninterrupted con-templation. **Rivers and lakes** are also favoured by those seeking relaxation. The activities associated with water – fishing and boating in particular – can be conducted at a gentle pace, ideal for those wishing to escape from the stresses and pressures of home and work. **Forests and heaths** are favoured by walkers, especially those with an interest in nature. They are attractive to walkers, bird watchers, campers and hunters.

Historic cities

Most overseas visitors to Britain include London in their itineraries. Part of the interest may be in its history, though it obviously carries many other attractions as well. It is noticeable that companies operating tours for visitors to the UK often include Stratford, Chester, York and Oxford on their routes. These are all cities with distinctive architec-ture and they all have strong associations with the past. Buildings are often a means of conjuring up images of what the past must have been like. They attract visitors both because of their intrinsic beauty, but also because of their capacity to evoke times which may seem more stable or exciting than the present. Aware of this interest in the past, developers have constructed attractions like the Jorvik Centre in York or the Oxford Story which attempt to bring the past to life by means of indoor rides through series of animated tableaux. A similar ride called 'The Spirit of London' has recently been opened by Madame Tussauds, and presents visitors with a series of impressions of London at times like the Great Fire, the Blitz and the Coronation of Elizabeth II.

Bath is a good example of a city whose history and architecture are strong attractions for visitors.

Bath – World Heritage City

For almost two millenia Bath has welcomed visitors of all kinds: the sick, seeking a cure from the healing waters, the wealthy seeking entertainment, and today's visitors drawn by the legacy of that past. This includes some of the most spectacular Roman remains in Britain and a city unique in being almost exclusively Georgian. Bath is one of the best-preserved eighteenth-century cities in the world. Such is its importance that in 1988 the city was designated a World Heritage Site, the only such site in Britain.

Roman Bath

Bath owes its existence to its hot springs – the only ones in the country. Long before the Roman invasion in AD 43, the Celtic population revered this miracle of nature, seeing in it the power of the goddess Sulis. But it was Roman technology that created a bathing establishment known throughout Europe. Work began on the baths and temple around AD 60 to 70. The great complex beneath the present day Pump Room formed the nucleus of the Roman religious and spa town of Aquae Sulis.

Health and hot springs

During the Middle Ages Bath was well known for its cloth-making. But as the wool trade slumped in the mid-sixteenth century, the hot springs reclaimed their status as the chief attraction of the town. The visit of Queen Elizabeth in 1574 set the seal of approval on Bath as a spa. The baths were enlarged and improved, and the nobility and gentry flocked to the town. Fine inns and lodging houses sprang up to accommodate them and in the seventeenth century Bath was considered one of the loveliest cities in the country.

City of fashion

As the eighteenth century dawned a new era opened for Bath. The seasonal influx of a wealthy élite acted as a magnet to the luxury trades. Artists, actors, musicians and gamblers peopled a playground for the aristocracy. Richard 'Beau' Nash, attracted to Bath as a gambler, became the city's Master of Ceremonies. His firm hand welded together polite society in a fashionable round of promenades, assemblies, and visits to the Pump Room. What better city in Britain to be the host of the Museum of Costume – the country's most complete collection of fashions from the sixteenth century to the present?

Age of elegance

Bath burst out of the cramped confines of its medieval walls in a great spurt of new building. Elegant terraces snaked out across the surrounding hills, capturing between them stretches of countryside that became the city's parks and gardens. John Wood the Elder was the visionary architect who led the way. Leasing land outside the city walls, he planned Queen Square, the Parades and the Circus as speculative ventures. Wood designed developments with the grandeur of palaces, but with the convenience of a row of private houses. Individual plots were sub-leased to building tradesmen, who were left to devise their own interiors, provided they conformed to Wood's splendid designs for the facades. These endeavours reached their zenith in Bath's second major landmark and attraction – the magnificent Royal Crescent.

Historic properties

Interest in history draws visitors to attractions as varied as country houses, ships, birthplaces of the famous and castles. It is estimated that there were over 55 million visits to historic properties in 1992. The most popular single attraction of this kind, the Tower of London, alone received over 2.2 million visitors. Properties with royal connections, such as Hampton Court Palace and Windsor Castle, have a strong appeal for overseas visitors. Many historic properties are owned by organizations like English Heritage and the National Trust. They will manage and maintain the sites, including the provision of information, catering and retailing services, as well as determining admission charges. Many larger properties stage special events like mock battles, craft fairs, and displays and exhibitions. Those with plenty of land available have often sought to broaden their appeal by developing attractions to interest children such as farm centres, nature trails and train rides. Table 3.7 shows the drawing power of the best-known historic buildings in the UK.

Table 3.7 Visits to historic buildings, 1990 and 1991

	1990	1991	1992
Tower of London	2,296,683	1,923,520	2,235,199
Roman Baths and Pump Room, Bath	950,472	827,214	895,948
Warwick Castle	685,000	682,621	690,000
Stonehenge, Wiltshire	703,221	615,377	649,442
Shakespeare's birthplace, Stratford-upon-Avon	603,899	516,623	577,704
Blenheim Palace, Woodstock	511,630	503,328	486,100
Hampton Court Palace	520,995	502,377	580,440

Source: statistics supplied to BTA/ETB

Museums and galleries

Museums and galleries are particularly attractive to visitors seeking to understand the culture of the people in the destination they are visiting. They appeal to people with a desire to understand the past, as well as those who appreciate artistic achievement. Recent research concluded that the most common reason given for visiting museums was 'the chance to learn and find out about things'. The second most popular reason was important, if less expected, and that was to take advantage of 'facilities under cover and protected from the weather'.

Apart from differences of size, most galleries and museums focus their interests on a particular theme. A small museum may concentrate on recording the history of a specific town, such as the Watford Museum. It may focus on a theme. For example, in the suburbs of London there are museums and galleries concentrating on each of the following:

- pianos
- ethnology
- astronomy
- motor cars
- steam engines
- postal history
- contemporary art
- silk
- William Morris
- butterflies
- Sigmund Freud
- artillery
- taxicabs
- the Great Eastern Railway
- the Royal Air Force
- maritime history
- childhood

The largest of the galleries and museums are very important in terms of attracting visitors from considerable distances. Over 5 million people entered the British Museum in 1991 and figures for the National Gallery stood at 4.2 million. Outside London,

49

Glasgow Museum and Art Gallery attracted 892,000 visitors while Birmingham's Museum and Art Gallery recorded 754,000.

The costs of major museums and galleries can be high. Not only are many of their exhibits very costly to acquire, but also the condition of these may make preservation and conservation a time-consuming task requiring considerable expertise. The value of the collections means that adequate security of the premises, including staffing levels, has to be a high priority.

There are about 2,300 museums in Britain, roughly a third of which admit visitors free of charge. However, many museums have found it necessary to raise their commercial awareness in order to survive. Recognizing that many of their visitors are from the higher spending end of the market, they have combined modern interpretive skills and better marketing as a means of generating more revenue from admission charges and retailing activities. Other methods of increasing the appeal of museums and galleries include offering evening tours and events, and introducing variety by featuring touring exhibitions.

For many years museums and art galleries were perceived as dark, dingy, uninteresting places. However, many have improved both the quality of their displays and information. For example, video presentations are used in some art galleries to show the process of restoring famous paintings. Museums employ modern technology both to enable visitors to understand exhibitions with the assistance of monitors allowing them to respond to questions and also to make judgements based on information displayed. Some museums employ staff dressed up in period costume who provide learning experiences by acting out roles. Visitors to Wigan Pier can experience a lesson taught in a Victorian classroom by an actor impersonating the teaching styles and attitudes common in the nineteenth century.

A recent trend in museum development is the appearance of more open air museums, like the Chiltern Open Air Museum in Buckinghamshire. Most of these attempt to recreate the past by reassembling old buildings on a single site. They provide an appropriate setting for demonstrations of old crafts and skills central to an agricultural or industrial way of life associated with the region's past.

Blists Hill Open Air Museum

On this 50-acre site the visitor steps back in time into a living community at the turn of the century. Along the gas-lit streets of this Victorian town, past railway sidings, yards and pigsties, shops and offices, hear the hiss of steam and clank of machinery, taste the butcher's pies, drink beer in the pub and smell candles in the candle factory.

Source: Leaflet advertising the Ironbridge Gorge Museum

Activity

Read the following description of a temporary exhibition, entitled 'Trawlers at War', mounted at the Grimsby National Fishing Heritage Centre:

During two World Wars, as a nation under siege, Britain's survival depended on materials, munitions and food imported from North and South America. Germany tried to cut that lifeline using U-boat wolf-packs and mines. The battles for control of the Atlantic were eventually won with the help of trawlers, hastily converted with makeshift protection. Thus equipped, they undertook minesweeping, convoy escort and U-boat patrols. Trawlers at War shows how Britain's fishing fleet helped to turn the tide of both World Wars.

Experience the harsh reality of being under enemy fire on the gun-deck of a trawler at war. An explosion rips away the sides of the vessel as a Focke Wulf 200 completes its attack run. Abandon ship, swap your tin helmet for a German soft hat as you enter the claustrophobic confines of a Type VII U-boat. Join the wolf-pack and stalk a North American convoy. Discovered, you are forced to lie low only to be depth charged. Feel the shudder, hear the tortured metal fracture and escape to the rest of this stunning exhibition which tells the gripping story of the Royal Naval Patrol Service in two World Wars.

1 Discuss who you think this exhibition is intended to appeal to.
2 Identify a number of examples where the writer of the text has attempted to make the exhibition sound exciting.
3 Suggest ways in which the design of the leaflet or brochure advertising the exhibition could also be made visually exciting.
4 What other information would be needed to persuade undecided visitors that they should visit the exhibition?

Leisure parks

Attractions like EuroDisney are commonly called theme parks. They are designed to provide entertainment for visitors through a range of activities based on a historical or fictional theme. Imaginative design and complex technology have been used to provide a mixture of thrilling 'white knuckle' rides and experiences intended to appeal to the imagination of children. They are dependent on the family market, though this may change, particularly bearing in mind that the leisure time and spending power of young families is noticeably less significant than that of older couples without children. Given the very high cost of purchasing new rides – major parks were paying in excess of £10 million by 1993 for more complex ones – many parks may opt for investment in attractions appealing to a wider audience. Gardens, restaurants and retail outlets are increasingly likely to play an important role in the future plans of theme parks.

Many theme parks would be more accurately described as leisure parks, since their activities do not all share a common theme. Some, like Chessington World of Adventures, have evolved from zoos. Though animals are still an attraction for many, the adverse publicity surrounding the keeping of some kinds of wild animals in captivity has resulted in a reduction in the number of visitors they receive. At Chessington the number of animals on view has been reduced, while a range of rides and entertainments has been introduced to the site. Other leisure parks, such as Beaulieu and Alton Towers, have grown up on the estates surrounding country houses. Others, like Thorpe Park, took the opportunity of the need to renovate

A scene from a popular leisure park.

industrial sites. In the case of Thorpe Park gravel excavation had left behind extensive lakes which needed landscaping and returning to an appropriate use.

The major disadvantage which British leisure parks face is the climate. Their indoor entertainments have a limited capacity, though they are constantly being expanded. The ability of new technology to simulate many of the thrills of the 'white knuckle' rides seems sure to present the parks with a challenge. Virtual Reality simulation enables participants to experience a range of exciting activities without moving out of their seats. Disneyworld in Florida, still the world market leader, attracting over 12 million visitors a year, has for several years incorporated rides in which audio and video effects are combined with programmed shifts of seating positions to give people the impression that they are taking part in a dramatic sequence of events.

Industrial heritage and factory tourism

The decline of many manufacturing industries has contributed to the development of industrial tourism. Areas once mainly dependent on single industries, such as mining in South Wales or ship-building in parts of the north-east, have seen the development of industrial heritage sites and museums as a means of bringing some revenue to the regions. Mills, mines, factories, warehouses and dockyard offices have been converted to accommodate visitors. Industrial processes and their history are explained through exhibitions of artefacts, and the use of models and video films. Visitors can see machinery demonstrated or witness at first hand the conditions in which miners worked.

A number of working factories have turned themselves into visitor attractions. The Dartington Glass Factory in Devon built a raised walkway above the factory floor. Paying visitors can follow the whole glass-making process from start to finish, having an overhead view of the various blowing and cutting processes. The tour route ends in a factory shop where the company's products are on sale. Similar factory tours are available at Wedgwood, Royal Doulton, and a number of breweries and distilleries. A tour at Cadbury's factory proved so popular that a separate visitor attraction, Cadbury World, evolved from it.

Cultural attractions

Some destinations attract visitors because of their associations with famous people. Elvis Presley fans may choose to visit Gracelands or lovers of Mozart go to Salzburg. Cultural events like the Oberammergau Passion Play in Bavaria or the Cheltenham International Music Festival will temporarily swell visitor numbers. An interest in cultural diversity motivates many long haul travellers. Dance, drama, food, dress, language, religion and artefacts can all attract visitors to destinations with distinctive cultures.

3.4 The provision of accommodation and catering

Hotels and catering services account for more than half of the people employed in tourism. These services together are often described as the **hospitality** industry.

Accommodation

Hotels provide food and accommodation in return for payment. This makes them **serviced** accommodation as opposed to **self-catering** villas and apartments where people provide their own food and service. Serviced accommodation requires the provision of both meals and housekeeping, the general term used for cleaning and replacing linen and towels. The additional staff required to run serviced accommodation – for example receptionists, waiters, chambermaids and accountants – makes it more expensive than unserviced rooms. Larger hotels may also have leisure facilities such as swimming pools, saunas and fitness centres. Entertainments such as live music or dancing may also be provided. Many will open their bar and restaurant facilities to people not requiring accommodation. Conference facilities are increasingly used as a means of attracting block bookings.

Hotels are able to belong to voluntary classification schemes, such as the crown scheme administered by the local tourist boards or the star scheme operated by the Automobile Association. These schemes indicate the facilities and services which are available in the hotels. They may be combined with a grading scheme which involves regular inspections leading to a grading based on the quality of the rooms, the food, the facilities and the service. The crown scheme allows the award of up to five crowns to hotels participating in the scheme. In order to achieve these awards, hotels have to comply with a detailed list of requirements relating to bedrooms, bathrooms, toilets, heating, cleaning, public areas and dining facilities. Fire precautions and public liability insurance cover must be satisfactory. Hotels which opt to be graded as well as classified will be judged on a series of criteria assessed by inspectors. Once they have met a minimum requirement, they can be judged as approved, commended or highly commended. If they provide ramps, reasonably wide entrances, reserved parking spaces and suitably adapted bathroom fittings they may also display a logo indicating that the tourist board inspection has judged them suitable for physically disabled guests.

THE KEY IS YOUR SURE SIGN
OF WHERE TO STAY

SELF-CATERING HOLIDAY HOMES

Throughout England, the tourist boards now inspect over 13,000 holiday homes, every year, to help you find the ones that suit you best.

THE CLASSIFICATIONS: **ONE to FIVE KEY**, tell you the range of facilities and equipment you can expect. The more **KEYS**, the wider the range (see below).

THE GRADES: **APPROVED, COMMENDED, HIGHLY COMMENDED and DE LUXE,** indicate the quality standard of what is provided. If no grade is shown, you can still expect a high standard of cleanliness.

ONE KEY: Clean and comfortable, adequate heating, lighting and seating, TV, cooker, fridge and full range of crockery and cutlery.

TWO KEY: Colour TV, easy chairs or sofas for all occupants, fridge with icemaker, bedside units or shelves, heating in all rooms.

THREE KEY: Dressing tables, bedside lights, linen and towels available, vacuum cleaner, iron and ironing board.

FOUR KEY: All sleeping in beds/bunks, supplementary lighting in living areas, more kitchen equipment, use of an automatic washing machine and tumble drier.

FIVE KEY: Automatically controlled heating, own washing machine and tumble drier, bath and shower, telephone, dishwasher, microwave and fridge freezer.

Every Key classified holiday home is likely to provide at least some of the facilities and equipment of a higher classification.

More detailed information on what is provided at each Key classification is given in a free *SURE SIGN* leaflet, available at any Tourist Information Centre.

We've checked them out before you check in!

THE CROWN IS YOUR SURE SIGN
OF WHERE TO STAY

HOTELS, GUESTHOUSES, INNS, B&Bs & FARMHOUSES

Throughout Britain, the tourist boards now inspect over 17,000 hotels, guesthouses, inns, B&Bs and farmhouses, every year, to help you find the ones that suit you best.

THE CLASSIFICATIONS: **'Listed'**, and then **ONE to FIVE CROWN,** tell you the range of facilities and services you can expect. The more Crowns, the wider the range (see below).

THE GRADES: **APPROVED, COMMENDED, HIGHLY COMMENDED and DE LUXE,** where they appear, indicate the quality standard provided. If no grade is shown, you can still expect a high standard of cleanliness.

Every classified place to stay has a Fire Certificate, where this is required under the Fire Precautions Act, and all carry Public Liability Insurance.

'Listed': Clean and comfortable accommodation, but the range of facilities and services may be limited.

ONE CROWN: Accommodation with additional facilities, including washbasins in all bedrooms, a lounge and use of a phone.

TWO CROWN: A wider range of facilities and services, including morning tea and calls, bedside lights, colour TV in lounge or bedrooms, assistance with luggage.

THREE CROWN: At least one-third of the bedrooms with ensuite WC and bath or shower, plus easy chair, full length mirror. Shoe cleaning facilities and hairdryers available. Hot evening meals available.

FOUR CROWN: At least three-quarters of the bedrooms with ensuite WC and bath/shower plus colour TV, radio and phone, 24-hour access and lounge service until midnight. Last orders for meals 8.30 pm or later.

FIVE CROWN: All bedrooms having WC, bath and shower ensuite, plus a wide range of facilities and services, including room service, all-night lounge service and laundry service. Restaurant open for breakfast, lunch and dinner.

Every Crown classified place to stay is likely to provide some of the facilities and services of a higher classification. More information available from any Tourist Information Centre.

We've checked them out before you check in!

English Tourist Board Key and Crown

Table 3.8 Number and size of hotels in England, 1991

Size of hotel	Number of hotels	Number in London
1–3 rooms	3,263	13
4–10 rooms	10,180	29
11–15 rooms	3,211	31
16–25 rooms	2,374	38
26–50 rooms	1,863	73
51–100 rooms	872	91
101–200 rooms	375	78
201+ rooms	145	87
Total hotels	22,293	440

Source: English Tourist Board

Hotels may have a variety of charges for rooms. The location of the hotel is likely to be a major factor in determining its popularity. As long as they are of similar quality, those on the seafront or close to city centre entertainments and attractions will probably be able to charge more than those hidden away in back streets. Rates will depend on size, quality and positions of the rooms. They are also likely to change according to the time of year and the day of the week. City hotels frequented by business travellers are often very quiet at weekends, when special rates are offered to attract weekend visitors.

Hotel overheads remain much the same whether the rooms are full or empty and so there is considerable incentive to try and raise **occupancy rates**. Occupancy rates may be measured in terms of rooms occupied or in terms of beds occupied. Single and double occupancy indicates the number of people using a room. In other words every room in a hotel might be occupied without its total capacity being used because many double rooms were being occupied by single people. This would result in less than the maximum revenue being generated. Since different room occupiers may also be paying different rates, hotels often measure their success rate by comparing the actual revenue they receive from room bookings against the maximum they could obtain if all rooms were fully occupied at the maximum rate. Where occupancy rates vary hotels have to decide whether to employ part-time staff at busier times, which may result in a reduction of the quality of service available, or to keep a full complement of full-time staff at all times, which raises their costs.

Many hotels are owned by international companies with a variety of interests. Holiday Inns, for example, were purchased in 1990 by the brewing company, Bass. Large hotel companies like Forte will introduce a degree of standardization in all their hotels. The decor, the tariff, the menus and the uniforms may be used to achieve this. It then enables the company to market them more easily, and to some extent makes different hotels familiar and recognizable to regular customers. Bigger groups will also brand the hotels within the organization according to their levels of service and the relative luxury of their interiors. Thus, within the Hilton group, Hilton International Hotels are bigger four- and five-star hotels, while Hilton National Hotels depend on a more local, commercial market. The centralization of marketing, sales and purchasing for a hotel group can also considerably reduce costs. However, over three-quarters of all the hotels in Britain have fewer than ten rooms and are therefore likely to be of less interest to international companies. Some hotels are independently owned while others are **franchised**. This means the hotel operator pays to use a company brand name and benefits from its marketing. The best-known examples are

55

Holiday Inn, Sheraton, Marriott, Ramada and Hilton International. Groups of independently owned hotels may join together to combine their marketing operations.

Table 3.9 gives an indication of the extent to which hotels are owned or franchised by parent companies.

Table 3.9 The top UK hotel groups, 1993

	Group	Hotels in UK	Rooms in UK
1	Forte	344	30,343
2	Mount Charlotte Thistle Hotels	109	14,071
3	Queens Moat Houses	102	10,407
4	Hilton UK	40	8,501
5	Whitbread Group of Hotels	94	4,438
6	Swallow Hotels	35	4,397
7	Accor UK	28	4,120
8	Holiday Inns Worldwide	23	4,052
9	Stakis Hotels	30	3,688
10	Jarvis Hotels	43	3,522

Source: Caterer and Hotelkeeper

Self-catering accommodation has proved an increasingly popular option for British holidaymakers. Most seaside resorts have a good supply of self-catering apartments, often developed from former guest house premises. Rural tourism has been stimulated by the successful growth of tour operators offering self-catering accommodation in country cottages and farmhouses. Owners of second homes in coastal and countryside areas often let them out to friends and relatives when they are not in residence themselves.

Holiday camps, using chalet-style accommodation, reached their heyday in the 1950s. Competition from relatively inexpensive Mediterranean package holidays resulted in their decline, but they still appeal to families seeking a holiday with plenty of planned activities and supervision available for children. Aware of the competition from foreign destinations with more predictable climates, Center Parcs successfully used new technology, enabling swimming pools, relaxation areas and leisure facilities to be covered so that a warm, light atmosphere is maintained. An increasing proportion of holiday camp accommodation is self-catering.

Timeshare accommodation schemes allow purchasers to use premises, usually furnished and serviced, for a specified time period each year. Some timeshare schemes allow participants to exchange the period they have purchased in a property with clients who have bought the same time period in a timeshare elsewhere. The schemes were initially very popular, especially with property developers in Spain, but adverse publicity about the tactics of timeshare sales teams has made people more wary of such arrangements.

Catering

Catering services also operate separately from accommodation. Cafes, restaurants, fast food outlets and pubs provide a range of choices from quick snacks to *haute cuisine*. Restaurants may offer fixed price menus, where the cost of all courses is included, as well as an *à la carte* **menu**, where customers pay individually for the items on the menu. Most restaurants will employ staff to wait at individual tables though some, such as carveries, may include buffet courses where customers help themselves from a choice of dishes. Some restaurants, particularly those specializing in Indian and Chinese food, have developed a tradition of takeaway services, some of which now include delivery to the customer's door. In 1992 it was estimated that takeaway services accounted for over a quarter of all food prepared in catering establishments.

Perhaps the biggest growth area in catering is in pubs. They have become extensive providers of cooked meals, hot snacks, salads and sandwiches. This may be partly the result of a fall in the consumption of alcohol, with pub operators turning to food services to boost their turnover. It may be too, that in an economic recession, they are seen as good value for money when compared with the higher cost of a restaurant meal.

Fast food outlets, offering items such as hamburgers, pizzas, pasta and baked potatoes, have also flourished by offering inexpensive food in an informal atmosphere. They appeal particularly to families with children. Many new shopping mall developments and large railway stations now have food courts, where a range of fast food outlets surround a common seated eating area. Companies like McDonald's have broadened their product range in order to keep themselves competitive. Other fast food providers, like Kentucky Fried Chicken (now KFC), have increased the seating capacity in many of their outlets in the belief that this can increase sales.

Catering operations also serve non-commercial organizations, sometimes on a wide scale. They will generally receive government subsidies in order to provide meals to schools, hospitals, prisons and to the elderly. With health and education increasingly being released from local authority control, more catering contracts are likely to go to private catering companies.

School meals service
- School meals services employ some 100,000 people
- The 1980 Education Act requires local authorities to provide catering only for those children who qualify for free meals
- The number qualifying for free meals has grown during the recession of the early 1990s
- The number of children taking school meals has declined steadily in recent years
- An estimated 2.64 million children take packed lunches to school each day
- Eighty per cent of school meals are provided by catering teams formerly employed by local authorities; commercial contract caterers provide the rest
- Most contracts to provide school meals insist on a fixed price arrangement
- Many school catering services now advertise their products
- Local authority subsidies for school meals are being phased out
- School meals catering receives an EU subsidy for milk, though this was cut by a quarter in 1993

It is difficult to make catering services supplied to passengers in transit profitable. **In-flight catering** requires food to be prepared and packaged in advance, rapidly chilled, and transported to the right plane under safe health conditions. Regardless of whether the flight departs on time, in-flight caterers aim to ensure that meals are reheated and consumed within 24 hours of being cooked. A single Boeing 747 flight may carry as many as 25,000 catering items and, since each food item has to be individually positioned in the right place on a tray, the preparation is extremely labour intensive. Companies seeking catering contracts with major airlines may be required to prepare more than 20,000 meals a day. Not surprisingly most are situated virtually on the perimeter of the airports they serve. Since many passengers will regard one flight as being much the same as another, in-flight catering remains an important means for many airlines of distinguishing their product from that of their competitors. It also has a practical value in that it relieves tedium and reduces the amount of passenger movement in the confined space available.

Food on British Rail InterCity trains is provided by InterCity On-Board Services. The food service is regarded as a 'value added' element, not necessarily profitable in itself, but helping to retain passengers who, without it, might opt for a different form of transport. Unlike airlines, the cost of food is not included in the rail fare and passengers may move to a restaurant car to be served, thus potentially occupying more than one seat. Two additional problems for InterCity rail caterers are that the average journey time is only two and a quarter hours and that, unlike airlines, it is very difficult to estimate in advance how many passengers will require food.

Table 3.10 Catering companies operating motorway service areas (MSAs), 1993

Company	No of MSAs	Locations
Road Chef Motorways	10	various including Clacket Lane on the M25
Kenning Services	2	both on the M5
Granada	19	various, including on the M4, M6 and M40
Pavilion	11	various
Welcome Break	17	various, including Barn Hill on the M40
Blue Boar	2	including Rothersthorpe on the M1

Activity

Recent deregulation has reduced the minimum permissible distance between two motorway service areas from 30 miles to 15 miles.

1 Study a motorway map of Great Britain and select three sites where there is no motorway service area for 15 miles in either direction.
2 Identify the kind of data a catering company would need to gather in order to decide whether any of the sites could be profitably developed as an MSA.
3 Discuss who you think would be the largest groups of frequent users of each of the three stretches of motorway – commercial heavy goods vehicles, other business traffic, tourists, travel to work traffic, local visitors to friends and relatives, shoppers, other groups.
4 Give a short presentation making out a case for choosing one of the three sites as having the greatest development potential and outlining the kind of catering services which would be most likely to meet the needs of frequent users.

3.5 The provision of agency, information and financial services

Travel agents

The main function of a travel agency is to sell holidays on behalf of tour operators, transport on behalf of airlines or other transport companies, or accommodation on behalf of hotel groups. Additional services connected to the holiday or travel may also be purchased through the travel agent. These include insurance, currency exchange, travellers' cheques, guided tours and tickets for entertainments. Travel agents are generally sited near main shopping centres and some retailers, such as W H Smith, have opened travel agencies within their main stores.

Travel agents provide information to clients to assist them in making holiday and transport choices. Much of the information is delivered through the medium of brochures, but specific data on travel and accommodation arrangements are checked through **computer reservations systems**. Counter staff who have been on educational visits to some destinations can also draw on this personal experience. Some agents will lend potential customers videos featuring popular resorts. Since the brochures are provided by the operators and the agents do not have to purchase stock before they sell anything, their setting up costs are relatively low. However, profit margins on package holidays tend to be low and so agents have to make a lot of sales in order to register a profit.

Increasingly travel agents are being taken over by a small number of 'chains' which, as much larger organizations, are able to negotiate better rates of commission than smaller operators, and invest more heavily in sophisticated reservations technology and marketing campaigns. Figure 3.1 shows the estimated market share of the major travel multiples.

Lunn Poly, part of the Thomson Travel Group, had acquired 578 holiday shops by the end of 1992 and these accounted for some 22 per cent of all the summer inclusive tours sold in the UK.

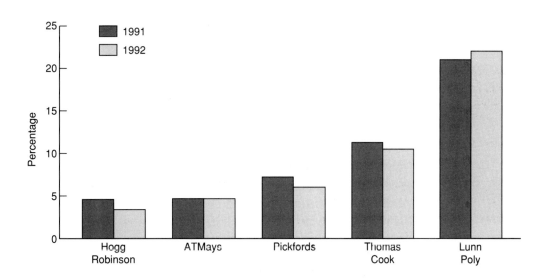

Source: Thomson Travel Group – Annual Report 1992

Figure 3.1 Percentage retail market shares of major travel multiples, 1992

One result of this growth of travel agency 'chains' is to make independent agents more inclined to specialize. They may focus on specific destinations or on particular markets, such as the business traveller. Business travel may appear an attractive option for an agent because the profit margins are generally higher than those on package tours, but there are drawbacks. Business travel differs from leisure travel in that the destination is often not a matter of choice. It may require reservations at short notice and travel plans may change without much warning. Companies generally settle their business travel accounts after the journeys have been made, whereas holidaymakers pay in advance.

Once the client has made a choice, the agent makes the reservation and handles all the necessary paperwork which follows. This involves sending out holiday or travel itineraries, issuing tickets and information, and responding to any questions which the client may raise.

Main Computer Reservations Systems (CRS) used by UK travel agents

Amadeus – a European CRS based in Madrid and owned by Air France, Lufthansa and Iberia airlines.

Galileo – a multinational CRS based in Chicago and half-owned by North American airlines United, USAir and Air Canada, and half-owned by European airlines including Alitalia, British Airways, KLM and Swissair.

Sabre – a CRS developed and owned by American Airlines.

Worldspan – a CRS owned by Delta, Northwest and TWA airlines.

Whenever agents sell a tour operator's holiday or an airline ticket, if they are licensed to do so, they automatically receive a percentage **commission** on the sale. The size of the commission will depend on an agreement between the agent and the providers of the holiday or travel or accommodation, often known as the **principals**. The commission rate may rise if the agent increases sales of a particular product.

Agents are required to hold a licence from the International Air Transport Association (IATA) to sell airline tickets. They may also register with the Association of British Travel Agents (ABTA), which for many years involved a **bonding** system. Each registered agent lodged a bond with ABTA or with a suitable alternative such as a bank and this fund offered consumers protection against any individual member going out of business and leaving holidaymakers stranded or out of pocket. New EU regulations applying to package holidays require all operators to provide adequate consumer protection based on turnover.

Activity

1 Look at the 1980 Standard Industrial Classification for accommodation and catering, below. Does it need modifying in any way in order to reflect how people are employed in catering and accommodation in the mid-1990s?

2 Discuss ways in which this classification might be used to estimate the importance of accommodation and catering as an employer in a single town.

3 How would you assess what proportion of the employment in accommodation and catering in the town was the result of tourism, and what proportion depended on local custom?

(A) Restaurants, snack bars, cafes, and other eating places
Eating places supplying food for consumption on the premises:

1. Licensed places
Eating places licensed to provide alcoholic liquor with meals but not normally providing regular overnight accommodation. Any entertainment provided is incidental to the provision of meals. Railway buffets and dining car services are included.
2. Unlicensed places
Eating places which do not provide alcoholic liquor: ice-cream parlours and coffee bars.
3. Take-away food shops
Fish and chip shops, sandwich bars and other premises supplying prepared food for consumption off the premises.

(B) Public houses and bars
Establishments wholly or mainly engaged in supplying alcoholic liquor for consumption on the premises; the provision of food or entertainment is ancillary and the provision of overnight accommodation, if any, is subordinate.

(C) Hotel trade
1. Licensed premises
Hotels, motels and guest houses providing overnight furnished accommodation with food and service which are licensed to serve liquor.
2. Unlicensed premises
Hotels, motels and guest houses providing overnight furnished accommodation with food and services but are not licensed to serve alcoholic liquor (including bed and breakfast places).

(D) Other tourist or short stay accommodation
1. Camping or caravan sites
The provision of camping and caravan sites for rent. Rented caravan or chalet sites providing food supplies from a retail shop.
2. Holiday camps
Provision of chalet or caravan accommodation having on site a place providing prepared food.
3. Other tourist or short-stay accommodation not elsewhere specified
Holiday centres, conference centres, holiday houses, apartments, flats, youth hostels, non-charitable holiday homes, private rest homes without medical care.

Tourist information centres

The 1969 Development of Tourism Act gave the English Tourist Board (ETB) powers to provide advisory and information services in England. The ETB pursued this major objective by setting up a network of tourist information centres (TICs). These easily recognizable centres aimed to improve the quality of visits by offering guidance about accommodation, attractions, tour routes and leisure facilities. From the early 1980s the

TICs, which were working in partnership with the ETB, were expected to provide an information service about places capable of being reached on an average day's excursion from the centre.

Staff in a TIC need to be familiar with local transport timetables and fares. They should have some knowledge of the availability and standard of local accommodation. They should know how to get to local attractions and what hours they are open to the public. Many of the questions they will be asked will be from people seeking directions, both to tourist attractions but also to places like shops, stations, bus stops, churches and hospitals.

Below are shown the symbols included in the official tourist board guide to Tourist Information Centres and a sample of some of the entries.

Tourist Information Centre symbols

Financial services

Insurance

For many families an annual holiday represents a major investment and taking out holiday insurance is the best means of protecting themselves against anything going wrong. From the beginning of 1993, anyone selling holidays was required as part of the EC directive on package holidays to offer clients travel insurance. Selling insurance is attractive to travel agents because they earn commission on all policies sold.

The most common insurance packages would provide financial compensation in the event of cancellations, loss of or damage to baggage, and any cost incurred in seeking medical help. Some policies also offer a measure of compensation for flight delays or other causes of late arrival at the destination. Particular types of holiday may involve specific risks and insurance cover can be purchased to apply in the event of skiing injuries or road accidents. In parts of the world where medical costs are extremely high, such as the US, cheaper insurance policies may set a maximum claim level which would not cover major medical treatment. Credit and charge card companies often offer purchase protection to people who use them to buy holidays. This would enable them to recoup their money if the holiday was cancelled by the operator, but it would not provide any cover for baggage, medical costs or client cancellation.

Tour operators often include an insurance quotation within the holiday price, indicating on the booking form that clients are not obliged to purchase the policy offered. The insurance quotations and claims are generally dealt with by a separate company. Policies will normally set a maximum sum which can be claimed for each possible event covered. They will also list circumstances, called exclusions, where they will not be held liable. These may include a sum called an **excess**, which represents a fixed sum which the policy-holder must pay before any claim is met. Other exclusions may involve people who have travelled against medical advice, or those who have failed to report loss or damage within 24 hours of its discovery.

Travel insurance is available from banks as well as from insurance companies linked to tour operators. Charges will vary considerably as Table 3.11 shows, but this is often because the amount of cover provided varies.

Table 3.11 Comparison of main outline provisions of sample worldwide travel insurance cover policies, 1993

	Barclays Bank	Nat West Bank	Kuoni Worldwide	Hayes & Jarvis Worldwide
Medical expenses	unlimited	up to £2m	up to £2m (£50 excess)	up to £2m
Hospital benefit	£15 a day – up to £500	£20 a day – up to £400	£30 a day – up to £900	£10 a day
Cancellation	up to £3,000	up to £3,500	up to full cost (excess £50)	up to £4,000
Travel delay	up to £100	up to £100	up to £150	up to £100
Missed departure*	up to £500	up to £350	up to £500	up to £200
Personal property	up to £1,500	up to £1,750	up to £1,200**	up to £1,250**
Personal accident	up to £15,000	up to £25,000	up to £10,000	up to £15,000
Personal liability	up to £2m	N/A	up to £1m	up to £500,000
Legal expenses	up to £25,000	up to £25,000	N/A	up to £5,000
Cost for 60 days' cover	£126	£75	£41	£42

* Where missed departure due to transport failure

** Separate limits set for cash and, with Hayes & Jarvis, certain individual items

Activity

1 Discuss the major differences between the four policies outlined in Table 3.11.
2 Select three contrasting destinations worldwide where travellers might expect to find very different geographical, social and political environments, and note briefly what you think might be the main risks for travellers intending to spend up to 60 days in each one.
3 Suggest in each case which of the four policies outlined might be the most suitable.
4 What details of these policies, not included in the outlines, would you want to know if you were actually intending to visit one of the three destinations you chose?

Currency and travellers' cheques

Holidaymakers going abroad need cash to pay for goods and services. Carrying sufficient cash for a family two-week holiday increases the risk of theft. One way round this problem is to pay, wherever possible, with charge or credit cards, or with cheques, but none of these are universally accepted. The most popular alternative is to carry travellers' cheques which can be converted into local currency at banks and, in some destinations, in hotels and shops.

The main advantage of travellers' cheques is that they can only be cashed by whoever buys them. They are signed in the presence of a cashier when they are purchased and signed again when they are cashed in. Most travellers take some foreign currency with them for immediate use. The exchange rates between different currencies fluctuates and can be a significant factor in making particular destinations attractive or otherwise.

Sellers of travellers' cheques profit from a small percentage sum above the face value of the cheques paid by purchasers. Companies like American Express, who supply travellers' cheques, invest the money they receive and earn interest until the time comes to repay the foreign banks where the cheques have been cashed. A condition of allowing agents to sell travellers' cheques is that they return payments received for them to the company supplying the cheques within an agreed time, usually one week.

American Express Travellers' Cheques

- If lost or stolen they can normally be replaced within 24 hours
- Hotels, shops and restaurants accept them all over the world
- Dollar travellers' cheques can be used like cash in America
- Ensure you have access to funds if your cash and/or credit cards are stolen
- Enable you to budget your holiday spending money
- Can be ordered in a variety of major foreign currencies
- Can be rapidly replaced through the 24-hour worldwide refund delivery service

---

Source: Lloyds Bank 'Travel Services' booklet

Travellers often need foreign currency when they arrive at an overseas destination. They may have to pay for taxis, give tips or pay for food and drinks. Banks may not keep regular opening hours and are closed at weekends. Exchanging currency before departure can be done through banks which will make a commission charge, usually based on the amount exchanged. In many countries currency can be exchanged in hotels and at exchange offices, but these will often provide a less favourable rate than banks. In countries with a high rate of inflation, such as the former Soviet Union, there may be shops which only accept certain 'hard' foreign currencies like US dollars. Since these hard currencies hold their value more consistently than local ones they are much in demand and often the subject of unofficial black market exchange arrangements.

3.6 The provision of sports participation facilities

Taking part in sport is only possible if access to the necessary facilities is available. In some cases, such as squash, this may require the construction of a very specific built environment. In others, such as fishing, the main resource needed may be a part of the natural environment. Obviously little can be done to control the location of naturally occurring sporting venues, but the provision of built ones is generally a response to a community need or a commercial decision that there is a potential market for a private sector development.

Table 3.12 shows the percentage of the population taking part in outdoor sports, games and physical activities in 1990. The survey sample was asked whether they had taken part in the activity in the four weeks leading up to the interview.

Table 3.12 Percentage of people participating in sports

Walking	41%
Cycling	9%
Golf	5%
Running/jogging	5%
Swimming	4%
Soccer	4%
Tennis	2%
Fishing	2%
Bowls	1%
Water sports	1%
Cricket	1%
Horse riding	1%
Field sports	1%
Sailing	1%
Hockey	1%

Outdoor sports facilities

Most people take part in organized sport for the first time at school. Some of the sports pitches on school and college sites are available for public use in the evenings and at weekends, especially those intended for soccer, hockey, netball and cricket. This is particularly true where all-weather surfaces have been installed, reducing the harmful effects of frequent use. Sports pitches are often located in public parks and administered by local authorities. In this case they are generally available for public hire and are often used without payment by casual visitors. Many sports pitches are owned by private sports clubs and by larger companies providing them as a benefit for their staff. Generally these can be used only by official club members or company employees and their guests.

The Register of Recreational Land

A recent estimate suggested that there might be as many as 70,000 pitches in England. Most of these are in urban areas and may come under pressure from the demand for new land for building development. Concern about this threat resulted in a £500,000 government grant being made available in order to establish a Register of Recreational Land. It is hoped that this register, to be completed during 1993, should identify where the current pitches are and help to protect those which are meeting an obvious demand.

Most towns and cities have a number of sports stadiums which can cater for spectators as well as participants. Though many of these are likely to be private and reserved for the use of professional players, some are used by groups like amateur athletes and hockey players. Synthetic tracks and playing areas are commonly used for both athletics and hockey, providing a truer and more reliable playing surface than grass. Though less regular maintenance is required the surfaces generally have to be completely replaced every seven to ten years. Access to such synthetic surfaces may be restricted to people who have achieved a high level of performance in their chosen sports. Sports stadiums are also often hired out for occasional leisure activities, such as firework displays or marching band competitions.

Golf, tennis and bowls are all sports to which the public have come to expect reasonable access. Facilities for tennis and bowls are often available in public parks, though it is noticeable that indoor facilities for both sports are increasingly fashionable. The indoor facilities are in the main private clubs, admitting only those who have paid an annual membership fee. The demand for golf increased more rapidly in the 1980s than the supply of golf courses. Golf courses consume extensive areas of land, and require generous supplies of water and staff to maintain. They can only accommodate a finite number of players at any one time and so their income is limited by this factor. Perhaps for this reason many golf clubs have developed driving ranges, sports goods shops and professional tuition services. Many golf courses are traversed by footpaths and public rights of way, and have thus become popular walking areas.

Artificial ski slope

Dry ski slopes
- The first outdoor artifical ski slope in the UK was opened in the 1960s at Crystal Palace in London
- By the end of 1991 there were over 120 in the UK
- The surfaces are constructed from plastic or PVC
- 80 per cent of the users are under 40
- More than 50 per cent of users are practising for snow skiing: 25 per cent have never skied on snow
- In 1990 an estimated one million Britons went skiing abroad
- A number of centres are planning ski slopes using snow machines to produce 'real' snow

---

Skiing is a more recent but extremely popular interest. The short European skiing holiday season and the shortage of suitable skiing locations in Britain has led to the construction of artificial ski slopes, sometimes by private developers and sometimes as part of local authority leisure provision. As with golf courses, artificial ski slopes consume space and they can also be visually unattractive unless they use existing natural land contours.

Water is an essential resource for a whole range of outdoor sports. Fishing, often claimed to be the most popular British sport, requires access to canals, lakes and rivers. The owners must be willing to grant fishing rights, which may be done by selling permits to anglers. In order to meet the needs of anglers, many lakes and waterways have been artifically restocked with fish. On some waterways the interests of sport and leisure may conflict. The needs of canal anglers are very different from the needs of people taking canal boat holidays. Larger water spaces, often artificially created by excavating gravel or constructing enclosed docks, are increasingly in demand for sports like windsurfing, rowing, water-skiing and power boat racing.

Rural areas have traditionally supported sports like horse riding and shooting. More affluent suburbs, especially those on the outer fringe of cities, are likely locations for facilities like equestrian centres and shooting ranges. They are close enough to the country to provide enough space, but near enough to population centres to attract custom. Both may have other reasons for not being too close to busy areas: equestrian centres because the horses will be more difficult to control in heavy traffic and shooting ranges because they have to be absolutely sure that the range itself is completely secure.

Outward bound centres can be found in more remote rural areas. They offer supervised instruction in sports like climbing, canoeing and orienteering. They are very dependent on natural resources like mountains, rivers and forests.

Indoor sports facilities

Swimming has long been regarded as a particularly valuable form of exercise, enabling good all-round muscle use. However the British climate means that opportunities for outdoor swimming are far from year round and the majority of regular swimmers in Britain make use of the estimated 1,300 public indoor swimming pools. Many of these were developed as part of local authority leisure provision. The introduction of compulsory competitive tendering, whereby private companies could put in bids to run various local services, has meant that a number of pools are now managed by companies in the private sector.

The paragraphs below were adapted from an article in a Hertfordshire local newspaper.

Swimming pools go up market

Do you remember the days when swimming pools were white-tiled halls with ugly wooden cubicles round the edge and with that pervasive smell of chlorine everywhere? The water was invariably freezing, changing an embarrassment and there seemed few concessions to those of us seeking to come to terms with a basic fear of getting into the water at all.

Well, it seems those days are long gone. Nowadays you are more likely to find a variety of water-based activities, including features like flumes and artificial wave machines which will keep the younger members of the family amused for hours. Learning to swim is no longer a matter of hanging on desperately to a bar in the shallow end – training and learning pools can be found in most modern pools. Even those of us who are older and more sober are as likely to be well catered for with specialist swimming lanes, jacuzzis, saunas and sun beds. Sitting recently in the comfort of my local aquatic centre's coffee bar, I felt only the slightest twinge of nostalgia for the paper cup of Bovril dispensed by a sullen matron in the lobby of the swimming baths of my youth.

Many indoor sports use the general facilities provided by sports halls. These usually consist of a large main room which can quickly be adapted for activities like badminton, keep fit, five-a-side football or judo. Smaller rooms may be equipped for use by specialist groups like weight-lifters. Squash courts may also form part of the sports hall complex. Increased exposure on television for indoor competitions featuring bowls and tennis, previously perceived as mainly outdoor sports, has encouraged the growth of indoor facilities catering specifically for these sports. In the case of tennis, a desire to improve the international competitiveness of future British professionals saw the 1986 launch of the Sports Councils's Indoor Tennis Initiative, a scheme aimed to make tennis available to a much wider cross-section of the population.

It has become increasingly evident that interest in health and fitness is growing rapidly. If this originated with the medical profession, it has been taken up by the media and by advertisers, both through their products and through the images of desirable lifestyles which they portray. Most population centres are now served by mainly private sector health and fitness clubs. These are generally equipped with a range of fitness monitoring machines enabling users to run, cycle, row and lift weights, according to appropriate personal programmes. They also often offer a range of classes and beauty treatments which can provide manicuring, skin care, dietary advice and stress management courses.

Table 3.13 shows the percentage of people participating in indoor sports within a four-week period prior to being interviewed in 1990.

Table 3.13 Indoor sports participants

Activity	% taking part
Snooker/pool/billiards	14
Swimming	12
Keep fit/yoga	12
Darts	7
Weight lifting/training	5
Tenpin bowling/skittles	4
Badminton	3
Squash	3
Indoor soccer	2
Table tennis	2
Indoor bowls	1
Self defence	1
Ice skating	1
Basketball	1

Source: adapted from *General Household Survey*

The David Lloyd clubs

69

Activity

Planning permission is being sought on the outskirts of a town in your area for each of the four following sports facilities:

- an indoor climbing centre featuring three walls offering a range of climbing routes from the basic to the international competition level;
- a synthetic all-weather athletics track to be laid at an existing leisure centre;
- a nine-hole golf course on land adjacent to a public park;
- an indoor tennis centre, providing four courts, to be run as a private members' club.

1 The planning authorities decide that they must first prioritize the four proposals. In what order do you think they would place them?

2 What local factors would they consider in deciding an order of priority?

3 If all four developments required financial investment from local companies, which proposals do you think they would be willing to support?

4 What conditions might they insist on in return for this investment?

3.7 The provision of sports spectator facilities

Outdoor sports

Well-established national sports like football, horse-racing and cricket have traditionally drawn large crowds of spectators. Where a stadium is used the crowds continued to grow as long as there was both space and a reasonable view. The biggest crowds were generally recorded before the Second World War. In more recent times the advent of televised sport, and the rapid growth in the number of leisure choices available, has resulted in lower attendances though, as Table 3.14 shows, sports like soccer are still capable of appealing to large numbers.

Table 3.14 Average attendance at Football League matches

Year	Division 1	Division 2	Division 3	Division 4
1961/2	26,106	16,132	9,419	6,060
1966/7	30,829	15,701	8,009	5,407
1971/2	31,352	14,652	8,510	4,981
1976/7	29,540	13,529	7,522	3,863
1980/1	24,660	11,202	6,590	3,082
1986/7	19,800	9,000	4,300	3,100
1991/2	21,622	10,525	5,423	3,404

Source: Football League

Crowd safety has become an increasing concern for the administrators of spectator sports. The tragedies at Hillsborough and Bradford in England, and the Heysel Stadium in Belgium, all resulting in the deaths of spectators, highlighted the need for improved crowd control and more thorough safety checks on the fabric of the stadiums themselves. The immediate consequence of these tragedies was the setting up of a government commission to report on stadium safety. The findings of this commission were published in the Taylor Report.

The need for better evacuation procedures was stressed by the report, which also led to legislation requiring all major Football League grounds to become all-seater stadiums.

Main safety problems at sports grounds

Underfoot conditions – poor building work and/or lack of proper maintenance can result in individuals falling or tripping. Individual incidents can rapidly escalate through crowd pressure.

Crowd pressures – can be caused by overcrowding, by sudden crowd surges, and by crowds converging on entrances and exits. Motion or swaying by sections of a crowd can cause individuals to fall and crowd pressures can make it very difficult to help them.

Emergency evacuation – crowd disorder or fire may require evacuation which should be orderly to be safe, but crowd pressure may be increased by panic. Spectators in elevated and covered areas can face greater evacuation problems. In the case of fire construction materials in the ground itself may increase the fire risk.

Source: adapted from 'Guide to Safety at Sports Grounds' (Home Office/Scottish Office)

Racecourses originally traversed suitable pieces of private or common land. The emergence of horse-racing as a major gambling sport enhanced its popularity and enclosed race tracks are now found in most parts of Britain. Like motor racing tracks, and indeed like most open air sports stadiums, they are only used on a limited number of days each year. In both cases the major events of the year, like the Derby, the Grand National and the British Grand Prix draw exceptional crowds, general substantial revenue and create chaotic local traffic congestion! Horse-racing contributes indirectly to the national economy through the revenue derived from taxation on betting. As the costs of maintaining racecourses and stables have risen, so has the demand for increased government support for horse-racing.

Indoor sports

The range of indoor spectator sports tends to be subject to changing fashions. Ice hockey has been through both highly popular periods as well as times when players had great difficulty in securing the use of an ice rink. Television has boosted interest in sports like snooker and darts, once perceived more as leisure activities than sports capable of attracting big audiences. Sports like show jumping and boxing attract loyal followers to indoor arenas, though both have their critics too. The presence of international stars will attract crowds to watch major tennis, basketball and squash events. The design of courts, playing surfaces and lighting systems has done much to make these sports more accessible to the indoor spectator.

3.8 The provision of entertainment facilities

Facilities dedicated to a single type of entertainment, such as a traditional theatre with a raised stage and tiered seating, are often under-used. The modern trend in many population centres is to develop flexible facilities which can be quickly adapted for use as concert halls, theatre or film auditoriums, dance halls or floor space for sports or indoor events like political rallies or antiques markets.

Most modern centres offering entertainment now include facilities intended to keep visitors there for longer. Rather than just coming in to see a film or for a swim, visitors are encouraged to have a drink and a chat in a bar area, or to take advantage of restaurant or snack bar facilities. The emphasis on this social element can both raise the importance of the centre as a community meeting place and increase the revenue derived from visitors staying longer.

In 1994 Stuttgart in Germany will open what is described as 'an entertainment city'. This scheme will include an 1,800 seat theatre, a health spa complex, and hotel and restaurant facilities. The centre will use a theatrical theme in the design of shops, bars and surrounding streets. The siting of the project in Stuttgart highlighted the fact that theatre productions, especially musicals, can draw large numbers of visitors to stay in cities. However, outside London's West End and New York's Broadway there are very few cities with a high concentration of theatres. It was felt that the presence of a major theatre in the city would significantly increase the number of short break visits to Stuttgart.

The Barbican Centre, York

The Barbican Centre in York is an example of a facility offering multiple uses. It has fixed seating for up to 1,500, but more than half of these seats can be automatically retracted. The main auditorium is sound-proofed by means of a surrounding acoustic corridor. Sports facilities, including a swimming pool and a climbing wall, have been incorporated into the whole design. Semi-sprung floors in side rooms make them ideal for use as dance studios. Local residents are encouraged to make use of the Barbican Centre in York by the issue of cards giving discounts on both admission to events and participation in sporting activities.

Any multi-purpose complex will need reasonable acoustics and lines of vision to accommodate a wide range of events. Modern concert halls are specially designed to encourage good sound quality throughout. Hi-fi and video equipment in the home has improved so much that people's expectations of the sound quality of public performances are high. Modern halls often use devices which can vary the acoustics according to different needs. Panels, curtains and ceilings form part of a retractable design which can alter the amount of reflected sound. An individual making a speech will require less sound to be absorbed than a sound system playing amplified music. A canopy capable of lowering the ceiling can make a room large enough to accommodate the performance of a full symphony orchestra adaptable enough to be used for solo recitals.

Cinemas have also undergone many changes in recent times. Many larger, old cinemas containing a single auditorium have had their interiors ripped out and have been rebuilt as multi-screen facilities. It is estimated that these centres, sometimes described as **multiplexes** and offering up to ten different film shows in the same building, now account for a third of all the cinema screens in the UK. Multiplex centres may have different seating capacities for different films so that highly popular films can be shown alongside some which are likely to attract smaller audiences. The centres aim to make cinema attendance more comfortable than was the case with many older buildings. They also need substantial parking areas to cope with audience capacities which can be over 2,000. Some multiplexes also feature facilities like ten-pin bowling alleys, ice skating rinks and night clubs. Table 3.15 gives an idea of how the level of cinema attendance among different age groups has varied since 1984. The figures represent a percentage of all those attending the cinema at least once in any given year.

Table 3.15 Cinema attendance: by age

Aged	1984	1986	1988	1990	1991
7–14	73	87	84	85	80
15–24	59	82	81	87	88
25–34	49	65	64	79	70
35–44	45	60	61	70	70
45 and over	13	25	34	41	39
All persons aged 7 and over	38	53	56	64	61

Source: Cinema and Video Industry Audience Research

Activity

Identify changing trends in the cinema attendance of different age groups from Table 3.15 and discuss the potential reasons for these changes.

The theatre as a form of popular entertainment has had to face increasing financial problems throughout the 1980s. These problems have often resulted in price increases putting many major performances out of the price range of many people. Attracting only the most affluent groups may also limit the range of theatrical events staged, increasing the perception that drama and opera are primarily for the well-off middle class. Another factor which limits the kind of audiences theatres attract is that obtaining tickets for popular shows necessitates booking weeks in advance, while cinema audiences can generally queue and buy tickets on the day of the performance. West End theatres, increasingly dependent on audiences of over-seas visitors, were also hit hard by the fall in the number of American visitors during and after the Gulf War. Unlike the cinema, whose audiences largely come from among the young, the theatre appeals more to older age groups. Theatres have traditionally provided more opportunity to socialize, with drinks intervals available mid-way through the evening, and bar facilities often available before and after performances. Many provincial theatres run clubs and workshops, as well as family membership schemes, designed to increase the interest of young people. The example below shows how many theatres see catering as a means of boosting their attendances and profits.

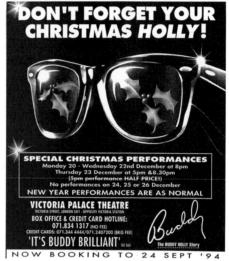

Newspaper listings of West End theatre productions

The Cafe Theatre Royal at the Drury Lane site, situated in the cavernous first floor bar, is decked out in oriental flavour to reflect the on-stage production of Miss Saigon.

Such theming extends to the menu where dishes such as chicken satay, shredded duck salad, sweet chillied beef and water chestnuts are on offer.

Dinner and theatre tickets can be booked in advance by credit card and the plan is that packages will eventually provide a major part of the on-site catering business.

Source: Caterer and Hotelkeeper

Technological development is now a major influence on new entertainment facilities. Advances in film technology means that realistic simulations, some incorporating synchronized seat movements, can give people the impression that they are taking part in fantastic adventures. People entering the *Back to the Future* attraction at Universal Studios in Florida are strapped into a car and taken on a rapid chase simulating a journey through time. Other film developments include 3D films and domed theatres where the audience can watch 180 or even 360 degree films. The capacity to relay video pictures on to large screens has been used in a variety of other entertainments. Rock concerts attracting large crowds to stadiums use them as a means of giving those at the back a close up of the bands. Spectators at major sports events also benefit in this way, as well as being able to see exciting moments and contentious decisions again.

Entertainment in many town centres is dominated largely by pubs and clubs. Pubs in particular have extended the range of entertainments they offer in order to attract more custom. Live music is common, while events like quiz nights, karaoke evenings, stand-up comics and pub games competitions are regularly staged in many pubs. These events are often intended to broaden customer range. In many areas pubs were traditionally male-oriented, and their exteriors made them difficult to see into and hence unwelcoming. In an attempt to get away from this image some modern pubs have been refurbished and renamed, often taking on a themed style intended to appeal to younger people.

Stricter laws on drinking and driving, and wider publicity given to the health risks involved in excessive alcohol consumption, have caused a fall in sales of beer, traditionally the main source of income for pubs. To counter this the majority of pubs now offer some sort of food service, varying from snacks to hot meals. Many country pubs dependent on customers arriving by car have seen a decline in business in recent years.

Pubs in town centres have to manage very different patterns of use from those in suburbs. They may be most busy for a couple of hours at lunchtime, and for an hour or so as people leave work on weekdays and, unless they are close to visitor attractions, very quiet at weekends. Suburban pubs are more likely to be busy during the evenings and at weekends.

Activity

Write the introduction for a new publication, titled *The Good Night Club Guide*. In it you should discuss the criteria that the editors might use to judge which clubs should be included in the guide. You might approach the task by including a personal account of a visit to your own ideal night club.

A study of existing hotel and pub guides might also suggest other ways of approaching this task.

3.9 The provision of other recreation facilities

Gardening is one of the most popular forms of recreation in Britain. A recent estimate suggested some 125,000 people are members of horticultural and gardening clubs. A choice of garden centres can be found in most towns and cities, and gardening books are much in demand. Between 1987 and 1991 attendance at the majority of Britain's most popular gardens showed a marked increase, despite the fact that attendances at other attractions were for the most part decreasing. Most public gardens also provide retail services offering seeds, plants, garden furniture, materials to improve both the soil and the garden design, and a range of gardening books. Municipal parks and gardens generally try to cater for a broad range of interest groups. They often contain sports pitches, tennis courts, children's play areas and quiet, enclosed flower gardens. Many users favour them for walking and they tend to be popular with dog owners.

The idea of garden festivals

The idea of rejuvenating industrial and urban dereliction by a massive concentrated effort on the part of government and other supporting bodies first appeared in Germany just after the Second World War. Hanover had been badly damaged by Allied bombing, but by 1949 plans were already under way to breathe fresh life back into that city by holding a Bundesgartenschau, a garden festival, there in 1951. The concept was at that time a revolutionary environmental initiative providing a means of restoring an infrastructure of roads, housing, industry, parks and gardens to an area that had become a wasteland.

Such was the success of the garden festival that the concept was soon taken up by other countries. It finally came to Britain in 1981, when Michael Heseltine, then Minister of the Environment, gave the go ahead for the International Garden Festival which was held in 1984 in Liverpool. Since then national garden festivals have been staged in Stoke-on-Trent (1986), Glasgow (1988), Gateshead (1990) and Ebbw Vale (1992).

A number of major events exploit this national interest in gardening. The Chelsea Flower Show attracts up to 200,000 visitors annually. National garden festivals held in Liverpool, Stoke-on-Trent, Glasgow, Gateshead and Ebbw Vale received government funding for major renovation of both inner city and industrially polluted sites. Apart from attracting visitors, the aim of these festivals was to encourage companies to see the potential of these renovated areas and to consider investing in them.

Though dancing is not perhaps as popular as it was before the Second World War, hotels still find that dinner dances bring in extra customers. There is still sufficient interest in ballroom dancing for this to be a valuable **niche market** in areas within reach of a reasonable number of people in the 40-plus age group. Disco dancing will appeal more to a younger market, though it is often a standard form of entertainment at family occasions like weddings and anniversaries. The majority of disco operations are mobile, with disc-jockeys and equipment being transported to a range of venues. Facilities which operate permanently as night clubs and discos are sometimes integrated into hotel or pub premises, and managed by the same company.

For many people increased leisure time has provided an opportunity for study. They may feel a need to make up for something they were unable to achieve at school. They may want further qualification to enhance their career opportunities or they may wish to learn new skills. For those with special interests, further education may be purely a matter of enjoyment. Facilities like libraries and adult education classes are invaluable in providing and supporting these learning opportunities. The fact that these services are generally provided solely out of local authority funding makes them vulnerable to cuts when economic times are difficult.

It could be argued that shopping is no longer simply a means of providing necessities like food and clothing. The design of huge new shopping complexes like the Metrocentre in Gateshead acknowledges that, for many people, shopping represents a pleasurable leisure experience. Window displays, public performances, piped music and a range of food outlets generate something of interest for most tastes. Some shopping complexes also contain cinemas and facilities for sports like squash or bowling; others include fairground rides for children.

3.10 The role of the different economic sectors in leisure provision

Industrial activity is frequently divided into three sectors – **public**, **private** and **voluntary** – though in practice much leisure provision may be difficult to categorize wholly into any single sector. The main distinctions between the three sectors are:

- **public sector** – organizations and facilities, often providing a public service, funded mainly by central or local government through national or local taxation, by means of grants or in the form of subsidies;
- **private sector** – companies providing products and services in order to generate financial profit;
- **voluntary sector** – generally non-profit-making organizations and facilities dependent on volunteers, and often serving special needs and interest groups.

It is now much more difficult to link specific types of leisure provision to public, private or voluntary sectors than it used to be. Government funded bodies like the Sports Council, on the surface belonging clearly in the public sector, increasingly raise additional funds from a mixture of commercial activities and sponsorship arrangements. Since the advent of compulsory competitive tendering, many public facilities are now managed by private companies. Major leisure and retail developments have been jointly planned and funded by partnerships between commercial companies and local authorities keen to stimulate regional economies. The growing presence of sponsorship, especially in sport, means that many voluntary organizations now derive direct financial support from the private sector in return for promoting company products. The distinctions between leisure services for the community, profit-making leisure developments and voluntary organizations run for the benefit of special interest groups are often far from clear.

Table 3.16 offers some examples of facilities which are commonly, though not always, mainly identified with either the public, private or voluntary sectors.

Table 3.16 Economic sectors and the provision of leisure facilities

Sector	Interests within sector	Examples of provision
Public sector	Central government	Royal parks, national sports centres, e.g. Lilleshall, Bisham Abbey
	Local government	Playing fields, swimming pools, leisure centres, parks, gardens, allotments, community centres, libraries, regional theatres
Private sector	Members' only sports clubs	Golf, squash, snooker, health and fitness centres, country clubs
	Payment on admission entertainment centres	Cinemas, theatres, bowling alleys, skating rinks, dance halls, professional sport, theme parks, bingo halls
	Employee benefits	Company-owned sports grounds, bars, dance and entertainment venues
Voluntary sector	Amateur sports clubs and arts groups	Amateur drama/opera groups, hockey, rugby, cricket and soccer clubs
	Interest groups and charities	Conservation and heritage groups, community action groups, youth organizations

Assignment 3
Present provision of leisure and tourism products and services

This assignment develops knowledge and understanding of the following elements:

1.2 Investigate UK leisure and tourism products
1.3 Investigate the variety of local services and products
1.4 Identify sources of income for leisure and tourism facilities
4.2 Identify market opportunities
4.3 Plan promotional activities

It supports development of the following core skills:
Communication 3.2, 3.3
Information Technology 3.2, 3.3, 3.4

Your tasks

Design a promotional campaign intended to attract companies to establish bases and/or new outlets in an area or region which has already successfully enhanced its leisure and tourism provision.

Among the things your campaign might seek to demonstrate about the area or region are that it:

- offers a pleasant environment in which to live;
- has an existing infrastructure capable of supporting business expansion;
- is economically 'on the up';
- provides local residents with easy access to a range of leisure activities.

4 The impact of the leisure and tourism industry

What is covered in this chapter

This chapter examines the major effects which tourism and leisure development has on a country or region. It points out that both benefits and losses can result, and that the leisure and tourism industry needs to be sensitive to impacts if it is not to destroy the resources on which it depends – in particular landscape, culture and people.

- The economic impact
- The social impact
- The cultural impact
- The environmental impact

4.1 The economic impact of leisure and tourism

Like all activities with economic consequences, there are both costs and benefits derived from leisure and tourism. Additional earnings of foreign exchange and increased employment are two evident gains. However, not all the revenue derived from leisure and tourism activities reaches and hence benefits the local community. This is especially true in countries and regions relatively new to leisure and tourism development, where the costs of developing and servicing facilities result in a flow of money out of the country or region.

These losses are often referred to as **leakages** and may include payments for:

- imported food for tourists;
- expertise, materials and sometimes labour for building and infrastructure development;
- the repayment of loans and interest secured abroad to finance leisure and tourism developments;
- commissions paid to foreign travel organizers;
- fees to foreign-based training companies.

> Travel and Tourism is the world's largest industry today accounting for more than 6% of Gross Domestic Product, 1 in every 15 workers, 7% of capital investment and 13% of consumer spending worldwide. We forecast that Travel and Tourism's contribution to the global GDP will grow by more than 100% in the period leading up to 2005, that capital investment will grow by 80% and that employment generated will rise by 33%. This last figure represents some 40 million jobs or, worldwide, one new job every 10 seconds.

Source: World Travel and Tourism Council – Progress and Priorities, 1993

Ownership of leisure and tourism developments frequently determines the extent of any leakages. A new hotel being developed by a multinational group is likely to buy all its expertise and materials from well-established sources of its own. Only where national or local government legislation directs the use of local labour and materials can this be limited.

The costs of establishing leisure and tourism developments include providing adequate **infrastructure**, including the provision of roads, sewage systems, telecommunications links, and water and power supplies. The presence of greater numbers of visitors brings labour costs other than those directly related to providing leisure and tourism services, principally in areas like cleaning and policing. In the case of tourism, rapid growth can stimulate other areas of the local or national economy too. A principle known as the tourism income multiplier, sometimes called more simply the **multiplier effect**, suggests that money paid by visitors to settle hotel bills or to buy local goods is spent by local people on goods and services which they need, so that a proportion of the money originally spent circulates among other local business interests. The extent to which tourism or leisure income does multiply in this way depends very much on the relative amount of leakage of revenue from the region or country.

Travel and tourism as an economic catalyst
- **Job creation** – travel and tourism creates jobs more rapidly than most other industries.
- **Multiplier effect** – a wide range of other activities are stimulated by travel and tourism development, including infrastructure projects, agriculture, manufacturing, high technology and communications.
- **New business formation** – travel and tourism encourages small and medium-sized businesses which in turn help to generate service and entrepreneurial skills.
- **Services stimulus** – spin-offs like insurance, financial services and communications emerge alongside travel and tourism development, creating further job and training opportunities.

Source: The World Travel and Tourism Council

Where leisure and tourism have been used to attract high spenders from outside the region, one negative economic result can be **price inflation**. Local communities might be relatively unaffected if this were restricted to luxury goods and items like souvenirs. However increased demand for food, land and property can put essential purchases out of reach of local people. This can offset the advantage of increasing employment opportunities by reducing the value of earnings. The potential in poorer countries for people to obtain higher earnings for employment in tourism can attract people away from traditional industries like agriculture and fishing. This migration may make food products scarcer, which can in turn inflate the prices of essential products.

The net economic value of leisure and tourism to a region or country depends on a range of factors. These include:
- whether it derives income from other industrial sources;
- whether demand for the specific attractions and facilities it offers is constant;
- whether the majority of leisure and tourism facilities and developments are locally owned;

- the systems of taxation and public spending in operation;
- in the case of international tourism, the strength of the local economy and its currency compared with those overseas;
- the ability of the standards found in developments and infrastructure to keep pace with the growing demands and sophistication of the market;
- the ability to persuade local residents not to counteract increasing earnings by going out of the region or country to spend them.

4.2 The social impact of tourism

The leisure and tourism industries both rely heavily for their success on contact with people. Many leisure activities require supervision; some require coaching. Tour operators often suggest that the main advantage of holidays in particular destinations is the friendliness of the people. Yet the meetings between the customers experiencing leisure and tourism, and the people supplying the services needed to support it can have considerable impact on society in general. This is particularly true where tourists from wealthier countries are travelling to areas where the general standard of living is lower.

There are often major cultural differences between tourists and the residents of the places they are visiting, incorporating differences of language, religion, food, dress and moral codes. Encounters between the two may in theory lead to a greater awareness and understanding of other people's beliefs and values, but this assumes that such contacts actually encourage genuine exchanges of ideas. Tourists do not stay very long, nor do they meet host communities on equal terms. Local people are often acting in the capacity of servants, which may lead them to feel either that it is not their place to initiate discussion with their visitors or that they resent the inferior status conferred on them.

Given that much tourist–host contact is impersonal it is perhaps not surprising that tourists often remain unaware of the social impact of their presence. They are in any case indulging themselves and would not wish their quest for enjoyment to be spoiled by concerns about tensions within the local community. In many countries new to tourism it is women and children who derive most direct financial income from its presence. This can put great strain on traditional family relationships, especially when cleaning, selling souvenirs or asking tourists for money brings more cash than traditional means of earning a living. The involvement of children is a further cause for concern because potential income from tourism, even though this may only be short term, is sometimes seen as more important than completing education.

Tourists on holiday often appear to local people to be wealthy, to spend all their time enjoying themselves and to have few worries. This leads, especially in areas where the standard of living of the host community is markedly below that of most of the visitors, to imitation. In a process often referred to as the **demonstration effect** local people will copy the clothing, food tastes, attitudes and values of people they perceive as being more sophisticated. This can be a major cause of social conflict, particularly between generations. It is often young people who imitate the visitors, while the older residents speak out for traditional customs and values. Ironically the tourists themselves may behave in a much less uninhibited way once they have returned to their own communities.

The effects of tourism on the Maasai people of Kenya

The Maasai people have pursued a pastoral life in Northern Tanzania for more than two centuries. However, over the last 30 years the government has introduced regulations designed to protect the regions which now form the Serengeti National Park and the Ngorongoro Conservation Area. These areas, with their outstanding wildlife, are major tourist attractions and, as such, are a major source of foreign exchange. The Maasai were forced to evacuate significant parts of their traditional lands, including grazing areas and land containing water sources for their cattle. The consequence of these impositions has been a considerable deterioration in the living conditions of the Maasai. Their livestock-keeping and their freedom to cultivate land in the area have been severely restricted.

Impoverished living conditions and the increased need for cash made many young Maasai try to earn money from tourism in an informal way. Many stood along the main road to Serengeti and the Ngorongoro Crater waiting for tourists and hoping that they would pay to take pictures of them.

A recent tourist survey showed that although tourists' main interests are in the wildlife and landscapes, they are also interested in the culture and traditions of Maasai society. At the moment, however, the tourist and the Maasai are alienated from each other. For both, their only interest is to profit as much as possible from each other – the tourists by taking pictures of the Maasai; the Maasai by getting money from the tourists. They don't see each other as dignified human beings.

The Maasai now want to secure other and better ways to show the tourists something of their traditions and culture. They have three suggestions as to how to do this: the women are very eager to start a project for making and selling necklaces and other souvenirs; a Maasai boma could be built in which cultural dances can be performed and where tourists could stay overnight in a Maasai hut, also serving as a village museum for the tourists; walking safaris with Maasai guides could be offered.

The survey suggested that 87 per cent of those who had bought souvenirs would prefer to buy them direct from the Maasai. A similar proportion would have liked the opportunity to visit a Maasai village and take a safe walking safari with a Maasai guide. It is clear that there is a large gap between the potential tourist interest in the Maasai and actual contact currently made.

Source: '*What about the Maasai?*' – an article by Tate Olerokonga in the Tourism Concern magazine *In Focus*

It is wrong to attribute the demonstration effect solely to tourism. The advent of satellite technology means that television programmes can now be received in areas previously considered very isolated. Images of the lifestyles of richer nations are received through this medium. Since many of the programmes are fictional, the picture which emerges may be a far from accurate reflection of the true standard of living experienced by the majority of those living in wealthier economies.

A rise in crime – especially theft, prostitution and drug trafficking – is generally considered to be one of the likely consequences of any major new growth in tourism. Tourists represent a group with money to spend, often unsure of their surroundings and unlikely to stay long enough to pursue identified criminals through the legal process. They may carry expensive possessions, such as video cameras or jewellery, which will give some local residents the impression either that they are targets for theft or that they will readily part with money without much return. Tourists themselves are not, of course, blameless. Arrests for drunkenness in the Costa del Sol and the continuing presence of child prostitutes in Far East destinations present strong evidence of their contribution to local social problems.

It is not surprising that resentment against tourists in some parts of the world has escalated to the point of physical attack. Recent cases of holidaymakers murdered in Florida, Kenya and Australia, tourist buses stoned in Egypt and tourist cottages burned down in Wales bear witness to the strength of feeling which can be generated against these 'outsiders'. One consequence is that the destinations concerned have to direct more money and resources into protecting tourists, perhaps diverting funds away from services for the local community.

Adventure holidays can pose a particular threat because they often seek out remote areas where the local communities have experienced only limited contact with the outside world. Here is an example of how one company attempts to minimize the social impact of its activities:

Small groups
A small group makes our impact upon communities and cultures both minimal and positive; a village can cope with a dozen people, but a coach load will often swamp it.

Accommodation
Where it's possible we like to use accommodation with a local character – not just because it's more interesting, but because it's more beneficial, too; our tourist and first-class hotels are often locally owned rather than multi-national, and we often use small family-run accommodation, providing a direct local benefit.

Food
When staying in hotels, we generally leave the choice of a venue for most main meals to the individual, which not only gives you more choice, it spreads the local benefit too. When we are camping, we try to purchase as much fresh food as is practical locally – another two-sided benefit. When we leave a site we dispose of our rubbish and leave the area as we would wish to find it.

Local staff
Wherever practical, our guides, porters and means of transport are recruited locally, in order to benefit the local people directly for the services they provide. In Pakistan, for example, we sometimes use different guides and porters in each valley, so that as many people as possible receive some benefit as we pass through their homelands.

Our own staff
We encourage our own staff to take an active interest in the environment and ecology of the places they visit, and to advise and assist groups to blend in with and respect the communities they meet.

Source: Exodus Adventure '93 brochure

Activity

1 Read through the extract from the *Exodus Adventure '93* brochure above.
2 Identify a small village in the UK which currently is relatively untouched by tourism.
3 Suggest an event or unexpected discovery which could suddenly make it very attractive to wealthy visitors from a specific overseas country.
4 Draw up some guidelines, intended to minimize any negative social impacts of a sudden growth in tourist visits to the village, which a tour operator from that overseas country might include in a brochure.

4.3 The cultural impact of leisure and tourism

For much the same reasons that contact between tourists and hosts is often superficial, so their awareness and appreciation of the local culture is often limited to a very basic level. They have little time to get to understand the full significance of the local art, crafts, beliefs and ceremonies. Nevertheless, because these are different from the world they are familiar with, they often come to represent the essence of the trip and need to be retained in the mind, either by souvenirs or photographs of people, buildings and ceremonies.

Ghana

Many countries keen to develop an expanded tourism industry use their native culture as a primary selling point. The following extract comes from a tourist guide to Ghana published by the Ghana Tourist Development Company:

Ghanaian cultural history is like a cloth woven with many multi-coloured threads forming diverse patterns incorporating an older traditional element originating from the indigenous West African situation, a Mediterranean and Oriental element as well as European and New World elements. In spite of this mixture born of dynamic history and cultural contacts, the pure indigenous traditions still survive as an active core of national modern lifestyle.

Ghana is especially renowned for its pottery, its metal work – iron has been locally smelted for nearly 2,000 years –carving, beadwork, basketry and leatherwork. Traditional methods of dyeing cloth are now rare and have been largely replaced by tie and dye and batik techniques. Though the styles and patterns are mainly traditional the dyes used are imported.

Music, dance and drama are an essential part of Ghanaian life. Traditional music can be heard most often at festivals and at funerals. 'High life' music is a blend of traditional and imported styles, using both African instruments and guitar bands.

Festivals take place all over the country, sometimes to express appreciation to the deity for a good harvest, sometimes to celebrate a good year and sometimes to celebrate landmarks of tribal history. The visitor to Ghana can count on participating in the many major festivals between May and November.

The presence of tourists may have an impact on local culture in two quite different ways. On the positive side the demand for souvenirs and performances may revive crafts and skills which had fallen out of use. However the demand is likely to be for products and performances which the tourists can readily understand. Craft souvenirs may reflect tourist expectations more than real local designs and their quality can suffer as a result of demand for products in large numbers. The end result is often described as 'airport art'. Performances can be restructured and shortened so that tours and excursions can be conveniently accommodated and tourists can grasp what is going on. This often means that the original significance of the performance is lost altogether and its true purpose debased.

Cultures change as a result of contact with and borrowing from others, a process called **acculturation**. This can be observed in the impact of tourism on the use of buildings and on the choices of available entertainment. Restaurants once serving local dishes have been turned into fast food outlets. Traditional ethnic musical instruments have been incorporated into the production of new kinds of popular music. Churches once used only for worship have become tourist attractions selling guide books and souvenirs. Cinemas showing American and European films have replaced local 'live' entertainments such as music and dance. It would be wrong to suggest that tourism alone is responsible for these changes. Moral attitudes and changes in fashion and taste are as likely to be affected by television as by tourism.

4.4 The environmental impact of tourism

Since tourism and, to a lesser extent, leisure demand a pleasant environment in order to provide a fully satisfying experience, it is not surprising that both can have adverse effects on the locations to which they are attracted. From the Caribbean reefs to the deforestation along the trekking trails of the Himalaya, there are many examples of direct physical damage caused by leisure and tourism activities. This impact is exacerbated by the extra rubbish and sewage generated by visitors, and the fact that they make demands on resources like power and water, often in places where local people already find these in short supply. The demand for facilities like hotels and swimming pools has led to many concentrated coastline developments which show little consideration for issues of space, matching shape and materials to land contours, obscuring views or traditional local building styles. Little regulation of the subsequent development of bars, restaurants, souvenir shops, and advertising and directional signs is also responsible for the destruction of the visual attractiveness of many settlements which have become popular with tourists.

The heavy use of air, water and land transport by both leisure and tourism interests often has a detrimental effect on the environment.

Airports

Airports often originated in the days of light aircraft when the disturbance to the city fringe areas in which they were generally sited was slight. The growth of air traffic has encouraged the development of housing around the airports, in part to cater for the large workforces required to run major airports. Airports consume a lot of land, particularly since their design ideally needs to leave generous space between the runways and the perimeter fence, both for safety and noise reduction reasons. Developers of new airports seek flat land and suitable sites may also be important wildlife habitats. The land may have to be drained, which in turn can lower the level of underground water in surrounding areas. Airports are also large consumers of energy because heat, lighting and power supplies are needed for catering and maintenance operations, as well as the public areas generally. Huge quantities of water are needed for cleaning, drinking, sewage disposal, fire services and aircraft maintenance. The disposal of the chemicals used for de-icing planes and the oil used in servicing them is a threat to the environment if efficient purification systems do not exist.

Frankfurt Airport

This description of the water system at Frankfurt's new airport suggests developers are increasingly aware of environmental concerns:

Water requirements for toilets in Terminal 2 will be covered by both rain water and industrial water from the River Main. The airport has opted for an environment-friendly rain water utilization facility. The system is suitable for purposes not requiring drinking water quality e.g. for supply of sprinkler systems and toilets, as well as air conditioning systems.

Aircraft

Aircraft engines make the most noise during take-off and landing. Most jet aeroplanes use reverse thrust to slow them down which reduces the length of runway they need but increases the noise level. Aircraft design has attempted to reduce the noise problem by fitting a series of baffles to muffle some of the engine noise. New aircraft are designed to climb more rapidly than their predecessors, so that they are within hearing range of local communities for a shorter time. They also use up to 40 per cent less fuel than older models, thus reducing the amount of polluting gases which they release into the air. However the greater demand for air travel at peak times, especially at the height of the holiday season, means that aircraft are often kept in a circling queue as they wait to land which means unnecessary fuel is being burned.

Road traffic

Increased road traffic at popular destinations increases air pollution as well as potentially causing damage to road surfaces, parking areas and verges. It is often argued that emissions from increased traffic causes damage to buildings and statues in cities like Athens, although not all this traffic is directly attributable to tourism. Heavy traffic and new road construction can also increase noise levels and spoil otherwise attractive views. The use of unleaded petrol and the fitting of catalytic converters to cars has eased, though not solved, the problem of air pollution. **Park and ride schemes**, such as the one operated from a number of points around the outskirts of the City of Oxford, can reduce traffic levels in popular city centres. Other proposals currently under review include the possibility of charging motorists to enter particular zones, permitting only certain registration numbers to enter city centres on different days of the week, and installing electronic devices capable of transmitting messages about specific traffic conditions to in-car receivers.

Traffic congestion in city centre

Off-road driving

Leisure activities using motor vehicles can cause environmental damage. Soil erosion on some long distance paths has been accelerated by cross-country motor cyclists, though in most cases hikers also bear a major responsibility for this kind of damage. Four-wheel drive vehicles, capable of traversing the most rugged terrain, have caused considerable damage to vulnerable surfaces. Sand dunes and soil systems in areas with very little rain are often held together by sparse vegetation which, if uprooted, can take years to re-establish itself.

New railway routes

New rail routes, such as the one linking London with the Channel Tunnel, often create heated debate about environmental issues. On the one hand they reduce traffic on the roads; on the other they require the construction of tunnels, bridges and cuttings, often traversing attractive countryside and valuable farm land, as well as passing through densely populated residential areas. The visual impact can be reduced by the use of tunnels and cuttings, but their construction can be noisy, dirty and disruptive. In city areas new line construction may require house demolition and those remaining which are close may suffer problems from regular ground vibrations caused by trains. As with motorways, if the banks of railway cuttings are grassed and planted with trees and shrubs they can create the environmental bonus of a new wildlife habitat, popular because they are rarely frequented by humans. It is difficult to disguise the appearance of overhead cables carrying power supplies to railways. However, the judicious use of building materials in keeping with the local environment can mean that railway architecture, including stations, bridges and viaducts, can in time come to be perceived as an attractive feature of the landscape.

Activity

Read the following comments made by Mr Ivor Porter, a railway enthusiast, about proposals for a Channel Tunnel rail link between London and Folkestone:

People worry about the environmental impact, of course. One thing they should remember is that only a proportion of the link, perhaps a quarter at most, will actually be a new route on the surface. The rest will either follow existing routes or else will be underground.

Certainly it will not be possible to hide completely the overhead wires required to carry the power supply to the trains but new technology should make it possible to keep visual intrusion to a minimum.

One major concern of conservationists is the quantity of land which the rail link will require. It is inevitable that some will have to be sacrificed but rail routes require considerably less space than, for example, current proposals for motorway expansion. There are plans to make the sides of cuttings and embankments as steep as safety will allow because this will reduce the width of the corridor of land required.

If the link is to provide a rapid service, it will need to be relatively free of gradients. This does mean that some cuttings and embankments will be needed. As with existing railway routes, these will be landscaped so that only grass, shrubs and trees are visible.

Noise is always an issue for those living close to major transport routes. The use of continuous welded rails means that modern trains are quieter than they used to be. More aerodynamic designs and the use of disc brakes illustrate how technology is constantly being used to tackle the noise problem.

So, on the whole, though I think we should not underestimate the potential environmental impact of the new rail link, I don't think we should exaggerate it either. The new route is far too important for that.

1 List what you think would be the major concerns of residents living along the proposed route of the rail link.
2 To what extent do you think British Rail would have been able to reassure residents about each of these concerns?
3 What methods might they have used to do so?
4 Can you find any evidence to suggest that British Rail's plans for the route have changed at any point during the last five years? What reasons were given?

Water sports

Many tourist destinations are affected by the spread of water sports. The small, high powered boats used for water skiing and power boat racing tend to leave a residue of oil on the water. They are noisy and do not generally improve coastal or lakeside scenery. The wash they create can sweep away plants from the shoreline, and destabilize lake and river banks, hastening the process of erosion, as has happened in the Norfolk Broads. The habitats of fish and other marine life are disturbed and areas with extensive coral reefs suffer damage as a result of the popularity of boat excursions.

Outdoor sports and the environment

Natural environments are also vulnerable to outdoor activities such as skiing. In the Alps alone there are an estimated 40,000 ski runs and 14,000 ski lifts. In years where there is not sufficient snow many ski resorts now depend on artificial snow machines. These compress air and water, spraying them at high speed when temperatures are below freezing. Extra snow is created but major additional demands are made on the local water supplies. The use of snow machines can extend the skiing season artificially, but often at a cost to local flora and fauna. Skiing over muddy patches of thawing snow can also accelerate soil erosion and damage emerging wild flowers.

It is the construction of new ski resorts which gives the greatest cause for concern. Thousands of trees first have to be cleared and then slopes are often reshaped by moving thousands of tons of earth and rocks. This can make areas more prone to avalanche, since to some extent the trees have a stabilizing effect. As a result many Alpine roads are covered by a succession of unsightly concrete avalanche shelters. In addition the appearance of the slopes themselves is not improved by the construction of pylons, overhead cables, lifts and tows.

The construction of golf courses, for which there is clearly a growing demand, raises similar concerns. Trees have to be cut down and earth moved. Huge quantities of water are required to keep the greens and fairways playable. Herbicides and fungicides may be required to keep the grass on the courses healthy and this can lead to a build-up of phosphates wherever water drains off the course. Nearby streams and ponds affected by phosphates will suffer from a build-up of algae, resulting in the suffocation of fish and other wildlife. Golf course development has also been used as a means of circumventing planning restrictions on green belt or former agricultural land. The presence of the golf course strengthens the developer's case for permission to build additional facilities like a club house, a club shop, a hotel or apartments.

Tourism threat to flora and fauna

As tourists seek out more remote places, the threat they pose to the ecology of such places increases. Islands are particularly vulnerable. Their animal populations are often small and prone to disturbance. The rapid clearing of land can easily render rare plants extinct. Land clearance can also reduce the available living space and feeding grounds for animals. The introduction of non-indigenous plants and animals can have the same result, in that the newcomers may compete more successfully for the available food, water and light. Unrestricted collection of attractive plants like orchids and ferns can mean they die out in the wild. Marine pollution represents a threat to both animal and plant life. Yet the fact that tourists will often pay to see rare or unusual plants and animals is itself an incentive to developers and local people to invest in their conservation.

Activity

Table 4.1 overleaf illustrates some examples of the environmental impact of tourism. Discuss which would be the most appropriate examples to use to fill in the blanks in the right-hand column.

Table 4.1 Environmental impact of tourism

Type of environmental impact	The effects it produces	Locations where these effects are evident
Overcrowding	– Traffic congestion causing delays and air pollution – Queues spoiling visual impact	– –
Pollution of seas and water courses	– Sewage – Oil – Litter	– – –
Inappropriate development	– Building out of character with locality – Developments which drain hard-pressed local resources	– –
Loss of natural habitat	– Use of distinctive habitat for land development – Land damage by erosion and excessive use	– –
Extinction of species	– Hunting – For use in souvenir manufacture	–

The Tourism Council of the South Pacific's advice to tourists about the protection and conservation of the local flora and fauna
Observe these simple rules:
- do not collect plant or animal specimens – take only photographs;
- do not chase, frighten or otherwise disturb animals;
- take care not to disturb the habitat of animals;
- have respect for subsequent visitors who will come to view and enjoy the fauna;
- only hunt in specified permitted areas;
- do not pick flowers;
- take care not to trample plants when out walking.

For more on the environmental impact of tourism, see also Chapter 13.

Assignment 4
The impact of the leisure and tourism industry

This assignment develops knowledge and understanding of the following elements:
1.3 Investigate the variety of local services and products
4.3 Plan promotional activities

It supports development of the following core skills:
Communication 3.2, 3.4
Information Technology 3.3

---

1 Choose any destination which you consider to be at risk from the environmental impact of tourism – Venice, Stonehenge, Windermere or a ski resort in the Alps might be good choices – and write a brief report outlining both the concerns which have been expressed and some of the solutions which have been proposed.

2 Write an account of an imagined visit to your chosen destination in the year 2010 which is intended for use as part of a current educational campaign aimed at warning what will happen if urgent action is not taken now.

5   Teamwork

What is covered in this chapter

This chapter examines approaches to the management of teamwork in leisure and tourism, showing why shared objectives are vital in any service industry. It explores some of the factors which stimulate or inhibit good teamwork. The important relationship between the task set and the team make-up is stressed. A look at organizational structures shows how teams need good lines of communication if they are all to pull in the same direction. Issues of conflicting roles and responsibilities are considered, and the value of induction programmes and good leadership in reducing the possibilities of conflict is shown. The chapter concludes by indicating how appraisal, self-evaluation and incentive schemes can contribute to improving the quality of teamwork.

- The importance of teamwork in leisure and tourism
- Setting up working teams
- Structures of leisure and tourism organizations
- Work roles and responsibilities
- Team leadership
- Evaluating team performance

5.1   The importance of teamwork in leisure and tourism

The travel counsellor making a holiday booking for a customer has to work with a number of other colleagues, both in the travel agency and in the tour operator through whom the booking is being made. They rely on their co-operation and their ability to provide accurate advice and information in order to do their own job in a way which satisfies the customer. Each employee at a tourist attraction makes the job of others easier if they provide an excellent service to visitors. Failure to do so usually means that another member of the attraction's staff will have to handle a disgruntled customer. Leisure centre staff who give contradictory advice about use of fitness equipment or swimming pool availability will drive away potential new users.

In most leisure and tourism organizations there are staff who have direct contact with customers, and staff who provide the back-up necessary for this contact to take place successfully. Leisure and tourism companies compete on the basis of the quality of service they provide and so they are increasingly organized in a way which puts the customers' needs first. Hierarchical management structures, where senior executives issue directives about company policy, too often leave individual employees having no solution to individual customers' needs. The team approach to management acknowledges that in order to respond to individuals employees have to feel confident that they are empowered to do so. A shared set of values, beliefs and direction has to be established within the organization. This sharing involves acceptance that everyone within an organization has the same objective in mind and hence shares some responsibilities. For example, although the managing director and a gardener at an open air leisure park would have some different responsibilities, they might have a shared responsibility to pick up any litter they passed or offer directions to a visitor who appeared to need them. The idea of shared responsibility also makes it less likely that problems will be deferred or ignored because the person who is considered to be mainly responsible is unavailable. A culture of teamwork means employees are more likely to consult their colleagues for help and advice. Communication within the organization will be more frequent so that individuals are better informed. Overall such management principles make the organization appear much more helpful and efficient to outsiders. As the Chessington World of Adventures staff handbook puts it:

> When you see other staff in need of help, lend them a hand and they will be happy to help you. Your customers don't enjoy seeing you struggling. It makes them feel a nuisance, so get help from others and offer your help when it's needed.

Good communication is an essential part of successful teamwork: Thorpe Park

Working teams may be made up of individuals with specialized skills contributing to a predictable process. In a small restaurant there may be a chef, a kitchen assistant, a waiter and a manager. Their roles will remain much the same, though in such a small team the manager might on occasions need to fill in for the waiter or even for one of the kitchen staff. Larger companies will probably have some kind of departmental structure with separate teams in each. However, many work functions, such as finance and accounts, will be company-wide and hence some work teams will need an understanding of the tasks being carried out by other working groups. In addition to these teams involved in a continuous work process, teams may be set up for the purpose of creating, testing the viability of or monitoring new projects.

The nature of working teams depends on a number of factors:

- the task they are undertaking;
- the mix of personalities involved;
- the style of leading or managing the team's work;
- the working environment and resources available;
- the perceived status of the team in the organization as a whole.

The attitude of the team members is an important factor in determining how successful the group is. Table 5.1 suggests some of the ways in which individuals can react to working in groups:

Table 5.1 Reactions to working in groups

Positive	Negative
Listens to and supports others	Attempts to dominate or distract others
Volunteers to follow up points for action	Leaves additional tasks to others
Reads all background material	Relies on others for information
Is willing to praise efforts of others	Is critical of others' contributions
Contributes positive and creative ideas	Looks only for faults and weaknesses
Treats others equally, regardless of status and seniority	Uses rank and experience alone to judge worthiness of others
Can accept counter-argument	Sees opposing arguments as personal criticism
Is willing to explore new ideas	Resents change

Working teams usually have some kind of internal structure. This structure will often be related to the roles carried out by different individuals. Someone may take on the role of **leader** if the task requires it. The leader may relate to the rest of the group in a number of different ways. They may:

- issue them with instructions;
- seek their collective views on what they are doing;
- attempt to persuade them to do things in a particular way;
- initiate discussion as a means of deciding how things should be done;
- indicate that they will take no active part in decision making themselves.

Some working teams, such as those assembling food trays for in-flight catering, operate on a permanent basis, only changing their personnel when individuals leave the company's employment. These are **organized teams**, usually operating under the guidance of a supervisor. However, sometimes working teams are established to develop a new aspect of a company's business. For example a tour operator might set up a **project team** to develop a new destination for a subsequent year's programme. The working life of this team would be short term, since its role would only be to set up the operation at the new destination, not to run it once it was actively part of the company's programme. All businesses are occasionally faced with unexpected issues or problems which need quick solutions. A successful leisure centre may suddenly find that it is receiving a number of local complaints about traffic turning into and out of its entrance. An **ad hoc team** might be set up to investigate the causes of these sudden complaints and to recommend some positive actions which might be taken.

Activity

Read the following schedule of activities showing how a historic house plans the approach to its annual firework display:

A Previous year's display is discussed, especially attendance, pricing policy and additional revenue from catering.
B Discussions are held with police, local authority, fireworks company and company providing musical laser show.
C Fireworks company proposes ideas for the firework programme.
D Safety and insurance requirements are discussed.
E Laser and music show plans developed with specialist company.
F Franchise caterers are interviewed and issued with permits to operate.
G Tickets go on sale.
H Event is promoted by mail shots using the attraction's customer database and through advertising in the local press.
I Power and water supplies to the site are laid on.
J Marquees and additional portable toilets are set up.
K Final briefing is held for all staff involved.

It has been decided to appoint an event team to handle this schedule of activities. Discuss the following questions:

1 What skills do you think the team would need?
2 Would they need to dedicate the whole working year to the task?
3 What kind of organization and communication systems would they need to work effectively with the other teams involved in the operation?
4 What kind of leadership do you think would be best suited to the task and why?

5.2 Setting up working teams

The success of any team depends on the ability of individuals to place the objectives of the team before their personal ambitions, their likes and dislikes, and their sense of their own individual importance. Establishing this belief in the overriding importance of a common goal is not easy. Frequent working contact with a small group of other people means that each individual's quirks, prejudices, inadequacies and skills are very evident to other team members. Setting up a working team which will operate successfully requires the establishment of some basic principles about trusting other team members, and respecting the contribution which their skills and abilities can make. For this reason many companies send working teams on training courses aimed at building up team spirit, learning to rely on and trust in others, and maximizing the contribution of all individuals to the whole team effort.

Deciding which combination of individuals makes the best team is complex. The size of the team needs to be appropriate to the task. Running a contract catering service for a leisure centre which served 2,000 meals to visitors each day would need a larger team than would be needed to operate a small cafe in a remote part of a National Park. Matching individual personalities and skills to appropriate work teams is clearly desirable, though it is not always easy to put into practice. In the case of the leisure centre, someone who was easily flustered might work less effectively with others than they would in the less intense atmosphere of the small cafe. Someone who was highly skilled at making home-made cakes would probably find that these skills could be better used in the cafe than in the leisure centre. Those who were easily bored or who wanted to learn more about business operations and management would be better suited to the leisure centre.

Working teams set up to handle specific projects or to propose strategies to improve particular aspects of a business are more easy to select on the basis of the skills they will need and the likelihood that the individuals will work together well. For example, a team set up to develop plans for modernizing the signage in a traditional museum may need to do all of the following things:

- conduct market research among visitors;
- consult the regional tourist board;
- research practices in other museums;
- contact organizations representing groups with special needs;
- draw up or commission some design proposals;
- evaluate feedback on the various proposals;
- cost various possible approaches within an agreed budget;
- present a final report to the museum directors.

The members of this project team will need diverse skills to enable them to design and evaluate their customer research, administer their contacts with and responses to outside organizations, create or suggest ideas for the new signage, cost each possible approach accurately, and present a clear and informative report which will enable a decision to be reached. It is unlikely that any one team member will be an expert in all of these fields and tasks will need to be allocated, where possible, to those individuals who have appropriate specialist knowledge or skill.

Another important aspect of setting up a working team is the question of where they will carry out their task. Sometimes the working environment is a major factor in the way the team operates. For example the cabin crew on an aeroplane have a very limited space in which to work. On shorter flights they are under pressure to serve meals at great speed. On longer flights they have to combat both the monotony of the experience from the passengers' point of view and their own tiredness. They may be called on to deal with fear of flying, illness, irritation, requests for information, antisocial behaviour or refusal to comply with regulations. Given that they are working in an enclosed space with no opportunity to draw on outside assistance until the plane lands, it is clearly essential that they offer maximum support to each other.

Teams set up to manage special projects may judge the importance of what they have been asked to do at least partly on the basis of the working environment provided for them. The amount of space, the degree of comfort, and the access to resources and equipment they are granted will all affect the team's work. Where they are required to liaise with other groups, their physical location may also help or hinder their ability to work effectively with others. Whatever they are doing good communication is likely to be essential to their success and this may in part be dependent both on the proximity of those they need to contact, as well as the equipment available to them.

Aircraft cabin crew at work

Activity

A large health and fitness centre, with 1,000 members, plans to investigate the feasibility of setting up a fee-charging on-site crêche to accommodate up to 30 children under the age of 5.

They intend to appoint a team of **three** to carry out a feasibility study, drawn from the following shortlist of six employees:

1 **Alison Harrison**, aged 50, and a mother of three grown-up children. Alison is a part-time receptionist at the centre, working 18 hours a week. She is a patient and placid person who gets on well with most people.

2 **James Ames**, aged 21, has two younger sisters and has worked full-time in the bar/cafeteria for the past 18 months. He is very enthusiastic and is keen to broaden his experience. Some people find him a bit opinionated. He has a first aid qualification. He was, until recently, engaged to be married to Judy Moody.

3 **Judy Moody**, aged 20, started work as a full-time fitness instructor at the centre a year ago. Prior to that she completed the first year of a primary school teaching qualification before dropping out so that she could spend more time with her fiancé, James Ames. This relationship has now ended and James is now dating Judy's flatmate, Anna Tanner.

4 **Hugh Pugh**, aged 27, was appointed assistant manager of the centre a year ago. He was previously employed in the accounts department of a large retail company. Hugh is extremely hard-working and very thorough, though he lacks confidence in approaching people he does not know.

5 **Mary Carey**, aged 34, works part-time (25 hours a week) in the centre office. Her responsibilities are mainly administrative, and she is very experienced in the

97

use of word processors and databases. She has two young children who are looked after by a child minder while she is at work. She applied unsuccessfully for the post of assistant manager when Hugh Pugh was appointed.

6 **Roland Bowland**, aged 43, has worked full-time at the centre since it opened five years ago. His responsibilities include maintenance, supervision of cleaning operations, receiving and storage of supplies, and a variety of odd jobs. He is easy-going, but very practical and versatile, when it comes to making sure everything in the centre remains in good working order. Not everyone shares his rather robust sense of humour.

- Identify what you think the main activities of the team should be.
- Discuss the relative advantages or drawbacks of each of the staff named on the shortlist.
- Write a short report to the manager of the centre, recommending which three employees should, in your opinion, be in the team and explaining why.

5.3 Structures of leisure and tourism organizations

How teams within organizations relate to others will be affected by the management structure of the company or organization. The traditional organization of a large company was often to employ a **pyramid structure** with a managing director at the top, and senior executives, heads of departments, supervisors and other employees ranked at different levels below them. This kind of structure clearly establishes who has responsibility for other employees and tends to rely on instructions passed down from above rather than negotiated or democratic decisions about how work should be carried out. The most important policy decisions are taken at the top; some operating decisions are delegated to lower levels of management.

At executive level staff would be likely to have a broad role, encompassing responsibility for areas like finance which would involve overseeing the work of a number of departments or sections. Managers or heads of department would then focus on more specific activities, such as sales, personnel or marketing. The chart in Figure 5.1 shows how the staff structure and lines of responsibility might be organized in a large hotel.

The larger the organization the more likelihood there is that there will be a greater number of working teams. Whether these teams are based on a departmental structure or whether they are set up to develop and manage specific projects, they will need clear guidance about their lines of communication with other working groups. In a departmental structure the processes of giving directions and reporting back may be clearly defined. A chairman or chief executive may work with senior directors with responsibility for major areas of the company, such as finance or public affairs. In the same way that these executives report to the chief executive, so departmental managers report to executives and supervisors to departmental managers. An example of how this structure, with its defined levels of seniority, might be applied in a leisure park is given in Figure 5.2.

This kind of vertical organization places emphasis on direction and orders moving downwards from the top of the organization and information moving upwards from the bottom. In leisure and tourism organizations this structure is increasingly felt to create too many levels of management, hindering the flow of ideas and information,

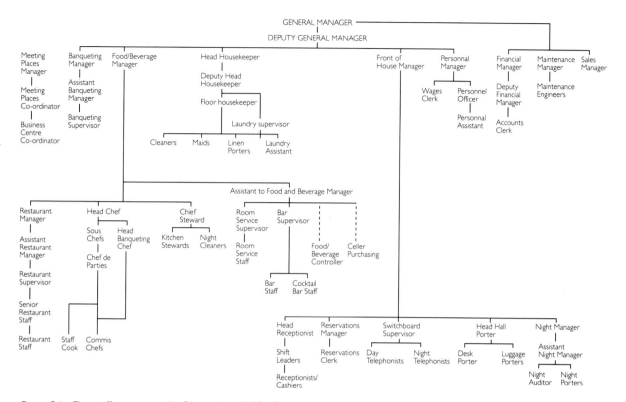

Figure 5.1   The staff structure at the Bloomsborough Hotel

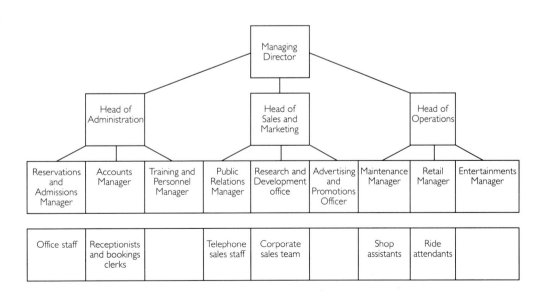

Figure 5.2 A management structure for a leisure park

and failing to exploit fully the abilities and potential of more junior staff. As one company managing director put it:

> People who do a job day-in day-out are the ones who usually know most about it. Only by showing them that we value what they do can we motivate them to improve the way they do that job. We must ask them about what will improve quality, safety, and productivity. Managers must be seen to be involved at this level.

Another reason for slimming down management structures, especially during times of recession, is that senior executives are more expensive to employ and so cutting out some levels of management to produce a flatter structure can be used as a cost-reducing exercise. For example the leisure park staffing structure could be revised to the pattern shown in Figure 5.3. This means more responsibility lies with section managers and smaller units have greater independence, perhaps controlled only in a few key areas, such as budgeting or training.

				Managing Director				
Reservations and Admission Manager	Accounts Manager	Training and Personnel Manager	Public Relations Manager	Research and Development Office	Advertising and Promotions Officer	Maintenance Manager	Retail Manager	Entertainments Manager
Office staff	Receptionists and bookings clerks		Telephone sales staff	Corporate sales team		Shop assistants	Ride attendants	

Figure 5.3 A slimmed down management structure for the leisure park

Whatever kind of structure is favoured, good communication between working teams is essential. As the Industrial Society's 'Guide to Team Briefing' says:

> For any organisation to operate efficiently and profitably, commitment and enthusiasm from employees is vital. However, it is very difficult to achieve either, unless people understand the importance of their contribution. Team briefing helps to achieve this.
>
> People will give of their best when they fully understand and appreciate the importance of their contribution.
>
> Team briefing is based on six basic principles:
>
> 1 face-to-face encounters;
> 2 working in small teams;
> 3 information through a team leader;
> 4 the regularity of meetings;
> 5 the relevance of information and agendas;
> 6 monitoring the effectiveness of communication.

In order to ensure that different working teams share similar general objectives, companies have to establish a clear corporate message, like the Forte company philosophy

Forte – Our Company Philosophy

- To increase profitability and earnings per share each year in order to encourage investment and to improve and expand the business
- To give complete customer satisfaction by efficient and courteous service, with value for money
- To support managers and their staff in using personal initiative to improve the profit and quality of their operations whilst observing the Company's policies
- To provide good working conditions and to maintain effective communications at all levels to develop better understanding and assist decision making
- To ensure no discrimination against sex, race, colour or creed
- To train, develop and encourage promotion within the Company based on merit and ability
- To act with integrity and to maintain a proper sense of responsibility towards the public
- To recognize the importance of each and every employee

described below. This message is constantly reinforced through briefings, manuals and training schemes. The image the company decides on must be communicated consistently. If a tour operator decides to promote itself as offering holiday products of luxury quality because that is what its customers say they want, the communication within the company needs to reflect this. If executives are seen not to employ the same high standards in working with employees as the company claims they use with customers, staff will receive mixed messages and morale will suffer.

Generally the content of an agreed corporate message is reflected in all internal and external communications, including annual reports, training manuals, promotional videos, press releases, advertising, memos, letters, staff handbooks and notices. It is also shown by the way working teams are managed and by the ways in which their efforts are rewarded.

Activity

'Top Dogs' is a new catering service operating 25 mobile hamburger and hot dog vans. Each van carries a driver and an assistant.

Kate Herring, the owner and manager of this new service, already runs a successful catering company which manages the following profitable operations:
- three pub-based restaurants (three teams of four employees);
- a local catering service providing for private dinner parties (two full time, two part-time staff);
- a bakery supplying three other retail outlets (four full-time employees);
- three mobile fishmongers' vans (each with driver only).

Kate feels that the expansion of her business needs additional management support, apart from her own input. She is also keen to make staff feel that they work for a coherent, ambitious, expanding company.

1 Discuss which areas of her business would most benefit from extra management support.
2 Draw up a staff structure, indicating responsibilities and lines of communication, which you think would enable all the parts of the business to operate efficiently and profitably.

5.4 Work roles and responsibilities

Not all working teams in the leisure and tourism industry are collectively employed in carrying out precisely the same task. Individuals will be given different levels of responsibility, so that some may have a managerial or supervisory role, while others operate machines or carry out directed tasks.

In a large hotel with restaurant and conference facilities there may be a number of small working teams employed to run the kitchen, attend to the bedrooms or market and administer the conference facility. However, the general manager of the hotel will want to create a sense of belonging to a team among all the hotel's staff, despite their differing roles and responsibilities. The variety of roles and responsibilities in this single workplace is illustrated in the examples below.

- **Accountant:** the accountant handles all wages and salary payments, keeps records of all revenue earned by the hotel, keeps track of what is owed to suppliers, settles bills and produces financial reports for the management.
- **Receptionist:** the team of receptionists greets guests to the hotel, checks them out when they leave, issues bills to be settled at the cash desk, and provides a range of information about services and facilities available locally.
- **Chef:** the chef is responsible for the whole of the kitchen operation, including menus, and the supervision of the preparation, cooking, and serving of food, cleaning and maintenance of equipment and the training of kitchen staff.
- **Floor housekeeper:** the floor housekeeper manages the team of room attendants, ensuring that all rooms are properly cleaned, and restocked with linen and bathroom items.
- **Bar manager:** the bar manager has to ensure that all bar items for which there is a demand are constantly in stock, to keep an accurate record of sales, and to make certain that an adequate number of bar staff is available to cover busier periods and special events.
- **Waiter:** the team of waiters and wine waiters is required to provide a prompt and efficient restaurant and room service, to offer informed advice about food and wine, and to have a thorough knowledge of the etiquette of good food service.
- **Sales and marketing manager:** the sales and marketing manager has the task of trying to attract new business to the hotel, as well as encouraging existing customers to return, a process involving the design of brochures, and the use of direct mail and advertising.
- **Conference and banqueting manager:** the conference and banqueting manager works with the sales and marketing manager to attract business and private parties to use the hotel's facilities, in addition to overseeing the planning and running of these events.

The diverse nature of the roles and responsibilities means that at one level there may often appear to be clashes of interest. For example, the bar manager may wish to give two of the bar staff a night off when the conference and banqueting manager has agreed to host a company celebration dinner. The accountant may wish to place the responsibility for restocking the mini-bars in the hotel bedrooms with the bar manager rather than the floor housekeeper. The task of the general manager is to take decisions which are in the best interests of the hotel's whole work team and then to explain to individuals the thinking behind the decisions. In other words, any conflict has to be resolved by compromise or by stressing the need for co-operation in the interests of the staff as a whole.

One of the best ways of securing this co-operation is through a carefully planned **induction programme** for all new employees. For example, the North West Tourist Board runs an induction programme for new employees which is also used to enable existing staff to refresh their knowledge. The scheme encourages co-operation by increasing the contact between different departments, and between staff with different levels of knowledge and experience.

The North West Tourist Board's induction programme involves an introduction to the staff and work of each of the board's departments. Information about facilities and conditions of service is supported by a pack of written materials. This pack is also used to develop local knowledge. Newcomers spend a period of time with the training unit, and are then attached for a short period to different members of staff who can familiarize them with procedures relating to documentation, publications, distribution, information technology and finance. They also spend a short period with reception staff so that they learn about handling enquiries. Outside visits are used to explain the way the board works with local businesses and organizations.

The programme includes a checklist so that employees can tick off subjects as they cover them. After three months a formal interview is arranged to review progress and to assess how well the newcomer is meeting the expectations of the organization. All new employees serve a probation period. Even if this is completed successfully, any continuing training needs are noted and arrangements made to meet them.

Activity

1 Suggest three steps which the general manager of the large hotel, referred to above, might take in order to develop a greater sense of team spirit in his or her staff as a whole.
2 Prepare a speech, including the preparation either of cue cards or of overhead projections, in which the general manager introduces these new approaches at a specially convened full staff meeting.
3 Write or design a message or illustration, copies of which can be hung in all staff areas of the hotel, which is intended to act as a reminder to employees that they are part of a team and should always act accordingly.

5.5 Team leadership

Despite the importance of the team ethos in many leisure and tourism organizations, it is generally individuals who provide the fresh ideas which motivate the group. Differences in personality and outlook mean that some people are always looking to lead and stimulate others, while other people are happier carrying out processes devised by someone else. The individuals who show themselves capable of thinking ahead and devising strategies often become leaders. Because they are willing to take on responsibility they also often become the representative of the group or team and speak on their behalf.

Leaders, however, are still part of the team and have to retain the confidence of its members. If the small contract catering team thinks its manager regards him or herself as superior to the rest of the team, communication about aspects of the job they will doing will be less open and the quality of the service will probably suffer. Winning the respect of the team is a vital part of leadership. This may be achieved in a number of ways:

- demonstrating a very high level of expertise;
- showing sympathy and understanding towards team members;
- acting decisively in a crisis or under pressure;
- showing a single-minded pursuit of objectives;
- recognizing, using and showing appreciation for the skills of individual team members;
- accepting responsibility when things go wrong;
- being willing to delegate some responsibility.

Naturally leaders who exhibit the opposite tendencies – such as impatience, panic or being hypercritical – are unlikely to win the confidence of the team.

The decision about how to lead a working team depends both on the personal strengths of the leader and on the make-up of the team. The leader has to judge whether individuals will respond better to coaxing, to the inspiration of personal example, to being given a degree of freedom or to a more structured approach. The nature of the task being performed by the team may also influence how it is led. The team performing the fairly mechanical task of manually laying out the food on trays for an in-flight catering company will need to be supervised in a way which ensures that they work in a precise and consistent way. The leader of a project team creating a proposal for a new ride at a theme park will need to ensure that the atmosphere within the team encourages inventiveness and does not stifle new ideas.

The idea of creating respect for others is an essential part of team leadership. It involves developing an attitude which encourages individuals to understand and value the other members of the team well enough not to want to let them down. This also means that on occasions individuals will need support by other members of the team with more knowledge or experience. It is important for the evolution of the team that younger members of it are able to learn from the expertise and experience of their seniors. Managing a team in a way that will allow all these things to happen requires all the qualities generally associated with good leadership, namely:

- tact;
- enthusiasm;
- foresight;
- integrity;
- a sense of purpose;
- determination;
- awareness.

Activity

1 Discuss what style of management you think would be most appropriate for each of the following work teams:

(a) 3 staff working in a busy tourist information centre in the middle of a historic city;

(b) 6 staff operating an outdoor activity centre specializing in canoeing and white water rafting, and providing low cost accommodation and catering for up to 40 visitors;

(c) 3 tennis coaches running sessions for schoolchildren at a local tennis club during the summer holidays;

(d) 30 students employed by a theme park for the summer peak months of July and August, as guides, entertainers and retail counter staff;

(e) a project team given the task of improving the low season occupancy rates of a large hotel in a traditional British seaside resort.

2 Write a series of guidelines for the leaders of each of these work teams indicating:

(a) what the organization expects from its employees;

(b) what strategies the leader might use to get the best from the members of the team.

5.6 Evaluating team performance

Policies about how people should work together effectively are intended to improve the overall performance of the company or organization. Yet without some means of measuring how successfully individuals and teams meet the objectives of these policies, no one can be sure how effective they are. Leisure and tourism, like most other industry sectors, has evolved a number of approaches to monitoring quality standards.

Quality standards – main entrance to Madame Tussauds

Guides are present and correctly dressed to uniform standard.
Guides do not eat or chew gum on duty.

End of queue:
- Guide is seen to be friendly and greets as many visitors as possible. Words used might be 'Good morning' or 'Good afternoon'.
- Guide gives information on how long the wait is likely to be, explains about All Star tickets and points out the advantages of seeing the Planetarium show first.
- Guide gives information on prices.
- Guide identifies those with special needs in the queue, such as wheelchair users or the elderly, and redirects them to the Group Entrance.

Middle of queue:
- Guide greets as many visitors as possible, saying 'Good morning' or 'Good afternoon'.
- Guide gives information on prices and general information about the exhibition.
- Guide observes the queue for queue jumpers and politely asks them to join the queue at the back.
- Guide mentions the availability of the cloakroom to anyone who may need it, e.g. parents with a child in a pushchair.

Front of queue:
- Guide greets as many visitors as possible, saying 'Good morning' or 'Good afternoon'.
- Guide splits the queue and explains the reason, saying, 'Both sides please, two cash boxes available.'
- Guide explains where cash boxes are and that souvenir guides are on sale inside.
- Guide gives any general information required, mentions the location of the cloakroom and asks visitors to have their money ready.

Quality standards are increasingly applied to the activities of working teams employed on repetitive tasks. A tour operator will monitor the amount of time it takes its staff to respond to incoming telephone calls; a theme park will monitor the average queueing times for attractions during busier periods. Some aspects of the work of employees working with the public might appear at first to be difficult to measure. However, many tasks can be broken down into stages as in the example above which shows the quality standards set for guides looking after the queues outside Madame Tussauds in London. This kind of analysis of tasks makes it easier to explain what is required of employees and also provides a checklist against which their actual performance can be judged. For other employees of Madame Tussauds, such as cashiers, the quality standards would include some similar requirements, such as greeting visitors, but also others relating to their specific activities. Cashiers would have standards relating to use of the tills, acceptable methods of payment, the price structure and required knowledge of different regulations about admission.

Staff at entrance to Madame Tussauds

The methods used to measure performance usually involve working with a manager or supervisor. Individuals may go through an **appraisal** process in which their personal strengths and weaknesses are identified. A key factor in most appraisal schemes is an assessment of how well individuals work with others. Appraisal should focus on positive things, establishing clear goals which both the appraiser and the employee agree are in the interests of both the company and the individual's career development.

Appraisal usually takes the form of an interview. When the person being appraised has a formal written job description, this document may be used in assessing their overall performance. Many companies use a standard form containing questions like this.

- Has the appraisee improved performance in specific areas?
- Has the appraisee achieved previously set objectives?
- Does the appraisee have a good knowledge of their duties?
- Does the appraisee have skills or abilities which are not used?
- What kind of working relationships has the appraisee established with colleagues?

The process gives the company the opportunity to judge whether it is making the best use of its employees and whether the constitution of the work teams in different departments represents the best mix of people that can be achieved from the existing personnel. It is important that the process of appraisal is not perceived as threatening. Its value lies in helping to improve the performance of individuals, by identifying strengths as well as weaknesses and by suggesting training gaps, and so benefiting the company.

One method of making assessment of performance less threatening is through a programme of **self-evaluation**. This is increasingly seen as a strong motivator. Employees collect their own evidence of how successfully they met customer requirements, what improvements they felt could be made in their performance and in their working conditions, and what aspects of the job have given them most satisfaction during the year. Most self-evaluation schemes are accompanied by guidance notes which may well highlight the issues of working with other people and other departments, as in the example below, drawn from the Tussauds Group's scheme.

What additional things might be done by you, or other colleagues, to further enhance your performance?

Consider ways in which you can help yourself further in raising your performance. You may want to consider changes to your working practices, delegating some responsibilities, improving the services from other departments, or developing specific skills among your staff.

Clearly some activities lend themselves to measurement more easily than others. A tour operator with regional sales teams or a hotel group recording the occupancy rates of its individual outlets can produce sets of statistics to show which teams are performing well. Where these statistics appear to ignore the inequalities of selling in different geographical areas with different populations and different numbers of visitors, performance is often measured by the team's achievement in a given period compared with their efforts at the same time in preceding years.

Some companies offer **incentives** to employees as a means of encouraging improved performance. For example the hotel group, Hilton UK, launched an incentive scheme for its employees in March 1994, aimed at rewarding excellent service and building staff loyalty to the company. Four incentives were offered:

1 a bonus scheme for hotel teams which achieved or bettered their profit target;
2 a voucher scheme, enabling staff who have made a special contribution to the efforts of their team to choose gifts;

3 childcare vouchers for women returning to work;

4 team membership cards, providing leisure and retailing discounts to staff with more than a year's service.

Assignment 5
Teamwork

This assignment develops knowledge and understanding of the following elements:

7.1 Investigate how leisure and tourism teams operate

7.2 Work with others in teams

7.3 Evaluate team performance

It supports development of the following core skills:

Communication 3.1, 3.2

Your tasks

1 Identify a local site with potential for development as a leisure or tourism centre or attraction. Consider the size of the site, the likely scale of interest in different types of development, the degree of potential opposition, and the effect of funding limitations, access and size on the capacity of the development. Taking these factors into account, agree on the basic details of a leisure or tourism development proposal for the site.

2 Select teams of three or four people to represent some of the following organizations:

   (a) an existing local tourist attraction;

   (b) a local tourist information centre **or** the Regional Tourist Board;

   (c) a local transport company (e.g. coaches, taxis, hire cars);

   (d) a large local hotel with a restaurant and conference centre;

   (e) an existing leisure facility (e.g. golf club, swimming pool).

   If possible visit the workplace your team is representing or invite one of their staff to come and talk about how they operate.

3 Each team must develop a strategy to demonstrate how their own organization would respond to the new development. The strategy should include:

   (a) a statement of the objectives and philosophy of their organization;

   (b) a suggested plan of action, with a time scale attached;

   (c) an allocation of roles and responsibilities within the team;

   (d) an indication of which other groups they would liaise with, and an outline of the methods of communication they would use.

6 Customer care

What is covered in this chapter

This chapter explains the importance of effective customer care in all service industries. It shows how companies and their outlets have to be ready to respond to a wide variety of customer needs, and gives examples of ways in which they achieve this response. The different types of contact between customer and employee are described. Typical advice which companies give new employees on how to handle these encounters is outlined. Three examples taken from the leisure and tourism industry are used to demonstrate the impact of good or bad customer service. The chapter identifies the key elements to be incorporated in a customer care policy, showing how these may vary in different workplaces. The importance and the benefits of monitoring customer care policies are stressed, and methods of measuring their effectiveness are discussed.

- The implications of being a service industry
- Meeting customer needs
- Different types of customer contact
- Customer care in practice
- Developing a customer care programme
- Monitoring and measuring standards of customer service

6.1 The implications of being a service industry

All industries are dependent on customers, but leisure and tourism, as a service industry, relies more than most on its ability to provide good customer service. It is a highly competitive industry and businesses which cannot provide customer satisfaction will suffer at the expense of rival companies. Customers who believe that a particular company will give them quality, service and value for money will be more likely to repeat their purchases and become loyal to the company's brands. Not only does this bring in more revenue, it can also reduce marketing costs if a high proportion of customers are already aware of the product. Recent research has estimated, on the other hand, that indifferent staff attitudes are responsible for two-thirds of all lost customers.

Beaulieu is a collection of leisure facilities which include a country house and gardens, the National Motor Museum, and a maritime village and maritime museum. The importance of good service in leisure and tourism is well illustrated by the comments from Beaulieu's staff handbook shown overleaf.

The fact that leisure and tourism is a service industry means that contact between employees and customers is frequent. Service is an important part of what is being purchased. Buying a television set allows the purchaser the opportunity to test the quality of the equipment themselves, though they generally do require some customer

The continued success of Beaulieu depends not only on the quality of the leisure facilities which we offer, but also on the ability and attitude to visitors of all our staff. You may be employed in an area in which you deal with the public face to face every day, or in a job in which you rarely meet them. Whatever your job, there is one point that you must never forget. At Beaulieu, VISITORS ARE OUR BUSINESS. That single fact makes your attitude to your job here absolutely vital. For the visitors, an entire day at Beaulieu or Buckler's Hard can be ruined by one contact with a member of staff who is bored, unhelpful, rude or abrupt. We expect you to be alert, considerate, courteous and cheerful. This positive attitude to your work will not only ensure that the visitors enjoy their time with us, it will also help you, by making your job easier, more interesting, more enjoyable, and more rewarding.

service, particularly in terms of advice about the product's specifications and the comparative merits of different makes. Purchasing an airline ticket, on the other hand, gives the buyer initially only a reservation. There is a major part of the purchase, namely the contact with airport staff and cabin crew, which represents something of an unknown quantity. Yet the way passengers are treated by the staff of different airlines is one of the most important differences between the airline products they can choose from. If the television breaks down, it can be returned to the shop for repair or replacement. The flight experience, however, is valid for the date and time specified, in just the same way as a ticket for a theatre performance would be. If the performance is inept, or the airline staff lack consideration, the customers are unlikely to give the company a second chance.

Customer service in the leisure and tourism industry, then, is of great importance because of the contact element in all aspects of consumption of the product or service. In marketing terms it means that a business hoping to sell products or services must pay close attention to the 'process, people and physical' evidence elements of the marketing mix (see Chapter 8).

Leisure and tourism customers do not all have the same needs and good customer service has to take account of individual differences. Young people may be happy to be addressed in a fairly informal style, whereas those who are older may not. Visitors from overseas will have different cultural values and may struggle to overcome language barriers. Not all customers will be patient and considerate; on the contrary, they may be naturally awkward, or circumstances may conspire to make them angry or irritable.

The industry is all about:
- making customers feel welcome;
- keeping them entertained and amused;
- looking after them well and safely – whatever their needs;

by people who:
- are willing to listen;
- are able to take trouble;
- are happy to be responsible and accurate;
- who enjoy working with people, whatever the time of day and whatever the pressure.

Attractions staff have to answer enquiries of all kinds and from all age groups

If it is possible to generalize about how all leisure and tourism companies would ideally wish to have their employees treat their customers, the following description from 'Skills for the Tourist Industry' might sum it up.

Great emphasis is placed on customer needs, even though these may appear to be exceptional. Airlines will now provide vegetarian, kosher or other special meals during flights. Some hotels have fitted ramps, lifts and bathroom fittings to provide access for wheelchair users. Attractions have printed guides and brochures available in a number of foreign languages. Sports centres have set up permanently staffed crèches. Museums have mounted tactile displays which can be experienced by those with sight disabilities. In other words individual leisure and tourism companies and facilities have taken practical steps to try and satisfy a wider range of customers.

Activity

1 Discuss examples of good and bad service which members of your group have experienced.
2 Write your own definition of 'good service'.
3 List 12 varied jobs in the leisure and tourism industry. Draw up a table indicating which would be the most important aspects of customer service that people carrying out these jobs would need to be skilled in providing.

6.2 Meeting customer needs

A small hotel with bar, restaurant and a conference room has to service a number of different customer needs. Between Monday and Thursday its main clientele are likely to be business travellers requiring accommodation and facilities to hold meetings with local business contacts and organizations. From Friday to Sunday there will be a higher proportion of customers taking weekend breaks or visiting the area for social occasions. The restaurant will have to provide both for residents and for local people dining out. To provide customer service to meet these different needs demands a careful analysis of what each client group is most likely to want.

Overnight business travellers require a booking procedure and telephone service which is fast, friendly and efficient. They may have special requirements relating to their business schedule, such as an early morning call or a taxi at a specified time. If they are often away from home and are frequent users of the hotel, they will appreciate being welcomed as regular customers whose needs can be anticipated.

Business travellers also staying for on-site meetings will have similar needs, but in addition will require a meeting room, appropriately set up with stationery and any audio-visual equipment requested. The nature of the meeting may call for the availability of a direct dial phone and fax machine. Lunches and tea breaks are likely to be part of the service the hotel provides.

Leisure travellers will be looking for a friendly, relaxed atmosphere, in which they can enjoy a break from their normal routine. One of their main needs will be information about the area. They will want hotel staff who can recommend interesting things to see and do, who can suggest the best routes and who can offer local advice about what to avoid.

Restaurant users will want to be able to book a table in advance. They will have considerable direct contact with hotel staff, and will look for a warm welcome, sound advice about the menu and wine list, and efficient service. The quality of the food, the cleanliness of the premises and the behaviour of other diners are all important factors which the hotel needs to address if it is going to provide high quality customer service.

An analysis of the needs of these customer groups should indicate some of the basic elements of good service practice. When the initial hotel booking is made the following four actions would help to ensure the customers needs were met.

1 Send out a confirmation as soon as the booking is received.
2 Send accompanying information about the hotel, its environment, the restaurant and a map showing how to find it.
3 Enquire about the general purpose of the clients' stay and whether they have any special requirements.
4 Accurately log clients' details into booking/records system for future use.

On arrival there are a number of ways that the hotel can ensure customers' needs are taken into account:

1 Greet customers in a friendly manner, by name where it is known.
2 Provide information relating to hotel, hotel layout and restaurant facilities.
3 Explain services available, e.g. room service, laundry, leisure facilities.

4 Explain how and where customers' enquiries can be answered during their stay.
5 Establish any special meal or other service requests they might have.

Activity

1 Discuss and make a list of the special requirements which you think business and leisure travellers might request on arrival at a small country hotel.
2 Devise a role-play exercise to be used with students training to become hotel receptionists that would enable them to respond confidently to these requests, even though the hotel may not be able to provide adequately for all of them.

6.3 Different types of customer contact

Some jobs in leisure and tourism will clearly involve more direct contact with customers than others. A hotel receptionist or an overseas tour representative will be in constant contact with customers. A marketing manager is less likely to be, though an essential element of the job is to ensure that customers' needs are being met. In some respects, the skills required to work successfully with customers have much in common with those required to work with other colleagues. Both require:

- a willingness to listen;
- good concentration;
- calmness under pressure;
- a willingness to accept responsibility and take action;
- a determination to be well informed;
- respect for others.

The type of contact between employee and customer will also vary between the various sectors of the leisure and tourism industry. Most companies will have contact by telephone, mail or face to face, but the nature of these contacts depends on the purpose of the communication. Customers may be:

- seeking information or directions;
- seeking advice about the comparability of different products and services;
- seeking practical help in an accident or emergency;
- making or confirming bookings;
- checking details of travel, leisure or accommodation reservations;
- seeking to change details of agreed bookings;
- requesting special requirements;
- offering praise or criticism;
- seeking compensation.

Contact by telephone

Telephone communication presents an initial problem in that it is more difficult to establish a good relationship quickly without eye contact. Both parties have to relay and receive information without being able to see it in print. If the customer is seeking information it is important that the company employee has all the necessary information close at hand. If the customer is making a reservation, requesting special requirements or making a complaint the receiver of the call will need to record details from the customer accurately. Many companies will give specific training in receiving and making telephone calls. Advice might take this form.

Receiving a call

1 Have some method of noting details of calls readily to hand.
2 Greet the caller and say who you are, giving your company name.
3 Listen carefully to what the caller wants.
4 Make notes of any important details.
5 Check with the caller that you have got your facts right.
6 Answer any straightforward questions immediately and ring back, as soon as possible, with any information which you have had to look up or check.
7 At the end of the call check that the customer is satisfied.

Staff taking notes while answering the telephone

Making a call

1 Check that you have all the information you need before making the call.
2 State who you are, the name of your company and the purpose of your call.
3 Check whether you have called at a convenient time.
4 Make a note of any details which have been agreed or actions which now need to be taken as a follow up to the call.
5 Give the customer the opportunity to respond to what you have to say.
6 Again, make sure that the customer is clear about details and satisfied with what has been agreed.

Of course none of this advice will be very useful if the company employee sounds bored, irritated or tired. Customers want to hear a bright, friendly voice on the other end of the line. Many trainers suggest that smiling while speaking on the telephone automatically makes the speaker sound more pleasant.

Face to face contact

Face to face contact is the most important form of contact in many leisure and tourism businesses. The attitude and professionalism of the theme park entertainer, the tennis coach, the waiter or the cabin crew are crucial factors in determining whether customers enjoy themselves and subsequently return for more.

Successful contact often begins with a warm welcome. Customers will probably make their minds up very quickly whether they like someone or not and so most companies strive to ensure that their employees make a good first impression. Appearance is often what governs first impressions of people. Apart from insisting on general smartness, the theme park or the airline, for example, will probably put their staff in uniform. This has the dual benefit of making a statement about the company image and also enabling the customer to identify staff easily.

New employees are often given very specific guidance about how they should look. Training often focuses on the idea that they are on show, giving a performance for the public and, as such, will attract attention and comment if they do not look presentable and relatively conservative. The following list gives some rules which staff at a theme park might be required to observe:

1 hair must be clean and tidy, with long hair tied back;
2 men should be either clean shaven or wear neatly trimmed beards and moustaches;
3 black shoes and plain dark socks should be worn;
4 shirts/blouses should always be tucked inside trousers/skirts;
5 moderate amounts of subtle make up may be worn by women only;
6 jewellery should be limited to wedding rings and ear studs;
7 name badges should be worn at all times;
8 no tattoos may be visible.

However, the theme park staff are not providing good customer service simply by looking presentable. They have to respond to customers' needs and the first skill required to do this well is an ability to listen. This skill will include resisting the temptation to interrupt, unless customers need encouragement in getting their message across. It is important to judge the mood of the customer too, since the response should show that the employee appreciates their feelings and why they are in this state of mind. Summarizing what the customer has said is a good means of indicating that they have been listened to, as well as often clarifying the situation.

Frequently the customer will be seeking information and it is important that they feel that what they are told is accurate, unbiased and helpful. Explanations should not be too technical or too hurried. Reference to maps, price lists, brochures or guide books may help to substantiate what is being said. It also requires employees to be given sufficient training about the product or service they are providing. A travel agency employee who tells a customer to take three brochures away and choose a holiday for themselves is providing less of a service than one who knows the product well and who talks the customer through the differences in the three brochures, and offers the benefit of their experience of the destinations concerned.

Few employees can hold all the information customers may ask for in their heads. The way in which information is stored and retrieved is a vital factor in giving good customer service. Whatever system is used, whether it be files, databases or small reference libraries, it must be possible to find information without lengthy delays. The system also needs to be flexible enough to be updated regularly. Promising to write or ring back with information is sometimes used as a means of putting off persistent customers. Failure to keep such promises can quickly damage a company's reputation.

Spoken communication on the telephone and in face to face contact is an essential factor in the impression created on the customer. The voice needs to be loud enough to be heard. Accents are not generally disapproved of unless they are so strong as to be incomprehensible. For obvious reasons, slang and bad language are discouraged. Much of the advice given about how to talk to customers implies that common sense should be used. The aim should be a pleasant, reasonably informal style which puts people at their ease, while giving a favourable impression of the company providing the product or service.

Contact by mail

Writing to customers may be necessary for a number of reasons, including:
- to respond to a written request for information;
- to send confirmations of bookings or orders;
- to acknowledge the receipt of payment or documents;
- to reply to a written complaint.

Whatever the purpose of the written communication, two factors are of prime importance to the customer, and they are clarity and accuracy of information. The content of the letter will be easier to understand if spelling and punctuation are accurate, paragraphing is logical and the layout of the letter is neat. Details should be checked, not only of information sent out, but also of the names and addresses of the receivers. Some written tasks, such as the acknowledgement of payment, may be adequately covered by a standard letter format, often generated by means of a word processing package. Even here failure to sign or date the communication may make an unfavourable impression on the recipient. The use of standard letters in other circumstances, such as in response to customer complaints, may bring the benefit of accuracy but will certainly give the impression of an impersonal organization, not particularly concerned about the individual customer.

Handling complaints

American Express gives its employees this advice about how complaints should be perceived:

> The complaining customer is one of our best customers. They give us the opportunity to put things right. If we react in a positive, constructive and timely manner, we will have a far more loyal customer in future.

If employees are going to be able to respond positively to customer complaints they need first to be able to anticipate likely potential areas of difficulty. Airport staff, for example, should be aware that common causes of irritation for passengers include:
- flight delays;
- incorrect, poorly displayed or missing information;
- poor service;
- lost luggage;
- inadequate catering facilities;
- lack of space.

The process of handling complaints effectively generally involves a number of key stages: listening to what they have to say; clarifying the details; explaining what actions can be taken; pursuing the most appropriate action; and notifying both customer and colleagues about what has been done.

Perhaps the first duty of an employee in the face of a customer complaint is to stay calm and to take a considered view of the nature of the complaint and the likely causes. Sometimes customers have unreasonable expectations, but it is important to avoid simply getting into a confrontation with them. Various tactics can be used to deflate situations, such as:

- initially apologizing for what has upset them;
- showing sympathy for their point of view;
- asking questions to establish exact details;
- appearing willing to take positive action to help and getting agreement from superiors to do something promptly;
- where it is an unavoidable circumstance, explaining the cause of their problem;
- taking them to a less public place to clarify their concerns.

Complaining customers do need to be heard, but good customer service may involve explaining to them that the company has a policy on some issues on which it insists. A squash club, for example, will probably not refund money paid in advance to hire a court if a customer turns up five minutes before the time they are due to play, saying that their partner is unwell. In the face of an aggressive customer, individual employees may be tempted to pass the blame on to the organization or company that they work for. However, this is less likely to satisfy them than an explanation of why the company operates the particular policy and the consequences of not doing so. If all else fails, the most difficult problems are best shared with a more senior member of staff.

Table 6.1 shows how one customer care programme summed up what to do and what not to do in handling complaints.

Table 6.1 Handling complaints

Never. . .	Always. . .
. . .walk away from a customer with a problem	. . .look at all the possible ways of satisfying the customer's complaint
. . .argue publicly with a complaining customer	. . .emphasize what can be done rather than what is impossible
. . .promise action which you don't actually know is allowed or possible	. . .take a friendly rather than an antagonistic approach
. . .just say there's nothing that can be done	. . .move the discussion from what went wrong to what can be done now
. . .blame work colleagues or the company system	. . .give a full explanation if there is a good reason why nothing can be done

The final part of the process of handling customer complaints should not be overlooked. Customers should be contacted to ensure that they are satisfied with whatever action was taken. Internally it is important that ways of avoiding future recurrence of the same problem are found. This may require products to be changed, information and guidance to be written more clearly, or staff policies and training to be changed.

Ensuring that customers with special needs are provided for

Good customer care has to take account of the special requirements of individuals. A guide taking parties around St Paul's Cathedral in London, for example, might encounter in the same day:

- elderly visitors;
- parents accompanied by young children;

- visitors with limited sight or hearing;
- wheelchair-using visitors;
- non-English speakers;
- visitors with very specialized interests.

Each of these groups will require a different kind of service. The provision of special facilities, like foreign language audio-tapes, large print notices or a reference library can help to meet some of these needs. Major tourist attractions can plan special group visits to accommodate some of these needs. However, it will take all the personal skills of an experienced guide to handle the conflicting needs of some of these groups, if they are within the same party.

Flying can be a difficult experience for those with special needs. Families travelling with small children have to keep them entertained. For wheelchair users the confined space can present problems. Qantas, the Australian airline, publishes guides to air travel for people with disabilities or special medical conditions, for first-time fliers, for older passengers and for children travelling alone. The extract below shows the kind of customer service available to those with disabilities:

> You can use your own wheelchair up to the door of the aircraft. It will be stowed in the hold for the duration of the flight. Wheelchairs are available on board for moving to and from the washrooms and will be provided at most transit stops. . .
>
> Specially designed toilets for people with disabilities are provided. . .
>
> If you have sight or hearing problems, your guide dog may accompany you in the cabin, free of charge. The dog will occupy a mat in front of a window seat and you will occupy the adjacent seat. However, it is important to note that guide dogs are not exempt from quarantine regulations in any country. . .
>
> All aircraft carry braille books showing a plan of the aircraft and its safety features.

Hotels and self-catering accommodation seeking to meet the needs of wheelchair users can have their premises inspected and given a rating in one of three accessibility categories. The criteria used to determine these categories are as follows.

Category 1: Accessible to a wheelchair user travelling independently
- Parking or drop off point at main entrance
- Permanent ramps or level access throughout
- All doors in public areas and bedrooms wider than 750 mm
- Lateral transfer to bed and toilet of more than 800 mm
- Handrails by toilet and bath
- Toilet and bath height between 450–500 mm
- Lifts must have a minimum clear door opening of 750 mm and an internal space of at least 1,200 x 800 mm
- In all areas used by guests there must be unobstructed space of at least 100 x 700 mm

Category 2: Accessible to a wheelchair user travelling with assistance
All criteria for category 1 apply, with the exception that a single step is allowed into the establishment, public areas, bedroom or shower, and the bath or toilet heights may be between 420 and 500 mm.

Category 3: Accessible to someone with limited mobility, but able to walk a few paces and up to a maximum of three steps

The criteria stipulate a maximum of three steps to the public areas and to at least one bedroom.

Activity

1 Allocate a particular special interest to each member of your group (see list of requirements for visitors to St Paul's listed on page 117 for examples). Make sure you include as broad a spread of special interests as possible.
2 Visit a local tourist attraction. Each individual should collect evidence of how successfully or otherwise their special needs have been catered for.
3 Each individual should read out a short summary of what they found.
4 The group should combine to plan and write a report on the special needs provision for visitors to the attraction, including recommendations for constructive but viable means of improving what is available.

6.4 Customer care in practice

Perhaps the best way of demonstrating the impact of good or bad customer service is to examine some examples of leisure and tourism products from the customer's point of view. The first example looks at taking a holiday, the second at using a keep fit gymnasium and the third at a stay on a health farm.

Taking a holiday

The majority of holidaymakers still book their holidays through travel agents. In order to make their choice easy a good travel agent should provide:

- a reasonable range of brochures covering different operators and different types of holiday;
- quick attention or an acknowledgement of their presence if the agency is busy;
- an efficient process to establish the details of when and where they wish to go, and of what individual requirements they might have;
- sensible advice about the comparative quality of the destinations advertised and how appropriate or otherwise each might be for their particular needs;
- a clear explanation of the pricing of the product, including any extras like travel insurance;
- details of how to contact the person who has served them, either to make a reservation or to check details in the future.

Once a holiday has been booked, much of the responsibility for whether the customer is well served or not passes to the tour operator. The travel agent's remaining task is to ensure that all relevant tickets and documentation, as well as notification of any late changes in holiday arrangements, arrive at the right address in advance of the time they are needed.

For most package holidays the airport may be the next customer–employee encounter. The tour operator may employ a handling agent here whose job is to ensure that passengers can be given guidance about the check-in procedures. The agent will also be responsible for ensuring that passengers are made aware of the cause of any flight delay and will organize the distribution of meal or accommodation vouchers, should these become necessary. They will inform delayed passengers about the compensation policy operated by the company concerned and the procedure for claiming this.

At the destination itself the prime responsibility for customer service lies with the resort representative employed by the tour operator. Their first task is usually to ensure that transfers from the airport to hotels run smoothly. In major resorts they will probably run a welcome meeting, with complimentary drinks, and an introduction to the destination and its major attractions. During the course of the visitor's stay the representative has to be available at a specified place and time to provide advice or information. They may also organize various social events, aimed at enhancing the enjoyment of holidaymakers. They must give all customers a reliable means of contacting them in an emergency, such as illness, injury or theft of money and belongings.

Using a keep fit gymnasium

Using a gymnasium does give the customer the opportunity to view the product before deciding to participate. The first service a potential customer needs is a guided tour of the premises. They might wish to be informed about:
- the most popular and the most quiet periods of use;
- the range of fitness equipment available;
- how different equipment can be used to monitor and improve different aspects of fitness;
- the range of classes and specialist activities catered for;
- the qualifications and level of guidance which instructors will offer;
- membership fees and facilities which incur hourly charges.

Each new customer will need a thorough induction programme if they are intending to use gymnasium equipment. Failure to do this will increase the risk of injury. Most fitness centres will offer the option of a personal fitness trainer to monitor and develop individual progress, though this will generally incur an hourly fee. Some fitness activities are highly repetitive and customers may wish for some form of distraction, such as background music or enhanced television pictures. Good ventilation, an available supply of drinking water and free paper towels will all help to make the gymnasium a more comfortable place. Other services may include towel hire, a bar and restaurant, a sports equipment shop, a crèche, car park video surveillance or a car valeting service. Clearly some of these services are only indirectly related to the gymnasium activity itself, but they are an integral part of the whole visit to the centre.

Staying on a health farm

Customers choosing to stay on a health farm may share a number of common characteristics. They may be concerned about their weight, they will probably be relatively well off and they may expect to be pampered. In other words they may be very demanding customers who expect a high standard of personal service.

As with a gymnasium a health farm's initial assessment of customer needs is very important. Staff need to be good at listening to what the customer wants but also knowledgeable about the products on offer and their likely effects. In centres where a range of diet and beauty treatments is available, staff will need both experience and qualifications to ensure that customers suffer no ill-effects. The quality of food provided is likely to come under particularly close scrutiny, especially from customers who feel they are depriving themselves of their normal, less health-conscious diets!

A health farm may call for the utmost tact and diplomacy from its staff. They need to impose a regime which will make people feel better when they leave. Yet, on the other hand, they cannot impose such severe regulation that customers feel the atmosphere is oppressive and unrelaxed.

Activity ──

Make notes covering what you consider to be the key elements of good customer service in each of the following situations:
1 buying a pair of running shoes in a sports goods shop;
2 making a telephone booking for an overseas campsite;
3 enquiring about arranging a visit to a medieval castle for a group of primary school children;
4 booking a restaurant for a family birthday celebration;
5 enquiring at a college reception area about available leisure and tourism courses.

6.5 Developing a customer care programme

The starting point for many customer care programmes is the company's **mission statement**. This document outlines what the company considers to be its main purpose and suggests routes by which it hopes to achieve this. A tourist attraction, for example, might describe its purpose as:

> to set the highest of standards for all aspects of our operation, both in the interaction between departments and in our dealings with visitors, so that we maximize both customer enjoyment and satisfaction which will in turn enable us to secure and sustain maximum financial benefit.

This mission statement tries to balance customer needs and company objectives. The attraction is in business to make a profit, but it must ensure that its customers are satisfied if it intends to maintain their interest and hence its revenue. The value of clear objectives and targets should be stressed. It makes the training of new staff more straightforward, and it gives the company a means of monitoring and measuring the quality of its customer service.

If the customer care policy is to be effective, the company has to find a means of making all staff believe in its importance. In other words, a means of motivating people to change has to be found. One way of doing this is to ask company personnel to put themselves in the customer's situation in order to get them to see things from their point of view. As Chessington World of Adventures staff handbook says:

> How often have you thought that the person serving you in the supermarket or the pub or the garage was just rude or uninterested? Did they keep you waiting while they talked to their friends, or did they just ignore you whilst they carried on filling out a form?
>
> All of us have suffered at the hands of such people at some time or another and when we have the choice we don't go back. We don't like being treated as if we were just a nuisance getting in their way, especially since our custom is paying their wages.
>
> So as the experts who know what the customer wants, we can show our customers how it's done properly.

The next stage in the customer care policy is to indicate some of the methods by which the company's overall purpose is to be achieved. Tour operator, Near and Far Travel, describes how they hope to be successful like this:

> The continuing success of Near and Far Travel will be based on innovation, the quality of our products, and the high standard of service to our customers and agents. We therefore strive to further this success and excel in all aspects of our business.
>
> In order to achieve this level of excellence, Near and Far Travel is dedicated to:
> - encouraging involvement from every employee, supported by the appropriate training to further develop each individual's capability
> - providing a working environment which encourages speed, efficiency and accuracy
> - growing profitably through offering exceptional quality, service and innovation.

The effectiveness of the customer care policy may depend on how much it focuses on general encouragement to staff to work together on shared principles and how much it concentrates on specific detail about an individual company's operations. A hotel, for example, may give a central focus to a complaints handling policy on the grounds that their business success depends on repeat bookings and word-of-mouth reputation. An essential part of this policy might be to offer guaranteed refunds to customers who demonstrated that their stay had been unsatisfactory. The policy would also define the internal procedures to be followed in the event of customer complaints. It might specify a meeting, a report to be completed, a time within which the customer should receive any compensation due and how the hotel would implement any perceived need for improvement of its service.

An American hotel management company, Ritz-Carlton, shows the same mixture of general and specific advice in the part of its customer service policy dealing with complaints:

> The Three Steps of Service which Ritz-Carlton expects its employees to follow are:
> - a warm and sincere greeting. Use the guest name, if and when possible.
> - anticipation and compliance with guest needs.
> - fond farewell. Give them a warm goodbye and use their names, if and when possible.
>
> The Ritz-Carlton motto states: We are ladies and gentlemen serving ladies and gentlemen.
>
> Any employee who receives a customer complaint 'owns' the complaint. Instant customer pacification will be ensured by all. React quickly to correct the problem immediately. Follow up with a telephone call within 20 minutes to verify the problem has been resolved to the customer's satisfaction. Do everything you can to ensure that guests will return. Guest incident action forms are used to record and communicate every incident of guest dissatisfaction. Every employee is empowered to resolve the problem and prevent a repeat occurrence.

In this case it is company policy to entitle individual employees to assess the seriousness of any complaint and refund up to $2,000 to any dissatisfied guest.

Customer care policy at Katzonderloos Safari Park
Welcome
Every visitor should feel at home in the park. It's up to you to greet them warmly, show a friendly interest in them and provide any help they need. Make sure no one wanting attention ever feels unnoticed. And don't forgot – a smile costs nothing but makes everyone feel better.
Appearance
If you look good, the visitors will have more faith in you. Your uniform identifies who you are and what you and the company stand for – concern and reliability.
Preparation
Whatever you need to do your job properly should always be at hand. It's no good running out as soon as you get a rush. Make sure you're equipped for the whole day before the visitors arrive.
Rubbish
Never allow this to be someone else's responsibility. Everyone from the MD to the first-day recruit should be willing to pick up litter and keep their own work area tidy. Customers will not return to a place whose overriding appearance is dirty or scruffy.
Information
Anticipate the kind of questions you will be asked and be ready with answers. Make yourself familiar with the site map and all the key locations on it. Don't be afraid to ask uncertain-looking visitors if they need any help.
Above all, remember you are part of the Katzonderloos TEAM. Enjoy your performance, support the other members of the side and be part of a winning combination.

Case study

Canterbury Cathedral's customer care programme
Some customer care programmes are very specific because of the nature of the workplace. For example **Canterbury Cathedral** was not built as a tourist attraction and employs voluntary staff to act as guides to the thousands of visitors which the building receives each year.

The cathedral authorities have produced a booklet for guides, concentrating on practical techniques to ensure that visitors enjoy the experience. The basic underlying principle of this booklet is that all guides need to learn how to combine knowledge and enthusiasm to produce a really professional performance.

The role of the guide is more complicated than might be supposed. They may be required to:
- explain and interpret all aspects of the cathedral and its work;
- welcome visitors on behalf of all cathedral staff;
- organize and time the group's activities;
- perform well enough to inform and entertain the group;
- represent the overall interests of the cathedral and its staff, and act as their ambassador.

Information for visitors approaching Canterbury Cathedral

In order to carry out these functions effectively guides will need to possess a number of qualities, including such things as stamina, a clear speaking voice, a smart appearance, an interest in people and enthusiasm. Guides who are late, or who grumble, or who criticize or argue will not be able to fulfil their roles adequately.

A critical point in the relationship between guides and customers is the first meeting and hence the booklet takes a detailed look at what the guide should aim to establish in the first few minutes of the encounter. The two fundamental principles here are:

- establishing mutual respect through the guide's confidence and manner;
- establishing rapport through friendliness and personality.

In order to establish rapport quickly the guide has to be sensitive to the mood and level of interest of the group. Often they can read clues which indicate whether the group is having a good day or whether there are circumstances which mean they have arrived in an irritable or uncooperative state of mind. It is also important to assess quickly what their main interests are. If they are on a general, fairly rapid guided tour of the sights of London, they will expect a different approach and technique from a group with an interest in heraldry or stained-glass windows.

Guides need to be sensitive to special needs, especially in terms of the speed at which the tour moves round the cathedral and in terms of the complexity of the language they use. Overseas visitors may have only a limited knowledge of English history and customs, and explanations will need to take account of this.

Good customer service is often a matter of planning. The cathedral guide can do much to prepare themselves for a tour beforehand. Research about the group may indicate their special interests, perhaps related to the organization to which they belong or the places they come from. For example Canterbury cathedral contains a number of items from overseas, such as the Swedish statue of St Thomas or Australian altar pieces. On some days areas of the cathedral may be out of bounds and guides are more likely to be able to explain the reasons for this tactfully if they have taken the trouble to find out in advance.

The tour itself also benefits from careful planning. If what is said has a clear structure it is more likely that it will be easy to take in. Essentially each tour has three phases: a beginning, a middle and an end. Each serves an important purpose, summarized in Table 6.2:

Table 6.2 The phases of a tour round Canterbury Cathedral

Beginning	Middle	End
Introduction and welcome	Moving through the cathedral	Asking for questions
Finding out about the group	Talking about background and items of interest	Giving a brief summary of the tour
Explaining the tour route	Keeping to required timing	Showing the exit
Giving policy on taking photographs	Avoiding other tour groups	Pointing out facilities such as bookstall, toilets, Welcome Centre etc.
Encouraging the asking of questions		Wish them a safe journey and an enjoyable continuation of their stay

The technique of speaking to visitors is an important part of a guide's work. They are given specific directions on how to position the group, where are the best positions for the guide to stand, what gestures should accompany the words and a warning to observe the golden rule of 'not turning your head away from the group when talking.' The use of small cue cards as an aid to memory is encouraged. Where technical terms are relevant, such as 'chapter', 'evensong', 'chantry' or 'clerestory', guides should be able to provide explanations. Techniques for handling questions are outlined, suggesting that the formula of **'listen, repeat, answer'** works best. Though there may sometimes be a temptation to try and respond to questions to which the guide does not really know the answer, this may misfire. Customers who genuinely wish to know things, however obscure, are better served by either an honest admission that no one knows the answer or by an attempt on the guide's part to find out the answer from another member of staff.

Because the cathedral exists primarily as a place of worship and not as a tourist attraction, guides need to be familiar with the schedule of services, ceremonies and prayers which may affect their tours. Sometimes interruptions will be necessary and customers are less likely to be irritated if they receive an explanation of what is about to happen. Similarly, certain parts of the cathedral, such as the crypt, may be subject to a rule of silence and groups need to be briefed about this before entering such areas. Respect for people at prayer is also a principle which guides have to encourage their groups to observe.

However successfully the booklet describes good guiding practice, the skill of guides depends on them adopting a self-critical approach which continually looks for improvement. Practical ways of doing this include the following.

Improving Cathedral knowledge:
- consulting the cathedral, city and county libraries
- using the education department's booklets and trails
- reading the range of newsletters produced for and about the cathedral
- revisiting the cathedral audio-visual presentations.

Communication and technique:
- practising in front of a mirror
- accompanying another guide on his/her tour
- making a video or tape recording of the guide's performance
- practising different introductions and endings
- planning alternative tours with different time constraints
- developing descriptive powers by planning a tour for the blind
- asking a friend to join a tour and make constructive comment about how it might be improved.

The Canterbury Cathedral booklet is a good example of the way many companies resolve the problem of conveying their customer care policies to their own employees. It is relatively inexpensive to produce but gives employees a reference guide. It does not require significant amounts of staff time to implement, since most of the message can be absorbed in the reader's own time. In many leisure and tourism companies and organizations this customer care policy will form an integral part of the staff hand book, which will also contain details of induction, conditions of employment, health and safety policy, and grievance and disciplinary procedures. Placing the customer care policy in this context indicates that it is an integral part of the company's whole operation.

The most common method of enabling employees to do their jobs more effectively is through training, either while they do the job or by means of dedicated training courses off-site. In leisure and tourism such training is often done by demonstration, using trainers skilled in performance and setting up role-play situations. Videos are increasingly used in customer care training. They have the advantage of being flexible. They can be interrupted at will and taken away by individuals wishing to review what they have seen.

Activity

1 Identify an attraction in your area either which already offers guided tours or which you think might benefit from doing so. Arrange a visit.
2 Compile a list of questions which you think visitors might ask and from this list identify **ten** which you think might prove the most difficult for a guide to answer.
3 Compose ten answers to your questions which you think the most professional of tour guides would give.

6.6 Monitoring and measuring standards of customer service

Though training should demonstrate how to improve customer service, it does not in itself guarantee that it actually happens. Transferring a company customer care policy into practice requires a system of monitoring how effective the policy is. Increasingly businesses are establishing **performance targets** for individual employees that set standards against which they can measure their own performance.

Some aspects of customer service are easier to quantify than others. A tour operator, for example, may employ a number of telephone sales staff. They can set performance targets relating to the average time taken to respond to each call or the average time taken in talking to each customer. The first measure is more objective than the second. If it takes more than five seconds to answer each incoming call, a large tour operator may well decide it needs more sales staff if it is not to lose some custom. The average time taken with each customer is a less reliable performance measure, since no two enquiries are identical. However, if the same employee persistently takes ten minutes longer to deal with incoming calls than anyone else, and is not achieving a correspondingly higher level of sales, their performance would probably be reviewed and further training recommended. Measuring certain aspects of telephone performance is made relatively easy by systems which will analyse timings electronically.

Other measures of performance may be more difficult to set. For example, measuring how friendly and helpful employees are towards customers is a more subjective matter. Generally these factors are monitored by means of customer surveys. The design and use of surveys is considered in more detail in Chapter 14.

Once performance targets have been set, there has to be a continuing process of monitoring how successfully the company and its employees are measuring up to them. The standards achieved have to be recorded, made available throughout the company, and the data generated must be the subject of meetings aimed at eliminating errors and weaknesses, and working towards and maintaining high quality service. The monitoring process may be conducted in a number of ways. Random checks by company personnel or outsiders are often used. A leisure park, for example, may brief an outsider to visit for a day and record specific detail of the levels of service received in various catering, retail and entertainment areas. Any mail received which comments on an aspect of the performance of employees should be used to build up a broad picture, which can be fed back to all employees, of the public perception of the company.

Some companies carry out a regular **customer service audit** in an attempt to get an independent, unbiased view of the quality of service they are offering. The audit is generally conducted either by a panel of outsiders, possibly customers, or by another company specializing in market surveys, or by other departments within the company. Any of the following methods may be used:
- random checks of telephone response times;
- inspections of locations and premises open to customers;
- analysis of mail and phone calls commenting on the company's performance;
- interviewing customers and employees;
- questionnaires to both customers and employees.

American Express identifies five elements of customer service within which it sets out standards to measure levels of service in its business travel locations: telephones, reservations, documentation, customer service and appearance. Eighteen standards are set in all, six of which are measured on a weekly basis:
- speed of answering the telephone;
- rate of lost telephone calls;
- completeness and accuracy of travel itinerary details;
- completeness, accuracy and timing of final package of tickets and documents;
- correctness and prompt handling of all customer complaints;
- speed in processing refunds.

It is important that customer service monitoring schemes are not perceived by employees as simply a process of checking up on them. Though there may be an element of truth in this, the overall benefits to the company, its profitability and future career prospects of its employees are usually stressed. American Express lists the following potential benefits of monitoring levels of service:
- it identifies areas needing improvement and enables action plans to be developed;
- it helps the company in making decisions;

- it can give early warning of problems ahead;
- it can identify problems experienced across departments and suppliers;
- it ensures that attention is paid to detail;
- it encourages all employees to get things right first time;
- it highlights training needs;
- it forms an integral part of the appraisal system.

Tour operators specializing in package holidays have a major problem in monitoring some aspects of their services to customers because much of the contact takes place overseas. They have to ensure that the product which the customer will be experiencing, and in particular the accommodation they are due to stay in, is of a high standard before the holiday season begins. The case study which follows shows how tour operator Near and Far Travel monitors the quality of its overseas properties and the service provided by the staff in them.

Case study

Near and Far Travel's system of quality control reports

A tour operator requires a great deal of information about the performance of its individual destinations if it is to keep ahead of its competitors. It also requires accurate information about any new destinations featured, since by law the brochure descriptions must not misrepresent features of the accommodation, facilities or the resort itself.

Near and Far Travel require their overseas representatives to complete weekly quality control reports which are forwarded to the company's area managers. The area managers then relay the contents of these reports back to Near and Far Travel in the UK. Overseas reports are compared with responses to customer questionnaires and customer letters to ensure that problems are properly resolved.

Management information about the overseas part of Near and Far Travel's operations comes from a series of reports and information-generating forms which include:

The Property Owner's/Manager's Declaration;
The Area Manager's Pre-season Brochure Declaration;
The Representative's Beginning of Season Report;
The Weekly Quality Control Report;
Resort Irregularity Reports;
The Resort Building Work Report;
Compensation in Resort Information;
Defect in Resort Form;
Representative's End of Season Report.

The Property Owner's Declaration confirms that the brochure gives an accurate description and photograph of the property for the coming year. In order to ensure that the information is accurate area managers are required to go through brochure entries thoroughly with each property owner featured. Once all details have been verified the Area Manager can sign *The Pre-Season Brochure Declaration* and return it to the UK.

The Representative's Beginning of Season Report provides a detailed assessment of the resort as a whole and of the individual properties within it. It is extensively used as a customer service tool back in the UK to answer requests for information from customers. The report is compiled under given headings relating to the size and type of properties, their facilities, locations, appearance, services available, suitability for families with children and any complaints made. A resort map has to be included, as does any other useful information or guidance likely to be helpful to first-time visitors. Throughout the holiday season this information is supplemented by *Weekly Quality Control Reports*. Representatives are asked to judge and report back on the standards of service, catering and cleaning of individual properties.

Resort Irregularity Reports are only required on an ad hoc basis when unexpected problems arise. They are a vital element in providing customers with an up-to-date information service about the resort they have booked. These reports may relate to brochure inaccuracies, the withdrawal of facilities, problems with power or water supplies, health risks, exceptional weather conditions, or falling standards of accommodation or transport. If construction or renovation work is due to begin in or near any of Near and Far Travel's properties detailed information is relayed back to the UK through the *Resort Building Work Report*. If this kind of work begins in the middle of a holiday season management will have to decide what information should be given to customers. Sometimes it proves necessary to provide compensation payments to customers actually in resorts, and *Compensation in Resort Forms* ensure that the company has an accurate record of exactly what sums have been paid out and for what agreed reasons.

Defect Report Forms are essential in ensuring the safety of Near and Far's clients. This form, agreed by the area manager, acts as a warning to property owners that a serious safety problem must be resolved. The area manager has the responsibility of ensuring that the defect is quickly remedied.

At the end of the holiday season overseas representatives have to complete their *Representative's End of Season Report*, similar in structure to the one they completed at the beginning of the season. This report will review the performance of each property during the season and will enable management to decide what action to take where any problems have arisen.

Assignment 6
Case study

This assignment develops knowledge and understanding of the following elements:
3.1 Identify the function of customer service in leisure and tourism facilities
3.2 Plan a customer care programme
3.4 Evaluate the operation of the customer care programme

It supports development of the following core skills:
Communication 3.2, 3.4

Consider the examples of Near and Far Travel's *Weekly Quality Control Report* and *The Resort Irregularity Report* shown below.

WEEKLY QUALITY
CONTROL REPORT

Property HOTEL BIANCO/PLAYA DAGAMA	Report for the week ending	03/06/93
Resort LANZAROTE	Number of customers – Adults	82
Total Customers in Hotel 250 80 % ALL COMPANIES	Children	38

THIS REPORT SHOULD BE YOUR PERSONAL ASSESSMENT
FULL COMMENTS ON PERFORMANCE **MUST** BE MADE PARTICULARLY IF UNACCEPTABLE

HOTEL/APARTMENT	Excellent	Good	Accept	Unaccept	Comments on performance
1. Reception/Manager Services		✓			FRIENDLY & HELPFUL
2. Porterage Services					NOT APPLICABLE
3. Security		✓			SECURITY GUARDS ON COMPLEX
4. Availability of keys		✓			24-HR RECEPTION
5. Food Quality		✓			PIZZERIA OFFERS GOOD CHOICE
6. Food Quantity		✓			& VALUE FOR MONEY
7. Dining Room/Bar Services			✓		BAR SERVICE SLOW AT TIMES
8. Grocery Pack					NOT APPLICABLE
9. Bedroom Cleaning		✓			CLEANED 5 TIMES A WEEK
10. Change of Bed Linen			✓		OVERLOOKED ONCE THIS WEEK
11. Public Areas		✓			COMFORTABLE & WELL-FURNISHED
12. General Cleanliness		✓			WELL-MAINTAINED
13. Lifts			✓		ONE LIFT OUT OF ORDER ALL DAY WED.
14. Water Supply/Plumbing			✓		WATER OFF 2 HRS THURS
15. Electricity/Gas Supply		✓			NO CUTS THIS WEEK
16. Heating/Air Conditioning					NOT APPLICABLE
17. Maintenance Services		✓			PROMPT & EFFICIENT
18. Swimming Pool/Cleanliness			✓		OK - BUT SEE GP.
19. Cots			✓		SPANISH COTS - SAFE FOR USE.
20. Furnishings		✓			COMFORTABLE
21. Beds			✓		VERY THIN FOAM MATTRESSES
22. Kitchen Utensils			✓		SOME ITEMS MISSING - REPLACED ON REQ
23. Kitchen Facilities		✓			WELL-EQUIPPED

WEATHER   Exc. ☐   Good ✓   Fair ☐   Poor ☐   TWO CLOUDY DAYS (TUES/WED)

BROCHURE ACCURACY: CHECK THE PROPERTY DESCRIPTION AND RECORD ALL VARIATIONS, ACTION TAKEN AND THE RESULT.

Variation ① NO POOL TABLE ② NEAREST SUPERMARKET NOW 300m AWAY ③ MAIN POOL OUT OF USE UNTIL APPROX 4-6-93.
Action taken ① + ② ERRATA ISSUED 6-10-92 & 20-04-93. ③ IRREGULARITY REPORT ISSUED 29-05-93.
Customer Reaction ① + ② NO COMPLAINTS ③ SOME COMMENTS RE 2ND POOL NOW TOO CROWDED.

REPRESENTATIVES' VISITING TIMES:

Monday 11AM - 1PM	Wednesday 2PM - 5PM	Friday 11AM - 1PM
Tuesday 11AM - 1PM	Thursday AIRPORT	Saturday GUIDING
		Sunday DAY OFF

GENERAL PERFORMANCE: THIS SECTION MUST BE COMPLETED EACH WEEK GIVING A SUMMARY OF ANY PROBLEMS, SPECIAL EVENTS AND THE ENTERTAINMENTS PROGRAMME.

MAIN POOL CLOSED - GUESTS HAVE USE OF 2ND POOL & POOL AT NEXT-DOOR CPLX. BUILDING WORK STARTED 30-5-93 NEXT TO APTS - REPORT MADE 30-5. GUESTS MOVED AWAY FROM THE WORK. DEFECT REPORT ISSUED 28-5 RE BROKEN TILES IN 2ND POOL - NOTICE ON BOARD. CIR PAID TO MR WOOD X4 - BKG REF - ARR. - DUR - AMOUNT - DUE TO LACK OF BALCONY 2NTS. NOW MOVED TO APT WITH BALC.. LINEN/TOWEL CHANGE OVERLOOKED ONCE THIS WEEK BUT REPORTED THIS TO RECEPTION WHO ARRANGED FOR THIS TO BE DONE. ENTS. THIS WEEK INCLUDED A BBQ AND A DISCO BY THE POOL.

I CONFIRM THAT I HAVE COMPLETED AND CHECKED EACH SECTION ABOVE FULLY AND TO THE BEST OF MY KNOWLEDGE

Prepared by   A. REP   (BLOCK CAPITALS)

Representative's Signature a. Rep   Date 4-6-93   Area Manager a. Manager   Date 5-6-93

RESORT IRREGULARITY
REPORT

Property Name __HOTEL   BIANCO__
Resort __PLAYA   DAGAMA__
Area __LANZAROTE__
Season __SUMMER 1993__
Brochure/s __ALL   NAF   MAIN S93__
__BROCHURES__

Completed by __A. MANAGER__
Position/Title __AREA   MANAGER__
Date __29-05-93__
Other Companies Affected _____
__ALL NAF- BRANDS__

Problem __MAIN POOL OUT OF USE AS OF TODAY'S DATE, DUE TO__
__REPAIRS NEEDED ON FILTER SYSTEM. MAINTENANCE AWAITING NEW__
__PART FROM ARRECIFE.__

Date identified __29-05-93__
Anticipated duration of problem __APPROX. ONE WEEK - SHOULD REOPEN 4-6-93__
Impact on customers __NOT TOO MUCH OF A PROBLEM - 2ND POOL AVAILABLE AND__
__POOL AT NEXT-DOOR COMPLEX CAN BE USED TOO.__
Are guests complaining? __SEVERAL HAVE MENTIONED THAT 2ND POOL IS TOO CROWDED.__
If facility withdrawn, state nearest alternative __SECOND POOL WITHIN COMPLEX, AND POOL__
__AT PLAYAMAR CPLX NEXT DOOR - APPROX 250 M.__
Action by Property __ATTEMPTING TO REPAIR POOL ASAP.__
Action by Representative __ADVISING GUESTS OF ALTERNATIVE POOLS AVAILABLE.__
Action by Area Manager __HAVE SPOKEN TO APTS. MANAGEMENT - THEY HAVE AGREED__
__TO GIVE ALL GUESTS A BOTTLE OF CHAMPAGNE DUE TO INCONVENIENCE.__
Is advice to future guests necessary? __YES - NEW ARRIVALS ON 2ND & 3RD JUNE.__
If applicable, state reason for error/s __NOT APPLICABLE.__

UK Section
Received by Quality Control __29-05-93   (FAX)__
Research/action by Quality Control __OPS ASKED TO PHONE - ADVISE 2/3 JUNE ARRIVALS.__
__SCREEN ERRATUM INPUT BY DATA CONTROL FOR RELEVANT DATES. NO C.I.R.__
__AT PRESENT (AS PER O'SEAS DIRECTOR) - SITUATION TO BE REVIEWED IF__
__POOL NOT OPEN AS OF 4-6-93. REQUESTED UPDATE FROM RESORT ON__
__3-6-93. ADVISED RESORT OF ACTION TAKEN 30-05-93.__

USE THIS FORM TO REPORT ON THE FOLLOWING:

1. Brochure inaccuracies/discrepancies
2. Withdrawal of facilities - permanent or temporary
3. Technical problems (water supply, lifts etc)
4. Natural conditions (Storm etc)
5. General hazards (defect reports)
6. Property services (cleaning, food etc)
7. Standard of transport suppliers
8. Standard of venues

'Mona's Castle'
Bridge Street
Easthampton
10 June 1993

Dear Sir/Madam,

I have just returned from a one week holiday (week ending 3 June), booked through your company, to the Hotel Bianco on Lanzarote. This hotel had been highly recommended by our local travel agent but we were frankly disappointed with a number of aspects of it.

1. the lift was out of order most of the time we were there
2. the service in the hotel restaurant was very slow
3. the swimming pool was being repaired so we had to use one next door which was very crowded at most times of the day
4. the nearest shops were nearly half a mile away
5. no English food appeared on the menu
6. youths were riding noisy motorbikes outside late one evening

The result of all this was that our holiday was thoroughly spoiled. We think that it should be the responsibility of Near and Far Travel to repay us the cost of the holiday because so many things were wrong that we might as well have stayed at home and saved our money.

   I look forward to hearing from you.

Yours faithfully,

Ivor Grudge

Ivor Grudge

Your tasks

1 Write a reply to the letter below from Ivor Grudge on behalf of Near and Far Travel.

2 In view of this and a number of other complaints the manager of the Hotel Bianco decides to develop a customer care programme for the hotel, before they lose their contract with Near and Far Travel. Use the *Weekly Quality Control Report* to determine which aspects of the hotel's performance are likely to have an impact on customers. Produce a plan for a customer care programme which you think would ensure a reduction in the number of complaints.

7   Identifying markets for leisure and tourism

What is covered in this chapter

This chapter outlines the elements involved in the whole marketing process. It stresses the importance in marketing of accurately assessing what customers want, and the way in which market research is used to establish this. A SWOT analysis is described, showing how it is used to assess the market potential of a new business idea. It concludes by identifying the main types of research undertaken and commenting on the contribution these can make towards a company's profitability.

- Consumer choice
- What is marketing?
- Market research
- Main types of research
- Cost-effectiveness of research

7.1   Consumer choice

All leisure and tourism businesses are involved in the process of selling either products or services. Their markets are the people with time and money who therefore have the potential to buy from these businesses. In making such purchases individuals are presented with choice, and leisure and tourism, in particular, offer a very wide range of options both in terms of the nature of the products and services and the competition between the different companies providing them. Potential purchasers can choose to book a stay in a hotel, visit a theme park, go to the cinema, or sample the pleasures of attractive landscape or historic cities. Even when the initial choice has been made, consumers have to decide which hotel to try, which attractions to visit or which country region would best meet their needs.

Providers of leisure and tourism experience have found that because the market place has such a vast range of choice and opportunity, this in turn has made the market extremely competitive. Twentieth-century communications and transport developments have made the world a potential global market place and exposed many markets to the pressure of competition on a scale never seen before. Many countries in the world have come to look upon tourism as the solution to their economic problems. Those with substantial budgets to spend are able to market their own tourist destinations and target markets elsewhere with a vigour that puts other destinations and products under threat.

Against this background of competition the leisure and tourism industry has had to become market orientated and focus more directly on its customers' desires. Without doubt marketing is now recognized as an important element in determining the success or failure of any business organization.

Range of holidays advertised in travel agency window

7.2 What is marketing?

It is often assumed, wrongly, that marketing is merely a matter of advertising, and promoting goods and services. However, in reality these factors are only part of the total marketing process. It includes all of the following stages:

- identifying the needs of customers;
- carrying out market research;
- developing products and services;
- pricing them;
- promoting them;
- distributing them.

Essential to understanding the function of marketing is acknowledging the difference between **needs** and **wants**. Needs are essential to survival. People need food, water and heat just to live. These are essential elements and without them we would not survive. Yet even these essential elements present certain kinds of choice. For example, there is the option to choose between different forms of heating: gas, electricity or solid fuel. Staple foods are available under different brand names and the products themselves may have distinctive ingredients or other qualities. The customer will express preferences in choosing these essential products.

Any kind of company faces a basic decision about the products or services it intends to produce. They can utilize their strengths in developing a well-made product or a highly efficient service. However, if they ignore changes in the market, they may find that, good as their services or products are, no one is willing to purchase them.

The provider of leisure and tourism services and products has to contend with the basic problem that these are wants rather than needs, and as such are things which people can manage without. The experience of leisure and tourism activities is not essential for survival, though it can add greatly to the quality of people's lives. They expect such activities to provide enjoyment, diversion and relaxation. Yet they can only choose to indulge in them if they have sufficient money and access to leisure and tourism facilities. Any attempt to market leisure and tourism must take account of these fundamental points.

Foreign countries compete for revenue from British tourists: the Swiss National Tourist Office in London

Leisure and tourism, then, represents an industry which competes for potential customers' **discretionary expenditure** and also for their time. In other words, customers make a choice about whether they spend their time and money on leisure and tourism, or on other things. Against this background any successful organization must constantly recognize the needs and wants of the customers it has. It has to be constantly in touch with its customer base. The following comment on achieving business success emphasizes this view:

> It is not the art of selling, but rather knowing what to offer, by identifying and understanding customer needs, that satisfies the customers and produces profit for the company.

The company which identifies what its customers want and offers the right end product can lose everything it has gained by not training all its staff to be aware of the expectations of its customers. A successful company should aim to provide a uniformity and quality of experience for its customers 100 per cent of the time. It can only do this by ensuring that the whole company is involved in the marketing process. Marketing should not be a separate function within a company restricted to an individual department. Every manager and employee should be aware of what the company's customers want and expect, and all the company's working practices should take these wishes into account.

Activity

1 List three leisure products or services, and three tourism products and services (see Chapter 1 for examples). Design and conduct a survey to establish which of the six is regarded as the most essential and which is regarded as the least essential. Summarize the reasons given by your respondents.

2 Write down a list of six products which might be regarded as essentials, perhaps including food products, clothing or energy supplies. Draw up a table comparing the issues and problems which face companies providing these products and services with the issues and problems which face the companies providing the leisure and tourism products and services you identified in Activity 1.

7.3 Market research

Market research has been defined as:

> The gathering, processing, analysis, storage and dissemination of information to facilitate and improve decision making.
>
> (Seibert, 1973)

No company can successfully establish the needs of its customers without research. In a competitive market place, it is essential to identify what existing customers are happy with and what potential customers want. It would be unwise, for example, to open a new cinema in a town simply because an existing one generally attracted full houses. Research might show that cinema attendance had reached its peak and that a new cinema would simply split the existing market which might even decline.

Recognizing marketing opportunities has become more difficult, and although some people still have hunches and end up very successful, these have become the exception more than the rule. Hunches need more than luck to be successful. They need a proper business and marketing plan, and this will include the financial requirements to realize the end result.

A financial institution will not lend money purely on the basis of a speculative proposal. It will want a concise, comprehensive business plan outlining the intended market, the expected sales, the methods of promotion and distribution, and the means of monitoring both the performance of the business and the reaction of the market. Gaining approval for a business plan will require sound researching of the market place and a realistic assessment of the internal strengths of the company.

Initial research can demonstrate the past record of an existing company in terms of sales and revenue. The company can compare its market share with that of its main competitors. Other data about existing customers can be analysed, alongside reports showing local and national trends which affect the industry concerned. All of this information is necessary in assessing what the market strategy and tactics of the company should be. An assessment of the company's overall position can be described in a **SWOT analysis**. SWOT stands for strengths, weaknesses, opportunities and threats and, as in the example given below, it can sum up both business potential and risk.

The strengths and weaknesses identified in a SWOT analysis are generally factors to be found within the company itself. The opportunities and threats, on the other hand, are likely to include factors relating to economic, political, social and technological changes and are therefore usually outside the control of the company.

Internal factors, which can be strengths or weaknesses, might include:

- **expertise** – specific knowledge and background of company personnel;
- **financial backing** – access to funds for business development;
- **age and outlook of the workforce**;
- **product** – the right product/service generating revenue;
- **premises** – suited to customers, function and company personnel;
- **location** – accessible to potential markets;
- **price** – profitable, but perceived as good value;
- **customer care** – appropriate programme of company objectives, training and evaluation.

External factors, which can represent opportunities or threats to a company, might include:

- **economic** – recession, inflation, exchange rates, competition;
- **legal** – laws such as the Health and Safety at Work Act, EU directives relating to tour operators;
- **political** – changes of local or national government, availability of grants;
- **social and cultural** –changes of attitude, taste and perception;
- **technological** – innovations in communications, transport, reservations, computer software.

SWOT analysis of proposal for Charles Dickens weekend in London

Strengths

- Charles Dickens is an internationally known name
- He has always been associated with London life
- No other company offers weekends using a similar theme
- London has many other attractions to offer

Weaknesses

- Few parts of London retain their Dickensian appearance
- Tour parties in London streets have to be kept small
- Those reading Dickens may be older and reducing in number
- Market is limited to those with a fondness for Dickens

Opportunities

- *Bleak House* and *Little Dorritt* attracted large TV and cinema audiences in the UK and overseas
- Interest in historical aspects of less well-known parts of London has been revived

Threats

- Outdoor tours can face unseasonal weather
- Unfavourable exchange rates make the UK an expensive destination for overseas visitors at present
- High level of competition from other tourist attractions

A SWOT analysis is a good method of assessing the potential for a new enterprise. A company planning to develop a new tourist attraction would probably begin such an analysis by looking at **strengths**. They would consider the location, access and parking, staff, facilities available, and the likely extent of interest. They would have to be honest about the **weaknesses**, looking carefully at what improvements were needed in their plans. As well as considering the features of the attraction itself, they would have to look at issues like how easy it would be to recruit and retain staff, what public transport services were like, and whether they would be able to afford to add new developments once they were up and running. **Opportunities** might include events elsewhere which could stimulate an interest in the attraction. The introduction of a new local radio station could provide an opportunity for successful promotion of the attraction. The **threats** which a new attraction could face might be national issues, such as a rise in taxation or unemployment leading to a reduction in the amount of money available for spending on leisure, or they might be local, such as a new road scheme directing the main flows of traffic away from the location.

Case study

Bed and breakfast or hotel?

Simon and Jill Smith inherit £280,000. Simon is 49 and can retire from his job in the insurance and financial services industry in a year's time on a good pension. He is a specialist in insurance and venture capital, is used to working with people and has travelled widely. Jill is a professionally trained chef with several years' experience of working in top hotels.

Both partners wish to continue working and see an opportunity in owning and running either a good quality bed and breakfast (B/B) establishment or a small hotel. They feel it would be especially worth while to target the North American market.

The SWOT analysis in Table 7.1 identifies the following:

Table 7.1 SWOT analysis

Strengths	Weaknesses
Cash £280,000	No experience of tourism
Good health	No marketing plans
Availability of good pension	Absence of research
Experience of working with people	Possibly age
Expertise in insurance and raising capital	
Professional catering experience	

Opportunities	Threats
To capture a good share of the B/B or hotel market	Competition
Finding an area popular with tourists	Strict health and safety regulations
Suitable properties available	Britain's lack of popularity as a tourist destination

The Smiths would appear to have a good chance of at least raising the extra capital they might need because of Simon's contacts and knowledge. They also have the essential skills needed for the project – both the professional catering ability and the extremely important experience of working with all kinds of people. The main concern about whether their idea might succeed would be the external state of the market in relation to the type of product they would offer. They need to research the trends in domestic and overseas holiday taking, and this would help them to decide:

1 if the option they are considering is worth pursuing;
2 if it is, where the ideal place to purchase a property would be;
3 what size and type of property they should look for, e.g. the number of beds;
4 what kind of marketing mix to offer, i.e. defining the product offer in relation to what the customer wants.

The SWOT analysis is a handy model to use and is extremely simple. It shows that there is possible potential in the Smiths' idea but it also reveals what is lacking. They must undertake further research before they can present a satisfactory business plan. Such a plan will be needed if Simon is to raise additional capital, since investors will want to be sure precisely where his income, and hence their repayments, are to come from.

Case study

A new venture

John Williams has never been short of financial resources and has never had to work for a living. His parents have their own haulage business and he has occasionally helped them out. However, his parents have never felt that he had the ability to make a serious contribution to the business. They have agreed to help him set up his own business, providing that it is a sound proposition. He is unhappy about his parents' attitude and feels he has a lot to prove, not only to them but to himself. He would like to set up his own business but has a distinct lack of business experience, either practical or theoretical. He is not even sure what he would like to achieve, only that he enjoys ten-pin bowling, having played it frequently on holiday. He knows that there is no bowling alley within a 100-mile radius of his home but does not know what planning applications have been submitted or are about to be on behalf of rival developers.

John realizes that such an undertaking as a ten-pin bowling alley will require considerable expertise which he does not have, but he has friends who might be able to help. Chris is a marketing manager with a major leisure company which includes such products as bingo halls, ice skating and holiday camps. Chris has said he would like a new challenge and that, providing he did not have to put any capital into John's ideas, he would consider being involved.

Frank is another of John's friends. He has been financial director with a major theme park and knows the leisure business very well, having worked his way up through the company. Frank would be interested in becoming involved, providing that he was made a director and was given shares in the company.

There are many immediate questions for John to face up to. He lacks knowledge about land purchase and planning permissions, though he feels his parents could help with the issue of acquiring land. He remembers reading that the locality has 'assisted area' status, and that developments which are likely to bring employment and revenue may qualify for development grants. Unfortunately he does not know how to set about locating these possible sources of financial support. One of his old teachers, whom he met on the golf course, suggested approaching the local college to see if they could help. Most important of all, though John enjoys ten-pin bowling, he does not know the extent of the interest in his own area or whether it is sufficient to sustain his business proposal.

Activity

Read the case study above featuring John Williams.

1 Compile a SWOT analysis for John Williams.
2 On the basis of the information gathered, what would be your advice to John Williams?

Once the SWOT analysis is completed, it becomes part of a logical process, usually leading on to further research, the setting of marketing objectives and targets, the agreement of a marketing budget and the marketing mix, and finally to evaluation. See also sections 8.6, 9.1 and 9.2.

7.4 Types of research

Case studies such as the one featuring the Smiths or the case of John Williams will, in most cases, need further research to enable sound decisions to be made.

Chapter 14 looks in more detail at the specific types of research which businesses need to undertake, both in setting up new enterprises and evaluating their continuing performance. Once they are operating many companies will conduct regular marketing audits aimed at judging their current strengths and weaknesses.

The two main types of information generated by research are generally known as **primary data** and **secondary data**. Primary data result from research commissioned in response to a particular set of questions a company wants answering. There is no access to information which would answer them from any other source. Secondary data are derived from existing sources, including reports, statistics and general market surveys.

In most companies there will be a host of facts and figures available which can help with the ongoing **development** of the business. This information is not necessarily easy to access, especially in large organizations, since it may be held in a number of different departments such as finance, personnel, distribution or sales. Chapter 10 explains how this information is collected and interpreted. Management information systems are developed in order to feed back relevant information to the different components of the company. The kind of information which will be available internally includes: sales figures; research records; location reports; press reports.

In some instances it may be necessary to carry out specific research. For example a coach company may wish to find out current attitudes of passengers towards similar services operated by competing coach operators. Major companies are more likely to undertake primary research, whereas small or medium organizations can find the procedure too costly and so they have to rely purely on secondary sources.

Activities

1 Design a questionnaire intended to establish a profile of the most frequent users of a local leisure facility.
2 Draw up a set of guidelines intended to ensure that those asking the questions to respondents collected data which was as reliable and valid as possible.
3 Discuss the main ways in which you think the leisure facility could use the data which your questionnaire would generate.

7.5 The cost-effectiveness of research

Before embarking on any type of research it is important to be specific about what is required and the costs involved.

Undoubtedly secondary research should be less expensive as the data already exist. However, it may take a considerable amount of time to locate and interpret the findings. Regional tourist boards, for example, will hold a range of statistics and reports about visitors to the region, levels of expenditure and popularity of attractions. The Sports Council will, from time to time, commission national reports about sports participation or the existence of different sporting facilities. Most of these can be purchased in the form of reports, a much cheaper option than commissioning consultants to carry out specific research. However, for a small business to make the best use of these, they need to develop some skills in interpreting statistics and identifying trends.

Primary research is more costly but has the advantage of leading to specific answers. The costs of any research identified as essential have to be included in the marketing budget.

The cost of internal research is more than recovered by the remedial actions it triggers. For example, a major theme park such as Alton Towers will know from its daily, weekly and monthly ticket sales which are its peak periods and which are its low ones. Feeding the information back to the sales and promotion team enables them to take the necessary immediate action. This may be a matter of planning a promotion to boost sales in the low period or it could be a matter of seeking ways to encourage people who came in high season to consider visiting in the quieter periods.

This information generated by research can also be of financial value to an organization like a theme park by suggesting that other revenue-affecting decisions need to be taken, such as:

1 staffing levels, roles, responsibilities and deployment;
2 pricing and payment issues, e.g. the number of pay desks;
3 reducing dissatisfied customers, e.g. providing more entertainment for queues;
4 rectifying failure to provide for special needs by analysing breakdown of types of people arriving, e.g. age groups, non-English speakers.

These become financially important because failure to act on them will seriously reduce the volume of visitors and hence the theme park's income.

Assignment 7
Identifying markets for leisure and tourism

This assignment develops knowledge and understanding of the following elements:
4.1 Identify market needs for products and services
4.2 Identify market opportunities
4.3 Plan promotional activities
7.2 Work with others in teams

It supports development of the following core skills:
Communication 3.1, 3.2, 3.3

The 1994 Winter Olympics at Lillehammer received extensive television coverage in the UK. Sports like skating, skiing, ice dancing and ice hockey become common topics of conversation for the duration of the Games.

Ice Incorporated, a leisure company specializing in the development of winter sports facilities, decides to offer a market research contract relating to a town in your area.

They wish to establish:

- what the current trends in leisure activity and spending of the residents are;
- what the real impact of the Winter Olympics was;
- what people's attitudes are to different winter sports;
- whether there would be sufficient long-term interest to justify additional research into either a new winter sports facility in the area or a winter sports club offering regular visits to winter sports facilities in other regions.

Your group is successful in winning the contract.

Your tasks

1 Specify the market research approaches you developed to win the contract.
2 Carry out this research and analyse the results.
3 Prepare a presentation to be made to the directors of Ice Incorporated, suggesting how you think they should proceed.

8 Targeting the market

What is covered in this chapter

This chapter shows how different criteria are used to divide up the market into segments. It explores how and why companies seek to identify the market segments they wish to reach. The use of the Boston Matrix is explained as it applies to the various stages of development of different products and services. Companies need to analyse their existing products and services in order to assess both future marketing strategy and profitability. However, it is not easy to define leisure and tourism products with precision, and hence their life expectancy can be hard to predict. The practical starting point of all marketing is the establishment of objectives, which enable the marketing mix, the major elements of which are described, to be determined.

- Market segmentation
- Targeting market segments
- Marketing a range of products and services
- The product life cycle
- Deciding on market objectives
- The marketing mix

8.1 Market segmentation

Not everyone will be interested in or able to buy the same leisure and tourism products. Companies have to calculate which people in particular represent their most likely markets, and also how they can match their products to the wants and needs of these groups.

In the same way that a whole orange can be divided into a number of segments, so markets for leisure and tourism products and services can be divided into groups, each with distinctive characteristics. This enables companies to target more accurately the people to whom they think their products and services will most appeal. They can make their objectives more specific and design products which meet needs more precisely, so enabling them to compete more effectively against their business rivals. This system of dividing up the market is known as **market segmentation**. School students or retired people, for example, could be targeted as market segments of interest to, in the first case, a manufacturer of computer games or, in the second case, a tour operator offering extended winter breaks in the Mediterranean.

Most leisure and tourism companies will deal with a range of market segments at the same time. Their aim will be to match their range of products and services as closely as possible to the different needs of the various identified market segments with which they deal. At the same time they will try to keep their whole operation as economic and cost efficient as possible.

A small organization, such as a three-room bed and breakfast establishment, may be able to tailor its product to suit the needs of each individual customer. A large hotel chain, on the other hand, may choose to brand its hotels, taking the view that each brand will meet the needs of different segments of the market. Some will provide for business travellers, some for overnight motorway stops and others for leisure breaks. As this begins to suggest, there are a number of ways of determining different market segments. The most common forms of segmentation are determined by geographic, demographic, psychographic or economic criteria. Table 8.1 illustrates some of these distinctions.

Table 8.1 Forms of segmentation

Geographic	Psychographic
Place of residence	Psychological make-up, e.g.
Distance from destination/attraction	active or passive,
	adventurous or inhibited,
	explorer or drifter
Demographic	**Economic**
Age, gender, occupation	Income
Family size and make-up	Past consumer preference, e.g.
Marital status	budget conscious, luxury
Nationality	

It has become increasingly common to link geographic, economic and demographic factors so that market segments can be identified which both share similar purchasing characteristics and are located in well-defined geographical areas. A combination of census data and postal code information has been used to identify different household types, each with their own age, family and income characteristics. This technique, commonly known as ACORN (**a** **c**lassification **o**f **r**esidential **n**eighbourhoods), can be linked with the sales records of major retail companies to enable very accurate targeting of appropriate market segments, particularly by means of direct mail.

8.2 Targeting market segments

An analysis of the market segment including all British people who take an annual holiday overseas would indicate that this group can be split further into various subsegments. These might include those opting for summer sun, for winter sports, for accompanied tours or for long haul destinations. They can be categorized by their means of transport or their choice of accommodation. Within the segment opting for summer sun, further divisions can be made on the basis of destination choice. The ability to draw these distinctions would be of great interest, for example, to a small company who wished to target its marketing purely at those people who customarily take a self-drive holiday in the south of France, using only self-catering accommodation.

Even when a company has identified the market segments it wishes to reach, there are still conditions which have to be satisfied before its marketing can be successful. The **size** of the segment needs to be taken into account. Large market segments are not necessarily more profitable, since the buying patterns of some small groups may generate more potential income than some larger groups whose average spend is lower. It is more important then to work out the **potential purchasing power** of different market segments.

A company has to try and calculate all of these things in relation to the market segments it is targeting:

- how many people will buy the product or service;
- how often they will buy it;
- what the life expectancy of the product or service might be;
- what price they will be willing to pay;
- what effect on price existing and potential competition will have.

Even if a company has successfully identified the market segments it wishes to target, it may not have sufficient staff or funds to reach them successfully.

Activity

1 Study holiday brochures offering any **three** of the following: coach tours; holiday camp accommodation; luxury hotels; adventure holidays; Caribbean cruises; self-drive camping holidays; Disneyworld holidays.
2 For each of your three examples suggest a number of geographic, demographic, economic and psychographic market segments which you think the operators of the products and services advertised would ideally wish to target.
3 For each of the market segments you have identified, suggest an appropriate method which the operator concerned could use to reach them most effectively.

8.3 Marketing a range of products and services

For a small company offering a very specialized service, such as holidays for disabled people in Cornwall, it is relatively easy to identify potential markets. However, many companies in the leisure and tourism industry offer a wide range of products and services. They may have sought **vertical integration**, giving them control of all stages of their business. For example, a tour operator may have purchased a controlling interest in an airline and a travel agency chain. Each of their different products will have different market strengths and be at different stages in their life cycles.

The advantage of having a range, or **portfolio**, of products is that the company is less vulnerable to external factors. For example, during the Gulf War hotels in London which relied heavily on American visitors suffered a drastic loss of income as more and more Americans decided that the risks of terrorism made travel to Europe too dangerous. Similarly, organizations specializing in accompanied tours for American visitors suffered a major decline in their business.

Careful planning is needed in marketing a range of products, some of which may be new, some of which are selling well and others which appear to be declining. A commonly used method of analysing a company's portfolio of products and comparing the performance of each one is through a matrix developed by the Boston Consultancy Group. This matrix divides products and services into four categories, as shown in Table 8.2 overleaf.

Table 8.2 Boston Matrix

Growth	**Question marks** High growth rate, but small market share. Need investment to increase market share and become stars.	**Stars** High growth rate and high market share. Likely to be profitable but will face competition.
	Dogs Low growth rate and declining market share. Not worth investment unless increase in market share predicted.	**Cash cows** Low growth rate, but high market share. Less competition and reduced marketing costs make them highly profitable.

Market share

Depending on where a company's products lie on this matrix, the marketing plan for them may be to try to increase their market share or sales, to attempt to maintain their current market share, to maximize the immediate revenue they are generating, or to take them out of the market altogether.

Each of these various products and services passes through a **product life cycle**. This means that first research determines whether the product is likely to be sufficiently profitable to be worth developing. The product then has to be launched which is its most costly stage, since none of the development and advertising costs have yet been recovered. As its sales increase it establishes itself in the market and its price may well fall as a result of competitors offering comparable products and services. The product comes to maturity when it has reached the limit of the potential market and is simply competing with others for market share. Once its sales fall significantly it will generally be taken off the market and replaced by other products or services.

The product life cycle of a brand of running shoes is likely to be shorter than that of a package holiday developed by a major tour operator to a Mediterranean destination. A London hotel which had suffered as a result of losing American custom during the Gulf War might naturally have chosen to target and penetrate new markets. In terms of the Boston Matrix they would hope to create a Question Mark which they would hope to turn into a Star. They would aim to preserve the existing product they were offering as a Cash Cow for as long as possible before it became a Dog.

All companies should know what stages their various products have reached. Their various product stages might be classified as follows.

- **Market penetration**: the company is seeking market share for existing products or services, possibly by setting a lower price than competitors, or else by offering exclusive, better quality standards at a higher price.
- **Market development**: the existing products or services are being used to attract new markets.
- **Product development**: existing products or services are extended, modified or branded in order to maintain or increase their market share.
- **Product diversification**: new products and services are added to the existing range, generally requiring the company to seek new markets.

Museums are less able to rely on subsidies than they once were and hence are much more conscious of the need to maximize revenue and ensure profitability. A local museum might identify the following potential market segments:

- school children;
- family groups;
- senior citizens' coach tours;
- overseas visitors;
- history societies.

It is also likely that its business will be uneven, with some very quiet periods. One way of addressing this problem would be to give priority to the schools market, on the grounds that schools are more likely than other groups to be able to visit in off-peak periods. The schools market will have specific needs which may, for example, relate to the National Curriculum. The current resources of the museum may not fully meet these requirements. They will have to decide how much to invest, not an easy calculation given that it is an untested market and will bring in little revenue in the initial stages. The market should grow if the museum develops an interesting and relevant product which clearly benefits student learning. However, retaining this new market will probably involve the museum in continuing costs. They may, for example, have to allocate a specialist member of staff to give talks and presentations to students, and to work with them on follow-up assignments. If the scheme begins to cost more than the revenue it is producing, it is likely that a decision to drop the service will be taken by the museum managers.

Party of schoolchildren at Madame Tussauds

8.4 The product life cycle

All products and services go through stages of development, growth, maturity and decline. Sales may be slow at first, mainly because the product is not widely known. These increase to a point where all likely purchasers have been reached. The life of the product or service may be very short or extend over many years, but it is likely to decline once markets begin to perceive it as inferior to others. The progress of a domestic seaside resort as a tourist attraction could be used to illustrate this cycle. At first only a few visitors appear. Greater numbers lead to an increase in hotels and facilities. This expansion eventually reaches the point where supply exceeds demand and where the very presence of so many hotels in itself makes the product less attractive. Overseas resorts, with their guaranteed sunshine, are seen as better value for money and so the resort declines. It can only be revived either by investment in the product or by a radical shift of taste in the market.

Understanding the product life cycle of its various products and services enables a company to assess where its current and future profits will come from. It is vital in devising a marketing strategy. Figure 8.1 illustrates the characteristics of the product life cycle:

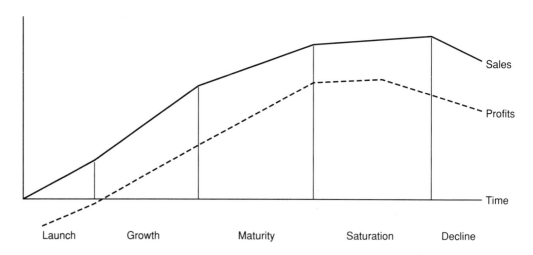

Figure 8.1 Characteristics of the product life cycle

The ideal product life cycle has a short research and development stage with limited expenditure, followed by a rapid growth and a long period of maturity. Finally the decline period is gradual and long. In practice, however, many products and services require considerable expenditure, and time spent on research and development. This is often followed by a long, gradual growth, a reasonable period of maturity and then a short, rapid decline.

Applying the principle of product life cycles to leisure and tourism is slightly complicated by the nature of the product itself. A holiday or a swim in a leisure centre is not a tangible article which can be inspected beforehand. A holiday represents such a combination of elements – flight, transfers, accommodation, facilities and services – that it is difficult to describe the standard product. Every package holiday, even to the same destination, is likely to be different and certain elements, for example the weather, cannot be guaranteed to satisfy the consumer. The holiday has to be sold to ensure profit. It cannot be held in stock in the same way that a manufactured product can wait for a purchaser. Finally, the quality of service received is an essential, but very unpredictable element of the tourism and leisure product. The marketing manager can advertise the quality standards of the company in general, but cannot predict with absolute certainty the relationship which will develop between clients and individual company personnel. It is perhaps as difficult, in leisure and tourism, to define the product as it is to estimate the length of its likely life cycle.

Two examples illustrate the point. The development of Quasar-laser gun games during the period 1992–3 began with rapid growth. Their popularity, especially with the young, led them to reach the stage of product maturity equally quickly. Perhaps because they appealed to market segments which liked new excitement, and hence constant change, the product declined fairly quickly. Such a brief life cycle gave the facilities which had developed these games only a short period to recoup their investment.

By comparison the demand by the British for theme parks such as Alton Towers appears to be insatiable, with visitor numbers rising from 2 million in 1992 to 2.5 million in 1993. Admittedly the theme park has to keep improving its product offer by developing new rides and other attractions, but the product life cycle for theme parks would appear to be still in the growth stage with an expectation of a long life cycle and period of maturity. The theme park example also illustrates the point that few leisure and tourism products and services are entirely new. Apart from individual novelties within a particular product, most lie somewhere along the product life cycle continuum, which in itself will affect whether companies wish to enter the market, to maintain their current market share, or to concentrate their activities on products outside the area of leisure and tourism.

Activity

1 Divide into groups of three or four, each representing the marketing department of an existing company producing leisure or tourism products or services. Each group should select **two** actual products or services which their chosen company produces.
2 Discuss as a group where you think each of the products or services you have chosen is on the product life cycle and note down the reasons for the conclusions you have drawn.
3 Suggest what marketing action, if any, would be most appropriate for each of the products at this stage.
4 Each group should report back their conclusions and proposals, and the class as a whole should assess what general conclusions can be drawn about the product life cycles of the range of products and services chosen.

8.5 Deciding on market objectives

Objectives are crucial in any marketing campaign. They are an essential part of the planning framework, as the diagram representing the marketing strategies of the Hancock Museum in Newcastle upon Tyne, shown in Figure 8.2 overleaf, illustrates.

Figure 8.2 Marketing strategies of the Hancock Museum

The organizational objectives of the Hancock Museum were to broaden audiences, to present a popular image, to provide a museum product that was both entertaining and educational, to demonstrate a commitment to quality and variety, and to increase the public and business profile of the venue. A robotic dinosaur show called 'Dinosaurs Alive!' was put on, with the marketing objectives of increasing attendances, attracting business sponsors, either breaking even or earning income for future projects, bringing first-time visitors into the venue, generating media attention and encouraging future visits by offering a satisfying experience. Table 8.3 shows the relationship between the organizational objectives and the marketing objectives of the Hancock Museum's 'Dinosaurs Alive!' exhibition:

Table 8.3 Organizational and marketing objectives

Organizational objectives	Marketing objectives
To broaden audiences	To increase attendances
To present a popular image	To generate media attention
To provide a museum product that is both entertaining and educational	To earn income for future projects
To demonstrate a commitment to quality and variety	To encourage future visits by offering a satisfying experience
To increase the public and business profile of the venue	To attract business sponsors To bring first time visitors into the venue

Any company can use a SWOT analysis as a starting point in determining its marketing objectives. Any number of immediate conclusions might be drawn, such as:
- the company's products have a limited life cycle and are approaching decline;
- the company's products are not being targeted effectively;
- the company's products need to be improved or developed to maintain its market share;

- the company's strengths make diversification into new products and new markets realistic objectives.

In order to respond to these conclusions a marketing strategy will be required which will, in turn, determine the **marketing mix**. The strategy could involve:
- keeping the product essentially the same but seeking new markets (market development);
- seeking to increase market share and revenue (market penetration);
- upgrading products to maintain market share and profitability (product development);
- identifying new markets and developing new products accordingly (diversification).

CERT, the Irish state tourism training agency, suggests the following examples to illustrate each of these four strategies.
- **Market development**: 600,000 Australians visit Britain each year. The Irish tourist boards are seeking to develop a market for Ireland from among these visitors, first researching the images that these visitors have of Ireland and then assessing what might motivate them to include it in their travels.
- **Market penetration**: a number of airlines operating the London–Dublin route have employed this strategy. Since most of the airline services are similar, customers have been attracted by competitive pricing and by promotional offers. The fierce competition that this kind of strategy encourages can undermine the perception of the product.
- **Product development**: perhaps one of the most common examples of product development in Irish tourism in recent years is the addition of leisure facilities to hotels. However, adding something like a swimming pool to a hotel only gives a commercial advantage for as long as it takes the competition to improve its own product. One effect of product development is that the market comes to expect the improvement as a matter of course rather than an exception.
- **Diversification**: this is the most radical of all strategies, because it involves the company in changes to its central operation. A number of Irish secondary boarding schools have seen the combined advantages of relatively inexpensive accommodation, attractive settings and periods of time when they are not in use as an opportunity to develop themselves as summer centres for foreign students learning English.

Activity

Choose a company with a diversity of leisure or tourism products and/or services. Give an example of how they might adopt each of the four strategies above in relation to a different product or service.

8.6 The marketing mix

The marketing mix is the term used for all the factors which a company can vary in its attempt to achieve its desired level of sales. Four major factors are involved: product, price, place and promotion. Each of these factors, often called the four Ps, poses a number of questions for the planners of marketing strategy. They include the following:

Product or service

What is its quality?

Could its design or organization be improved?

Would it benefit from branding?

What are its distinctive features?

What is the company's range of products and services?

Price

What is its normal price?

Is it subject to discounts?

What commissions have to be paid on its sales?

Is it liable to surcharges?

Are there any other additional charges?

Place

Where is the product or service available?

How many different methods of reserving the product are there?

Is access to the product sufficiently widespread?

Promotion

Where is the product or service advertised?

How are its sales promoted?

What kind of sales technique is required to sell it?

What publicity, other than advertising, does it achieve?

Three further factors are sometimes added to the marketing mix: physical evidence, process and people. These factors all relate to aspects of leisure and tourism products and services. **Physical evidence** would include decor, lighting, music and layout, and could be applied to a product such as a hotel. **Process** would relate to the way services are delivered and what the customer experiences. **People** are often said to be the major factor in any leisure and tourism operation since their numbers, training and attitudes will have a major effect on what the market thinks of the services and products it experiences.

A closer look at each of these factors of the marketing mix suggests what sort of circumstances would lead to a company deciding to change the balance of its marketing strategy.

The product or service

The main difficulty in marketing leisure and tourism often lies in the complicated nature of the product itself. As we have seen, buying a holiday is very different from buying a television set. A holiday consists of a number of elements, each of which could fail to satisfy the high expectations which most holiday purchasers have. Companies marketing holidays are really offering a range of services and products combined into a single package – travel, accommodation, information, service, the destination and facilities. Some of these elements are beyond their control. A leisure centre faces the same issue with a client booking a game of squash. Though the court itself and the cost may be the most important factors of the product, service, refreshment facilities, access and atmosphere are all likely to be perceived as part of the total product.

Price

Sales revenue is dependent on volume of sales and price. Prices of some leisure and tourism products can vary considerably. Items like holidays have to be priced some time in advance of the product being consumed. They are also subject to external changes such as fuel surcharges, while fierce competition may lead to frequent discounting, especially in the months after Christmas. Tour operators will often use price cutting as a means of increasing market share.

The price of tickets for pop concerts using larger venues like the National Exhibition Centre (NEC) in Birmingham may appear to be high, particularly when the target market may be relatively young and hence not generally high earners. In order to set the price, however, the organizers have to cover the costs of all of the following:

- hiring the venue;
- support bands;
- any new equipment needed;
- catering for performers and back-up staff;
- transport of personnel and equipment;
- hiring the main performers;
- press and PR;
- accommodation.

Costs are not the only factor governing the price of the tickets. International stars are in bigger demand and so people will be willing to pay more in order to acquire concert tickets when they perform.

Place

Most leisure and tourism products and services are, unlike manufactured goods, consumed at the place of origin. So, for example, the holiday product is consumed mainly at the destination and the leisure experience at the sports centre or on the golf course. In other words where the product is, is itself likely to be a factor in its success. A pub at the end of a 3-mile dirt track will probably attract fewer customers than one easily reached from a major trunk road.

Attractive roadside pub

Promotion

Promotion is the essential communication which creates an image of the product or service in the minds of the potential consumers. It is particularly important in leisure and tourism because the product cannot be sampled or often even seen beforehand, certainly not in the same way that a particular make of television set can be tested in the shop. Demand for leisure and tourism is often seasonal and promotion is needed to stimulate sales during off-peak periods. Customers have a wide range of choice of products and, indeed, may choose to do without holidays and leisure products altogether when economic conditions are hard. Both these factors make promotion essential for leisure and tourism companies wishing to stave off the competition.

Physical evidence

This is particularly important in the leisure industry as indoor sports, health and fitness centres and dancing have all grown in popularity in recent times. Some factors of physical evidence, such as comfortable furniture in relaxation areas, clear signage or flowers in reception areas, will probably appeal to all market segments. Others, such as ramps, may be specifically intended to appeal to specific groups such as wheelchair users or mothers with babies in prams.

Process

The perception of the leisure and tourism product can be affected by the various processes involved. Lengthy queues to check in at a hotel or computerized ticketing and billing systems can irritate or please customers sufficiently to affect their future purchasing choices. The process element is often closely linked to the people involved in delivering the service, in that if they are knowledgeable, efficient and able to handle people well, many of the potential difficulties with customers can be nullified.

People

In many leisure and tourism businesses the people who work for the company are its most important resource. If a hotel has a sullen receptionist, a lazy waiter, an absent manager, a dirty chef and dishonest chambermaids, it may inspire good television comedy but is unlikely to attract many customers. Appearance, personality, product knowledge, efficiency and integrity are all key priorities for companies seeking to employ leisure and tourism staff. Training programmes will often place great emphasis on consistency, so that staff are perceived as part of a trusted and reliable product.

Assignment 8
Targeting the market

This assignment develops knowledge and understanding of the following elements:
1.3 Investigate the variety of local services and products
4.1 Identify market needs for products and services
4.2 Identify market opportunities

5.1 Propose options for an event

5.2 Present a plan for an event

It supports development of the following core skills:

Communication 3.2, 3.4

Information Technology 3.1

Your tasks

Identify a theatre or arts centre which serves a local community.

1 Describe the range of performances, and other activities and services which it currently offers.

2 Collect evidence from local newspaper reviews and eye-witness accounts, and use it to assess how successful one or more recent performances or activities have been.

3 Consider the characteristics of the local community and suggest two market opportunities which you think the theatre or arts centre does not exploit. Prepare a SWOT analysis for two products or services which you think might take advantage of these opportunities. These could be events, performances or other services made available to the community.

4 Write a brief summary of the two products or services you would propose, including a list of marketing objectives for each one.

9 Running and evaluating marketing campaigns

What is covered in this chapter

This chapter identifies some of the major costs of marketing and indicates how marketing budgets are set. It points out the need to monitor campaigns in order to estimate their impact on the performance of company products and services. The impact is measured against targets related to marketing and company objectives. The most commonly used means of promoting products are shown and a case study illustrates how the promotional mix is matched to each target market.
- Setting a marketing budget
- Monitoring marketing strategies
- Promotional campaigns

9.1 Setting a marketing budget

To continue our example from Chapter 8, if a museum decides to expand into the schools market, it will incur a number of costs in doing so. It may, for example, purchase a database containing the addresses and names of potential customers or of local coach operators which it can use for a direct mail promotion. It may send an employee with display materials to a schools exhibition or it may advertise in the local press. The cost of undertaking these activities has to be met before any new business is generated, and so the museum has to judge in advance what the likely business benefits will be and use these as specific targets. If the cost of pursuing all these approaches cannot be met from existing funds or borrowed, the museum will have to set priorities and concentrate on what it considers are the most important marketing activities.

In larger leisure and tourism organizations the marketing budget is generally determined on a company-wide basis, rather than in relation to a range of separate product promotions. It will often relate to the previous year's figure, perhaps increasing or decreasing by a small percentage. It may be based on an estimate of what competing companies are spending on marketing over the same financial year. Larger changes may come about if there are significant changes in revenue or turnover, or if external factors such as major changes in economic conditions or the performance of competitors make urgent action necessary. Smaller companies may find it easier to determine specific marketing tasks and work out the costs of implementing these.

The Tussauds group owns a number of different tourist attractions, each with its own internal market research. Every year each trading location prepares an initial marketing pack, in which they summarize their proposed marketing approach for the coming year. The marketing pack is then used as a basis for discussion of the marketing budget for the year. The pack requires managers of each trading location to produce the information shown in Table 9.1.

Table 9.1 Information to be included in the Tussauds group marketing pack

Admissions	– predicted and actual for current year, and monthly – categories, e.g. groups, school parties – number of discounted tickets – adult/child ratio
Prices	– numbers of adult/child tickets issued – family tickets – group tickets – dates and details of price changes
Holidays and major events	– school holidays – major competing local events
Ticket and other net revenue	– forecast and actual revenue less discounts – other revenue, e.g. merchandise, catering etc.
Publicity and promotion spend	– space/time bought in the media – media production – public relations – leaflets/direct mail
Capital expenditure (less proceeds of sale)	– new building work – motor vehicles – plant and machinery
Profit for the year	– net revenue (admissions and sales) less costs of merchandise, catering and overheads (salaries etc.)
Cash flow	– cash surplus or deficit for the year
Budget prediction for future years	– expected turnover and profit, allowing for an estimated rate of inflation

As part of this annual process site managers are asked to calculate the main changes which they think are appropriate for their business. In order to provide a background against which they can judge the impact of any proposed changes, each manager has to calculate the effect on their business of three factors:

- a significant number above or below the predicted volume of visitors;
- a specified change in ticket price for the year;
- an increase or decrease in the total sum spent per head by visitors.

Thus, if a manager suggested spending 10 per cent more on media publicity and public relations, this cost could be analysed against the possibility of linked or unexpected shifts in revenue resulting from changes in visitor numbers or visitor spend.

9.2 Monitoring marketing strategies

Once a marketing plan is put into operation, the outcomes need to be compared continually with the objectives which have been set. If the Forte Hotels group planned a national advertising campaign with the objective of increasing overnight weekend occupancy by 20 per cent, the company would have to set up a system to monitor how effectively this target was being met. The system would have two basic elements:

- statistics showing present occupancy rates at weekends;
- similarly formatted statistics for occupancy during the various stages of and after the campaign.

This information alone would be insufficient to judge the effectiveness of the campaign, since it would not indicate why any additional overnight stays were made. Reception staff at individual hotels would also need to record where weekend guests found out about the hotel. This would indicate what proportion of weekend visitors were influenced by the advertising campaign.

The easiest kinds of marketing objective to monitor are those which set specific numerical targets, such as an airline stating how many passengers it aims to carry in the coming year or the tennis centre predicting how many members it will recruit in a given period. If sales performance or membership falls below the set objectives the marketing manager will need to establish the reason for this and plan a strategy to remedy the situation. A tourist attraction would probably monitor its visitor numbers according to market segments. In this way it might identify a fall in group attendance at a particular time of year, calling for a response such as a sales promotion for local coach tour operators. Of course, if sales reach considerably higher levels than targets, it may be that the marketing budget can be reduced. In all of these examples, there is no doubt that advances in computer technology have speeded up the collection of sales and quality performance data, enabling marketing responses to be much more rapid.

Activity

The tourism officer for a small seaside resort decides to run a marketing campaign through two national newspapers and two different regional television networks. The main objective of the campaign is to increase the number of families with small children taking a traditional summer seaside holiday.

1 What information would be needed to monitor this campaign effectively?
2 Outline a plan for gathering the relevant information, showing where it will be collected, and how it will be collated and presented.

9.3 Promotional campaigns

Promotion is concerned with communicating about products and services to targeted market segments. Table 9.2 summarizes the most common ways in which this communication is established:

Table 9.2 Establising communication

Advertising	local and national newspapers, magazines, trade press, posters, hoardings, bus sides, local and national radio, television, direct mail
Sales promotion	point of sale material, prizes, price discounts, promotional evenings, in-store promotional events, branding of products
Personal selling	visits by sales teams to retail outlets, presence of sales teams and sales presentations at: trade forums, trade shows, workshops, trade exhibitions
Publicity and public relations	press visits, press releases, special events, product placement in film and TV programme locations, community projects and charity donations

Each of these four basic methods has applications within the leisure and tourism industry.

Advertising

A basic principle of advertising is often called **AIDA**. This stands for **a**ttention, **i**nterest, **d**esire, **a**ction. In other words advertisements must do something initially to capture attention. A newspaper advertisement for a holiday destination may do this

Magazine advertisements for holiday products

by use of a large print headline or a picture of dramatic scenery. A television advertisement for sports shoes may combine music rhythms with slow-motion action film shot from unusual angles. The ultimate aim of the advertisement, however, is to stimulate enough interest to persuade people to purchase the product.

The type of advertising chosen and the medium used depends on the target audience. Advertising may be aimed at consumers but, as in the case of promotional material produced by tour operators, it may also be aimed at sellers of the product, for example travel agents. Cost will also affect this choice. Television and the national press may reach the widest audience but they are also the most expensive of the media.

Advertising leisure and tourism products will generally focus on one of the following approaches:

- stressing price in relation to competitors, e.g. discounts;
- stressing extra value over competitors' products, e.g. all villa rooms provided with *en suite* bathroom and direct access to swimming pool;
- stressing the uniqueness of the product, e.g. the only hotel on the island.

The second approach (stressing extra value over competitors) is perhaps the one that is most commonly used. Larger companies like Thomas Cook use the approach to try and establish an image in the public mind associating the company with a high quality product.

Sales promotion

The purpose of sales promotion is usually to generate immediate sales. Bargain offers in a travel agency window are intended to draw in consumers who are willing to make a quick decision about a purchase because they are more interested in price than brand. Sales promotion, therefore, often has more short term objectives than advertising.

Sales promotions aimed at consumers are common in the leisure and tourism industry. Examples include the habit of some hotels and airlines of giving away products like toiletries and wash bags bearing their company name and logo. Sometimes promotions are jointly launched with companies outside leisure and tourism. These may encourage consumers to buy extra retail goods for the vouchers which accompany them. These vouchers can be redeemed against the cost of travel or the entrance fee to a tourist attraction.

Some types of sales promotion are intended to encourage others to sell the product. A hotel chain, for example, might take a stand at a major exhibition like the World Travel Market, promoting the quality of its individual outlets. Their purpose would be to negotiate with tour operators attending the exhibition and persuade them to consider including the group's hotels in their future tour programmes. This type of sales promotion may lead directly to involvement in personal selling.

Personal selling

The effectiveness of personal selling is, not surprisingly, dependent on the relationship which the sales staff develop with individual clients. Personality, appearance, personal hygiene, confidence, honesty and efficiency are all therefore likely to be highly valued by companies seeking to employ sales staff.

A common criticism within the travel industry is that, although product knowledge and customer care may have improved, the ability to complete a sale does not match up to this progress. Sales staff do have to establish a rapport with clients, and be aware of their needs, but they also have to find ways of persuading them to commit themselves. This is not best achieved simply by trying to apply pressure. An ability to give a good professional presentation about the product and a sensitivity to the client's reactions to it are ultimately the best route to closing a sale.

Publicity and public relations

The public reputation of a company will almost certainly affect its business performance, even though this may be hard to quantify. Good public relations concerns a much wider audience than the company's known customers. It should include other companies with whom they do business, like trade organizations and regulatory bodies, professional associations and trade unions, the local community, public figures, and both national and local news media.

One essential difference between PR and advertising is that the message about a company delivered through publicity or PR is perceived to be more objective. The information provided about a tourist attraction by a visiting journalist or television reporter is regarded as the view of an outsider with no vested interests in the company.

Good press relations are important if any leisure or tourism facility hopes to gain regular coverage of its activities. It takes time to build a good reputation and the sustaining of good press relations is important to the facility's long term objectives.

Successful PR requires both a good instinct for what is newsworthy and also an awareness of the likely impact of different kinds of publicity. For example, the presence of Nick Faldo opening a new club house should provide good publicity for a local golf club. A television programme featuring an internal argument among a club's committee members will probably not enhance its reputation, though it may make it more widely known!

Choosing which methods of promotion to use will then depend on the intended target market, the overall marketing objectives and the marketing budget. The case study of the promotional plan for Caledonian Hotels in Cheltenham which follows shows how these promotional principles are applied in practice.

Case study

Promoting Caledonian Hotels, Cheltenham

Caledonian Hotels identify the following target markets:
- the business traveller (Monday–Thursday)
- conference groups (both one-day and overnight)
- group travel
- short breaks/leisure traveller
- overseas independent leisure traveller.

A decision is taken to set individual objectives for each of the market segments identified. For example, the group aims to increase bed nights in the short breaks market by 10 per cent over a period of 12 months. In order to achieve these objectives a separate **promotional mix** is agreed for each market targeted. The overall promotion plan is shown overleaf.

Target market: The business traveller

Advertising	local press, trade magazines and journals, new exterior signs showing price
Personal selling	sales staff visiting local companies holding meetings with personnel requiring overnight accommodation
Sales promotion	incentive discounts for existing business travellers bringing in new business, discounts shown on exterior signs

Target market: day and overnight conference attenders

Advertising	conference manuals, regional tourist board manual, city or county conference manual, direct mail to companies
Personal selling	sales calls on local companies known to hold regional and national sales meetings and annual conferences
Publicity/sales promotion	incentives such as discounts and free use of audio/ visual equipment, attendance at conference trade exhibitions

Target market: short breaks leisure market

Advertising	entries in: English Tourist Board's *Let's Go*, regional tourist board publications, RTB accommodation guides
Sales promotion	special offer of two nights for price of one or one child free with two accompanying adults
Publicity	press release publicizing special offers available

Target market: overseas leisure market

Advertising	inclusion in regional tourist board advertising distributed through British Tourist Authority offices overseas
Personal selling	part-time overseas representative in major overseas tourist-generating country, stand at World Travel Market

Target market: group travel

Direct selling	direct mail to tour operators requiring overnight accommodation or lunch/dinner/afternoon tea stop
Sales promotion	attend travel trade exhibitions, e.g. British Travel Trade Fair at the NEC, Birmingham
Personal selling	personal contact with overseas tour operators, offer of inspection visits to tour operators

---

Each market segment requires a different approach. Advertising is likely to be the most effective channel of communication for the short break leisure market but personal selling is more appropriate for dealing with the business and trade segments.

Promotion can take a number of forms, not all of which involve sales teams or working through the media. Restaurants, for example, are often faced with the problem of considerably fewer diners on Mondays and Tuesdays than later in the week. There are several strategies they can adopt to try and counter this. They can:

- run special evenings to celebrate festivals such as Easter or May Day;
- put on themed events for Valentine's Day, Guy Fawkes Night or Hallowe'en;
- design menus based on seasons of the year, local festivals or local famous people;
- promote evenings featuring the cuisine and perhaps music of other countries.

This type of promotion can be advertised by local posters, a press release to the local newspaper and perhaps the distribution of leaflets to nearby households.

Running and evaluating marketing campaigns

Assignment 9
Running and evaluating marketing campaigns

This assignment develops knowledge and understanding of the following elements:
4.1 Identify market needs for products and services
4.2 Identify market opportunities
4.3 Plan promotional activities
5.1 Propose options for an event

It supports development of the following core skills:
Communication 3.1, 3.2
Application of number 3.1, 3.2

In 1990 the Southern Tourist Board began a campaign, since supported by other regional tourist boards, aimed at celebrating the fiftieth anniversary of the D-Day landings in Normandy in June 1944. The campaign was intended to stimulate an increase in the number of overseas visitors to England in 1994.

A major market targeted by this promotion was the US. Thousands of Americans stayed in southern England in the run up to the Normandy landings. The campaign set out its major objective as attracting an additional 100,000 visitors. Since the average spend of overseas visitors is currently £565, achieving this target would bring in substantial revenue. Mindful of the potential benefit to the national balance of payments, the Department of National Heritage decided in early 1994 to give £1 million towards supporting the campaign.

A range of events and special occasions all across the south and west of England has been planned to commemorate the events and deeds of 1944. Among the proposals already put forward are:
'We'll Meet Again' themed weekends;
Glenn Miller tours;
a garden party for D-Day veterans;
a Channel crossing by a flotilla of boats;
museum exhibitions featuring the events of D-Day;
a national competition to promote further interest in the campaign.

Your tasks

1 Choose a facility, attraction or organization in your area which might be able to take advantage of this national promotion because of its own wartime or D-Day connections. Visit the place or organization and establish, either by making notes or interviewing personnel, the nature of the wartime connection.
2 Plan a campaign to promote the D-Day tourism initiative in a local facility or in your local area generally. Your plan should include:
(a) a statement of the objectives of the campaign;

(b) an analysis of the potential target markets;

(c) an assessment of the potential benefits of the campaign;

(d) a schedule of the planned activities or events;

(e) a more detailed plan of one specific event, including the allocation of human resources;

(f) a summary of the probable costs of the campaign.

10   Providing and using management information

What is covered in this chapter

This chapter explains what management information is, and describes its range of uses within leisure and tourism organizations. It indicates which people are likely to require management information. The variety of systems used for collecting, recording and presenting management information is demonstrated, supported by specific examples of the generation and use of information in three leisure and tourism contexts.

- Definition of management information
- The role of management information in decision-making
- The variety of decisions requiring management information
- Range of decisions made by Airtours management
- Management information in practice
- Methods of presenting management information.

10.1   Definition of management information

Management information is the range of information which can be collected **within** an organization to inform any decisions taken by members or representatives of that organization. This information can cover a number of diverse areas, as the following examples illustrate:

details of guests' individual bills in a hotel;

booking patterns of individual members of a sports or leisure club;

the number and nature of group visitors to a theme park.

Information is needed in order to judge the current performance of a company. Some of this information will be numerical, such as sales figures, room occupancy rates or admission numbers. However, information about the quality of service being provided or about the performance of the company's personnel is more likely to be in written form. It may be gathered from responses to surveys and questionnaires, from letters, inspections or, in the case of personnel, from appraisal procedures.

However, this internal information almost always has to be supplemented by information collected, presented and analysed about external factors which influence any decision-making process within the organization. So, for example, a London hotel chain planning a marketing campaign in the US would need information about the US economy, about dollar exchange rates, about any political issues which might be perceived as a threat by potential visitors and about any likely changes in air fares.

10.2 The role of management information in decision making

The range and variety of management information required within different organizations is immense. Appropriate management information is used to aid decisions in any leisure or tourism organization. These decisions may concern any of the following areas of a company's operation: finance; administration; personnel; marketing; controls; purchasing; safety; security; quality; strategic planning; day-to-day operations.

Nor is it only the managing director who has to use management information to make decisions. They may be taken at a number of levels, for example by: directors; senior, middle or junior managers; supervisors; individual employees with delegated responsibility.

The timing of decisions will also vary, with some being required on a regular basis and others being taken quickly in response to something unexpected. Decisions might be taken: moment to moment; weekly; monthly; annually; on a one-off basis.

The systems used for the selection, collection and recording of management information need to be appropriate for the purposes to which it is going to be put. **Selection** is often important where quick decisions have to be taken. Decision makers will often require information to be summarized so that a clear overall view of its significance can be easily established. This is invaluable in meetings where excessive amounts of information could prove both time-consuming and disruptive. The methods of **collection** of management information have to reflect the needs of the users, since otherwise much useless information can be generated. For example there is little point in a theme park surveying visitors about the daily newspapers they read if the company has a policy of never advertising in the press. The way in which the **recording** of management information takes place is important because it will determine how accessible the information becomes. A large hotel which stored its records of guests' previous visits on a manual filing system would find it more difficult to generate further data than a hotel which had used a computer database.

Depending on the nature of the information and the policy of the organization, information systems can be one, several, or a combination of the following:

formal – informal
manual – automatic
all-embracing – selective
confidential – with open access
in-house – external.

10.3 The variety of decisions requiring management information

The management of any leisure or tourism operation depends on the scope, accuracy, currency and relevance of its information supply.

- **Scope** – information needs to be drawn from reasonably wide and representative sources, e.g. the managers of a hotel chain of 50 hotels should not base company-wide decisions on information from two outlets.
- **Accuracy** – information should be checked for accuracy, and clear distinctions made between verifiable figures, estimates and conclusions drawn from samples of an organization's total activity.
- **Currency** – information relating to leisure and tourism quickly becomes out of date and decisions should always be based on the most recent figures available.

- **Relevance** – information, especially from external sources, needs to be sifted so that time is not wasted on data which has no bearing on management decisions.

Once it has been agreed that information meets these four criteria it can be used by a company or organization to monitor its own performance, analyse the market situation and plan successfully for the future. The range of decisions which will need to be made could include any or all of the following:

- what sort of products/services are to be sold or provided;
- what additions to or deletions from the product/service range should be made;
- how products/services should be priced;
- what returns on overall investment should be targeted;
- what policy on discounting should be adopted;
- what are appropriate sources of funding for current or future operations, including the negotiation of loans and negotiation with investors;
- how suppliers should be selected;
- how negotiation with suppliers for goods/services and payment terms relating to these should be handled;
- how techniques to control costs and to manage cash flow effectively should be applied;
- how image of the organization – locally, nationally and internationally – can be established and conserved;
- how marketing strategies are determined, including
    the level of investment in market research,
    the identification of target markets,
    the selection of appropriate advertising, public relations and other forms of promotional activity,
  the selection of products/services requiring urgent promotion;
- how quality assurance techniques to monitor standards throughout the organization are to be established, including
    customer service,
    organizational methods,
    personnel methods,
    communications;
- how staffing can be organized to ensure that numbers, selection procedures, pay, bonuses, commissions, conditions of service, rosters and training strategies are appropriate;
- how operations times in daily and seasonal terms should be reviewed;
- how health, safety and security issues and practice are to be monitored.

As this by no means exhaustive list shows, the range of management decisions is considerable and extends from long term strategic planning to issues which relate to the practical day-to-day running of a business operation. For example, how to establish the image of an organization is likely to be part of a long term plan, while drawing up a roster to cover a bank holiday requires immediate one-off decisions. Any organization must look simultaneously at improving its long term performance and at ensuring that its day-to-day operation runs smoothly. At any one time a host of decisions will need to be made:

- some based on extensive and detailed internal and external research, consultation and discussion;
- some where there is little or no time for reflection;
- some which can be considered routine and where existing or previous practice is likely to be repeated or adapted;

- some which will involve facing unfamiliar issues;
- some which will require direction from the most senior levels of management;
- some which can be taken by staff with delegated responsibility.

Many of these decisions are made after taking account of much external information, such as research among competitors and in the market environment. They may be preceded by discussion of demographic changes or analyses of current consumer trends. However, all decisions depend heavily on effective management information about the operation of the organization itself. In other words, both external and internal information is often required.

10.4 Range of decisions made by Airtours management

A good way of illustrating the range of decisions which are dependent on reliable management information is to take a look at a specific company's operations during a calendar year, in this case Airtours during 1993.

Airtours, at the time of writing, is the second largest outbound tour operator in the UK, carrying around 1.7 million holidaymakers a year to destinations around the world. It is a vertically integrated company, having launched, acquired and assimilated other organizations at different stages of the supply and distribution chain. It has also expanded horizontally, adding other tour operators to the group.

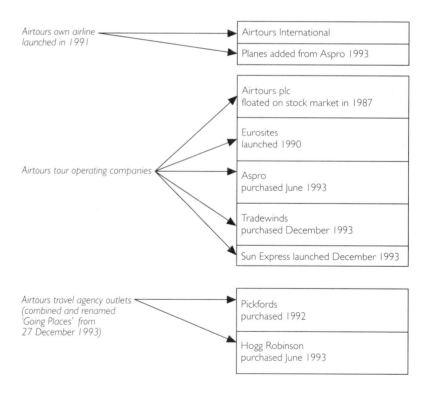

Figure 10.1 Organizations within the Airtours group

The range of decisions being taken at any one time in an organization like Airtours is extensive, ranging from those affecting multi-million pound policies to those concerned with daily operations. What follows is a summary of some of the decisions which would have been under consideration at various levels and in various departments within the company at particular moments in 1993.

Senior management

An attempted buy-out of Owners Abroad for approximately £269 million, the purchases of Aspro Holidays, leisure travel agency chain Hogg Robinson and the long haul operator Tradewinds, the introduction of Cuba into the Airtours programme and the persuasion of the government of the Cayman Islands to allow charter flights to take in Airtours holidaymakers were all completed in 1993. The organization ended 1993 contemplating its relationship with the Association of British Travel Agents (ABTA), now that the status of that organization has been changed.

Marketing

Pricing decisions for both the first and second editions of Airtours brochures are crucial for the success of their tour programme. Staff in the marketing department spent long hours in front of their computer screens, creating pricing structures which would both appeal to customers and meet targets for the season's income. Comparisons were made with prices offered by competitors' brochures and precise calculations were done to assess the financial impact overall of various permutations of price adjustments. As the year advanced, quick decisions were required on the pricing of late availability holidays.

Decisions about the best means of launching the new ski programme for the winter of 1993/4 to the travel agencies and to the general public were the subject of keen discussion early in the year.

Sales

Decisions were taken on levels of incentives and support to be offered to travel agencies to ensure prominent racking of the Airtours brochures. The sales department had to identify which agencies needed what support and incentives.

Administration

Everyday decisions included selecting and sending relevant information to the resorts featured in the Airtours programme. This included customer details, amendments and queries. Information and documents also had to be sent to travel agencies, including confirmation invoices, tickets and notification of any changes to accommodation or itineraries.

Overseas offices

While some of the overseas staff were involved in critical negotiations for accommodation and ground handling arrangements for next season, others were making day-to-day decisions to ensure that visitors enjoyed a pleasant and trouble-free stay. Such decisions ranged from something as simple as organizing a surprise birthday cake for a customer to taking appropriate action in a crisis, such as a client falling seriously ill. The communications links between the overseas offices and the duty office at Airtours' Headquarters in Lancashire were constantly open.

Personnel and training

The seasonal nature of the business means that every year new overseas representatives have to be recruited and trained. Many of the decisions involved in this process were similar to those of previous years. However, the dynamic nature of this particular industry means that personnel and training decisions require constant adaptation. In 1993 Airtours added new destinations, creating a need for more staff and fresh product information to be available. The EC directive on package travel increased the direct responsibilities of overseas representatives and they had to be trained accordingly.

Airtours introduced National Vocational Qualifications into its training and staff development strategy. This involved extensive planning and decision making at all stages of the process.

Airline dealing

Airtours International does not have enough aircraft to fly the entire Airtours programme. This meant that the company had to purchase seats on flights operated by other airlines. Decisions about the precise number of seats which were actually needed, and about what was an acceptable price to pay for them, are critical to the company's annual profitability. These decisions are never easy because demand for particular destinations can fluctuate, often boosted or reduced by factors outside the tour operator's control, such as bad weather or a sudden increase in reported crime. Plans made early in the year sometimes have to be modified later by instant decisions to increase or reduce seat purchases.

Customer service

Some companies issue standard letters as their first response to any complaint. The staff in the customer service department of Airtours write a separate letter for each query or complaint they receive. The decision to adopt this policy was taken in 1993 as a result of an analysis of customer feedback. That strategic decision now means that each member of staff replying to an individual query or a complaint has to decide on the most appropriate response.

Activity

1 Identify the information *about its own operation* which Airtours would have to have available before each of the following decisions could be made (the first example has been completed to guide you):

Decision maker	Subject	Internal information needed
Senior management	Purchase of tour operator Aspro	Funds available for the purchase; similarities/differences between Airtours and Aspro product; identify personnel in Airtours to effect successful integration of the two operations; estimate of on-going costs of acquisition and integration
Senior management	Purchase of Hogg Robinson leisure travel agency chain	
Marketing	Pricing strategy for brochure entries for new resort in the Caribbean	
Personnel	Recruitment of overseas reps for new ski programme	
Training	Designing courses for Head Office junior and senior staff	
Customer services	Replying to letter of complaint about flight delay on return from holiday	

2 Create a grid like the one below for a leisure or tourism facility in your locality. Identify the different sections or departments in the facility. For each one list a range of decisions which need to be made, whether on a one-off or a regular basis, and indicate what internal information needs to be gathered within the organization to inform these decisions. To complete this activity as effectively as possible, you will need to be aware of the aims, objectives, structure and operation of the facility you have chosen.

Decision-making in _____ (name of facility)

Departments/ sections	Decisions made	One-off/regular	Internal information required

The following example shows some of the decisions taken within a leisure centre:

Decision-making in _____ (name of facility)

Departments/ sections	Decisions made	One-off/regular	Internal information required
Marketing	Selection of advertising media for year	Annual	Research on success of last year's adverts
	Promotion of particular activities	As and when required	Monitoring of which activities need support
Management	Rostering of reception staff	Weekly	Booking patterns and busy periods/staff available
	Purchase of new equipment	One-off	Establishment of priorities of needs/funds available
Fitness instructors	Selection of individual fitness programmes for customers	On-going	Customer fitness profiles, details of general health Availability of equipment
Cafe manager	Buying supplies	On-going	Popular and not so popular consumables

10.5 Management information in practice

The systems used for the selection, collection and recording of management information need to be appropriate. Every leisure and tourism organization has its own set of management information needs, and the systems it uses for collecting that information vary accordingly. The size of the organization, the sectors in which it operates and the resources available, both human and technological, are all factors helping to determine individual approaches. The four examples which follow illustrate different responses to different management information needs.

Farmhouse accommodation

The owners of a farmhouse near Dorking in Surrey converted three twin-bedded rooms in their seventeenth-century farmhouse to accommodate overnight guests. Having looked at other similar operations in different parts of the country, they decided to offer bed and breakfast accommodation at a rate of £20 per person per night if sharing a twin room and £30 per person per night if taking a twin room on sole occupancy. They referred to this type of occupancy as 'single'. They joined the Farm Holiday Bureau so that their accommodation could be advertised in the publication *Stay on the Farm*. They also produced leaflets and cards which they handed round to local shops and pubs. A sign was erected at the roadside offering 'Farmhouse Bed and Breakfast'.

After a few months business began to take off and by the end of their first year they were not only regularly achieving full occupancy of the rooms, but were having to turn people away. They noted that many of their bookings were repeat bookings and that there seemed to be a lot of business people during the week, with a few couples coming for weekends. Indeed some of the business people who came to stay in the week returned later for a weekend with their partners.

After 18 months of operation the owners started to think about expanding, perhaps converting some outbuildings or just using more of the vacant rooms in the house. Before making any decisions, particularly because any expansion of the business would be both expensive and very complicated legally, the couple decided to embark on the collection of relevant management information about their current business.

They identified three questions to which they needed answers, before proceeding any further with their plans. These were as follows.

- How far could they expand while still maintaining high occupancy levels?
- What type of accommodation and board should they consider offering?
- How best could they publicize their expanded product?

They chose to set up a manual information system, part of which was in fact already in place, in order to obtain the following information:

Customers' names

Customers' addresses and telephone numbers

Distances travelled by customers

Reasons why customers were in the area

How customers had found out about the farm

Dates of bookings

Lengths of stay

Amount of advanced notice of bookings

Numbers of cancellations

Ratio of single bookings to twin bookings

Numbers of repeat bookings

Number of potential bookings lost through being full

Any significant booking patterns

Customers' preferences for any new accommodation

In order to acquire this information, the farmhouse owners redesigned their **reservations book** and their **register**, and they created a **customer questionnaire** which they asked each guest to complete before leaving.

The reservations book

This was an ordinary diary used solely for reservations. When a booking was taken either over the telephone, or by fax or letter, it was noted down on the page covering the dates of the reservation. Details were taken of the customer's name, contact number, booking type (single or twin), date of the receipt of the booking and the number of days' notice. If the booking was subsequently cancelled, this was marked in red, together with the number of days' notice given. If a booking could not be accepted because the rooms were already occupied on the required dates, this was also noted.

Here is a typical extract from the reservations book:

Room no.	Customer details	Single/twin	Date of Booking	Days' notice	No. of bookings turned away
—	Thursday 26th August.	—			
1	Ms Jane North	S	22/8	4	///
	tel. 0923 45732				
2	Mr. Alan Dean +1	T	20/8	6	
	tel: 0904 72311				
3	Mrs. A. Porter	S	24/8	2	
	tel: 0705 42715				
—	Friday 27th August	—			
1	Ms Jane North (from 26/8)				1
2	Mr. Peter Duncan	S	15/8	12	
	tel: 0473 92915				
3	Mr & Mrs Edwards	T	1/8	27	
	tel: 071 493 1111				
—	Saturday 28th August	—			
1	Mr. & Mrs. Smith	T	28/8	none	
	tel:				

The register
The register in use was slightly redesigned to provide appropriate information. Each customer was required to enter their full name, address and telephone number, and to indicate the length of their stay and the purpose of their visit to the area. A page in the new register looked like the example below:

Date	Name	Address and telephone no.	No. of nights	Purpose of stay	Room number

The customer questionnaire
The farm owners were thorough about collecting the rest of the information they needed, using a carefully constructed questionnaire. They also used the questionnaire as a public relations instrument to demonstrate to their customers that they were committed to providing a service of the highest quality.

They kept their questionnaire simple, brief and relatively easy to complete. By gently reminding all customers of the value of a high proportion of information returned from their customers, they achieved a return of 366 completed question-naires, in fact almost all of those distributed.

Customer questionnaire

It would be of great assistance to the proprietors, Jean and David, if you would spare a few moments to answer the questions below about your stay at Fieldfare Farm. We are always look-ing to improve the quality of our guests' stay here and are considering extending the provision of rooms in the near future.

For questions 1-4 please tick the appropriate box and for question 5 enter the appropriate number in the boxes provided.

---

1 How many times have you stayed at Fieldfare Farm?
  Once ☐
  Twice ☐
  Three times ☐
  More than three times ☐

2 Where did you learn about Fieldfare Farm?
  Recommendation ☐
  The book 'Stay on a Farm' ☐
  Road sign ☐
  Other, please specify below ☐

3 Are you staying here for:
  Leisure ☐
  Business ☐
  Both leisure and business ☐

4 If additional accommodation were to be offered at Fieldfare Farm, would you prefer:
  A single room ☐
  A double room ☐
  A family room ☐
  A family suite ☐

5 If additional accommodation were to be offered at Fieldfare Farm, which features would be most attractive to you? (Please list 1 as the most important and 4 as the least important)
  En suite bathroom ☐
  Television ☐
  Tea and coffee-making facilities ☐
  Full self-catering facilities ☐

6 Please add below any comments you may have which could help us improve your stay at Fieldfare Farm:

Thank you for completing this questionnaire. We hope you have enjoyed your stay with us and look forward to seeing you again soon.

Jean and David Brook

Activity

1 Discuss the range of questions which the couple might initially have considered including in their questionnaire.
2 Discuss why you think they selected the ones they did and comment on the style and layout of the questionnaire itself.

Improving customer service at a seaside holiday centre

It has been decided by the management of a UK seaside holiday centre to take urgent action to improve the quality of customer service at the centre. This follows the analysis of customer report forms which have been completed by guests over the first four weeks of the season. These forms are already in use to supply management information. Those analysed so far show:

2 per cent of clients felt that the customer service was excellent;

22 per cent of clients felt that the customer service was good;

56 per cent of clients felt that the customer service was satisfactory;

20 per cent of clients felt that the customer service was unsatisfactory.

Among the comments expressed by the clients on the questionnaires were observations such as: 'The staff seem very young and here to have a good time themselves'/ 'Only one or two people seemed to know what was going on'/'The staff are quite friendly, but are often unable to help straight away with enquiries'.

The management is aware that British people on the whole still tend neither to expect good service nor to complain about poor service. The likelihood is, then, that their real views are even less supportive than indicated on their customer report forms. Low ratings by customers are likely to result in:

• lack of repeat business;

• poor 'word of mouth' publicity.

At the moment the centre opens throughout the summer, with the season beginning in April and finishing at the end of September. The centre can accommodate up to 450 people at any one time and is usually at least 80 per cent full. The majority of clients are families, with up to three children. Entertainment on the site is planned to cater for family interests, and includes fun competitions such as talent shows, swimming races and fancy dress occasions. There are magicians who perform regularly, and discos catering separately for both teenagers and adults.

Most of the staff who come into contact with the guests are recruited on a seasonal basis, usually from outside the locality. Three of the full-time staff in the centre conduct a two-day induction course for new staff at the beginning of the season. Any member of staff joining later in the season is assigned to a mentor who will supervise them for their first few days and train them 'on the job'. Staff turnover is relatively high and many employees often do not complete the full season. All staff are accommodated in the centre during their period of employment.

In this case, management accepts that it must act very quickly to improve customer service and relations for the remainder of the season. It decides to use management information collection both to establish practical training needs for the staff and to provide a motivational tool for them. Collecting the information will demonstrate an interest in the individual training needs of staff and incentives are to be offered for ideas which improve existing training methods.

The management is in a position to organize 'in-house' half-day courses in basic first aid, telephone techniques, consumer contact skills, sales and cash handling, entertaining adults, entertaining children and on the subject of the centre's goals for the current year. It will also instigate other training if a particular demand is established. It is decided that each section manager will conduct a short interview with each of their section members over the next two weeks so that a training programme based on the results of these interviews can be in place within a month. Each section manager is equipped with a **personal review sheet** for each person employed in their section, and this will be completed and agreed during the interview. It is stressed that this is an activity intended to motivate staff so that managers should see it as an opportunity to support and encourage, as well as agreeing what training needs remain. A personal review sheet is shown below.

Personal review sheet

Name

| **Job title** | |

Key roles within the organization	Levels of competence within each role	Training or help required

Specific courses or help required (in priority order)

1   4
2   5
3   6
                   7

Choose from:
* Basic first aid   * Telephone techniques
* Customer contact skills   * Sales and cash handling
* Entertaining adults   * Entertaining children
* The centre's goals for the current year

Date:...........................
Signed:.......................and   Names:........................and
      ....

The information from the completed interview sheets can then be collated, so that the numbers requiring specific courses can be determined. Any previously unidentified training needs will also come to light at this stage and arrangements can be made to cater for these in an appropriate way. It will be of key importance to schedule any training to fit in with duty roster planning.

For an ambitious training and motivation strategy such as this to work, particularly given the brevity of the season, the staff will have to see the training up and running within the time specified. This in turn means that analysis of the results of the interviews needs to be carried out very rapidly.

Activity ———————————————————————————

Devise a summary chart for each manager to use, on which they could show the training needs within their section. For this activity you should assume that each manager is responsible for up to 25 people.

Promoting a modern town centre museum

Many town centres now have museums which depend largely for their financial survival on being commercially successful. Museums such as The Oxford Story, The Canterbury Tales, A Day at the Wells in Tunbridge Wells and The White Cliffs Experience in Dover are all run on a commercial basis, relying on admission charges and customer spend on site for their continued success.

Such museums can use a wide range of promotional activities as part of their marketing strategy. These include radio, television and newspaper advertising, posters, leaflets, letters to schools, billboards, bus advertisements, membership of regional tourist boards, attendance at trade fairs and exhibitions, the offer of discounts to tour operators, coach companies and group organizers, and public relations schemes. One practical way for a museum to decide how to spend its promotional budget wisely is to check on the success rates of previous promotional campaigns.

Many tourism and leisure facilities build management information or 'feedback' into promotional activities so that the information is being gathered constantly, ready for use in decision making at a later stage. An example of a very simple method of doing this would be to include a voucher of some sort in each type of promotional literature used. Vouchers might offer a 10 per cent entry charge discount, or a free place with every two full admission payments, or perhaps a free cup of coffee in the facility restaurant. Suppose a museum were to include such vouchers in:

- leaflets displayed in local tourist information centres and hotels;
- advertisements in two or three local newspapers;
- mailshots sent out to schools and colleges within a 50-mile radius;
- leaflets displayed in other similar attractions in different parts of the country.

The museum would be in a position to measure the effectiveness of each advertising medium over a set period of time. Each set of vouchers distributed by one of these four methods would have to be clearly distinguishable so that the museum staff could keep accurate records of how many from each source were actually used. When it came to deciding where to focus future promotional activity, the redeemed vouchers should give a clear indication of which of these four routes achieved the maximum impact on customers.

Another simple method of collecting information about which promotional activities have been successful in attracting customers is to conduct research among visitors while they are at the museum. It would be feasible simply to ask each customer as they arrived at the ticket office how they learned about the museum and to note down their responses on a pre-prepared form. However, this might lengthen queues at busy times and create an unfavourable first impression among visitors. Such information is more commonly collected by means of a customer questionnaire which has the added advantage of allowing further questions intended to generate information to be used in making other management decisions. Visitors out to enjoy themselves may regard filling in a questionnaire as a chore and consequently many attractions offer them an incentive to do so. For example, completed questionnnaires may go into a prize draw.

One of the drawbacks of voluntary customer questionnaires is that they only provide data from a random selection of visitors and so managers making decisions based on this information need to be aware that it may not be fully representative of the views of all visitors.

Activity

An example of a typical museum questionnaire is shown below. The range of questions covered is quite considerable. Draw up a list of management decisions in the museum which could be affected by the responses of the customers to the questions set.

Questionnaire for visitors to Easthamptom Museum

SOME SAMPLE QUESTIONS

1. Please state the date of your visit and your time of arrival at the museum:

Date: __/__/__   Time of arrival: _____

2. Are you travelling from home or staying in the area on holiday?

Home ☐   On holiday ☐

3. If you are on holiday, which of the following are you staying in:

Hotel ☐   Guest house/Bed & Breakfast ☐
Caravan/camp site ☐   With friends and relatives ☐

4. Please indicate the distance you have travelled to reach the museum today.

Less than 3 miles ☐   4-7 miles ☐
8-15 miles ☐   16-30 miles ☐
30-50 miles ☐   more than 50 miles ☐

5. What transport did you use to reach the museum?

train ☐   car ☐   coach ☐   bus ☐   other ☐

if other, state which _____

6. Where did you hear about the museum?

local paper ☐   local radio ☐   leaflets ☐   from friends ☐
magazine article ☐   other ☐

if other, state where _____

7. How satisfactory did you find each of the following aspects of your visit?

	Very good	Good	Fair	Poor
Direction signs around the museum	☐	☐	☐	☐
Quality of the exhibits	☐	☐	☐	☐
Attitude of staff	☐	☐	☐	☐
Refreshment facilities	☐	☐	☐	☐

```
8. Please indicate the number in your party.
Adults
One ☐    Two ☐    Three ☐    Four ☐    More ☐
if more, please indicate how many _____

Children
One ☐    Two ☐    Three ☐    Four ☐    More ☐
if more, please indicate how many _____



9. To which of the following age groups do you belong:
Under 12 ☐    13-18 ☐    19-30 ☐    31-45 ☐    46-65 ☐    Over 65 ☐



Please add any other comments you have in the space below








Thank you for completing this questionnaire. It should help us to continue to provide
the sort of service you want.
```

Note that there are limitations to the practical use of management information on its own. The collection and analysis of internal information like this must be complemented by external research activity before it can be used as a basis for decisions. For example, there could be many untapped sources of promotion for the museum which are worth using, but analysis of previous strategies will never identify them!

A foreign exchange bureau within a travel agency

Some major travel agency multiples operate foreign exchange bureaux within their travel agency branches, offering their customers the opportunity to buy both foreign currency and travellers' cheques at the same time as collecting their travel tickets. The service is also available for customers who have not made their travel arrangements through the agency. As in any commercial enterprise, the management needs to ensure that the foreign exchange bureau operates at a profit, and so information is collected constantly to monitor both income and overheads. One example of this type of information is the figures gathered to demonstrate the **gross** income from the foreign exchange bureau in one branch of a travel agency chain. Once gross income has been established, operational costs such as salary, and share of premises, heating, lighting, communications, insurance and security are deducted to show the actual operational profit of the bureau.

Foreign exchange bureau in an American Express travel shop

Income from buying and selling foreign currency is made in two ways.

Service charge or commission

Most bureaux have a minimum and maximum transaction fee, with a percentage charged on amounts that come between the minimum and the maximum, e.g. a bureau charging a 1 per cent fee, with a £1 minimum and a £10 maximum, would charge the following when **selling** the amounts shown:

French francs   100 @ 8.50 =   £11.76 + min £1 commission   =   £12.76
French francs   1,000 @ 8.50 =   £117.65 + 1% £1.18 commission   =   £118.83
French francs   10,000 @ 8.50 = £1,176.47 + max £10 commission   =   £1,186.47

If it were **buying** currency from customers, it would always deduct the service charge or commission from the sterling equivalent calculated.

US dollars ($)   100 @ 1.70 =   £58.82 minus £1 fee   =   £57.72

Rates of exchange

Any currency rate board in a bank or travel agency will show rates at which foreign currency will be bought or sold. The rates at which a bureau will buy foreign currency are higher than the rates at which they sell it. This means that the bureau pays less for currency than they charge for it, just like any other retailer selling a commodity. The margin between buying and selling rates for any currency is usually somewhere around 2 per cent.

Thus, if a customer brought 1,000 French francs back from holiday, the bureau might pay them £114.45 (1,000 @ 8.65 = £115.61 minus £1.16 = £114.45).

If another customer came into the bureau to buy 1,000 French francs, the bureau might charge £118.83 (1,000 @ 8.50 = £117.65 plus £1.18 = £118.83).

Income from selling travellers' cheques is also made in two ways.

Service charge or commission

As with currency transactions, most bureaux have a minimum and maximum transaction fee, with a percentage charged on amounts that come between the maximum and the minimum.

Interest

For all the time that the travellers' cheques remain unused, the issuing organization earns interest by investing the money the customer has paid for them. This income is not seen at the bureau which sold the travellers' cheques, since the bureau must credit its supplier immediately for all cheques sold. This income will therefore go to the company supplying the travellers' cheques.

Some bureaux also buy and sell currency travellers' cheques, which generate income both from service charges and rates of exchange.

On the surface it appears that a foreign exchange bureau cannot fail to be profitable. However, the process is not as simple as it appears. A bureau usually has to obtain most of its currency supplies from a supplier, rather than from returning travellers and, mindful of the need to ensure their own profits, suppliers will not sell at high rates. In addition rates of exchange can fluctuate overnight and the value of the different currencies held in the bureau can rise or fall sharply. Holding high levels of cash, in any currency, also has a significant opportunity cost, in that the money could be being used to earn interest if it were invested rather than sitting in a till or safe waiting to be purchased. For this reason currencies which are less in demand generally have to be ordered specifically.

The only way to calculate how the business is performing financially is to monitor currency stock values, sales, purchases and commissions over set periods. The simplest way to collect this management information is to summarize once a month figures collected every day and then to summarize these monthly figures at the end of each financial year.

The information required to show the **gross** profit on the foreign exchange bureau is as follows:

Value of stock at financial period end

plus (+)

Sales figures for the period

minus (-)

Value of stock at financial period start

plus (+)

Purchase figures for period

equals (=)

Profit made on exchange rates

PLUS

Commissions or charges made on

exchange or travellers' cheques

EQUALS

TOTAL GROSS PROFIT FOR PERIOD

The two documents reproduced below illustrate this collection of management information, the first showing the daily totals for a foreign exchange bureau and the second showing the monthly summary sheet. The same sheet can be used to summarize the profit for one month or for one year, according to the figures used for its completion.

It is interesting to note that when the bureau carries out its currency valuations, it always uses the current 'buy' rates, so that it does not overestimate the potential value of the currency.

The information can be collected manually or by using information technology. In either case, the key is to organize its collection from the beginning and throughout the accounting period.

FOREIGN EXCHANGE BUREAU MONTHLY SUMMARY

MONTH AND YEAR   February 1993

Date	Sales	Purchases	Exchange commission	T/cheque commission
01 Feb	7100.24	6044.11	42.17	25.00
02 Feb	5296.17	5332.12	33.12	18.00
05 Feb	6144.18	6486.24	15.81	13.00
06 Feb	6522.11	5711.19	52.10	8.00
07 Feb	7055.16	8422.67	36.50	19.00
08 Feb	4222.12	4076.89	92.10	6.00
09 Feb	5173.18	5042.66	45.16	15.00
12 Feb	6466.21	6267.74	72.13	14.00
13 Feb	5481.19	5166.14	27.90	11.00
14 Feb	6222.22	6000.19	36.52	7.00
15 Feb	8161.14	8222.11	41.80	12.00
16 Feb	5611.11	5422.73	57.60	19.00
19 Feb	7234.18	7511.22	91.20	22.00
20 Feb	6477.32	6618.34	47.50	3.00
21 Feb	5223.19	5084.76	32.50	–
22 Feb	3746.18	3236.88	25.00	18.00
23 Feb	5433.94	5211.23	46.50	22.00
26 Feb	1500.18	11462.92	110.50	14.00
27 Feb	8777.54	4604.17	47.00	15.00
28 Feb	9104	988.94	15.40	17.00
TOTALS				

MONTHLY CURRENCY VALUATION AND REVENUE REPORT				
Currency amount	Currency	Rate	Equivalent	Date: 28 Feb 1993
	Aus $		53.33	Monthly sales (Currency)
	Austrian		269.61	Current month's valuation
	Belgian		53.28	**Total 'A'**
	Canad $		420.51	Monthly purchases (Currency)
	Danish		11.37	Previous month's valuation
	Dutch		84.24	**Total 'B'**
	French		764.14	Profit on exchange (Total 'A' less Total 'B')
	German		295.05	Foreign exchange commission
	Greek		105.26	**Sub Total 'C'**
	Italian		756.06	Travellers' cheque commission
	Norwegian		21.56	Total revenue
	Spanish		39.32	
	Swedish		38.03	
	Swiss		249.00	
	US $		352.58	

Activity

1 Complete the calculations for the month of February to establish gross profit in the foreign exchange bureau. (The currency on hand at the end of January was £4,051.79.)

2 Estimate what the annual gross profit will be if the February figure is likely to be 5 per cent of the annual income.

10.6 Methods of presenting management information

Every leisure and tourism organization has its own set of management information needs, and the systems it uses for collecting that information vary accordingly. In the same way the methods each uses to present management information will vary. The subject of the information will be a factor in determining its presentation, depending on whether it relates to finance, personnel, customers, suppliers or agents. The information may be sensitive, in which case it will need to be kept confidential and secure. It may also be subject to the Data Protection Act or to copyright laws.

Financial information is now almost exclusively generated by computer software packages. Spreadsheets can be used to display information in a form or layout chosen by the user. Formulae can be set up so that frequent calculations, such as the sales figures for each of a tour operator's sales teams, can be carried out instantly. Most other numerical information, such as room occupancy figures, attendance figures or stock control, is now commonly generated by the same means.

Information of a more descriptive kind, such as the appraisal reports on company employees, is just as likely to be stored in a computer network. Larger companies will probably hold a database of all their employees. Individual records can quickly be accessed and hard copies made in a format to suit their specific use. The use of desktop publishing software means that even relatively inexperienced users of information technology can create professional looking paper information, including things like the integration of graphs and illustrations into the text. Codes and passwords are used to limit access to sensitive information.

Tour operators provide a good example of specific information needs. They require up-to-the-minute statements about the performance of the different travel agents who are selling their holidays. They want to know:
- how much each agency owes them at a given time;
- how long each agency spends on their reservations system before completing a booking;
- how the sales of each holiday product are progressing.

Up-to-date information is invaluable because it enables:
- negotiation with travel agents about different commission levels;
- negotiation with travel agents about the level of sales support they receive, e.g. in educational visits to destinations for their staff;
- increased sales efforts for destinations which are not selling well.

This information must not only be delivered fast, it must also be kept confidential so that competitors do not have access to it. In the light of these two criteria it is easy to see why the travel industry has quickly become dependent on information technology.

Travel agencies in turn generate their own management information. For example, a large business travel agency will need a system which identifies the amount and type of business generated by each of its corporate customers. That information must, however, be kept totally secure and confidential, since it would be of great value to competing business travel agencies. Similarly, the clients themselves would not wish their competitors to have details of their travel and expenses budgets.

A key item of management information for most leisure and tourism organizations is their mailing list or database of clients. It is particularly valuable because it enables communication by mail with a very specific market which is already known to have expressed an interest in the product. This information has often taken years to develop and would clearly be of interest to other companies with similar business interests. One indication of this concern is that when senior managers leave one company for another, the terms of their departure may exclude them from working for particular competitors within a specified period of time.

The need for security and confidentiality is best illustrated through specific examples. The example which follows looks closely at the financial management information produced in a fitness centre. It shows how the leisure centre presents its annual figures, by means of a **profit and loss account** and a **final balance sheet**. It illustrates how management information needs to be presented in a way which aids analysis in preparation for decision making.

Definition of terms used in financial reports

Debtors: those who owe money to the organization whose figures are being presented

Creditors: those to whom the organization owes money

Share investment capital: money invested in the business by shareholders

Drawings: money paid out to investors each year

Assets: value belonging to the organization, including any debts owed to the organization, as well as property, equipment, stock and moneys held

Fixed assets: assets deemed to be long term, such as property, fixtures and equipment

Current assets: assets whose value is likely to fluctuate in the short term, such as debtors, cash on hand, stock, current account balance

Liabilities: amounts owed by the organization – long, short, mid term or current

---

Case study

The Silhouette Fitness Club

At the end of a financial year, the following management information has been collected about a fitness centre, the Silhouette Club. The way it is set out, however, means that it would be of little use to the management or shareholders in either monitoring the company's success or in planning decisions about its future.

```
Facts and figures about the Silhouette Club

                                                  £
Bank overdraft                                5,231
Premises valuation                          100,000
Value of fixtures and fittings                3,000
Electricity costs                               842
Telephone costs                                 524
Salaries and payroll                         15,400
Insurance                                       622
Stationery                                      163
Advertising                                     226
Sundry expenses                                 400
Bar sales                                     9,785
Food sales                                    4,692
Bar purchases                                 2,811
```

Food purchases	1,186
Value of stock at start of financial year	482
Membership subscriptions	3,822
Fees for sessions	6,820
Debtors	310
Creditors	650
Drawings	Nil
Investment capital	95,000
Cash on hand	34
Value of stock at close of financial year	351

By extracting some of the figures from the list given a clearer picture can be created, demonstrating how the Silhouette Club is performing financially. Below is a simple version of how a **profit and loss account** can be set out:

Silhouette Club profit and loss account		
Sales (Bar)	9,785	
Sales (Food)	4,692	
Closing stock	351	14,828
Purchases (Bar)	2,811	less
Purchases (Food)	1,186	
Opening stock	482	4,479
Gross profit on food and drink		10,349
Membership subs	3,822	plus
Sessions fees	6,820	
Income from activities		10,642
TOTAL GROSS PROFIT		20,991
OVERHEADS		**less**
Electricity	842	
Telephone	524	
Payroll	15,400	
Insurance	622	
Stationery	163	
Advertising	226	
Sundries	400	18,177
NET PROFIT BEFORE TAX		2,814

From the profit and loss account it is immediately clear that the Silhouette Club achieved an operational profit of £2,814 during the financial year.

Activity

Discuss what analysis of the account would reveal about the following questions and what kind of decisions might be taken in the light of the conclusions drawn.

1 Assuming the club currently has 150 members, what is the average membership subscription being charged?
2 If the subscription had been £15 higher, what would the subscription income have been increased to?
3 What is the highest overhead cost in the centre?
4 What percentage of gross profit is retained after overhead costs?

Another set of figures which can be compiled from the original list is known as the **balance sheet**. By incorporating the operational profit figure for the year, a clear picture can be created of the current value of the company.

```
Balance sheet for the Silhouette Club
ASSETS                            LIABILITIES
Fixed Assets
Premises                100,000   Capital           95,000
Fixtures and fittings     3,000   Profit             2,814
                        103,000   less Drawings        Nil
                                                    97,814
                                  Current Liabilities
Stock                       351   Overdraft          5,231
Debtors                     310   Creditors            650
Cash on hand                 34
                       £103,695                    £103,695
```

The simple balance sheet shows that the Silhouette Club is in a very 'tight' situation. Even though it achieved a profit for the year, its overdraft is actually almost twice that profit. The shareholders could not take any drawings, and would be lucky to get their capital back if they were able to sell the business for its premises and equipment.

Faced with a set of figures like these, any management team would need to obtain more detail of the day-to-day running of the centre, with a view to increasing revenue and keeping down costs. However, it would not be enough to rely solely on internal information. The situation at the Silhouette Club demands serious research into the market environment, competition and opportunity in the locality.

While management information can be collected and presented manually, it becomes very time-consuming to do so once the turnover of the organization begins to grow. Information technology saves time in recording, collating and analysing data. Whatever the system used, three key principles apply to the way management information is collected, recorded and presented:

1 the systems for collecting, recording and presentation of management information must be integrated into the overall operation of the facility or organization;
2 security and confidentiality must be built into the system;
3 policy decisions should always rely on a combination of management information and research and analysis of external factors.

Assignment 10
Providing and using management information

This assignment develops knowledge and understanding of the following elements:

6.1 Plan a management information service
6.2 Select and provide management information
6.3 Record and process management information

It supports development of the following core skills:
Communication 3.4
Application of number 3.2, 3.3

Breaktime Travel Agency

By analysing the figures shown in this assignment the management of the Breaktime Travel Agency will be able to judge its performance over a period of time, identifying strong and weak points in the operation so that it can make decisions about the way forward.

In order to come to a full understanding of the significance of the profit and loss account of Breaktime Travel, it is necessary to be clear about the basic principles involved in running a travel agency.

Sources of income

Although travel agency income can be generated in several ways, Breaktime depends on one source of income only – the commission paid by **principals** (travel suppliers such as airlines, ferry companies, tour operators).

The level of commission received varies according to the product, as indicated below:

Package holidays	10%–15%*
Car ferries	9%
Scheduled air flights	9%
Charter flights	10%–15%*
Travel insurance	50% or more*
Hotel sales	8%–20%*

* Depending on particular agreements between suppliers and particular agencies

Typical travel agency business targets

Most travel agencies' business objectives will aim to achieve an operational profit of between 10 and 15 per cent of their total income.

Sales figures for leisure travel sales clerks are generally accepted as satisfactory if they reach between £250,000 and £300,000 per annum.

Bearing in mind that the main source of operational income in a travel agency is sales commission, it is much more important to improve **both sales volume and mix** than simply to increase sales volume alone. Improving mix would involve trying to sell a higher proportion of high revenue, and hence high commission, products. The point is illustrated in the example below:

Example A
£1,000 holiday booking   @ 10% commission yields **£100**
4 brochure insurance policies @ £20   @ 10% commission yield **£8**
                                                  Booking commission = £108

Example B
£1,000 holiday booking   @ 15% commission yields **£150**
4 agency organized insurance policies @ £20   @ 50% commission yield **£40**
                                                  Booking commission = £190

The following pages provide data relating to Breaktime's financial performance for the year ending 31 October 1993.

BREAKTIME TRAVEL AGENCY SUMMARY
Financial year ending 31 October 1993

ANNUAL PROFIT AND LOSS ACCOUNT

Travel sales	973,310
Actual income (commission on sales)	98,420

Overheads	
Salaries	42,500
Rent	9,000
Rates	1,200
Advertising	850
Telephone and Viewdata line	4,500
Postage	900
Electricity	1,250
Manuals etc.	260
Cleaning	1,872
Insurance	1,500
Security	820
Terminal rental	3,200
Stationery	830
Write-offs	620
Credit card commissions	6,020

Operational profit	**£23,098**

The following information has been provided in support of the profit and loss account, to allow management analysis to be more comprehensive:

Breakdown of travel sales for financial year

Sales area	*£*
Air	220,300
Rail	3,340
Ferry	65,720
Cruise	6,140
Hotels	12,560
Inclusive tours	640,210
Seat only	12,220
Insurance	8,420
Other	4,400
	973,310

Inclusive tour bookings

Main operators	Bookings	Pax	£'s
Thomsons	320	750	245,000
Airtours	222	376	121,300
Owners Abroad	90	220	80,000

Headcount (number of staff employed)

Travel sales	3.5	£23,000
Support*	1.5	£19,500
	5.0	£42,500

*Support staff are those not actually involved in selling, such as an administrative clerk or perhaps the manager. The figures suggest that one person spends half their time selling and the other half in a supporting role, or that the agency employs at least two part-time members of staff.

Your tasks

Put yourself in the position of the manager reading the figures provided, with the intention of using them to plan for the future operation of the agency. By answering the following questions, you will be able to assess the performance of the agency and make recommendations for its future operation.

1 Calculate the percentage of total travel sales of each sales area. *This will tell you where the branch's main business is focused.*

2 What percentage of the total inclusive tour sales go to each of the three main operators – Thomson, Airtours, Owners Abroad?

3 How much is the average package tour price for passengers with Thomson, Airtours and Owners Abroad? *This will give some indication of client price profile.*

4 What is the average party size for bookings with Thomson, Airtours and Owners Abroad? *This will provide more information on client types.*

5 Taking an average per person package tour price for the three operators for whom you have figures, estimate the total number of inclusive 'heads' sold in this agency. Then multiply that number by £17, the average cost of an insurance premium, to determine possible insurance sales **just** for package holiday customers. *When you compare this figure with actual insurance sales, it will tell you if there is room for improvement in travel insurance sales techniques within the branch.*

6 What is the average annual travel sales figure for each of the travel sales clerks? *This will tell you if they are achieving acceptable levels of sales.*

7 What was the average percentage commission achieved on travel sales overall this year? *Remember – the higher, the better!*

8 Can you identify any cost areas which you think are excessive and which you think could be reduced?

9 What other information would you need before you could draw up an action plan to improve the agency performance over the next financial year?

11   Planning: objectives

What is covered in this chapter

This chapter shows how leisure and tourism enterprises may aim to make a profit, supply a public service and provide job satisfaction. It shows how meeting short term objectives is essential in enabling long term objectives to be achieved. It shows what maximizing profits means and why seeking to do this does not always improve a company's overall performance. It shows how companies can increase market share by adding extra products, price-cutting and opening new branches, and how companies seek to expand their activities. It shows how non-commercial leisure and tourism organizations exist which seek to ensure public access to sport and the arts. It explains how companies create a corporate image and use brands.

- Introduction
- Short and long term objectives
- Maximizing profits and setting satisfactory profit targets
- Increasing market share
- Diversification
- Public service
- Corporate image and branding

11.1   Introduction

The leisure and tourism industry includes every size of organization from the sole owner of a souvenir stall right up to multinational corporations. An individual who sets up a small tea shop in an area which attracts tourists may be as much concerned about finding a satisfactory, reasonably rewarded use of their time as with making a large profit. Leisure enterprises in particular may be government owned and may exist primarily to provide services. In other words, although the majority of organizations which make up the leisure and tourism industry have the long term objective of making the best profit possible, many suppliers of leisure and tourism products set this alongside other short term needs.

Short term objectives might require increased sales or improved service within months; long term objectives might seek an improved national awareness of a company's products over a number of years. Of course the majority of companies providing leisure and tourism products do aim to see many of the objectives they set met within a specified period of time. Their objectives may include:

- an intention to increase sales;
- an aim to improve profitability by a certain percentage within a set trading period;
- a desire to achieve a certain percentage of the market for the product they are offering by introducing new improvements and winning customers from their competitors, known as increasing market share;
- a determination to strengthen their business position through broadening their range of products, known as diversification.

The objectives of Montagu Ventures Ltd., the organization managing Beaulieu

The Aims of the Organization

Activities at Beaulieu and Buckler's Hard today are many and varied, but it must be remembered that all individual activities serve one over-riding aim, namely:

To ensure the continued existence and continual enhancement of the Beaulieu Estate as an entity in family ownership, an area of outstanding beauty and an integral part of the New Forest and to make appropriate areas of the Estate accessible for public enjoyment.

In order to achieve this overall aim, a number of different organizations exist, all under the direction of Lord Montagu. These have specific objectives, which may be summarized as follows:

Montagu Ventures Limited

1 To provide public access to sites suitable for leisure and recreational activities at Beaulieu and Buckler's Hard, while protecting more sensitive areas of the Estate.
2 To manage leisure facilities at Beaulieu and Buckler's Hard including Palace House and gardens, Beaulieu Abbey, the National Motor Museum, and at Buckler's Hard the village, historic cottages and Maritime Museum.
3 To market these facilities to attract the maximum number of visitors which may be accommodated without detriment to either the physical environment or visitor enjoyment.
4 To apply income from leisure activities to either the improvement of visitor services and facilities or the restoration and conservation of heritage buildings and landscape within the boundaries of the Estate.

Activity

Can you explain the following?
1 Why is making as much profit as possible not the first concern of all businesses involved in leisure and tourism?
2 What different ways do leisure and tourism companies use to judge improvements in their business performance?
3 Why might a company specializing in selling camping holidays to France decide to develop French tours based in five-star hotels?

11.2 Short and long term objectives

Long term objectives

Many company objectives will be long term, particularly if they involve significant changes to products or major diversification. One long term objective of a hotel might be to develop a range of new leisure facilities in order to attract a wider market. In order to achieve this the owners are likely to have to borrow money. The long term objectives of many leisure and tourism enterprises can only be met by raising finance. An airline, for example, cannot introduce new routes if it does not invest in the aircraft to fly them, whether it be by direct purchase or by leasing them from other companies.

Short term objectives

Short term objectives involve planning for the immediate future. A hotel, for example, may have a short term objective of increasing its occupancy rate during the early summer months. Such short term objectives are important in maintaining the day-to-day running of a business. The hotel may need to increase its occupancy rate in order to ensure that there are sufficient funds to pay the increases in bills and wages which become due in the summer.

The actual payments received by a business and the sums they pay out to settle bills and other costs are called the **cash flow**. Some leisure and tourism companies have to be particularly wary of cash flow problems. Tour operators often have to pay out money to secure accommodation before they receive payment from potential customers. They have to repay with interest any money they borrow to offset these costs and still convince their banks, other lenders and shareholders that they are able eventually to operate profitably.

Short term objectives have to ensure that sufficient cash is always available to enable the business to continue operating. This means that achieving longer term objectives is usually dependent on meeting short term goals satisfactorily.

Activity

Henley Hall is a small, eighteenth-century country house recently opened to the public at weekends between May and October.

The owners have agreed the following six objectives:
1 to raise £50,000 to renovate the two derelict gatehouses at the entrance to the estate;
2 to develop a range of family attractions and activities within the grounds;
3 to produce a leaflet advertising the Hall;
4 to open a small tea shop for visitors in a vacant wing of the Hall;
5 to establish the Hall as an international conference centre;
6 to set up a charitable company, 'The Friends of Henley Hall', to raise funds.

In small groups discuss which of these objectives you would classify as long term and which would be more short term.

Produce a chart showing a possible time frame for the implementation of these developments.

11.3 Maximization of profits and setting satisfactory profit targets

Maximizing profit

Setting objectives involves a company in trying to plan ahead. One obvious intention to aim for would seem to be to extract as much profit as possible. If successful, this would please investors, as well as raising capital for new developments.

Extracting maximum profit is achieved by two policies:
1 trying to establish what people would be willing to pay for a particular product;
2 cutting the costs of supplying it to a minimum.

Maximizing profit tends to work if a company has virtually no competitors. It can also be effective if the product is something on which customers are very dependent, for example fuel. Most leisure and tourism businesses face strong competition. Customers generally have a range of products to choose from, often, as in the case of holidays, quite an extensive one.

A hotel hoping to maximize its profits may establish what it thinks people will be willing to pay for a room. However, various seasonal factors and the influence of fluctuations in the national economy are likely to mean that this figure will be constantly changing. Keeping prices high may also encourage more competition from other local hotels calculating that they can provide a similar standard of service for a lower price. Cutting costs severely may seem an attactive option, particularly since a major cost in running a hotel relates to the employment of staff. Yet the resulting poorer standard of service might drive customers away to other firms.

Row of competing seaside hotels

An airline, where the majority of costs are fixed, might find it easier to maximize profits, since they could do so by attempting to fill unused flight seats. However, if most airlines are in a similar position of having significant numbers of unsold seats and all attempt to sell these off cheaply, it is likely that overall seat prices will drop, resulting in a corresponding fall in profits. In fact, companies have to take day-to-day decisions, depending on what they believe customers will pay, aiming to achieve the best profit practicable.

Setting satisfactory profit targets

Given the difficulties of maximizing profit, many leisure and tourism organizations develop business objectives which set what they consider to be a satisfactory or target profit. The target profit may be based on:

- a percentage of their sales;
- a proportion of the money invested in the company during a financial year.

Setting targets in this way is common in leisure and tourism organizations which are too large and diverse to establish easily what maximum revenue could be achieved.

Other leisure and tourism organizations would find it difficult to maximize profits for different reasons. Since the introduction of compulsory competitive tendering, private companies have often put in successful bids giving them contracts to manage local authority services such as leisure centres. However, the contract will often stipulate the type and level of service they must offer, which in turn prevents them from minimizing their costs completely. A national organization, like English Heritage, whose main function was conservation rather than generating income, would find it equally difficult to maximize profits. Small leisure and tourism enterprises, especially those which are family run, may be content simply to make sufficient profit to live on. In such cases profit maximization is perceived as far less important than job satisfaction.

Activity

The English Tourist Board (ETB) has a statutory responsibility to encourage the development of tourism in England. It is required to provide advice to the government on all matters relating to tourism in England. It plays an important part in promoting existing tourism areas and in spreading the benefits of tourism more widely. These responsibilities do not mean that the ETB does not have to manage its spending and set its own financial objectives.

Study Table 11.1 below which gives a summary of the ETB's accounts over the five-year period between 1987 and 1992.

Table 11.1 Five-year summary of ETB accounts

Key financial statistics	1987/8	1988/9	1989/90	1990/91	1991/2
Turnover (£ million)	28.3	31.2	28.1	24.6	23.8
% increase (decrease) p.a.	17	10	(10)	(13)	(3)
Staff costs (£ million)	2.7	3.2	3.0	3.0	3.3
% of turnover	10	10	11	12	14
Average staff numbers	139	150	128	111	130

1 Turnover represents the total of the government grant and the income from other sources received by the ETB. What factors might account for the changes in turnover from year to year?
2 What relationship, if any, is there between staff costs and turnover over the five-year period?
3 What possible consequences might be predicted if staff costs as a percentage of turnover continued to rise?
4 Though staff numbers fell in 1990/1, staff costs remained as high as in the previous year. Can you suggest a reason for this?

11.4 Increasing market share

Setting profit targets is an objective against which actual company performance can be measured. Aiming to increase market share is also a quantitative objective in that the extent to which it has been achieved can be shown numerically.

If a company increases its share of the market, this means it will be generating a greater volume of business, always at the expense of its competitors. If more people travel with one major holiday company like Thomsons than had done so in the previous year, unless they are new customers who had not bought a holiday in the last 12 months, competing firms will have lost the custom of those who changed to Thomsons.

There are a number of ways in which companies may achieve an increase in market share. They may add extra products which they think will appeal to a wider market. A tour operator may introduce new destinations, for example. They may embark on a price-cutting campaign to entice customers away from their competitors. In recent years price wars between tour operators resulted in the profit margins on package tours being cut to a minimum, with the result that a number of companies have gone out of business while pursuing the largest possible market share. Forced to cut prices to match those of their competitors, they still could not achieve sufficient volume of sales to make a net profit.

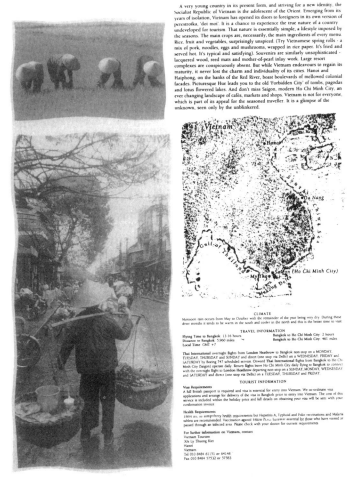

Brochure extract featuring new destination: Vietnam

A travel company with offices in a number of different cities may also attempt to increase its market share by opening new branches. Such companies, often called **multiples** or **chains**, have a number of long term objectives in wishing to increase their number of outlets. They may hope to:

- increase the profile and reputation of the company;
- as major outlets, negotiate better deals with suppliers.

A firm supplying stationery to a company with a chain of 100 retail outlets will be more dependent on that company than on a single independent retailer and is therefore more likely to be persuaded to offer discounts on bulk orders. A tour operator carrying 20,000 passengers is likely to pay proportionally less for the same flight seats and accommodation than a company arranging similar tours for 500. The abilities of large purchasers to negotiate better rates are often referred to as **economies of scale**. The money saved in this way can be used to finance various incentive and discount offers, hence making life even more difficult for these companies' smaller competitors.

Activity

Easthampton, a medium sized market town in the Midlands, has three rival coach companies all offering week-long summer coach tours to France. Table 11.2 shows their market share of all passengers booking coach tours from Easthampton to France and the average cost per person of each company's tours:

Table 11.2 Market share of passengers booking coach tours

	Market share				Average tour cost			
	1989	1990	1991	1992	1989	1990	1991	1992
Ted's Tours	31%	25%	33%	35%	£130	£170	£175	£190
Cope's Coaches	51%	52%	46%	49%	£175	£190	£220	£230
Bus De Luxe	18%	22%	21%	16%	£250	£275	£300	£330

What effects on each company's 1993 market share and potential profitability do you think the following would have?

1 Ted's Tours invests in two new coaches, renames the company Edward James Tours Ltd, hoping that this will expand the company's target market, and raises the average tour cost to £230.

2 Cope's Coaches decide to go all out to improve their market share by holding their average tour price at £230.

3 Bus De Luxe decide to concentrate on gourmet tours, with a consequent increase in average tour price of £370 and to advertise these beyond Easthampton.

4 Easthampton Aeronautics, employing some 30 per cent of the town's workforce, goes out of business in early January.

11.5 Diversification

A long term objective for many firms is to grow. They may see this as offering greater potential profit, which is important if the company has raised capital by issuing shares. Shareholders will expect to receive some financial return on their investment. Growth may also be thought to offer a more secure future for the company's employees.

Apart from opening new branches or offices, companies may grow by merging with or buying out other companies. They may choose to merge with companies which operate in similar fields, since they will already have expertise in managing the same activities. For example the tour operator, Thomsons, purchased another well-known operator, Horizon. Thomsons also own the 600 branches of the travel agency chain, Lunn Poly. This makes aspects of their business operation easier as it gives them control of a greater proportion of the total process of creating and selling package holidays. Airlines such as British Airways now sell package holidays under their own name. The ownership of transport companies, tour operators and travel agents is less likely to be in the hands of a single specialist company than it once was.

However, a recent trend has seen a number of large companies, whose main activities have not been in leisure and tourism, expand by buying into the industry. For example the brewing company, Bass, has major interests in hotels. Scottish and Newcastle Breweries own the Center Parcs holiday complex. The Pearson–Longman Group, best known as a publishing and newspaper group, owns a number of leisure attractions including Alton Towers and Madame Tussauds.

This spreading of business activities is known as **diversification**. Its main advantage is that it broadens a company's interests and makes it less likely that they will fail if one area of their activities comes up against financial problems. The main risk attached is that the company will mismanage its new acquisitions through a lack of experience and relevant expertise.

Activity

Which of the following do you think might benefit from diversification and for what reasons?
1 A new record label which has signed up three highly promising, but as yet relatively little known, bands.
2 A farmer providing strawberries for hospitality areas at major sporting events like Wimbledon and Ascot.
3 The owner of an open air swimming pool in Scotland admitting paying customers.

11.6 Public service

Not all organizations working within leisure and tourism have a function which is mainly commercial. The most obvious examples are those whose main role is conservation, such as English Heritage or the Countryside Commission, or those concerned with the national promotion of sport and the arts, such as the Sports Council or the Arts Council.

These organizations tend to have very broad objectives, though the extent to which they are able to achieve them is very likely to depend on the level of funding they receive. So the Countryside Commission is able to list its main objective as being:

> to improve and extend opportunities for the public to enjoy the countryside. But in doing so, to re-emphasise the link between the conservation of an attractive countryside and its enjoyment by the public.

In addition to this long term objective, a number of short term approaches help the Commission to achieve its aims. These include:

- agreeing principles about the development of tourism in the countryside;
- persuading the industry to see the value of these;
- establishing more accurately the expectations of visitors to the countryside;
- educating people to get the most out of such visits without harming what they have come to see.

The need to provide public services may produce conflict when commercial interests are introduced. Until the late 1980s local authorities provided a number of leisure facilities for the public, including swimming baths, playing fields, sports halls and community centres. However the Local Government Act 1988 required local authorities to put the management of sports and leisure facilities out to tender, as part of compulsory competitive tendering. This meant that commercial organizations could compete for the contracts to run these centres. Their objectives would still be to provide leisure and sports facilities for the community, while working to tight financial objectives. Some people are concerned that the need to undercut competitors and to generate profit will lead to a reduction in services as a result of concentrating on those which generate the most income.

Some organizations work with commercial companies but have a public service role that may include regulating an industry and representing its various members in public and political issues. For example, the International Air Transport Association (IATA) counts among its members representatives from over 200 airlines. It acts as an important regulatory body. Its influence and expertise enables it to support airlines in solving international problems, to advise governments, and to arbitrate between airlines and the interests of groups representing passengers, cargo agents and equipment manufacturers. These broad aims are translated into two practical objectives:

- to ensure that people, freight and mail can move on the vast global network as easily as if they were on a single airline within a single country;
- to ensure that the aircraft used to carry the world's passengers and goods are able to operate with maximum safety and efficiency – under clearly defined and universally understood regulations.

Many commercial companies increasingly believe that it is good commercial and corporate practice to contribute to the community in some way. Their aim in doing so is generally to establish a favourable local image, since most of their customers, and current and future employees are likely to have local connections.

This community support often takes the form of sponsorship of local sports and arts facilities and events. Contributions to charities and social care programmes are also common, particularly since they generate favourable publicity. Also they may result in direct or indirect benefits to the company. For example, helping to support a day nursery for children in the community may enable potential employees to surmount a major barrier affecting their ability to seek work.

Activity

Read the following article about the role of the brewing industry in promoting sensible drinking.

The problems of alcohol misuse by the small minority of problem drinkers does have an impact on how the public perceive the drinks industry.

One of the best ways the industry can respond to this problem is by the formation of an industry-wide group with two broad objectives, namely to:

- recommend new practical and effective initiatives to reduce health and social problems associated with alcohol misuse;
- encourage a more sensible and responsible attitude to drinking.

There are at least three areas relating to alcohol consumption which are current public concerns. These are: the effects of excessive alcohol on health and social life; campaigns to restrict drink-driving; under-age drinking. If the brewing industry is to retain public support and investment, it needs to do more than simply acknowledge these concerns. It needs to be seen to be taking an active part in confronting them.

1 What benefit is there to a brewing company in supporting campaigns that appear to find fault with some of their regular customers?
2 How do you think the long term objectives of a brewing company which also owns hotels and leisure companies would be affected by a significant increase in public support for campaigns which aim both to discourage people from drinking and driving, and also to discourage under-age drinking?

11.7 Corporate image and branding

Creating a corporate image

As well as quantitative objectives which can be numerically measured, companies are also likely to set a number of qualitative objectives. These relate to the quality of the goods or services they offer. The leisure and tourism industries are highly competitive which means that for individual companies:

- their public image distinguishes them from their competitors, especially where their products are similar;
- their ability to sell their products may in part depend on public recognition of the company name;
- their public image becomes strongly associated with a particular type of product or quality of service.

Larger companies are often involved in diverse business activities and so it is not always easy to create a picture in the public mind of exactly what they do. American Express, for example, is generally perceived in the UK as a charge card company, but the company is also a major provider of business travel services and of travellers' cheques.

Designing a corporate identity may include standardizing aspects of a company's products or services, for example the layout of a range of travel brochures, the decor of a chain of hotels or the uniforms of museum staff. It is likely to include a review of all its written and telephone communications, to ensure that a consistent style and standard is being achieved.

One simple but common method of communicating a company image to the public is the use of a logo, in the form of a specially designed name or symbol. A good logo will provide a simple, single message about the company and its activities. It can be used on stationery, vehicles, advertisements and signs in the hope that it will become readily identifiable by a wide audience.

Developing corporate image may lead to greater centralization. A multiple wishing to improve its corporate identity may issue very precise specifications about how its individual outlets should be designed and run. American Express commissioned the design of a model office and all its individual branches are refurbished in keeping with this design. Customers entering one of the company's travel shops are thus likely to encounter familiar features which they come to associate with the company. As with most aspects of corporate image development, this familiarity is intended to reinforce customer confidence in a service or product which they have experienced before, so that they will purchase from the same company again.

Branding

A large hotel group, like Forte Hotels, owns a variety of properties including five-star hotels, small country inns, motels and roadside restaurants. It would be difficult to bring them all to the notice of the people most likely to use them if they were all marketed under the same name.

A common means of improving a company's image is to develop its products through brand names. Branding is used to make individual products easy to identify and to distinguish them from those of competitors. Companies operating motorway service stations use different coloured signs, different decor and different uniforms in an attempt to establish themselves in the minds of people who also use the services of their competitors.

Branding generally includes both the name of the company, product or service, and the symbols or designs used to identify it. For example, airlines use different coloured livery and logo designs to demonstrate which aircraft are theirs.

Example of company logo

Apart from making the product distinctive, branding is also used as an indicator of quality. Even though they generally benefit from branding, this presents particular difficulties for many leisure and tourism companies, where the product they offer customers may include some kind of service and hence is more difficult to control. Consumers can predict that a Mars bar will taste much the same each time they eat one. It is more difficult to tell in advance precisely what a visit to a theatre or a night's stay at a hotel will be like. Branding is used as a means of persuading customers that repeat purchases or visits will result in an equally good experience. If this objective is successfully achieved and customers consistently choose the same brand, the company concerned can claim to have established brand loyalty.

Successful branding will itself have clear objectives. These may include an intention to appeal to a particular market, for example the very wealthy, or to create a perception that the product in question represents good value for money.

Activity

A national hotel chain purchases a number of motorway restaurants which it intends to rebrand as its own. A competition within the company yields the following eight suggested brand names:

Roadside Diner	Snacktime	Stopgap	Motormeals
Nifty Nosh	Inside Lane	Autoqueue	Grub's Up

Decide what you think the characteristics of both the product to be offered and the intended market are likely to be.

Then discuss the image conveyed by each of the suggested brand names, suggesting how appropriate or otherwise each would be.

Assignment 11
Planning: objectives

This assignment develops knowledge and understanding of the following elements:

1.3 Investigate the variety of local services and products

8.1 Research the organizational objectives of facilities

8.2 Plan the evaluation of a facility's performance

It supports development of the following core skills:

Communication 3.2, 3.4

Your tasks

Collect statements of the objectives of three leisure and tourism companies or organizations based in the region in which you live.

Write a report comparing these three sets of objectives in which you:
- identify and account for the differences;
- establish the priority given to different individual objectives;
- assess how comprehensive the objectives are and identify any omissions;
- describe various ways in which each company or organization's ability to meet these objectives could be evaluated.

12   Planning: resources

What is covered in this chapter

This chapter shows how leisure and tourism compete with other industries for resources. It shows how materials and equipment must be suitable for specific tasks. It shows how managing labour in leisure and tourism involves overcoming problems of difficult hours, and part-time and seasonal work. It shows how projects considered to be of local or national importance may receive government or local authority funding, and how private sector finance generally comes from a company's own capital reserves, share issues and loans. It explains how loans are obtained, and the benefits and disadvantages of sponsorship and grants. It shows how budgets are prepared and analysed.

- The variety of resources
- Materials and equipment
- People and time

- Public and private sector sources of funding for leisure or tourism projects
- Financing specific projects
- Budgeting

12.1 The variety of resources

Successful tourism ventures are highly dependent on a variety of resources. These may include:

- **natural resources**, like scenery and weather;
- **human resources**, to provide a workforce;
- **capital resources**, including such things as existing buildings, and infrastructure investments such as piped water and airports.

Leisure and tourism has to compete with other industries for some of these resources. For example, the development of a new leisure complex may require land which is also sought after for agricultural use or for building development. However, many of the resources which are most valuable to tourism are either already publicly available as services, such as roads, or else are simply freely accessible as part of the environment, such as the weather or good views, or national and regional cultures. Most leisure and tourism developments require a combination of resources. Hence a ski resort requires:

- natural resources, in particular slopes and snow;
- human resources, including ski instructors and hotel staff;
- capital resources such as roads, hotels and ski lifts.

Resources involving a cost create a number of investment choices for leisure and tourism developments. A hotel will have to budget how much it intends to spend on staffing and how much on equipment. Installing a new lift may be similar in cost to employing one additional member of staff and a decision will be needed about which option will bring the greatest benefit. The lift may make the hotel accessible to new markets like elderly people, but an extra member of staff may improve the service provided, thus giving the hotel a better reputation and attracting more customers.

By comparison with other industries, tourism in particular is **labour intensive**. The frequent demand for face to face contact with customers and personal service requires high staffing levels. Sectors such as catering include activities where manual dexterity, and human taste and judgement are still regarded as more practical than automation. Other areas, such as travel and tourism reservations, are increasingly reliant on computer systems and are less labour intensive than they once were.

12.2 Materials and equipment

Suitability of materials

The development of specific leisure and tourism events or facilities is likely to require the supply of materials and equipment. Decisions about which materials are appropriate will depend on a number of factors, the most obvious one being their suitability for the use to which they are to be put. Building a new toilet block for a camping site out of glass would clearly be inappropriate, as would the provision of steak and kidney pudding and three vegetables for a summer Greek island beach party.

The suitability of materials may be judged by four criteria:
- appearance;
- durability;
- safety;
- cost.

Appearance
Appearance is particularly important where built leisure or tourism developments are taking place in sensitive areas. In parts of the Cotswolds, for example, new buildings must use the local stone. The appearance of materials is important in any leisure or tourism product which is marketed in terms of its quality. Fireworks which do not provide a spectacle or a buffet which looks limp and unappetizing will affect perceptions of the event at which they are offered.

Durability
Durability is a requirement for the majority of materials and equipment, but it is a factor which generally has to be set against cost. Gold might appear to be both attractive and durable, but few hotels would consider decorating all bathrooms with gold fittings. Similarly, investment in computer technology requires careful budgeting. The cash value of expensive equipment reduces with time, a process known as **depreciation**. Even if the hardware is durable, the software may date quickly. Changes in the company's business activities may render the software incapable of performing the task for which it was originally purchased.

Safety and cost
In many leisure and tourism contexts safety is a critical factor in choosing materials and equipment. Re-laying the surface of a children's playground might reqire a decision about the use of bark or one of a number of synthetic surfaces. Equipping a leisure centre gymnasium would require careful checking of the assembly and recommended use of fitness equipment. Yet, within a range of materials and equipment considered safe, cost is still likely to be an influential factor in the final choice. In some areas, such as 'white knuckle' rides in leisure parks, the equation between cost and safety has to err on the side of safety, since not to do so would be to put lives at risk.

Safe floor surface in children's playground

Generally planners of events and functions, and operators of facilities are reliant on suppliers for materials and equipment. The suppliers have a responsibility for the quality of what they provide, though purchasers should operate a system of checking this quality. This is not always easy since leisure and tourism enterprises sometimes buy in complete services, catering being perhaps the most obvious example. An airline may receive thousands of meals daily from a catering service, and the quality of the food is dependent on safe food preparation practices and rigorous temperature controls from the completion of the cooking through to the actual supply. However, since supplier and purchaser are dependent on each other, if their respective businesses are to flourish, it is in the interests of both parties to ensure that a reliable supply service is established and maintained.

Activity

You run a small country hotel which has ten rooms, all with *en suite* bathrooms. The bathrooms are all approximately 3 m x 4 m (i.e. 12 m²).

You plan to resurface all the bathroom floors. Table 12.1 shows the relative merits and demerits of each of five materials you could use.

Study Table 12.1 and then answer the following questions.

I On cost and durability alone, which surface would appear to offer the best value for money?

207

2 What would be the total cost of reflooring all the hotel's bathrooms with each separate floor covering?

3 How highly would you regard the importance of the safety and comfort issues listed against each of the five suggested coverings?

4 Is the cost of supplying and fitting the floor coverings the only cost consideration likely to affect the final choice?

5 What advantages and disadvantages could you see in a local firm offering a protective treatment for synthetic tiles which should increase their expected life to 15 years?

6 What arguments would you put up in favour of choosing one particular floor covering?

Table 12.1 Merits and demerits of flooring materials

Material	Cost (per sq metre)	Durability (expected life)	Appearance potential	(1) Safety (2) Comfort (3) Maintenance
CARPET with thin underlay	£15	2 years	Reasonable colour matches available. Stains/marks more easily than other materials	(1) no obvious risks (2) warm/soft underfoot, as long as kept dry (3) easy to hoover, but stains/marks difficult to remove
NATURAL WOOD FLOOR (sanded and polished)	£35	10 years	In keeping with antique furniture and panelling in hotel's bedrooms, halls and dining room. Would add character	(1) slippery if too highly polished (2) acceptable (3) requires either special equipment or hard labour to polish
SYNTHETIC TILES	£20	5 years	Available in very wide colour/pattern range. Could be used to 'jazz up' bathroom appearance.	(1) offer good grip underfoot (2) reasonable – can be cushioned at extra cost of £10 per sq metre (3) easy to wash – may take time to dry
LINOLEUM	£10	2 years	Wide range of colours/patterns. May be perceived as cheap.	(1) could be slippery if wet (2) can be cold underfoot (3) easy to wash
CERAMIC TILES	£40	10 years	Available in styles to match/contrast wall tiles. Would give 'classy' look.	(1) Could be slippery if wet (2) can be cold underfoot (3) easy to wash; grouting may need occasional repair

12.3 People and time

People are very important resources in leisure and tourism. The success of a project or a facility will depend in part on the adequacy of the staffing provided. This means:

- there must be sufficient numbers to do the job efficiently;
- there must be enough time to perform tasks effectively;
- the abilities of those employed should be established;
- the level of training which they need should be established.

Ideally the skills and qualifications of any workforce need to be matched to the tasks they are set.

Leisure and tourism employs significant numbers of seasonal and part-time staff. Sectors like catering and entertainment often require people to work unsocial hours.

Both these factors can make it a complex task to match sufficient trained and qualified staff to the needs of a specific event or facility. The hours that employees are able to work may also be governed by regulations. EC regulations, likely to be applied in the UK, exclude people from working night shifts longer than eight hours.

Some large multinational companies are beginning to introduce computerized labour management systems. These systems can help to manage staff rosters, payrolls and personnel files. They can be used to generate information about the time individual tasks take to complete and the skills which they require, about the hours employees have worked and about the performance of staff involved in sales. Their main value to a large organization is in calculating its labour costs and improving its efficiency by deploying staff more effectively.

As with other resources, the cost of spending more on employing more staff has to be set against the improved service and profits it is capable of bringing.

Activity

Growmore Court is a large country house surrounded by formal gardens open to the public between May and October. In the gardens is a garden centre and shop.

The shop is open on weekdays between 9 a.m. and 5 p.m. On Saturdays it opens between 10 a.m. and 4 p.m., while on Sundays it opens from 10 a.m. until 1 p.m. The shop is staffed by three employees on weekdays and by four at weekends which tend to be busier. Weekday shifts can be split between two employees each working half a day, but weekend staff are expected to work through.

Lavinia and Hamish are the most senior employees, with considerable gardening expertise. Both work a 33-hour week, and are on duty on both Saturdays and Sundays, and both prefer to have a day off on Monday. Dawn, Warren and Julie also work in the shop and it has been agreed that the hours worked by these three should be as similar as possible, and all are guaranteed at least 30 hours' employment. Warren and Julie are taking a part-time course at the local horticultural college which requires their attendance all day on Tuesdays and Thursdays.

1 Draw up a staff roster for a single week which would meet all of these conditions.

The popularity of the shop at weekends leads to a decision to open from 10 a.m. until 5 p.m. on Saturdays and Sundays. Lavinia and Hamish agree to increase their hours to 38, including both weekend days.

2 Draw up a staff roster to cover the new opening times while still guaranteeing the original conditions for other employees.

Lavinia and Hamish are paid £5 an hour while Julie, Warren and Dawn receive £3 an hour. Compare the average daily shop takings before the opening hours were changed and those after the longer hours were introduced:

	Mon	Tues	Wed	Thurs	Fri	Sat	Sun
before	£35	£50	£100	£60	£110	£400	£520
after	£30	£55	£105	£55	£95	£450	£610

3 Does the change of hours appear to have been financially worth while?

4 What recommendations about the use of people and time would you make if the owner of Growmore Court came under pressure to make the garden shop more cost-effective?

12.4 Public and private sector funding for leisure and tourism projects

Public sector funding

National government may be involved in financing some aspects of tourism projects. For example, there may be a national policy relating to the preservation of our national heritage, both in terms of the built environment and the countryside. Direct government grants may be made to organizations like the Countryside Commission who may use some of these funds to ensure that new projects are sensitively developed. The British Tourist Authority (BTA) is funded largely by grant-in-aid from the Department of National Heritage under the provisions of the Development of Tourism Act 1969. The BTA's 1993 annual accounts show the grant to be £30 million, while a further £15 million is raised by joint activities with the trade, public and private sector interests.

Local government may also be involved in funding leisure and tourism projects. Councils may receive grants from central government, particularly in areas in need of economic regeneration. They can also raise money from local taxes or sometimes from the sale of assets such as property or land. Where tourism is considered to be of local economic importance the council may set aside a budget for specific tourism initiatives. These may include paying the salaries of regional tourism development officers, supporting the publication of brochures and leaflets, and providing grants for signs, exhibitions and campaigns. Councils will also fund important parts of the infrastructure which supports local tourism, in particular by maintaining roads, providing and staffing car parks, and restoring buildings and canals. Table 12.2 shows an example of a local authority's spending on marketing during 1990/1:

Table 12.2 Local authority's marketing spending

Local country holidays promotion	£20,137 (offset by £4,912 of revenue)
New promotional brochure (joint campaign with private sector)	£8,000 (offset by £4,000 revenue)
Point of entry signs for main town	£3,000
European Year of Tourism	£5,000 (£3,500 EC grant)
Area Visitor Guide	£2,000
Trade campaign	£3,500
Conference campaign (joint with private sector)	£3,000 (offset by £1,500 revenue)

Private sector funding

Organizations in the private sector may, if they have been operating successfully for some time, finance new projects from their own capital reserves. Alternatively, there may be sufficient public confidence in their performance for them to be able to raise capital by issuing new shares or arranging other sources of finance such as loans.

Small businesses are likely to need finance for the land, buildings and equipment they need to start up. Even before a new hotel opens it will have to meet the fees of builders, architects, interior decorators and lawyers, among others. Though a completion date for the opening may have been agreed, interest payments on any money borrowed will have to be met even if, as often happens, there is any delay and no income is being achieved. **Inflation** may mean that estimates of the cost of completing the project rise during the course of its construction. Funds will also be needed for initial advertising and marketing. Hotels very rarely make an immediate profit and generally need to borrow money during the first two or three years of trading, as they build up their clientele, to avoid cash flow problems.

Minimum Period Rental Agreement Terms

1. **If the Equipment you are renting includes a number of different items, this Agreement operates as a separate agreement for each item.** We can give you details of the rentals of individual items of equipment if you so wish.

2. **We accept liability** for any damage caused by our fault, but not for any consequential loss nor for loss of data.

3. **You must insure** the Equipment on our behalf against all risks from the date it is installed. You must tell us immediately of any damage to the Equipment.

4. **You must pay the rentals** when they are due. We will have the right to end this agreement immediately if you fail to pay any rental when it is due, and may obtain compensation from you for our losses.

5. **Where you agree** to pay us by Direct Debit, we will allow you a discount in the rentals you pay. If you cancel your Direct Debit, we may cancel that discount.

6. **If you so wish,** we will consent to this Agreement being ended before the end of the Minimum Rental Period if you pay us:

   (a) any unpaid rentals already due; and

   (b) all rentals which would have become due and payable from the date on which you want the Agreement to end until the end of the Minimum Rental Period. We will allow a discount on this amount at the rate of 5% a year.

7. **You can only transfer your rights and duties** under this Agreement if we give our written permission.

8. **When this Agreement ends,** you must either return the equipment to us or make it available for collection by us.

A rental agreement for office equipment

One means of reducing initial investment costs is by **leasing**. This is often used to secure expensive equipment without having to pay the whole purchase cost before the company has derived any income from its activities. Ownership of the equipment remains with the leasing company which will generally offer contracts covering both the hire and maintenance of the leased goods. Company cars and office equipment are frequently acquired by this means.

Activity

Which of the following are examples of public sector finance and which are examples of private sector finance?

1 Capital raised by a football club selling part of its ground for a supermarket development.
2 A bank loan enabling a hotel owner to build an extension.
3 A grant from the Wales Tourist Board to support the development of a regional farm tourism project.
4 A payment from English Heritage towards the cost of restoring a listed building.
5 A sum drawn from the previous year's profits at a leisure park which is invested in the purchase of a new ride.
6 A grant from a local authority towards the cost of developing a new sports stadium.

12.5 Financing specific projects

Bank loans

Business plans

The first thing anyone thinking of starting up a caravan park, converting a house into holiday apartments, or developing any other leisure or tourism scheme needs to obtain is sufficient finance. They must also be sure that there is enough demand for the product or service to enable them to pay the costs of this finance and to provide them with an adequate income.

Banks will lend money for projects, but only if they are satisfied that the proposition is viable. The major banks recommend that potential borrowers prepare a business plan. The plan should cover a number of important areas:

- the scheme's objectives;
- its potential market;
- the nature of the product or service being offered;
- the pricing policy envisaged – the supplies, premises and equipment needed;
- any extra personnel to be employed;
- the expertise and experience of the proposer of the project;
- the marketing plans;
- the book-keeping and recording system to be used.

Perhaps the most difficult part of the business plan is estimating accurately the level of sales which can be achieved. A hotel proposing an extension will have to calculate what rate of room occupancy it can reasonably expect to achieve and what it would require in order to break even. Cash flow is also important. A travel agent specializing in business travel may find itself waiting for accounts to be settled by its customers at the end of a quarterly period, and not having sufficient cash to pay its weekly and monthly bills.

Before banks will agree to lend money, they need to be sure that businesses can cope with unexpected setbacks. If the cost of building extra hotel rooms proves greater than expected, they may wish to know whether the hotel owner would raise prices and so risk attracting fewer guests, or whether they would reduce costs by dismissing staff and thus risk a lower level of service. Since hotels are often dependent on repeat business, it would be counter-productive to cut the costs of a new development if, by doing so, the resultant facilities or services appeared to the guests to be inferior.

Reducing the risks to lenders

Few banks will lend a large sum for a business project without some kind of security. The value of the security will need to be higher than the amount lent, with a **safety margin** between the two sums so that both parties have some degree of protection if things go wrong. Many borrowers will offer freehold land or property as security against the loan, while others will remortgage property in order to raise cash to invest in a business scheme. As hotel owners found in the early 1990s, the latter practice can harm a business if property values fall sharply so that the renegotiated mortgage is for a higher figure than the market value of the property. Machinery or equipment is rarely accepted as security.

Banks will probably expect business borrowers to invest a similar amount from their own funds as the sum the bank is lending them. This is seen as an indication that the borrower is committed to making a success of the project, as well as limiting the extent of the bank's loss if the scheme should fail. Most lenders will also insist on the borrower taking out an insurance policy so that the loan is repaid if the borrower dies, or is rendered incapable of work as a result of an accident or ill-health.

Repayment of loans

The structure of loan repayments may vary considerably too. The interest to be repaid may be at a fixed rate or may vary according to changes in the bank's base rate. Special terms may be available for business starters which postpone all repayments for an agreed period while the business is getting established. A government loan guarantee scheme will, in some circumstances, guarantee most of a loan in return for a premium payment of 2.5 per cent of the guaranteed amount.

Sponsorship

Potential benefits

Sponsorship enables companies to promote their products and services through an association with an event, function or facility. The company benefits in two ways. It receives advertising opportunities which may enable it to reach a wider market. It may also be allowed to deduct the sponsorship payment from the profits on which it has to pay annual taxation.

Many companies are very aware of the potential of events and functions in terms of providing good publicity. This kind of sponsorship is a common method of raising funds for leisure and tourism enterprises. Events like festivals or sports competitions, particularly if they have an evident local or regional focus, attract the attention of the media read or watched by the sponsors' actual and potential clients. Sponsoring companies use logos, competitions and personal appearances to identify themselves with the event. In this way they can be seen to be supporting community needs.

Possible disadvantages

Though finance by sponsorship has the advantage that the money tends to be a gift rather than an interest-carrying loan, there can be drawbacks. Potential disadvantages include the possible desire by the sponsors to influence the nature of the product, event or service in a way which conflicts with the wishes of its providers. There is also a risk that sponsorship will be withdrawn in times of economic recession, or if the public perception of the event or product changes. So, for example, Pepsi withdrew their sponsorship of Michael Jackson's 1993 world tour once individual events had been cancelled as a result of his admitted addiction to pain-killing drugs.

Sponsorship and company image

Since the prestige sponsors gain is likely to depend on the success of the event and whether, by its nature, it is likely to appeal to the company's target market, the choice of which event to sponsor is critical. Sponsors generally look for events or functions which are compatible with their image, so, for example, American Express would be more likely to sponsor a Rembrandt exhibition than an exhibition of punk rock record sleeve designs. A sport like cricket, as long as it can maintain a reputation for entertainment and fair play, may find it easier to attract sponsorship than boxing or fox hunting, which tend to have more critics.

Some types of sponsorship are very specific. For example a number of zoos invite visitors to adopt a particular animal. In return for a flat fee which goes towards the annual cost of the animal's upkeep, the sponsor may receive a certificate or reports describing the animal's progress. Zoos and leisure parks have successfully attracted sponsors willing to fund individual attractions or areas. At Chessington World of

Poster for photographic exhibition at National Portrait Gallery sponsored by American Express

Adventures, for example, different features within the park are sponsored by Kodak, Coca-Cola, the AA, Singapore Airlines and Schweppes.

Sponsorship is particularly widespread in sport. For example soccer competitions have been sponsored by Littlewoods, Coca-Cola and Barclays, while cricket has attracted support from Gillette, John Player and Cornhill Insurance. Many companies are attracted to this kind of sponsorship because it enables them to secure tickets and hospitality at major sporting events. These occasions are then used as opportunities for entertaining important potential business clients. Those sports which receive national television coverage are rarely short of sponsors, since the use of logos on the players' clothing ensures a wide audience at less cost than a television advertising campaign would involve.

Grants

Eligibility

Grants are funds usually provided by government or public organizations in order to support particular individuals or projects. In times of recession, grants tend to become increasingly scarce, and leisure and tourism projects are likely to have to meet some very specific criteria in order to secure this kind of funding. The rules of qualification may be strict, excluding many applicants for grants. For example, a new leisure development may have to guarantee the creation of a specified number of new jobs before it is eligible. Planners of a festival may have to prove that they can raise 70 per cent of the finance necessary before they might qualify for a grant.

Local and national government grants

Though in general grants for leisure and tourism are less widely available than they once were, some developments can still qualify for government financial support. Regions identified as in need of economic assistance can qualify for regional enterprise grants, some of which may go to leisure and tourism. The Rural Development Commission may assist the financing of projects aiming to diversify employment opportunities in country areas. Government ministries may give grants towards the cost of schemes with leisure and tourism implications. The Ministry of Agriculture and Fisheries may financially support changes in agricultural land-use, while the Department of the Environment may help further to develop a regional airport.

Schemes which involve conservation of landscape or listed buildings may be able to secure some financial assistance from organizations like the Countryside Commission or English Heritage. Local authorities may support the establishment of a local museum or leisure centre. Some regions may seek grants from the European Commission's European Regional Development Fund. However, they would have to demonstrate why the region's needs should be a priority and would also have to secure guaranteed investment from other sources.

Activity

In January 1993 a bank agrees to lend Mrs May Kitterbrake, owner of the Highcliff Hotel, £10,000 towards the cost of a new health and fitness centre. Three possible methods of repayment are offered by the bank.

Method A: Interest will be charged at a fixed rate of 16 per cent per annum. Four quarterly charges of 4 per cent will be made on the sum outstanding at that time. At each quarter the interest charge will be added first to the sum borrowed and the borrower will be required to pay off one-twelfth of the sum then owed.

Method B: No repayments of any kind will be required in the first year. Interest will then be charged at a fixed rate of 20 per cent per annum. Four quarterly charges of 5 per cent will be made on the sum outstanding at that time. At each quarter the interest charge will be added first to the sum borrowed and the borrower will be required to pay off one-tenth of the sum then owed.

Method C: No repayments will be required until the end of the first year when a single lump sum of £2,000 will be repaid. A single quarterly interest charge, equalling $4\frac{1}{2}$ per cent of the original sum borrowed, will be added to the sum of the debt still outstanding at the beginning of the second year. Interest will then be charged at a fixed rate of 18 per cent per annum. Four quarterly charges of $4\frac{1}{2}$ per cent will be made on the sum outstanding at that time. At each quarter the interest charge will be added first to the sum borrowed and the borrower will be required to pay off $\frac{1}{10}$ of the sum then owed.

1 Which method of payment will clear the amount owed to the bank most rapidly?

2 Which method will involve the highest overall repayment cost to the hotel owner?

Mrs Kitterbrake predicts that the hotel's occupancy rate will rise gradually as a result of the new health and fitness centre. Promised investment in marketing the region more widely leads her to estimate the following growth in additional revenue generated:

1993	1994	1995	1996	1997
£500	£1,500	£2,500	£5,000	£6,500

3 At the end of 1995 which repayment method shows the largest deficit when the extra revenue earned is subtracted from the sum still owing to the bank?

4 At the end of 1997 which repayment method shows the greatest overall gain for Mrs Kitterbrake?

5 At the end of 1997 which repayment method would show the cost of the loan still exceeding the extra revenue that had been generated?

12.6 Budgeting

Budget analysis

The preparation of any budget involves an analysis of expected income and expenditure. Most companies will prepare an annual budget, generally several months before the beginning of a new financial year.

In starting a new business it is helpful to draw up a **profit and loss forecast** and a **cash flow forecast**:

> - **The profit and loss forecast** will show in tabular form what sales the company hopes to achieve, what costs it will incur and what profit it expects to earn.
> - **The cash flow forecast** will estimate how much money the business will have available to use each month. This allows for delays between issuing invoices and receiving payments, and will show where financial help may be needed to cover the gap between income and expenses.

Cash flow forecast for cafe/souvenir shop at Aylott House and Gardens

	Jan	Feb	Mar	Apr	May	Jun	Jul	Aug	Sep	Oct	Nov	Dec	TOTAL
Anticipated Receipts													
Sales of goods	480	520	560	600	700	1000	1200	1500	800	540	440	560	8900
Sales of refreshments	600	660	700	800	900	1020	1100	1300	960	800	600	540	10000
TOTAL	1080	1180	1260	1400	1600	2040	2300	2800	1760	1340	1040	1100	18900
Anticipated Expenses													
Stock	0	0	750	750	0	0	500	0	0	0	250	0	2250
Food supplies	100	110	120	130	150	170	180	220	160	130	100	90	1660
Wages & benefits	700	700	700	700	950	950	950	1200	700	700	700	700	9650
Rates	80	0	0	80	80	80	80	80	80	80	80	80	800
Rent	175	175	175	175	175	175	175	175	175	175	175	175	2100
Utilities	90	100	100	90	80	80	70	70	80	90	100	100	1050
TOTAL	1145	1085	1925	1925	1435	1455	1955	1745	1195	1175	1405	1145	17510
Surplus/deficit	-65	95	-585	-525	165	585	345	1055	565	165	-365	-45	1390

Income

The accuracy of the budget predictions of income will depend on the quality of the information about current or previous trading. A tourist attraction, for example, will have to base its income assessment on its visitor numbers, the admission charges they pay less VAT and the discounts they offer. It will also have to study carefully the profit made in any other activity, for example, retail outlets it owns on the site.

Expenditure

The budget will set expenditure against this income. Expenditure will include both fixed and variable costs. **Fixed costs** include items such as rent, rates, heat and light and administrative expenses. Sometimes called overheads, these fixed costs remain the same, regardless of how much profit the company is making. **Variable costs**, on the other hand, include items like materials and labour, and do change according to the volume of business the company is transacting.

At a tourist attraction the variable costs would include wages and salaries, marketing, maintenance and repairs, cleaning and possibly bank charges. Each year budget discussions would consider whether costs in each of these areas were reasonable. If one area, such as cleaning, appeared to be rising in proportion to other expenses a decision might be taken to reduce the frequency or the extensiveness of the cleaning service. However, the budget decision would also have to consider whether reduced cleaning levels may create dissatisfied customers, a reduction in the number of visitors and hence a reduced income in the coming year.

Profit margin

The budget will need to take account of the level of **profit margin** which has been set. Profit margin is the amount added to the actual cost of producing an item or service in order to provide a return on the invested capital. Therefore, the price charged includes the profit margin within it. The profit margin is often expressed as a percentage of the total or gross price. Because the profit margin is calculated on the total price, overhead items such as rent, light and heat have to be deducted in order to arrive at a truer profit figure, called the net profit. Figure 12.1 illustrates this:

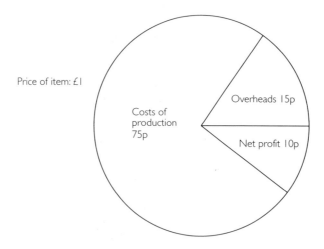

Price of item: £1

Costs of production 75p

Overheads 15p

Net profit 10p

Figure 12.1 Illustration of profit margin

Once the position has been reached where total sales just cover the total costs of providing a product or service, **break even point** has been reached. So, if a souvenir shop's total sales are £60,000, the costs of sales are £50,000 and the overheads are £10,000, the break even point has been reached. Only sales about this point enable a profit to be made. The calculation of the break even point enables a company to decide on the viability of individual products and services.

In planning margins and likely net profits margins of safety have to be included to cover as many of the predictable and possibly unexpected costs as is possible. Self-employed traders dependent on sunny weather, for example ice-cream sellers, have to work out what they must charge to earn a living, even if their sales are affected by bad weather. Unless there is some sort of positive return on the investment in a vehicle and the goods to be sold, the ice-cream seller has no incentive to take the risk.

Budgetary adjustment

Setting a budget is only the first part of an on-going process. Factors during actual trading may render some of the original budget predictions unreliable. A spell of particularly fine weather could increase visitor numbers and the income of a leisure park. This could lead to a temporary reduction in the funds allocated to marketing. Figures relating to admissions and retail sales are likely to be analysed on a weekly and a monthly basis. This analysis may show up trends which demonstrate the need for a budgetary adjustment. They may show that a particular food outlet is failing to meet its sales targets by some way. Closing it down would reduce costs. Admissions data may show that the percentage of children under 12 years of age has fallen sharply. This could suggest that the original pricing and discount policy was not sufficiently attractive, and pricing policy changes could reduce the income derived from individual child visitors, but increase overall income by attracting greater numbers.

Activity

In the left-hand column of the list below are eight terms commonly used in business financial planning.

Match each of these terms with a definition drawn from those listed in the right-hand column.

Term	Definition
1 **Cash flow**	(a) A document which analyses your business activities in detail and predicts expectations of the business for at least the coming year. Usually presented to the bank to support a request for loan and/or overdraft facilities.
2 **Asset**	(b) Expenses such as materials, labour and energy, which vary according to the number of goods produced or services offered.
3 **Capital**	(c) A short term line of credit from the bank granted for a fixed period, normally up to 12 months.
4 **Business plan**	(d) These are also known as overheads. These are the costs of the business which do not vary in proportion to changes in sales or output. Examples are rent, rates, administrative expenses etc.
5 **Balance sheet**	(e) Usually refers to the amount of money in the business belonging to the proprietors or shareholders, or backers such as banks, including cash from profitable transactions.

6 Fixed costs   (f) A statement of assets and liabilities of the business at a particular point in \
time.

7 Variable costs   (g) Something which is owned by or owed to the business which has a
measurable value (e.g. cash, property, machinery) and is therefore in its
favour.

8 Overdraft   (h) The pattern of total cash coming in and going out of a business over a
period of time.

(Answers will be found at the end of the chapter.)

Assignment 12
Resource planning

This assignment develops knowledge and understanding of the following elements:

5.2 Present a plan for an event
5.3 Allocate roles and personnel in an event
8.2 Plan the evaluation of a facility's performance
8.3 Evaluate the performance of a facility

It supports development of the following core skills:
Communication 3.2, 3.3
Application of number 3.1, 3.3

You decide to set up a new business providing a catering service which will deliver food direct to the homes of local residents **or** which will provide food for special events.

Your tasks

Draw up the first draft of a business plan which will enable you to do the following things:
- decide whether the business will work;
- identify the income and expenditure involved;
- monitor the progress of the business;
- provide your bank with sufficient background for them to judge whether and how they might help you.

(Answers to quiz on business financial planning: 1(h); 2(g); 3(e); 4(a); 5(f); 6(d); 7(b); 8(c))

13 Planning: constraints

What is covered in this chapter

This chapter shows how leisure and tourism can create new employment and recreational opportunities for local communities. It shows how many leisure activities are home-based, and yet at the same time the range and popularity of outdoor leisure pursuits are increasing. It shows how crowd control at major events can be properly managed. It shows how tourist activity is a factor in causing erosion and may also pose a threat to some wildlife habitats, contribute to traffic congestion, noise and litter problems. It shows how new buildings should fit in with their surroundings. It shows how national planning can both stimulate and hinder leisure and tourism development.

- Social and cultural impact of leisure and tourism development
- Public order
- Leisure needs of the local community
- Design constraints
- Regional and national tourism planning.
- Environmental impact of leisure and tourism

13.1 Social and cultural impact of leisure and tourism development

Potential benefits to the host community

The advent of leisure and tourism developments rarely provokes a single united view among the host community. Differences of age, interest, employment and wealth usually result in some groups being more in favour of development than others. Those in favour may feel that the local environment presently has too little to offer in terms of:

- entertainment;
- employment;
- contact with the outside world;
- infrastructure.

Leisure and tourism development may offer an encouragement for younger people to stay in the region rather than moving away in search of jobs or entertainment. If this trend is not halted, the future survival of the community may be put at risk. Leisure and tourism can stimulate a reawakening of interest in and a market for local crafts, as well as direct employment in new facilities. Successful leisure and tourism development may in turn attract new industries to an area because it is perceived as both forward-looking and able to offer an attractive environment.

Potential costs to the local community

Successful development can lead to year-round population growth, as visitors who are attracted to the area decide to settle there. This is rarely unaccompanied by social

Local crafts may be stimulated by tourism

problems, particularly with housing. Increased demand prompts a rise in house prices, putting many properties out of reach of young local people and offering further encouragement for them to move away. Sought-after locations may be purchased by occasional visitors as second homes. These can easily become a source of resentment among local people, who see them empty for much of the year while people in the local community are not satisfactorily housed.

One social consequence of increased tourism is the impact it has on local identity. As this resident of a small coastal fishing village which attracts ten times the number of its own population in the summer months says:

> Residents get to feel like strangers here, specially in summer. You go shopping in your own street and you find the stores crowded with people you don't know. My husband comes back early from fishing off the harbour wall because as the day goes on he knows he'll be surrounded by families on holiday. You can't even go down to the pub for a quiet evening drink with friends because most nights all the seats and tables will be occupied by outsiders and you have to wait ages to be served. A lot of the traditional fishermen's pubs have been painted pretty colours and given silly names like 'The Jolly Jack Tar'. Fishing nets and anchors are more

likely to be used as ornaments or decorations than to catch fish. I think it is insulting to our parents and grandparents, many of whom risked their lives to feed their families and who made this place what it is.

Competition between tourists and hosts

The idea of competition between visitors and local people extends to other areas. Lack of parking spaces, for example, may cause resentment, particularly if local people attempting to work or shop feel they are being obstructed by visitors who are at leisure. Traffic congestion is another area of potential conflict, as is the competition for the use of public sector resources. Local residents may feel services to local people, such as leisure or transport, are not generously funded by comparison with services and facilities developed to meet the needs of visitors.

Pedestrian numbers stretched by tourism in Winchester

The growth of tourism generally leads to an increase in the number of shops. More visitors may result in local residents having to queue longer to be served in shops, but may also provide them with a greater choice of produce and price. It may create a greater diversity in the type of shops available. Local shopkeepers, particularly suppliers of essential goods such as bakers or greengrocers, are likely to see an increase in trade. However, they may have to set this against an increase in the rental charges made for their premises.

Pubs, restaurants and cafes are generally found in tourist resorts. Local people may feel that these have been taken over by visitors. Sometimes the presence of tourists means that these outlets can stay open longer and perhaps offer even local residents more opportunities to use them than they might have had otherwise. This is often equally true of recreation facilities. Use by local people alone would not make them economically viable. Funded largely by the admission charges made to visitors, these facilities can provide a spin-off for local people.

Interaction between tourists and hosts

The degree of interaction between tourists and local residents may be an indicator of the social impact of tourism. Aside from making purchases, asking directions and booking accommodation many visitors may feel little need to talk to local people. For their part, the residents' reactions to visitors will depend to some extent on the stage of development which tourism has reached. The first visitors to previously isolated communities are often met with a degree of curiosity and are accepted while the numbers remain small. As more visitors follow, conflicts of interest can lead to irritation and, in some cases, to open antagonism. Residents of destinations with a long history of tourism eventually become resigned to the changes it brings, once these are too entrenched to be reversed.

This social cycle may be matched by the physical development of the resort itself. Residents may initially be involved in providing facilities for the first tourists. If significant growth occurs, outside business interests such as hotel chains may play an increasingly significant part in development. Mass market tourism may produce tourist enclaves and, as long as the resort stays popular, it may reach its full capacity. Crowds and congestion may then reduce its appeal, leading to a fall in profits and a consequent reduction in maintenance. Once the resort's attractiveness appears to be in decline, the relative merits of other destinations draw potential visitors elsewhere. Some of the accommodation provision then ceases to be profitable and may be converted to other use, for example homes for old people. This in turn changes the character, the social make-up and the appeal of the resort as a whole.

Opponents of leisure and tourism development may fear that their privacy will be threatened by encouraging more visitors. If the community is a close one, with long-standing traditions, there is likely to be a fear that an influx of outsiders will erode cultural values and create social conflict. Tourism can instigate a process known as the **demonstration effect**. The tourists demonstrate a way of life which is the result both of their own wealth and culture, and the fact that they are at leisure far away from the constraints of home. Hosts, feeling that there is something superior in this display of material success and apparent freedom, may imitate patterns of behaviour which do not find favour in their own communities.

Activity

All of the following are examples of contact between tourists and local residents on the Caribbean island of Grenada.

1 At Point Salines Airport a Grenadian customs official asks an incoming tourist to wait while her medication, prescribed by a doctor in England, is checked by one of his superiors.

2 A Grenadian walking along Grand Anse beach stops to ask a tourist for two dollars to buy a Coke.

3 A Grenadian asks a tourist, when they have returned home, to purchase some Ray-ban sunglasses and post them back to him.

4 A tourist asks a busy Grenadian market trader if he can photograph her selling her produce.

5 A tourist asks a Grenadian spice sorter about the rates of pay he receives for collecting and sorting spices.

6 A tourist tells a Grenadian seller of black coral bracelets that she won't buy one because this trade is responsible for damaging the coral reefs.

In each of these six encounters, what thoughts might go through the mind of the listener?

What conclusions could be drawn about the social impact of tourism in Grenada on the basis of these six encounters?

13.2 Leisure needs of the local community

Use of leisure time

Leisure refers to the time people have aside from work, sleep and study. They are free to decide how to spend this time and may choose to pursue hobbies, sports or cultural interests. Some of these interests are likely to be home-based, such as reading or watching televison, while others, like playing sport or going to see a film, involve travel from home.

Most people probably spend the majority of their leisure time at home. They may spend much of it watching television, reading, making home improvements or gardening. A number of facilities, particularly retail outlets like garden centres and bookshops, have been developed to exploit these leisure interests. The growth of available leisure time during the second half of the twentieth century has encouraged more people to travel in their spare time. Evidence of this can be seen in the countryside where the increase in footpath signs, nature trails, farm and craft centres, tea shops and designated picnic areas show that owners and managers of land recognize the opportunities presented by the rising number of visitors.

Securing balanced provision

Most communities regard sport and the arts as essential. For example, a community may benefit from sports provision through:
- better health and less time taken off work;
- the encouragement of community spirit;
- channelling people's energies away from anti-social activities;
- improved prestige and morale.

Arts provision can provide similar benefits to the community, as well as offering entertainment, insight into human thought, perception and feeling, and the chance to preserve both national and regional cultural heritages.

Providers of leisure facilities have to compete with the attractions of home entertainment. Though some leisure services are provided for the local community out of local government funds, such as public libraries, others, like squash clubs, depend on the number of participants they attract. Though leisure facilities are provided with local users in mind, most are also open to visitors. They need to attract as many people as possible, particularly since leisure is a volatile market. This means that a minority of people go to see a film or play ten-pin bowling with great regularity, while the majority of participants are occasional.

The vast range of potential leisure activities makes it very difficult to secure a balanced provision, especially in smaller communities. Access to a basketball court is likely to be easier in Central London than in a small, rural village. Provision has to cater for participative activities, like playing tennis, as well as passive ones, like watching a film. Different age groups within the community are likely to express some differences of taste in their leisure needs. Discos are more likely to appeal to younger people; bowls and whist drives will probably attract older participants.

Leisure activities serve the same purpose as holidays for many people. They act as a means of escape from the stresses of work and life at home. They provide the exercise, excitement or interest which other areas of their everyday life may lack. They provide opportunities to take up new interests or to acquire and update skills. A lack of leisure facilities in any community contributes to feelings of boredom, tension and disaffection. New leisure and tourism developments create hostility when they ignore the leisure needs of the local community.

Activity

Market research provides one method of establishing what the demand for leisure is within a given community.

Study the results in Table 13.1 taken from a survey conducted among the regular users of Easthampton Hall, a large room capable of holding 150 people, and used both for sports activities and for performances.

Table 13.1 Survey at Easthampton Hall

Numbers taking part in sporting activities once a week:

badminton	32	gymnastics	12
volleyball	20	aerobics	180
ballroom dancing	30	keep fit	130
yoga	70	5-a-side football	30
indoor cricket	36	weight-lifting	16

Numbers wanting to attend performances once a week:

cinema films	230	classical music concerts	50
pop concerts	120	dance performances	30
theatre plays	80		

The Hall is managed by the local authority which is determined to offer a range of leisure activities appropriate to local demand. Sporting activities are programmed from 4 p.m.–7 p.m. and performances from 7 p.m.–10 p.m. However, it has set the Hall manager a target which indicates that the Hall must not run at a loss. The costs of keeping the Hall open, including staff, amount to **£2,600** a week for the following hours:

Monday–Saturday (inclusive): 4 p.m. – 10 p.m.

Sunday: closed all day

A standard charge of **£3** is made for all performances, while sports are charged at **£2** per person per hour.

Any activity can be put on twice in the week, as long as it is on separate days.

Complete a timetable of activities for a week which both offers a broad leisure provision and also ensures that no loss is recorded.

13.3 Public order

Crowd safety

Leisure events frequently attract large crowds and these raise a number of safety issues which the organizers must take into account. These include:

- predicting the size of the crowd;
- assessing its likely character and mood;
- analysing which areas of the venue will be under the greatest pressure from crowding;
- implementing protective measures to reduce risks of crushing or other injuries.

Crowd safety is primarily a management responsibility. Events which take place on large sites can only be safely managed through good teamwork and effective communications. People with direct responsibility for crowd control need effective training and well-defined statements of what their roles are. Experience may also be invaluable in helping to prevent the unexpected from becoming a disaster.

The **Health and Safety Executive** advises that all those involved with ensuring crowd safety should carry out all the following actions:

- research the type of visitor expected and anticipate likely crowd behaviour;
- collate and assess any information available about the conduct of previous events at the venue;
- assess the risks attached to current crowd control arrangements and change these where necessary;
- inspect the venue and review crowd safety arrangements at regular intervals;
- set targets for crowd management, for example the control of queue lengths;
- liaise with outside organizations such as the police and emergency services.

Assessing the risks at individual venues

The layout of a venue holding an event is a major consideration in crowd control. Small entrances or a limited number of turnstiles may create crushes, and also provoke unrest and disorder. The use of barriers can help to direct crowd flows, and the placement of attractions and food outlets can help to disperse visitors. Well-placed signs and information can also help to keep crowd flows moving, as well as avoiding the frustration and potential aggression which a lack of information can generate. Where large crowds are present a good public address system is invaluable in encouraging people to use less congested routes and ensuring safe evacuation in an emergency.

Certain physical features at a venue may carry particularly high risks. These include:

- steep slopes;
- dead ends and locked gates;
- points where several routes merge into one;
- uneven or slippery flooring or steps.

The hazards which are particularly likely to provoke unrest or disturbance include:

- reverse or cross-flows in dense crowds;
- long queues;
- pedestrian flows mixing with traffic;
- moving attractions within a crowd.

Crowd behaviour can become a public nuisance. Spectators at a sports stadium or a rock concert are often witnessing something they feel passionate about. The excitement of the occasion can turn into hostility if the crowd controllers are not sensitive to the particular characteristics of the participants. If parts of the crowd cannot see or hear very well, the risks of disturbance or unrest are increased.

Activity

The Guide to Safety at Sports Grounds lists six basic duties which stewards are called on to carry out:

> (a) to control and direct spectators who are entering and leaving the ground, to help achieve an even flow of people to the viewing areas;
>
> (b) to recognise crowd densities, signs of crowd distress and crowd dynamics in order to help ensure safe dispersal of spectators on the terraces or viewing slopes;
>
> (c) to patrol the ground to deal with any emergencies, e.g. raising alarms or tackling the early stages of fires;
>
> (d) to staff entrances, exits to and from the viewing accommodation and other strategic points, especially exit doors and exit gates from the ground which are not continuously open while the ground is in use;
>
> (e) to assist the police as appropriate or as requested with crowd control;
>
> (f) to undertake specific duties in an emergency.

List the attributes you think would be required to enable a steward to carry out these duties effectively. You should include comment in each of the following areas:
- attitude and personality;
- physical appearance and capabilities;
- specific knowledge of the venue;
- skills and previous experience.

13.4 Environmental impact of leisure and tourism

Landscape damage

The popularity of some areas of the countryside has resulted in marked soil erosion, especially on footpaths. Popular long distance walks, such as the Pennine Way, seem particularly vulnerable, perhaps because people walk them in all kinds of weather. People who stray off the main paths quickly widen the eroded areas, as well as causing additional damage to plants and flowers. Serious erosion is also caused by cycling, horse riding and off-road use of motor vehicles. Local areas of erosion can often be caused by the presence of such things as food kiosks or signs and monuments which encourage continual movement in the same direction.

Dunes, coastlines, lake shores and river banks are also susceptible to erosion. Though the originating cause of this may not be the presence of tourists, it is often accelerated by their activities. River banks, for example, may be subject to a certain amount of natural erosion from the flow of water, but this is made considerably worse by the waves created by passing boats. Dune erosion can be checked by the provision of wooden or metal walkways and by the planting of marram grass, the roots of which bind sand or loose soil together.

Erosion caused by walkers on coastal footpath

Water areas present their own particular problems, apart from bank erosion. Places like Windermere and the Norfolk Broads have been popular magnets for boating enthusiasts for many years. In addition to the noise they make, boat engines have increased pollution levels and disturbed sensitive marine ecosystems. Responses to this problem on the Broads include a scheme to renovate three of the old shallow sailing boats known as wherries. Their original woodwork and intricate decoration has been restored. Each has a single large sail, traditional on the Broads and a more environmentally-friendly means of propulsion than petrol engines.

These issues clearly represent a constraint on tourism development in some country areas. There are two general approaches which can be taken to try and halt the damage. One strategy is for tourism to be confined to areas where such things as footpath repair can be strictly monitored and where there are sufficient resources to construct hard-wearing surfaces. Tourism can also be confined by restricting car parking spaces. Another is to use marketing and systems of waymarking to try and disperse visitors over a wider area. The development of more bridleways, especially in popular horse riding areas, would reduce the pressure on some footpaths.

Tourists are often attracted by fragile environments such as small islands, remote mountain ranges and undeveloped coastlines. Coral reefs around Caribbean islands have been damaged both by boating and by souvenir collectors. Visitors trekking in the Himalaya have cut down trees for firewood, leaving slopes vulnerable to erosion and landslides in wet weather. Wildlife, such as the loggerhead turtles which lay their eggs on some Greek island beaches, can be seriously threatened by a growing tourist presence. Most of these problems can be tackled through a combination of both long

229

term planning and financial investment to encourage alternative practices, and also education.

Damage to the built environment

Cathedrals, historic houses and other heritage sites are particularly prone to wear and tear caused by visitors. Churches and cathedrals have a long tradition of openly welcoming visitors. Floors and floor coverings are prone to wear and tear, and this is a particular concern where floors incorporate original tiled designs and mosaics.

The openness of places of worship has also resulted in an increase in theft and vandalism. The presence of large numbers of unguarded small objects like statues has proved a temptation to thieves. Increasingly, sensitive areas of churches and cathedrals are being cordoned off to protect them, while valuable objects on public display are replaced by replicas. The response to vandalism has generally been to increase the levels of security by means of voluntary wardens and video camera surveillance.

Traffic congestion

Destinations which attract tourists are not always in easily accessible areas. Access to well-known beauty spots may be along narrow roads. Improving access is likely to be undesirable because it would lessen the attractiveness of the landscape itself. In hilly areas, like the Peak District, the landscape means roads are often narrow, steep, twisting and bordered by stone walls – all factors slowing the flow of traffic. The topography of such areas may also restrict the number of available parking spaces, and result in cars blocking exits and thoroughfares.

At Dovedale, in the Peak District, a deliberate decision was taken to reduce the number of parking spaces from 900 to 500 as a means of reducing the negative impact of tourism. Another method of protecting attractive rural villages from summer traffic congestion is to avoid giving them any publicity in guides and brochures featuring the area as a whole. The growth in traffic affects local communities in terms of noise, pollution and delay. However, in some rural areas it is claimed that tourism can help to sustain local public transport services.

Road traffic in the vicinity of Chessington

Traffic to tourist attractions is rarely consistent throughout the year. A proportion of the traffic may be the result of increases in local car ownership. Visitors to Chessington World of Adventures contribute to general traffic volumes on the A243. However, research studies suggest that periodic congestion is caused on only 13 days a year and that some traffic increase can be measured on 70 days a year. A traffic survey indicated that visitors to Chessington contributed less than 3 per cent of the annual traffic flow on the A243. The plan to build a new road link between the A3, from where many of the visitors approach Chessington, and the A243 is expected to reduce traffic problems considerably.

Other approaches to solving traffic congestion caused by outside visitors include **park and ride schemes**. Visitors to Oxford can park on the outskirts of the city and catch a bus into the centre, thus avoiding the severe parking problems which are often found there. A number of popular tourist spots in town centres, such as the Pantiles in Tunbridge Wells, have been converted into pedestrian-only areas.

Overcrowding

Crowds can easily spoil the appearance and atmosphere of a place. Inside cathedrals and abbeys, the presence of large numbers of visitors makes it difficult for individuals to find a place for quiet reflection. In art galleries crowds tend to gather in front of famous pictures, so that the only way of getting a clear view of them is by being first in the queue when the gallery opens.

Table 13.2 Perceived positive and negative aspects attributable to tourism by residents of Calderdale

Perceptions	Number	%
Perceived benefits of tourism		
Don't know/nothing	50	20%
Economic	134	54%
Social/cultural	18	7%
Promotion of area	20	8%
Environmental	11	4%
Pressure on council	7	3%
More facilities	8	3%
Perceived negative aspects of tourism		
Nothing/don't know	104	42%
Traffic/congestion	71	29%
Vandalism/pollution	16	6%
Higher prices	10	4%
Overcrowded	29	12%
Less originality	9	4%
Dependency/jobs	3	1%
Less for locals	2	1%
Other	5	2%

Table 13.3 Perceived effect of tourism on different factors

	Better (%)	Same (%)	Worse (%)	Don't know (%)
Employment	52	18	8	20
Income	45	27	9	19
Relaxation/entertainment	47	26	11	16
House prices	21	14	50	16
Condition of buildings	47	23	9	21
Traffic	5	8	76	12
Parking	5	8	73	15
Public transport	23	32	18	27
Access to countryside	32	36	12	20
State of countryside	19	33	29	18
Environmental quality	30	35	15	20
Shopping facilities	32	34	16	17
Community spirit	19	45	14	22
Own identity with region	17	49	11	22
Others	2	3	1	95

One of the consequences of overcrowding at popular sites and attractions is an increase in the amount of litter. The problem is greatest where litter collection and disposal is inadequate. The volume of litter on British beaches during the summer months represents a considerable cost to local authorities. They have to employ staff and equipment to collect, compact and dispose of the rubbish daily. Disposal must be regular since the presence of litter at a site increases the likelihood that new visitors will add to it.

Development not in keeping with surroundings

The provision of facilities to meet the growing demands of tourists can result in unsightly developments, especially where commercial interests are placed before concerns about appearance. Brightly coloured signs and advertisements, food outlets, shops, toilets, camp sites and visitor centres all need to take account of the surrounding buildings and landscape. New developments should use materials which are compatible with local styles. The scale of new buildings should not be out of proportion with those adjoining them.

A tourist resort at Ayers Rock

The settlement of Yulara in Australia was built in a deliberate attempt to reduce the environmental threat posed by tourism in and around Ayers Rock. The fragile sand dune environment had suffered so much damage from visitors and off-road vehicles that it was decided to build a tourist resort some miles away and channel the great majority of visitors through it. All buildings in the new resort were low level and the same colour as the surrounding sand dunes. The buildings followed the base of the sand dune formations, in order to reduce their visibility. The settlement was designed with energy conservation in mind. Individual buildings provided some mutual shade. Windows faced away from the sun and solar heating provided 70 per cent of the energy needed for heating and air conditioning. Room keys automatically deactivated the electricity supply, and the water system treated and reused water from the swimming pool, using it for watering lawns and native plants.

Activity

Read the following comments on the environmental impact of skiing:

Skiing has grown so rapidly in the Alps that it is estimated that there are now some 40,000 ski runs and 14,000 ski lifts.

Skiing is totally dependent on snow. In years when there is not enough ski resorts have started to depend on artificial snow machines. Compressed air and water are sprayed at high pressure when temperatures are below freezing. This creates extra snow but is a serious drain on the local water supply. Some methods of making artificial snow also use chemicals to speed the formation of ice crystals. The use of snow machines also means that the skiing season can be extended. This can affect the habitat of local wildlife. It can also increase the damage to the slopes themselves, particularly if people ski over muddy patches. This can accelerate soil erosion and damage wild flowers.

Alpine pastures hold about 90 litres of water per cubic metre but when they are dug up and prepared for skiing they retain a mere 40 litres. A higher proportion of water produced by rain and snow falls runs downhill, increasing the likelihood both of soil erosion and flooding.

However it is the construction of new ski resorts which perhaps gives the greatest cause for concern. In order to produce suitable ski runs thousands of trees are cleared. Slopes are reshaped, often involving the movement of thousands of tons of earth and the blasting of rocks. This can noticeably increase the dangers from avalanches, since trees give some protection. It has meant that many Alpine roads are covered by a succession of unsightly concrete avalanche shelters. The steel pylons, overhead cables, lifts and tows which are necessary in ski resorts are also visually unattractive.

Outline the main elements of a strategy aimed at ensuring the long term survival of an already popular Alpine ski resort where several proposals for the creation of new ski runs are under consideration.

13.5 Design constraints

It is more likely that new leisure and tourism developments will be well received if local architectural styles and materials are used. As far as possible the colours chosen should mirror those found in the surrounding landscape. In a village where the majority of cottages were whitewashed, a resident choosing to paint a cottage purple would probably not be popular! The colour of surrounding vegetation, the network of paths, roads and fields, the colour of local rock and stone are all factors which should be taken into account by the designer. Similarly, the profile of the buildings, hills and trees which form the skyline need to be taken into account in designing new buildings. The height of a new building may be legally restricted in some areas, particularly if it is likely to affect seriously the view or light available to nearby residents.

Landscaping and the use of trees and shrubs are increasingly employed in the design of new developments. By using the natural contours of the land it is often possible to hide the less attractive parts of a new building. Trees and shrubs can provide a two-way screen, both preserving the appearance of the landscape, and protecting the building from noise, wind and public view. Selecting the right trees is important. Fast-growing varieties may rapidly become barriers to naturally attractive views. Other plant forms like mosses, ferns, vines and creepers can also break up the stark appearance of large expanses of wall.

Using existing structures

Design does not always involve starting from scratch. Buildings particularly are subject to changes of use. There have been many recent examples of buildings which were originally mills, factories, warehouses or railway stations being converted for use as recreational facilities. The materials and the design used in the original buildings represent constraints on the style of any adaptation of their use.

233

The Musée d'Orsay

The Musée d'Orsay was originally a railway station built in the nineteenth century on the banks of the River Seine in Paris. It was due to be demolished but it was decided that it would be better for the appearance of this part of the city if the existing structure were to be redesigned for a different use, particularly since the exterior style of the building blends in well with neighbouring ones. The original design contained massive open spaces, many arches and more complicated iron structures, and vast areas of glass. Some of these features were particularly valuable since the new use of the building was as a museum. The fact that there was so much glass, for example, made it easier to avoid the kind of glare and shadow which can make viewing works of art difficult.

The modernization of Covent Garden in London shows evidence of the use of original design features within a new and different context. The former fruit and vegetable market now houses a variety of small shops, cafes and restaurants, and has become a major tourist attraction. The original iron and glass structures have been incorporated in the roof design. Many of the shops have had their facades modelled on the way they must have looked during Victorian times. These characteristic styles are complemented by features like the Victorian-style lamps suspended from the ceiling.

Coastline development

Good beaches have traditionally attracted roads, promenades, and eventually accommodation and other building. Hotels were often built high, because the sea front land was expensive and the owners wished to get as many bedrooms into the designs as possible. This created a visual barrier between the land and the sea. It also meant that the coastal road became very congested and difficult to cross. On particularly popular coastlines separate developments began to merge so that the coastline became a continuous series of hotels.

Sometimes natural features prevented this. In Skegness the coast was known to be subject to a steady process of erosion. Perhaps for this reason hotels were set further back from the edge of the sea. The strip of land in between could be used for parks, gardens, boating lakes and a broad promenade. Many new seaside developments, such as La Grande Motte in the south of France, are planned to give easy access to the beach. The maximum number of people the beach can carry was a major factor in planning this development. Landscaped footways were designed to encourage people to walk to the beach rather than taking their cars.

Design and construction of Port-Grimaud

The construction of the purpose-built resort of Port-Grimaud began in 1966 on swamp land. Iron piles were driven into the ground and bridges built across the swamp. Canals were dug and the excavated earth used to construct small islands. A sea access was created which helped to prevent water stagnation. Two thousand houses were built with no two identical. Size, shape, window design and position, colouring of shutters, doors and railings were used to establish differences. The planners intended any future restoration to be carried out using the original colours. The curved pier, constructed from 24,000 tons of granite, used a traditional design. An extensive network of canals and wharves provided easy access and mooring for boat owners.

Port-Grimaud

Activity

Identify someone who is about to visit a traditional British seaside resort. Ask them to take a selection of photographs which illustrate the range of buildings, facilities and signs in the areas most popular with tourists.

Write a short illustrated report indicating whether development has, on the whole, successfully taken account of the surroundings or not.

Identify one building in the resort not currently used for leisure or tourism purposes. Outline a proposal which would give it a recreational use while at the same time taking care not to make it less visually attractive.

13.6 Regional and national tourism planning

National constraints

Governments are most likely to take decisions affecting leisure and tourism development, where these are thought to be capable of improving the national balance of payments and creating new employment. Leisure developments may be part of a social policy intended to increase recreational facilities for urban populations.

Improving the balance of payments through tourism is likely to be dependent on four factors:

- the number of incoming visitors and the amount they spend;
- the proportion of the resident population taking holidays abroad;

- the extent to which national planning and improved marketing can increase the number of high-spending visitors and the numbers taking domestic holidays;
- the amount of foreign exchange spent in order to provide for the visitors.

Table 13.4 shows a summary of visitors to the UK and to London and their expenditure. Only visitors spending at least one night in the UK or London are included and all figures are in millions.

Table 13.4 Summary of visitors to the UK and London

Visits	UK (millions)			London (millions)		
	1990	**1991**	**1992**	**1990**	**1991**	**1992**
Domestic	95.3	94.4	95.6	7.0	6.5	7.0
Overseas	18.0	17.1	18.5	10.3	9.2	10.0
All	113.3	111.5	114.1	17.3	15.7	17.0
Nights						
Domestic	399.1	395.6	399.7	19.2	19.0	19.4
Overseas	196.1	186.4	186.0	76.6	69.8	68.7
All	595.2	582.2	585.7	95.8	88.8	88.1
Expenditure (£s)						
Domestic	10,460	10,470	10,665	680	720	640
Overseas	7,748	7,386	7,807	4,227	3,924	4,152
All	18,208	17,756	18,472	4,907	4,685	4,792

Sources: International Passenger Survey; UK Tourism Survey

A national decision to target high-spending visitors, attractive because fewer are needed in order to generate income, would have consequences for individual leisure and tourism developers. There would be more investment support for luxury developments. Building restrictions would discourage the erection of ugly, high-density hotels and apartment blocks. Greater environmental concern would be essential in preserving the features which attracted high spenders in the first place.

National planning is sometimes needed to eradicate some of the inequalities which new tourism can bring. If coastal towns acquire new wealth, while villages in the interior do not, apart from the tensions which this can create, population shifts will occur and traditional agriculture may decline. National governments may seek to disperse the tourists, as well as distributing the income they bring. Many are coming to the view that it is inadvisable to base a national economy on a single activity, particularly one like tourism which is so vulnerable to external factors like wars, exchange rates, recessions and fuel charges.

National planning will also have a hand in which areas receive government financial support. Such decisions may depend on:
- the levels of local unemployment;
- the quality of the existing infrastructure;
- the anticipated social and environmental impacts;
- the number and location of different attractions.

Regional constraints

Restrictions may be placed on leisure and tourism developments because they do not fit in with an existing overall strategy for the region. This may be a matter of imposing height restrictions on buildings or of limiting the hours an attraction is permitted to open. Proposals for facilities likely to draw large crowds, such as football grounds, tend to come under particularly close scrutiny because of the evident impact this will have on the local community.

In the UK the English Tourist Board has worked in partnership with regional tourist boards, local authorities and private sector industry on a series of Tourism Development Action Programmes, often referred to as TDAPs. These are short term schemes aimed at creating a longer term strategy for tourism and economic development in specific regions. These programmes undertake research and marketing for the region, and attempt to involve local businesses in setting common goals for the development of tourism in the region. By this means they hope to stimulate additional employment and income in the area, as well as providing leisure and recreational facilities to the benefit of both local residents and visitors.

Local Area Initiatives

The English Tourist Board works with a number of regions of the UK that have been identified as areas of special need. For example, seven seaside resorts received funds during 1992 and 1993 intended to encourage new investment by local businesses and councils. These Local Area Initiatives are intended to revive the popularity of resorts like Eastbourne, Weymouth and Weston-super-Mare. The funds, more than matched by local investment, are generally spent on marketing, seafront renovation and new attractions.

In some cases regional planning is essential to protect fragile environments. The pine forests of the Landes region of south-west France were planted primarily to conserve an unstable land surface. Coastal dunes and thin soil layers in the forest are vulnerable to both the Atlantic sea breezes and the feet of the many visitors. The coastline has been divided into sectors, and the road system is planned to take account both of through coastal traffic and local sightseers. Small inland lakes provide an alternative to the beach and help to distribute the tourists more widely.

Activity

One constraint affecting leisure and tourism development would be the lack of a trained workforce. The London Tourist Board, in its 'Strategy for London', says this of employment and training:

The tourism industry faces the challenge of attracting and retaining a sufficiently skilled workforce in the face of demographic change. To do this, the industry needs to improve recruitment and training practices and employment conditions, work with schools and colleges and develop links with disabled groups and women returning to work.

List a number of actions which regional planners might propose to ensure that there is a large enough and a well enough trained workforce to sustain further leisure and tourism development in the region.

Include these suggested actions in a letter to your regional tourist board.

Assignment 13
Planning: constraints

This assignment develops knowledge and understanding of the following elements:
4.2 Identify market opportunities
5.2 Present a plan for an event
8.2 Plan the evaluation of a facility's performance
8.3 Evaluate the performance of a facility

It supports development of the following core skills:
Communication 3.1, 3.2, 3.3
Information Technology 3.3

Your tasks

1 Select a site or existing building with potential for development as a leisure or tourism facility **or** one with potential for hosting a leisure event.
2 Outline a proposal for a specific development or event intended to operate in your chosen location. You should include:
   (a) basic ground plans and/or sketches/artist's impressions;
   (b) an indication of the scale of the operation;
   (c) an explanation of the intended market.
3 Draw up an action plan showing how you intend to assess the potential impact of the development or event on each of the following:
   (a) the local community;
   (b) the local infrastructure;
   (c) the local environment.

14 Evaluation through research and data analysis

What is covered in this chapter

This chapter shows how data about leisure and tourism are often derived from surveys. It shows why businesses feel a need to measure their performance, especially in financial terms. It shows how reliable data can only be produced if questioning and sampling techniques are appropriate. It shows how external surveys and reports can indicate trends which affect individual leisure and tourism businesses.

- Data collection
- Types of data
- Interpretation of data

- How businesses assess their performance.

14.1 Data collection

Types of market research

Much of the data used to evaluate the performance of leisure and tourism facilities are derived from market research. Seibert defined market research as:

> gathering, processing, analysis, storage and dissemination of information to facilitate and improve decision making.

Victor Middleton, in his book *Marketing in Travel and Tourism,* identifies six main types of market research. These are as follows.

Market analysis and forecasting
This is where a company seeks to find out what its share of the market is and how much revenue each different market segment could contribute to the company's overall sales of products or services in the future.

Consumer research
This is information which a company collects about its existing customers, including their needs, awareness of the company's products and their spending habits.

Products and price studies
These studies test the reactions of consumers to new products and to different pricing strategies.

Promotions and sales research
This research is used to find out how people respond to different kinds of advertising and sales techniques.

Distribution research

Many products and services are sold through retailers like travel agents, and the company developing them will need to gather information about how effective the distribution of their products is and whether all retailers are equally informed about them.

Evaluation and performance monitoring studies

These studies identify how satisfied customers are with existing products and services which a company is supplying.

Research methods

Market research can be either **continuous** or **ad hoc**. If it is continuous, it is conducted on a regular basis at daily, weekly, monthly, quarterly or annual intervals. Ad hoc research is specially commissioned to investigate a specific question. A hotel, for example, might carry out ad hoc research to establish whether it would be worthwhile to open a snack bar at weekends.

As we have seen in section 7.4 the data provided in a research study may be either **primary** or **secondary**. Primary data come direct from the source and will be the result of specially commissioned research. Asking a sample of residents to judge aspects of their local transport service would yield primary data. Secondary data, usually the result of **desk research**, are derived from existing sources of information such as reports, press articles and cuttings, published statistics, past sales figures or past survey results.

Market research is sometimes described as **omnibus research**. This term is used of broad, general data covering a number of areas of activity. The data may be tabulated using criteria based on age, socio-economic group or area of domicile. Individual companies can purchase relevant sections of this data which apply specifically to their own operations. A number of companies may join together to commission a survey in order to generate data. This is called **syndicated research**.

One of the most common forms of market research is the **retail audit**. This type of survey measures sales volume and price in a number of retail outlets. The resulting data are assumed to be representative and are multiplied to give a picture of the overall sales performance. **Consumer audits**, on the other hand, monitor the purchasing habits of a representative sample of consumers and use the resulting data to predict the spending habits of different market segments.

Survey techniques and design

Surveys represent one of the commonest ways of acquiring business data. All surveys, except the National Census, depend on selecting a sample of respondents. Sampling can be random but most survey designers use a system of sampling which they think will give them answers representative of the range of views within the categories of people they are aiming at. They may do this by selecting a proportion of respondents by age, gender and socio-economic class which reflects the proportions of these groups in the population as a whole. (An example of a questionnaire used for museum visitors can be found in Chapter 10.)

The design of the actual questions to be included in surveys is critical. Carelessly worded questions may encourage all respondents to give the same answer. Questions which are ambiguous or which rely on jargon may prove difficult to answer. The ease with which responses can be collated into the form of usable data often depends on the format of the questions asked. Asking for boxes to be ticked or numbers to be circled both makes the questionnaire easier to complete and simplifies the task of processing the data later.

Closed questions and questions which offer a limited choice of answers are generally used since open ones allow too many variable responses. Yes or no answers may be required or respondents may have to choose a single answer from a number of alternatives. Opinion can be measured by offering a scale of fixed points, running from a positive view to a negative one, though it is important to ensure that there are as many positive options available in each question as there are negative ones.

Activity

Choose **three** different methods of selecting a sample of 50 students from your school or college. Ask each sample to complete the short questionnaire set out below.

Summer holiday choice survey

Tick the boxes after the answers which apply to you.

1 **Age**   under 12 ☐   12-14 ☐   14-16 ☐   over 16 ☐
2 **Gender**   Female   ☐   Male   ☐
3 **Destination of main holiday** taken between 1 June and 31 August last year:
   Town/nearest town: _____
   Country: _____
4 **Length of the holiday:**
   Less than one week ☐   One week ☐
   Between one and two weeks ☐   Two weeks ☐   More than two weeks ☐
5 **Distance travelled to destination:**
   Less than 50 miles☐   50-100 miles ☐
   100-200 miles   ☐   over 200 miles ☐
6 **Transport used to get there (mark more than one where appropriate):**
   own car ☐   hire car ☐   coach ☐   bus ☐
   taxi ☐   ferry ☐   hovercraft ☐   ship ☐   aeroplane ☐
7 **Number travelling in the party:**
   alone ☐ two ☐   three ☐   four ☐
   larger family group   ☐   organized group ☐
8 **Type of accommodation used:**
   tent   ☐   caravan   ☐   apartment   ☐   holiday camp ☐
   chalet   ☐   guest house ☐   small hotel ☐   large hotel   ☐
   house   ☐
9 **Attractions visited:**
   historic building ☐   museum ☐   art gallery   ☐
   sports event   ☐   dance/music festival ☐   funfair☐
   gardens   ☐   amusement park☐   ancient monument   ☐
10 **Activities participated in:**
   walking   ☐   swimming   ☐   sunbathing   ☐   fishing☐
   other sports   ☐   sightseeing ☐   shopping   ☐

---

1 Collate the results provided from each of the three different samples.
2 Discuss the possible reasons for differences between the three sets of results.
3 Decide which sample you think would yield the most reliable results and explain why.

14.2 Types of data

Quantitative data

Quantitative data, as the name suggests, are data which can be counted or measured. A large hotel, for example, might collect daily figures for all of the following:

- the average room rate guests have paid;
- the rate of occupancy of rooms;
- the actual number of guests;
- the number of covers in the restaurant;
- the debts still owing and the bills due to be paid;
- the payroll costs compared with the turnover.

The main objective of most businesses is to make a profit and therefore it is important that they continually evaluate their financial performance using all the relevant data obtainable. This often involves working to targets or standards which can differ, depending on the section of the business to which they are being applied. A marketing department cannot be evaluated in the same way as a kitchen. A restaurant or hotel kitchen will probably measure its performance on the basis of its percentage gross profit. This figure is produced by subtracting the cost of food from its selling price. Many hotels will operate on a figure of about 65 per cent, in other words if the cost of the food for a meal in the hotel restaurant is 35 pence, the selling price will be £1.

Restaurants can manipulate their gross profit in a number of ways. They can change the weight or size of the portions they are serving. If they buy an apple pie for £3, the cost of serving individual meals can be reduced by dividing the pie into eight portions rather than six. The number of covers, or individual customers, they serve is another profit factor, since the cost of individual meals is lower per unit if 100 are being prepared rather than 20.

Businesses also have to evaluate the level of service they are providing in relation to the profit they have to make. A ratio of 1 waiter to 25 covers produces higher costs than 1:50, but on the other hand the level of service is improved. Staffing levels in larger facilities have to be monitored constantly. If holiday bookings show a sharp upturn in January a travel agency may have to consider taking on an extra travel counsellor; if a hotel's advanced bookings are low for the month ahead, the managing company may take on an extra sales executive or someone with the marketing expertise to set up and manage a special promotion.

How pricing policy can have an impact on company figures

Leisure and tourism facilities need to monitor closely how much they are charging for the services they offer. An airline may carry passengers on the same flight and in the same class who have paid different prices for their tickets as a result of different deals. Some may have obtained reductions because they are part of a group booking, others may have done so as a result of advanced booking. An aeroplane with a capacity of 200 may sell all the seats on a flight at £50, bringing a total revenue of £10,000. Selling half the seats at £100 each would bring the same revenue but leave passengers with more space, better service from the cabin crew and the chance of late sales of the remaining empty seats. A hotel which sells 50 rooms at £100 derives the same revenue as if it had sold 100 rooms at £50 but the staff costs of serving 100 rooms would be higher. Some hotels deliberately seek to target those willing to pay a higher rate, such as business clients, even though this may mean a lower occupancy rate than some of their competitors.

A large hotel will monitor its average room rate daily. Though they will have a rack rate, the standard charge used when the hotel is advertising its services, clients will actually pay different rates as a result of deals agreed between the hotel and tour operators, and discounts offered dependent on the length of stay. If the daily average room rate looks low the hotel may respond in two ways:

- they may send out a sales team to try and attract more custom from the corporate business market;
- they may also raise the minimum room rate at which they will accept any new business.

Room occupancy is clearly a very basic measure of a hotel's performance. Data will include the number of guests in each room because this information will be required in order to plan staffing levels. Single occupancy of 200 rooms would demand resources for preparing and serving 200 breakfasts, some of which would require room service. An average room occupancy of 1.5 would result in the figure rising to 300. Similarly, the numbers taking lunch and dinner in the restaurant have to be closely monitored so that sufficient staff are always available to provide the expected level of service. Occupancy is also measured by representing the number of rooms occupied as a percentage of the total number of rooms. In other words, if 100 of the 200 rooms are occupied the occupancy rate is said to be 50 per cent.

An aspect of the day-to-day running of a business which receives close daily attention, especially in difficult economic times, is sometimes called the **debtors' factor**. Tour operators often sign contracts with hotels which involve the block booking of rooms. They pay for these on agreed dates but are able to cancel any they do not require. They are usually required to pay a proportion of the cost of the rooms they book and then cancel, on the principle that the later they cancel, the higher the charge. At any given time a large hotel may be owed payments by other companies, while at the same time they themselves also owe substantial sums to suppliers. The debtors' factor involves managing the collection of debts and the settling of bills at times which will be most beneficial to the company, and which will avoid cash flow shortages.

Payroll, as a major business cost, is subjected to regular scrutiny by most leisure and tourism companies. Payroll includes the gross pay of all employees, as well as the employers' contributions to national insurance and, where applicable, superannuation schemes. Payroll is often expressed as a percentage of turnover and regular reviews seek to ensure that this percentage does not rise above an agreed level. It is likely to be higher when business is quiet, but will fall during months of peak business. If the average percentage is regarded as too high, a company could take any of the following actions:

- reduce the number of staff employed;
- reduce the hours of employees;
- hold pay rates at their current level;
- take no action to fill staff vacancies.

Qualitative data

Qualitative data about a leisure and tourism facility would give a means of evaluating how it was performing in areas which were impossible to measure numerically. These would include areas like levels of service, efficiency, politeness of staff, quality of equipment and cleanliness of the premises.

Five of the most common methods of gathering qualitative data are:

- customer questionnaires;
- complimentary and complaint letters;
- observations and reports compiled by duty staff;
- employee surveys;
- company inspections and reviews.

Visitor questionnaires are commonly used to gather evidence of how facilities and attractions are rated in terms of value for money, appearance, service and comfort. Attractions may distribute these to selected visitors as they leave; hotels may leave them out in bedrooms and in restaurants. They are likely to be much more general than reviews conducted by the company owning the facility. Hotel groups, for example, may conduct a detailed **quality audit** which checks very specific details such as when the mattresses were last turned, whether the coffee served was hot and how many rings were heard on reception telephones before they were answered.

Crown classifications at a hotel entrance

Some leisure and tourism facilities are subject to regular inspections. The purpose of these may be to check that they are complying with health and safety regulations or they may be to check their quality on behalf of another commercial organization such as a publisher. For example, a restaurant may be inspected anonymously on behalf of the publishers of a restaurant guide. Various schemes to grade the facilities and service available in hotels depend on similar inspections. The AA and RAC will grade hotels mainly according to the facilities they offer. Guides appearing under the names of Egon Ronay and Michelin will also focus on the quality of food, accommodation and service provided. The English Tourist Board, through the regional tourist boards, has introduced the crown classification scheme which also lists three quality levels for hotels – approved, commended and highly commended. Classification is awarded on the basis of inspections and a highly commended grading requires at least 60 per cent of all the aspects inspected to be judged 'excellent'.

Activity

Below is a set of standards developed for a national scheme called 'Investors in People'. The standards are intended to reflect successful business practice and to help companies to evaluate their own performance as an employer by providing information which will enable them to answer questions like these.

- Are our employees getting the most out of their jobs?
- Are our customers getting the most out of our staff?
- Do our employees have the skills which the company needs?

Choose a leisure or tourism facility which intends to seek recognition as 'An Investor in People'. Draw up a plan of action, identifying what the main priorities should be.

National Standard for Effective Investment in People

An Investor in People makes a public commitment from the top to develop all employees to achieve its business objectives.

☐ Every employer should have a written but flexible plan which sets out business goals and targets, considers how employees will contribute to achieving the plan and specifies how development needs in particular will be assessed and met.

☐ Management should develop and communicate to all employees a vision of where the organisation is going and the contribution employees will make to its success, involving employee representatives as appropriate.

An Investor in People regularly reviews the training and development needs of all employees.

☐ The resources for training and developing employees should be clearly identified in the business plan.

☐ Managers should be responsible for regularly agreeing training and development needs with each employee in the context of business objectives, setting targets and standards linked, where appropriate, to the achievement of National Vocational Qualifications (or relevant units) and, in Scotland, Scottish Vocational Qualifications.

An Investor in People takes action to train and develop individuals on recruitment and throughout their employment.

☐ Action should focus on the training needs of all new recruits and continually developing and improving the skills of existing employees.

M All employees should be encouraged to contribute to identifying and meeting their own job-related development needs.

An Investor in People evaluates the investment in training and development to assess achievement and improve future effectiveness.

☐ The investment, the competence and commitment of employees, and the use made of skills learned should be reviewed at all levels against business goals and targets.

☐ The effectiveness of training and development should be reviewed at the top level and lead to renewed commitment and target setting.

14.3 Interpretation of data

Reliability

It is important that data used for evaluation purposes should be reliable. Users of data derived from surveys need to be confident that identical surveys carried out with different groups of respondents would produce similar information, as long as the sampling methods were the same. The reliability of data will also depend on factors like the consistent use of questions selected and the approaches taken by interviewers who ask them. Unreliable information will result if not all respondents are asked the same questions or if interviewers take different approaches to different respondents.

Some types of data collection require particular care in ensuring reliability. For example, a retail audit of travel agencies assessing their brochure displays could produce a very unrepresentative picture. Brochures are seasonal and what is on display in an individual agency one week may be quite different from what is there the following week. Their presence in sufficient numbers may depend on others meeting schedules, such as printers and distributors. Another difficulty in such a survey is the impossibility of predicting the frequency with which individual brochures will be requested or removed from displays by customers. Some travel agency chains, especially those which have business links with major tour operators, may have a policy to display only a limited number of brochures. Any of these factors could produce an untypical brochure display in an agency forming part of a survey sample. Data based on a sample containing several untypical displays would not give a reliable picture of the situation as a whole.

The type of sample used will also be a factor in deciding how reliable survey data are. Asking every tenth person whether they enjoyed a visit to Alton Towers might not reflect the full spectrum of visitor types. In other words it would be possible by this method not to have asked the question to anyone over 50 years of age. **Quota sampling**, which asked the question according to the proportion of different types and ages of visitors received overall, would provide more reliable data.

Validity

For a survey to be valid, it must demonstrably measure what it is intended to measure. A survey designed to test the degree of interest in sailing nationally would be unwise to use a sample based solely in Birmingham, where sailing facilities are limited, or Cowes, where they are much more common. The data gathered would be valid for those particular regions but would be unlikely to reflect the national level of interest.

Issues connected with surveying consumer attitudes towards various alcoholic drinks could illustrate the question of validity well. A survey may set out to measure general likes and dislikes, regardless of brand. If the whole content of the survey was 20 short questions, 15 of which concentrated on beer and lager, the data produced would probably be reliable in the sense that the data would indicate some facts about beer and lager. However, the data produced from such a survey could not be a valid measure of consumer views about alcoholic drinks generally. The data would be invalid because only five questions would have been devoted to all other types of alcoholic beverage and also because at least one question should have been used to establish which respondents do not like alcoholic drinks at all.

Difficulties of comparing data

In order to judge business performance over a particular period, data are often compared with previous performance. There are a number of reasons why a set of financial figures do not always tell the whole story. These include:

- the time period compared may not be exactly identical (e.g. months with different numbers of trading days);
- costs may be affected by seasonal factors (e.g. in catering the varying costs of meat);
- costs may increase towards the end of a financial year because more staff are required to attend meetings and replacements have to be taken on;
- external factors such as the Gulf War, recession or rail strikes may affect business in particular years;
- leisure and tourism businesses may be affected by movable holidays such as Easter, and many are particularly susceptible to changes in the weather;
- the poor performance of a single area of business can be hidden by its inclusion in a larger, more successful area.

The data shown in Figure 14.1 analyse the age groups of visitors to the Imperial War Museum, the Cabinet War Rooms, HMS Belfast and Duxford Airfield. Though a number of conclusions could be drawn from this data alone, it would be unwise to do so without also looking at the total number of visitors surveyed at each site, the location of the four sites, the type of marketing each carries out and the different facilities available at each one.

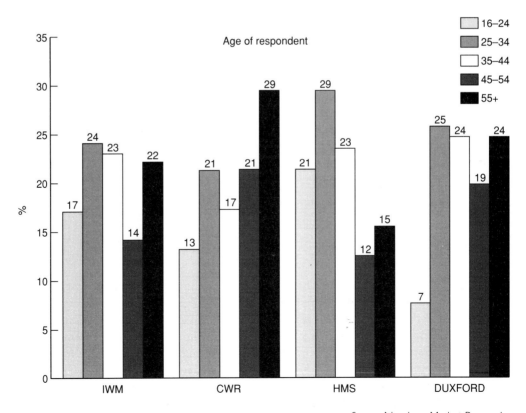

Source: Numbers Market Research

Figure 14.1 Imperial War Museum sites visitors survey

Qualitative data raise even more difficulties. The data collected are determined largely by the nature of the questions asked and the sample to whom they are presented. Asking tourists whether they enjoyed their holiday will generate different responses from asking them what complaints they had. An additional problem is that, whatever the question, responses about quality are subjective and may even be contradictory. Hotel guest questionnaires may receive responses on the same day from guests indicating that the hotel was both too hot and too cold. Guests may say identical beds are either too soft or too hard. Whether or not a tourist destination is judged to be too noisy depends very much on the expectations of individual tourists.

Activity

Easthampton has two leisure centres, East Vale and West Vale, both built at the same time and in a similar condition. Lack of funds means that one of the two will have to close. Study the data in Tables 14.1 and 14.2 about the performance of the two centres.

Table 14.1 East Vale Leisure Centre

(a) Number of users who have made previous visits (%)

	1989	1990	1991	1992
none	71	56	51	48
one	25	35	36	30
two or three	4	7	9	15
four or more	0	2	4	7

(b) % of visitors using different facilities (surveyed 6/92)

main hall	35%	swimming pool	42%
bar	67%	keep fit centre	11%
squash courts	2%		

(total users 1,380 for survey week 7–14 June 1992)

Table 14.2 West Vale Leisure Centre

(a) Number of users who have made previous visits (%)

	1990	1991	1992
none	32	30	24
one	27	21	15
more than one	41	39	61

(b) Number of users of each facility during week ending 14 June 1992

	Sat	Sun	Mon	Tue	Wed	Thu	Fri
swimming pool	412	288	73	53	45	35	70
main hall	85	*	61	77	70	51	64
weights room	*	*	16	*	22	*	30
bar	495	339	76	69	72	46	185

* facility closed

Write a short report indicating which of the two centres you would recommend for closure on the basis of this data alone.

Conclude your report by indicating:

- what difficulties there are in comparing the data provided for the two different centres;
- what other data would be useful in helping you to make a more informed decision.

14.4 How businesses assess their performance

External research

Many businesses purchase research from market research companies. In the case of a leisure and tourism company they may also purchase surveys and reports from the British Tourist Authority (BTA). Data derived from these sources can then be compared with data obtained from the company's own research. In this way a company can decide how it is performing in relation to the overall travelling and purchasing habits of its likely markets. It can also estimate how its performance might stand alongside that of its competitors.

These types of data are commonly used in major tourist attractions. Madame Tussauds, for example, buy in all of the following research:

Visits to Tourist Attractions (statistics compiled by the BTA);
The International Passenger Survey (a government survey);
Insights (a tourism marketing intelligence service);
The London Visitor Survey;
The UK Tourism Survey.

Such reports will provide information about the number of visitors to different attractions. The accuracy of the data are dependent on how carefully the criteria for categorizing the data are applied. For example, it is much easier to count admissions to a tourist attraction where a standard entrance fee is applied. Where there is a range of admission charges or where entrance is free, the methods of establishing exact visitor numbers may be less precise. However, increasing competition between attractions has led to more standardization of surveys so that comparisons of one set of data with another can be made more directly.

Another difficulty with using purchased data is the fact that they are often not sufficiently up to date. Attractions like Madame Tussauds, making planning decisions in June 1993, find that the most recent national tourism statistics are for 1991. The UK Tourism Survey may not be available until the October following the year to which its data relate. The leisure and tourism industry is very susceptible to both economic and political change, and this makes the use of data from previous years particularly problematic.

Internal research

Internal research, though not necessarily carried out by the company itself, is conducted on-site. With tourist attractions this often takes the form of a visitor audit. Madame

Tussauds interview a random sample of 3,500 individual visitors annually, covering the following areas:

- nationality;
- age and social class;
- party size and mix;
- day of the week and time of year of visits;
- method of entry into London;
- length of stay;
- first and repeat visits to London and to the attraction;
- awareness of the attraction and how they found out about it;
- length of the queues;
- satisfaction with different aspects of the exhibition;
- value provided by catering and merchandising;
- familiarity with different media.

The internal research conducted with a known sample size enables Tussauds to weight data derived from the visitor audit as a proportion of the total number of visitors annually. In other words, if the nationality of 35 of the 3,500 interviewed was French and the annual admissions totalled 1 million, the attraction could estimate that it had received 10,000 French visitors a year.

It is much easier to keep internal research up to date. Tussauds' managers will meet to discuss quarterly results. Comparisons may be drawn, with figures produced in the corresponding quarter of the previous year. Data may indicate that visitors from specific countries have fallen, a trend which might lead to more sales trips to these places. The figures could suggest that the travelling habits of people from these countries has changed. They may be travelling more as individuals than in group parties, so that Tussauds might decide to promote the attraction at public shows rather than trade fairs for tour operators.

Financial targets

Attractions like Alton Towers will evaluate their performance against financial targets. They will aim to achieve a return on the capital which has been invested during the year, as well as achieving a profit in their trading activities. New attractions, such as EuroDisney, need high investment for construction, fees and salaries before they have achieved any income. Newer attractions will aim to use a proportion of their own assets to invest in research and development. Banks and other financial backers could have secured interest by investing their money elsewhere and so they expect some financial reward in return for putting money into a project whose financial success is not yet certain.

Example of performance measures used to set targets in two travel shops, both retail outlets of a national company

The two sets of figures which follow in Tables 14.3 and 14.4 are for a small Midlands travel office and a larger travel office in the south-east of England.

Table 14.3 October 1993 Operating statement – small Midlands office

	October actual	%	October budget	%	October last year	%
Sales						
Air business	59,655	46.2	78,228	46.5	91,651	58.8
Air tickets for leisure	21,770	16.9	26,220	15.6	25,281	16.2
Total air	81,425	63.1	104,448	62.1	116,932	75.0
Package holidays	20,721	16.0	33,194	19.7	15,490	9.9
Hotel accommodation	11,487	8.9	7,983	4.7	4,834	3.1
Car rental	4,138	3.2	6,675	4.0	6,920	4.4
Insurance	1,160	0.9	3,013	1.8	2,476	1.6
Sea/cruise	2,840	2.2	3,157	1.9	414	0.3
Rail/ferry	7,349	5.7	9,624	5.7	8,783	5.6
Other	3	0.0	90	0.1	0	0.0
TOTAL	129,123	100.0	168,184	100.0	155,849	100.0
Travel commissions						
Air business	5,084	8.5	6,884	8.8	8,504	9.3
Air tickets for leisure	2,262	10.4	2,622	10.0	2,797	11.1
Total air	7,346	9.0	9,506	9.1	11,301	9.7
Package holidays	3,022	14.6	3,319	10.0	1,876	12.1
Hotel accommodation	423	3.7	595	7.5	457	9.5
Car rental	515	12.4	496	7.4	610	8.8
Insurance	580	50.0	1,624	53.9	1,343	54.2
Sea/cruise	114	4.0	316	10.0	54	13.0
Rail/ferry	812	11.0	866	9.0	852	9.7
Other	3	100.0	0	0.0	0	0.0
Total gross revenue	12,815	9.9	16,722	9.9	16,493	10.6
Card discount	(1,202)	0.0	(1,209)	0.0	(1,391)	0.0
Business discount	(897)	0.0	(840)	0.0	(1,124)	0.0
OCT discount	(444)	0.0	(631)	0.0	(248)	0.0
TOTAL	10,272	8.0	14,042	8.3	13,730	8.8
Income from foreign currency and T/C sales						
Foreign money	9,137	46.6	9,215	51.2	8,760	53.9
Foreign exchange	5,025	25.6	3,949	21.9	3,210	19.7
T/C sales commission	4,036	20.6	3,313	18.4	2,288	14.1
T/C incentives	0	0.0	511	2.8	1,503	9.2
Service fees	919	4.7	835	4.6	327	2.0
Other finance and service revenue	499	2.5	175	1.0	179	1.1
TOTAL F & S	19,616	100.0	17,998	100.0	16,267	100.0
Other income	(350)	0.0	(292)	0.0	(230)	0.0
TOTAL REVENUE	29,538	22.9	31,748	18.9	29,767	19.1
Expenses						
Regular payroll	7,595	25.7	7,420	23.4	7,235	24.3
Temp payroll	1,120	3.8	470	1.5	952	3.2
Overtime	102	0.3	95	0.3	155	0.5
Commissions	(30)	-0.1	196	0.6	521	1.8
Employment costs	1,707	5.8	1,736	5.5	1,455	4.9

Table 14.3 *Continued*

	October actual	%	October budget	%	October last year	%
Outside temps	0	0.0	0	0.0	270	0.9
Employee activity	151	0.5	80	0.3	88	0.3
TOTAL EMPLOYMENT COSTS	10,645	36.0	9,997	31.5	10,676	35.9
Rent	2,036	6.9	2,917	9.2	2,406	8.1
Property taxes	485	1.6	679	2.1	334	1.1
Utilities	163	0.6	458	1.4	225	0.8
DP	2,397	8.1	1,317	4.1	1,154	3.9
Equipment costs	423	1.4	808	2.5	496	1.7
General office supplies	1,038	3.5	459	1.4	631	2.1
Telephone	1,608	5.4	1,826	5.8	1,862	6.3
Postage/courier	759	2.6	597	1.9	402	1.4
Travel and meeting	307	1.0	251	0.8	(256)	-0.9
Other operating	540	1.8	367	1.2	501	1.7
TOTAL OPERATING COSTS	20,401	69.1	19,676	62.0	18,429	61.9
Advertising	(580)	-2.0	292	0.9	1,401	4.7
Provision for losses	194	0.7	83	0.3	387	1.3
Interest expense	0	0.0	0	0.0	54	0.2
TOTAL EXPENSES	20,015	67.8	20,051	63.2	20,271	68.1
Pre-tax income	9,523	32.2	11,697	36.8	9,496	31.9
NET INCOME	9,523	32.2	11,697	36.8	9,496	31.9

Headcount: 8 employees

Table 14.4 October 1993 Operating statement – Large south-east office

	October actual	%	October budget	%	October last year	%
Sales						
Air business	275,343	53.0	248,040	45.9	225,721	48.7
Air tickets for leisure	103,966	20.0	125,400	23.2	117,605	25.4
Total air	379,309	73.0	373,440	69.1	343,326	74.1
Package holidays	89,173	17.2	111,577	20.7	68,529	14.8
Hotel accommodation	23,145	4.5	18,040	3.3	21,496	4.6
Car rental	9,681	1.9	9,922	1.8	11,169	2.4
Insurance	7,293	1.4	10,734	2.0	7,888	1.7
Sea/cruise	200	0.0	3,608	0.7	1,962	0.4
Rail/ferry	10,853	2.1	12,628	2.3	8,567	1.9
Other	31	0.0	361	0.1	104	0.0
TOTAL	519,685	100.0	540,310	100.0	463,041	100.0
Travel commissions						
Air business	24,833	9.0	22,324	9.0	20,032	9.3
Air tickets for leisure	10,418	10.0	13,148	10.5	10,835	9.2
Total air	35,251	9.3	35,472	9.5	31,867	9.3

Table 14.4 *Continued*

	October actual	%	October budget	%	October last year	%
Package holidays	10,537	11.8	11,546	10.3	9,144	13.3
Hotel accommodation	2,009	8.7	1,624	9.0	1,935	9.0
Car rental	959	9.9	1,091	11.0	935	8.4
Insurance	3,627	49.7	5,773	53.8	4,324	54.8
Sea/cruise	0	0.0	361	10.0	101	5.1
Rail/ferry	1,192	11.0	1,173	9.3	799	9.3
Other	30	96.8	289	80.1	101	97.1
Total gross revenue	53,572	10.3	57,329	10.6	49,206	10.6
Card discount (1)	(2,472)	0.0	(2,977)	0.0	(2,460)	0.0
Business discount (2)	(1,139)	0.0	(2,385)	0.0	(1,409)	0.0
OCT discount	(1,632)	0.0	(631)	0.0	(291)	0.0
TOTAL	48,329	9.3	51,336	9.5	45,046	9.7
Income from foreign currency and T/C sales						
Foreign money	16,284	56.2	18,868	52.4	16,374	57.7
Foreign exchange	7,473	25.8	8,557	23.8	6,198	21.8
T/C sales commission	2,841	9.8	4,169	11.6	2,473	8.7
T/C incentives	0	0.0	658	1.8	1,164	4.1
Service fees	1,692	5.8	2,414	6.7	1,508	5.3
Other finance and service revenue	676	2.3	1,316	3.7	669	2.4
TOTAL F & S	28,966	100.0	35,982	100.0	28,386	100.0
Other income	(1,330)	0.0	(1,667)	0.0	(2.030)	0.0
TOTAL REVENUE	75,965	14.6	85,651	15.9	71,402	15.4
Expenses						
Regular payroll	23,309	30.7	22,075	25.8	18,186	25.5
Temp payroll	525	0.7	257	0.3	675	0.9
Overtime	63	0.1	306	0.4	753	1.1
Commissions	3,936	5.2	1,014	1.2	1,117	1.6
Employment costs	4,984	6.6	4,797	5.6	4,225	5.9
Outside temps	0	0.0	0	0.0	0	0.0
Employee activity	0	0.0	200	0.2	0	0.0
TOTAL EMPLOYMENT COSTS	32,817	43.2	28,649	33.4	24,956	35.0
Rent	8,738	11.5	9,717	11.3	10,535	14.8
Property taxes	2,333	3.1	2,500	2.9	1,997	2.8
Utilities	1,650	2.2	1,250	1.5	1,651	2.3
DP	3,996	5.3	3,250	3.8	1,455	2.0
Equipment costs	800	1.1	1,928	2.3	1,386	1.9
General office supplies	1,846	2.4	1,193	1.4	779	1.1
Telephone	(151)	-0.2	2,739	3.2	272	0.4
Postage/courier	2,513	3.3	1,652	1.9	1,552	2.2
Travel and meeting	827	1.1	418	0.5	766	1.1
Other operating	5,910	7.8	1,075	1.3	1,173	1.6
TOTAL OPERATING COSTS	61,279	80.7	54,371	63.5	46,522	65.2
Advertising	(389)	-0.5	667	0.8	1,386	1.9
Provision for losses	1,515	2.0	167	0.2	446	0.6

Table 14.4 *Continued*

	October actual	%	October budget	%	October last year	%
Interest expense	0	0.0	0	0.0	75	0.1
TOTAL EXPENSES	62,405	82.1	55,205	64.5	48,429	67.8
Pre-tax income	13,560	17.9	30,446	35.5	22,973	32.2
NET INCOME	13,560	17.9	30,446	35.5	22,973	32.2

Headcount: 25 employees

The performance of the two travel offices can be compared in a number of ways. The performance is usually measured as a percentage since this enables easy comparisons to be made, either over a period of time or between different units of the business. The main performance measures used are as follows.

Total expenses to revenues (per cent) Total expenses must be covered by revenues or else a business will make a loss and eventually have to close down.

Return on revenue (net income as percentage of total revenue) If total expenses account for 67.8 per cent of total revenue, as they do in the October figures for the small Midlands office, the net income is the remaining 32.2 per cent because net income = total revenues – total expenses. This return on revenue figure (ROR) is very important to business proprietors because if it is very low they might choose to give up their businesses and merely invest capital for very little risk and without any labour, and enjoying at least an equivalent rate of interest. Percentage figures enable easy identification of trends in revenues, expenses and, therefore, income. They are also important in setting targets. A travel company with a chain of outlets is likely to set an ROR target somewhere in the region of 30 per cent.

Employment costs to revenue (per cent) Employment costs are frequently one of the highest costs to an employer and therefore the percentage which employment costs show when compared to revenues is a key indicator. Employment costs on their own might eat up 36 per cent or more of total revenues. Performance here will have to take account of regional differences in wage and salary levels. Headcount in a company with a number of outlets may be used to calculate the amount of revenue each employer generates. For example, for each £1 it costs to employ them, they may generate £1.50 in revenue.

Return on sales (net income to total sales as percentage) This indicates the amount of money which can be made from a particular volume of sales. For example £9,523 can be made on total sales of £129,123 in the small Midlands office, representing 7.37 per cent return on sales. It might be that there are products with better margins and therefore, even with lower total sales figures, net income would be increased. A net income of £10,000 from total sales of £100,000 would represent a 10 per cent return on sales.

Sales per head (total sales divided by headcount) Employers often look carefully at staffing levels. In the small Midlands office 8 people selling £129,123 achieve £16,140 each. The larger south-east office has 25 staff and sells £519,685 or £20,787 per head. Though the smaller unit appears to be performing less well, factors like location, staff time spent on administration and sales potential may account for the diffference. The larger office is likely to be able to profit from economies of scale, particularly in terms of having a lower ratio of higher paid managers to general office staff who can devote all their time to sales.

All companies aim to make a trading profit. They expect their sales to exceed their costs by a wide enough margin to enable them to generate a return on capital investment. The data needed to evaluate profit usually take the form of a **profit and loss account**. This gives a measure of financial performance over a period of time. Such data are often produced on a quarterly basis in order to avoid the problems of comparing monthly figures, which can be subject to unpredicted fluctuations.

Drawing conclusions from internal research

Quarterly financial data are often used to compare business performance in different years on a seasonal basis. If results improve, fresh research and development may be planned. If they deteriorate, it may prove necessary to reduce costs. Various ways of increasing income may be sought. A visitor attraction might seek to increase its number of visitors by offering discounts. They could raise admission prices but, unless they are able to demonstrate that they have added value to the product, this might deter potential visitors. The need for additional value in order to attract more people and raise income demonstrates the close connection between profit growth and capital investment.

The results of internal research are also compared with data from external research. For example, the International Passenger Survey can be used to show the number of people from a particular country coming to London for a holiday or to visit friends and relatives. Madame Tussauds can use its own visitor audit to establish the number of visitors it receives from the same country and, by comparing the two figures, can assess its own share of that particular market. If half of all Germans visiting London come to Madame Tussauds, but only 1 in 25 of all Americans do so, the company will need to assess the potential reasons for this difference and to establish whether they can do anything about it.

Not all internal research is quantitative. Qualitative data are needed particularly for advertising research and for new product development.

Internal research for 'The Spirit of London' ride

In 1993 Madame Tussauds opened a dark ride tracing the history of London. Research was needed to ensure that the development would be well received by the public. Eight discussion groups were established, each with a different character. These included groups of children, teenagers, young independent people and families. Half the members of each group had visited Tussauds before and of these half expressed a keenness to visit the attraction again.

The groups were taken through the existing Tussauds exhibition and their comments were taped. They were then shown stimulus material relating to the new ride, including models, commentary and examples of animatronic figures to be featured. A professional moderator was used to encourage discussion and to analyse what lay behind the responses. The prime objective of the research was to help the company to decide how to communicate the new ride successfully to the public. Broad issues about what to call it were considered, alongside more specific ones about the impact of the commentary.

Quality standards

Quality standards are increasingly used as a means of evaluating leisure and tourism companies. Induction training will set out these standards and communicate them to individual employees. American Express, for example, sets out company standards which cover telephone use, reservations, documentation, customer service and employee appearance. Some of the standards, such as the time taken from the receipt of a ticket to processing it, can be measured on a weekly basis in individual travel centres. The internal publication of results provides one measure of the company's efficiency.

Quality standards generally cover all forms of communication. General guidelines or specific structures may be applied to written documents. Most leisure and tourism companies will offer their staff quite specific training in how they should approach and communicate with customers orally.

An example of an American Express Quality Standard
The quality standard: All customers awaiting service to be acknowledged and/or greeted correctly as soon as possible.
Definition: Although you may be unable to give a customer your attention immediately, make them aware that you know they are waiting:
- Establish eye contact
- Always smile when you greet the customer
- Greet them with 'Good morning/afternoon'
- Use the customer's name when known
- Ask open questions showing enthusiasm

Contingency plans need to be developed to ensure that the quality of service does not fall when a company is hit by staff absence or by unforeseen emergencies. When things do go wrong it is important to assess the causes so that preventative measures can be introduced. Often problems can be avoided by making sure all staff are well versed in company policy, as well as in any relevant laws and regulations which govern the company's activities.

Activity

Study the data in Table 14.5, based on opinions sought from visitors to London about the quality of food provided in restaurants and pubs:

Table 14.5 Quality of food in restaurants (waiter/ess service) and pub/wine bars

	Summer 1991	
Base: All overseas visitors 1200	**Restaurants**	**Pubs/Wine Bars**
Very Good (5)	13	8
Good (4)	38	28
Average (3)	20	17
Poor (2)	6	6
Very Poor (1)	2	1
Don't know	22	40
*Mean Score**	3.68	3.59

* The mean score has been calculated on the sample base which excludes the 'don't knows'.

Source: London Tourist Board

Discuss, offering reasons in each case, which of the following conclusions can be supported by the data and which cannot.

1 The quality of food was thought to be better in restaurants than in pubs.
2 Visitors to London tend to find food prices more expensive than at home.
3 Service in restaurants was thought to be better than that in pubs and wine bars.
4 Almost half of those questioned had not eaten in either a pub or a wine bar.
5 Sixty-two per cent of those questioned did not know what the quality of food was like in either type of facility.
6 Overall the quality of food was thought to be above average.
7 People don't like to be too critical when responding to questions asked by natives of the country they are visiting.
8 The survey doesn't give an accurate picture because it includes opinions of those who didn't eat in restaurants and those who didn't eat in pubs.

Assignment 14
Evaluation through research and data analysis

This assignment develops knowledge and understanding of the following elements:
1.1 Describe the scale and contexts of the leisure and tourism industry
1.4 Identify sources of income for leisure and tourism facilities
8.3 Evaluate the performance of a facility

It supports development of the following core skills:
Communication 3.2, 3.3, 3.4
Application of number 3.3

Your tasks

1 Collect the annual reports for the same year of three companies operating in the leisure and tourism industry, either by writing to a selection of businesses, or by referring to school or college travel and tourism resources.
2 Prepare a report for a potential investor, reviewing and commenting on the performance of the three companies over the year in question.

You should explain, using evidence drawn both from within the reports and from other sources commenting on the economic prospects for various sectors of leisure and tourism, which of the three you think would prove the most profitable investment for the coming year.

15   Legal constraints on leisure and tourism development

What is covered in this chapter

This chapter gives an introduction to the need for legislation and regulation. It discusses the manner in which legislation both constrains and facilitates development, and analyses the basic legislation affecting organizations. It examines the fundamental legal constraints on private, voluntary and public sectors, and the role of the Department of National Heritage and other central government departments. It shows the nature and role of statutory organizations in the regulation of leisure and tourism development, and identifies development regulations which particularly affect the leisure and tourism industry.

- The need for legislation and regulation
- Statutory bodies
- Organizational legislation
- Development regulations
- Fundamental legal constraints

15.1 The need for legislation and regulation

The key to understanding the need for regulation and legislation in today's society lies in analysing human behaviour. While it is true that humans have become social beings – living in rational, civilized communities – they still retain certain characteristics which make legislation and regulation necessary. Such rules attempt to ensure that people live together harmoniously, despite basic human competitive instincts. Although competition is encouraged in a free enterprise economy such as that in Britain, this rivalry must be conducted under fair and safe conditions. The framework that has been developed to guarantee these conditions is called the legal environment.

The study of law is a complicated process. Briefly, the law can be divided into four categories:

- **common law** – derived from custom and practice but now interpreted through case law:
- **civil law** – law governing the rights and responsibilities of individuals towards each other;
- **criminal law** – regulation protecting individuals and organizations from criminal actions;
- **statutory law** – laws and regulations created by Act of Parliament.

This analysis of legislation and regulation is concerned with laws passed by Parliament, the UK's principal law-making body. Successive governments over the past 100 years have passed innumerable Acts of Parliament which form the basis of statute law. These Acts include many specific pieces of legislation designed to amend previous statutes, tidy up legal loopholes or cope with the demands of a constantly changing society. The Health and Safety at Work Act 1974 is a good example of legislation which updates and unifies a mass of previously unconnected Acts. Similarly, the Development of Tourism Act 1969 is an example of new legislation designed to cope with the comparatively recent phenomenon of mass tourism.

If legislation is designed to ensure that people and organizations compete fairly and safely, then one can deduce that such legislation has a **constraining effect**. This may be true where, for example, new consumer legislation prohibits tour operators from making claims about holidays which cannot be fully substantiated. Holiday brochures are no longer allowed to talk about beaches being 'a stone's throw away' from the hotel. The complexity of such legislation may thus discourage new operators from entering the market. Yet, paradoxically, legislation may also have a **facilitating effect**. Any newcomer to package tour operations will know that there are basic rules governing the industry. The knowledge that established rivals are also bound by the same legislation will at least enable a new business to plan and compete on an equal footing.

This chapter does not set out to describe all legislation with relevance to this industry since there are well over 200 Acts of Parliament which affect leisure and tourism operations and development! It does, however, attempt to do two things:
- raise awareness of the breadth and complexity of this legislation;
- assist in finding more detailed information from appropriate sources.

Activity

The Monopolies and Mergers Commission is a statutory body which fulfils numerous functions. Under the terms of the Fair Trading Act 1973, one of these functions is to monitor any potential mergers of business organizations. The Commission scrutinizes such plans to guard against the creation of monopolies which may be deemed unfair or contrary to a competitive, free market business environment.

1 Suppose the two biggest tour operators, Thomson and Airtours, were proposing to merge, giving them a 75–80 per cent share of the package tour market. List the possible benefits and disadvantages which might be experienced by the consumer.
2 Explain why it was necessary to create a body such as the Monopolies and Mergers Commission. Try to illustrate your answer with examples from the leisure and tourism industry.
3 How does the existence of the Commission have both a constraining and facilitating effect on this industry? Give examples.

15.2 Organizational legislation

All organizations, like individual citizens, are subject to legislation and regulation. Whether in the private, public or voluntary sectors, managers in these organizations need to be aware of, and abide by, such legislation. Business law is a broad and complicated area. A wise manager ensures that he or she conforms to any operational procedures or, where appropriate, consults a professional adviser such as a solicitor or accountant. It is also a key role of management to ensure that staff are informed of their responsibilities and are trained to carry out any procedures prescribed by these rules.

Some legislation is general and applies to all organizations that employ staff or deal with the public. The Health and Safety at Work Act 1974 is a good example, being a crucial piece of legislation designed to protect the welfare of both staff and customers in any organization. Other legislation is quite specific, aimed at certain sectors, industries or even types of business. An indoor sports licence, for example, is only required by an organization holding a sporting event to which the public have been invited.

Activity

1 Why do you think public sporting events need to be licensed? Consider each of the following three examples: a football match; a rifle shooting championship; a sheep dog trial. What do you think would be the main criteria for granting each of these three public events a licence?
2 How do you think a professional adviser such as a solicitor or an accountant might help someone planning to start a leisure or tourism business?

15.3 Fundamental legal constraints

The private sector

Many businesses in the private sector are sole traders or partnerships. In other words they are owned by one or two individuals. Bed and breakfast establishments, small health and fitness studios, and even some travel agencies are businesses which can fall into this category. There are several advantages to this legal form of ownership, including:

- close control;
- ease of decision making;
- simplified operation;
- comparatively few legal requirements when setting up or closing down.

However, there can be disadvantages, especially when a business is trying to expand.

Expanding sole traders or partnerships often find it prudent to become limited liability companies. This can reduce the owner's liability in the event of financial problems and can sometimes make it easier to attract extra funding. However, limited companies are subject to a much more complicated range of legal obligations enforced by the Companies Act 1985. This Act is designed to protect the interests of investors and involves the business in much extra responsibility and paperwork, including:

- share issues;
- articles and memorandum of association;
- company taxation;
- annual general meetings;
- registration of audited accounts with the Registrar of Companies.

The decision to expand a successful business may also be constrained by much other relevant legislation. Expansion implies increased turnover and the inevitable crossing of the **VAT exemption limit**. This is an indirect tax on goods or services, collected for the government by businesses, requiring extensive record-keeping and quarterly reports. Increased turnover can usually only be achieved by increased staff levels. This in turn means the business has more complicated liability under the large range of employment legislation (see Chapter 16). In addition, all businesses are subject to much other basic legislation involving tax on profits, tax on capital gains, payment of business rates and insurance requirements. Small wonder that any guide to developing a small business advises consulting an accountant, a solicitor and a bank manager!

Activity

Imagine you are a small business adviser counselling Freddy Fence when he was selling ice-cream from a wheelbarrow. Freddy has told you of his plans to make his own ice-cream, the Trumpetto, into a household name by selling it through a nationwide chain of shops.

What would you advise him regarding the pros and cons of his plan?

The voluntary sector

Sport and recreation clubs and organizations in this sector make a huge contribution to leisure provision in the UK. Indeed, local organizations such as Sunday football teams or amateur dramatic groups play a crucial role in ensuring mass involvement in leisure activity. However, voluntary or amateur status does not exempt such organizations from the rules of the legal environment. They, too, are subject to fundamental legislation in terms of health and safety, events licensing, and food and hygiene. Thus bar and catering staff at a suburban theatre are just as bound by the Food Safety Act as their counterparts at the Royal Albert Hall. Cooking utensils must be properly cleaned and stored, regardless of the size or nature of the facility.

Many voluntary or amateur organizations take advantage of legislation allowing them to operate as charitable trusts. Charities can benefit financially from:

- grant aid for capital projects;
- rates or council tax discounts;
- tax exemptions and benefits;
- access to funding not available from the public sector.

However, charities are closely regulated by the Charities Commission. They too must be operated in accordance with the Companies Act, keeping proper records and submitting these to the Charity Commissioners annually.

The public sector

Although the public sector does not need to choose a legal 'form', its role in tourism and leisure development is still strongly affected by government legislation. For example, local authorities are obliged by law to maintain library services, allotment provision, and youth education and leisure facilities. However, due to economic or ideological reasons, recent governments have attempted to reduce public sector funding as much as possible. Through legislation such as the Local Government Act 1988, local authorities are being forced to involve private sector organizations much more. This Act, for example, made it compulsory for local authority leisure departments to put the management of their leisure services out to tender. This 'compulsory competitive tendering' forced local authorities to use competition between suppliers to obtain the best value for money.

The public sector is perhaps more affected by legislation than any other. It is not only obliged to abide by fundamental legislation affecting day-to-day operations such as employment and health and safety laws. Policy making and implementation in local authorities, statutory bodies and **quangos**, are also directly affected by central government legislation. For example local authorities are now forced, by law, to write development plans to ensure that resources are allocated and used in an efficient manner.

These organizations are also closely and crucially involved with both private and voluntary sector activity. Local authorities, for example, are large providers of leisure facilities, particularly of activities not profitable enough for private sector involvement. However, because of increasingly tight central government funding, many authorities are cutting back on non-mandatory expenditure which often includes leisure provision. Thus the role of local government is changing from that of leisure provider to leisure facilitator, encouraging private or voluntary sector involvement.

Tourism development in the UK has been similarly influenced by government legislation. The Development of Tourism Act 1969 authorized the establishment of the British Tourist Authority (BTA) and the national tourist boards of England, Scotland and Wales (ETB, STB and WTB). The BTA has sole responsibility for the marketing of Britain, as a tourist destination, to the rest of the world. The ETB, STB and WTB are responsible for the development and marketing of tourism products in their respective countries. These national boards combined with local authorities and private investors to create a network of regional tourist boards.

Originally, these public sector tourist organizations used central government funding to provide financial assistance for tourism development. Indeed one major part of the 1969 Act was the provision of financial assistance for the development of new or existing hotels. These 'section 4' grants and loans were used by the private sector to significantly upgrade the standard of British hotel accommodation, until funding ceased in 1989. Since that time the public sector has played a much more indirect role in tourism development in Britain. As with local authority leisure services, public sector tourism organizations are becoming promoters and facilitators rather than providers and funders.

Central government possesses and uses the power to influence directly development in all areas of the tourism and leisure industry. In addition to controlling public sector funding, government can pass legislation to change the statutory role of those public sector organizations charged with the provision and promotion of tourism and leisure facilities. Central government is thus severely constraining public sector tourism and leisure development while encouraging the expansion of private or voluntary sector involvement. Figure 15.1 illustrates the relationship between legislation and organizations from the public, private and voluntary sectors.

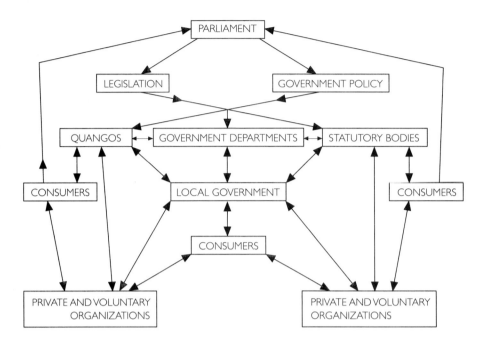

Figure 15.1 The relationship between legislation and the public, private and voluntary sectors

Activity

Teddy is a highly qualified and experienced swimming instructor at Horton Leisure Centre. He has been employed in local authority leisure facilities for nearly 20 years but only recently came to Horton. Like many staff at the centre, he is not happy with the current working environment and atmosphere. He feels that the centre has become too profit orientated and as a result staff are under a great deal of pressure. Due to personnel cutbacks, Teddy's general duties are now so onerous that he has little time for customer relations. Dealing with people was what had originally attracted him to the industry. He has also become frustrated with the increasing number of rules and regulations that he has to cope with. His favourite expression over the past few months has become 'Things aren't what they used to be' – and he is thinking of resigning.

1 Compose a letter on Teddy's behalf tendering his resignation and outlining the main reasons for his action. Treat this letter as a protest at the way local authority leisure provision has altered since his service began.
2 Imagine you are the manager at Horton Leisure Centre and you wish to improve staff/management relations. Write an article for the staff newsletter defending the changes that have occurred in the industry over the past few years.
You may find it helpful to visit your nearest local authority leisure facility and interview members of staff for further information or opinions.

15.4 Statutory bodies

It is clear that central government plays a crucial role in the regulation of the tourism and leisure industry, but the conversion of Parliamentary Bills into Acts of Parliament is only the beginning of the regulation process. In order to administer an ever expanding body of legislation, the government relies on a complex network of statutory organizations. Overseeing the tourism and leisure industry is the Department of National Heritage under the control of a full cabinet minister, the Secretary of State for National Heritage, who is responsible to the government for all activity within the industry. The department controls the many statutory bodies set up to regulate the industry such as the British Tourist Authority, the Arts Council and the Sports Council. These bodies also liaise with and sometimes control (either directly or indirectly) the myriad of private sector organizations which make up the industry. Figure 15.2 on page 266 outlines the main areas of responsibility of the Department of National Heritage.

In addition, the National Heritage department liaises with the numerous other government departments and bodies, which have a bearing on tourism and leisure development and regulation. For example, the National Heritage Minister has responsibility for tourism. Tourism is generally categorized into various sectors such as accommodation, transport and attractions, but clearly activity in any one of these sectors will involve other government departments. Expansion of the domestic tourism industry will mean job creation, something of vital interest to the Department of Employment. A new airline route to a major British city will need to be approved by the Civil Aviation Authority, a quango ultimately responsible to the Department of Transport. Tourism growth can lead to financial prosperity but often leads to severe environmental and social impacts. Both the Treasury and the Department of the Environment have vested interests in such developments. Table 15.1 on page 267 illustrates UK government departments and some of their areas of responsibility:

Activity

1 In groups of three or four, prepare a promotional booklet highlighting the role and activities of the Department of National Heritage. Concentrate on the three main sections which make up the Department: the Arts Group; the Broadcasting, Film and Sport Group; and the Heritage and Tourism Group. Pay particular attention to the way in which the department affects tourism and leisure development in public, private and voluntary sectors.
2 The Department of National Heritage was only established in 1992. Prior to this date, responsibility for tourism and leisure was divided between the following government departments:
   Environment – heritage policy;
   Employment – tourism policy;
   Education – sports policy;
   Home Office – broadcasting and media policy;
   Trade and Industry – film policy.

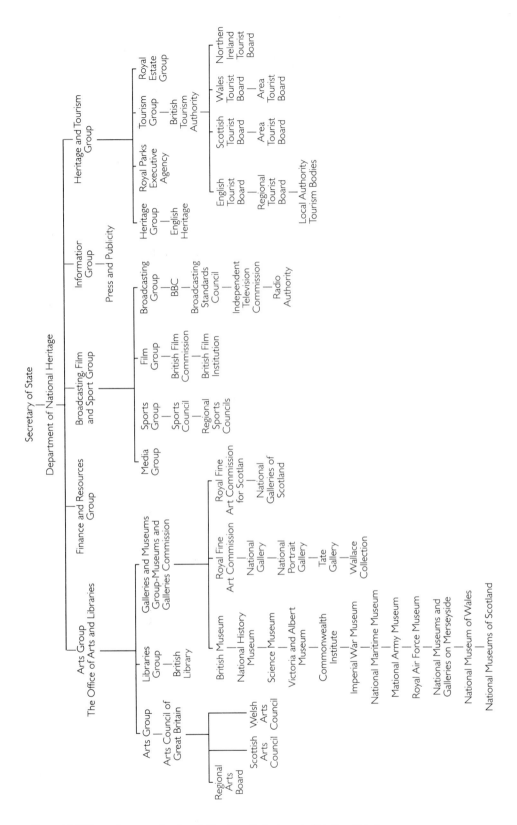

Figure 15.2 The main areas of responsibility of the Department of National Heritage

Table 15.1 UK government departments

The Treasury Bank of England Board of Customs and Excise Board of Inland Revenue	**Department of Trade and Industry** British Standards Institution The Charity Commission Office of Fair Trading
The Foreign Office The British Council	Monopolies and Mergers Commission National Consumer Council
The Home Office Police Department Equal Opportunities Department Commission for Racial Equality Immigration Department Nationality Department Equal Opportunities Commission Gaming Board for Great Britain Horserace Totalisator Board	**Department of Transport** Public Transport – London Regional Transport Railways – British Railways Board Urban and General Highways, Safety and Traffic Aviation, Shipping and International – Civil Aviation Authority – Port of London Authority British Waterways
Department of the Environment Local Government and Inner Cities Office Environment and Countryside Office Housing and Planning Office Local Commissioners Countryside Commission English Nature Joint Nature Conservation Committee Ordnance Survey	**Department of National Heritage** – see Figure 15.2 **Department of Agriculture, Food and Fisheries** Audit Commission Food Safety Countryside, Marine Environment and Fisheries Forestry Commission National Rivers Authority
The Welsh Office Countryside Council for Wales Historic Buildings Council for Wales Ancient Monuments Board for Wales National Library of Wales Land Authority for Wales	**The Scottish Office** Historic Buildings Council for Scotland Ancient Monuments Board for Scotland National Library of Scotland Scottish Law Commission Scottish Legal Aid Board Scottish Natural Heritage
The Lord Chancellor's Office Law Commissio Land Registries Legal Aid Board	**Department of Employment** Health and Safety Commission Health and Safety Executive
Department of Defence The Northern Ireland Office Department of Social Security Department for Education Department of Health	

Why do you think each particular department was allocated its area of tourism and leisure policy? What do you think were the main reasons for the creation of the Department of National Heritage?

3 Using your college or local library, name the secretaries of state responsible for each of the government departments listed in Table 15.1. Explain briefly how each of these departments may be affected by, or have an effect on, the tourism and leisure industry.

15.5 Development regulations

Any organization planning to build, expand, convert or even modernize premises will be subject to development regulations. It is compulsory to submit detailed plans for scrutiny by local authority planning departments before such work can be carried out. The basic legislation governing this type of development is the Town and Country Planning Acts and the Public Health Acts. Under the terms of these Acts local authorities are charged with enforcing any appropriate regulations governing the development of property. Table 15.2 outlines the main types of development regulations.

Activity

1 Suggest **four** examples of contrasting proposals for new leisure or tourism developments, such as the provision of catering facilities.
2 Discuss which of the regulations listed in Table 15.2 you think would be likely to apply to each of the development proposals.

European Community legislation

In addition to the wide range of UK legislation to be observed, tourism and leisure staff must also be increasingly aware of the impact of the European Community. EC member states now form one common trading block with many internal controls removed. The creation of this 'Single European Market' will enable workers to move and work freely in any member state. Similarly, organizations will now be able to exploit the creation of a huge domestic market, thus opening up innumerable opportunities for business expansion. The tourism and leisure industry will naturally be affected by these events. The removal of immigration and work permit controls will clearly affect employment patterns and conditions. Controls on the movement of capital between member states have also been removed. This may result in more investment funds reaching Britain, particularly for growth industries such as tourism and leisure.

EC member states are also subject to European legislation which takes three forms:

Decisions – binding instructions issued to specific organizations or individuals rather than to an entire country.

Table 15.2 Main types of development regulations

Regulation type	Activity	Regulating Officer
1 Planning permission	Required for any new building, site development, or major structural alteration or addition to an existing building. The addition of a squash court to a hotel would require such permission	Local authority planning officer
2 Change of use	Required if any plans are made to change the original use of a property. The conversion of a large house to a bed and breakfast establishment is clearly a 'material' change of use. Permission under this regulation is required even if no building work is needed.	Local authority planning officer
3 Building regulations	Any work involving structural alterations or change of use must be approved by a building control officer, before commencement. This is to ensure that design, materials and workmanship are all of an acceptable standard to guarantee public health and safety.	Local authority building control officer
4 Fire regulations	Designed to protect staff and customers. A fire certificate is required if, for example, more than six people are accommodated in a small hotel. These regulations also cover fire escapes and exits, the use of fire resistant materials and fire prevention measures.	Local fire authority fire safety officer
5 Food regulations	Based on the Food Safety Act 1990 and concern most organizations serving meals to customers. Local authority environmental health officers ensure that food is stored, processed and served in a safe manner. Food sales can be a lucrative way of increasing secondary spend in tourism and leisure but any business wishing to develop catering facilities must consider these regulations.	Local authority environmental health officers

Directives – instructions to member states that only become law by enactment via domestic legislation. For example the EC Directive on Package Travel, Package Holidays and Package Tours only came into force after regulations were drafted by the Department of Trade and Industry and passed by Parliament.

Regulations - automatically become law in each member state, superseding any original domestic law. From December 1993 the EC package holiday directive became a European regulation, thus becoming law in the UK regardless of domestic regulations or legislation.

Activity

Discuss the ways in which the Single European Market may both constrain or facilitate the development of tourism and leisure in the UK.

Assignment 15
Legal constraints on leisure and tourism development

This assignment develops knowledge and understanding of the following elements:

1.4 Identify sources of income for leisure and tourism facilities

2.1 Report on the health, safety and security arrangements in a facility

2.2 Propose ways of enhancing the health and safety of customers and staff

2.3 Propose ways of enhancing security in leisure and tourism

It supports development of the following core skills:

Communication 3.2

Information Technology 3.3

A small business proposal

You have recently inherited a very large house set in expansive grounds near a small coastal resort area. Although the property is in need of renovation, you feel it has considerable development potential. Tourist activity has been increasing in the resort for the last four years, largely due to an aggressive marketing plan devised and implemented by the local tourism consortium. After careful consideration you decide that the house would make an ideal country hotel. The only immediate problem is the acquisition of funding.

You have a colleague who has access to sufficient funds but he is worried about your lack of business experience. He agrees that the development is a potential profit maker but he is particularly worried about the legal ramifications of the plan. This is an opportunity to impress your colleague with your business acumen, and knowledge of the tourism and leisure industry.

Your tasks

Write a business report to your colleague outlining your proposal. This document must be set out in a professional manner using appropriate language. It must include the following.

1 A plausible outline convincing your associate that the proposal is viable. Figures are not required at this stage but remember that you are attempting to sell your idea.

2 A discussion of which legal form you think the business should take. Give your colleague the pros and cons of each different form and explain why your choice would be the best.

3 Details of what professional advice you would seek before implementing your plan and what you expect to receive from such people.

4 A list of the legal requirements to be addressed in the conversion of a domestic property to a hotel. Include the relevant enforcing bodies you would need to contact before work commences.

5 The name and address of any professional associations you think you should join and the reasons for doing so.

16 Health and safety legislation

What is covered in this chapter

This chapter provides an introduction to fundamental health and safety legislation. It analyses the Health and Safety at Work Act and discusses its main implications for the tourism and leisure industry. It identifies other relevant health and safety legislation, the role of the public sector and the impact of the EC. It shows the specific nature of regulations and their link to Acts of Parliament, and analyses the importance and range of licensing law. It discusses voluntary codes of practice, the role of the British Standards Institute in maintaining health and safety standards, and other sources of information regarding health and safety. It shows the practical measures to be taken to ensure the health, safety and security of staff and customers, and identifies preventative and remedial measures. It looks at the safety audit, the working environment, and the importance of plant and equipment maintenance, storage and handling, including work performed by contractors. It discusses accident and emergency procedures and reporting requirements.

- Health and safety
- Health and Safety at Work Act 1974
- Other health and safety legislation
- Enforcement of health and safety regulations
- Regulations
- Licensing
- Codes of practice
- British Standards

- Further information
- Practical health, safety and security measures
- Preventative and remedial measures
- Communication and training
- The working environment
- Plant and substances
- Building operations
- Accident and emergencies

16.1 Health and safety

> A basic principle of safety management is that accidents are caused and do not just happen. Investigations of accidents reveal that many could have been prevented had someone taken the trouble to inspect and examine the risk potential in the building or facility; followed of course by suitable prompt action. It may only be the repair to a faulty tread on a staircase; correction of a worn mat or uplifted floor tile; or some equally straightforward attention to detail to reduce the numbers of accidents caused by trips and falls.

Source: Sports Council's Recreation Management Facilities Factfile 1, 1994/5: Safety Audits

The above quotation illustrates the concept of individual responsibility. Under common law, each individual is responsible for his or her actions where they affect the health and well-being of others. Any injury or damage caused by negligence may lead to legal action in a civil court.

The main purpose of health and safety legislation is to ensure that preventative action is taken to avoid accidents before they happen. Organizations are compelled by law to adopt and maintain a comprehensive range of measures to ensure the health and safety of any individuals who may be affected by the facilities' operations including:

staff – management, part-time or full-time employees, casual staff, trainees, students undergoing work experience, sub-contractors, casual maintenance or repair staff;
customers – either on the premises or using equipment provided or sold by the facility, paying customers, invited guests, customers hiring the facility or its equipment;
outsiders – neighbours or passers-by who may be affected by activities connected with the facility.

Although these regulations affect all organizations, they are clearly of particular importance to the tourism and leisure industry. This industry relies heavily on part-time and sub-contracted staff. It is also an industry which sells or hires goods and services to its customers. Facilities and events can attract large crowds, and may take place well into the evening or over weekends, thus affecting many non-participants. Staff in the tourism and leisure industry must therefore be aware of the wide extent of their responsibilities under health and safety legislation.

Activity

1 One of the first daily tasks a sports centre duty manager performs is a safety tour of the facility. List three things which should always be checked.
2 How are the occupants of a row of terraced houses adjacent to a Premier League football ground affected by the club's activities? What can the club do to reduce any risk to the health and safety of its neighbours?

16.2 Health and Safety at Work Act 1974

The Health and Safety at Work Act is a crucially important piece of legislation designed to protect and save lives. Under its necessarily complex and wide-ranging terms, everybody – management, staff and customers – is responsible for following its guidelines. Although customers have an obligation to follow procedures and directions, it is management and staff who must take the lead in ensuring health and safety in the workplace. Their main responsibilities are summarized and illustrated in Table 16.1 overleaf.

Customers also have responsibilities under health and safety legislation. Using equipment properly, observing signs and co-operating with staff in the execution of normal or emergency procedures are some examples of these. Whereas misuse of personal leisure equipment such as weights or parachutes could endanger the user's safety, ignoring ground safety supervisors or stewards could endanger large numbers of innocent people.

Table 16.1 Main responsibilities under the Health and Safety at Work Act

Role	Responsibilities
Management	The provision and maintenance of plant, systems and premises in a safe condition
	Ensuring there is no risk to health or safety in the handling, using or storing of articles and substances
	The maintenance of places of work, entries and exits in a safe manner
	The provision and maintenance of a safe working environment, including facilities and arrangements concerned with staff welfare
	Ensuring that all staff are adequately informed, instructed, trained and supervised in workplace health and safety regulations
	The publication of an up-to-date health and safety policy
	Consultation with health and safety representatives
Employees	Considering the health and safety of themselves and others who may be affected by their actions
	Working in co-operation with employers to ensure that the conditions of the Act are fulfilled
	Correctly handling and maintaining plant, fixtures and fittings provided, in the interests of health, safety and welfare
	Reporting any health and safety risks or accidents

Activity ————————————————————————————————

1 Table 16.1 lists seven areas where employers are responsible for health and safety. Select three of these areas. For each one, identify a specific course of action which a leisure and tourism operator might have to take to ensure good health and safety practice. Two examples to guide you are:
   (a) the landlord of a pub with a children's playground must ensure that the equipment is maintained in a safe condition;
   (b) the stewards at a football ground must be trained in crowd control procedures.

2 Liverpool Football Club, one of Britain's best supported clubs, has been at the centre of two tragedies which have profoundly affected the sport in the UK. In 1985 Liverpool played the Italian club Juventus in the final of the European Cup at the Heysel Stadium in Belgium. Eighty-five Juventus fans died when a wall collapsed under the strain of crowd disturbances largely blamed on Liverpool supporters. This was the most serious incident involving the hooligans who have dogged English football, both at home and abroad, for almost two decades. UEFA, the European football governing body, decided enough was enough and banned all English clubs from European competitions for 2 years. This disgrace particularly affected England's bigger clubs causing loss of prestige, revenue and valuable international experience. Football hooliganism has not been eradicated in the UK but has been greatly reduced through costly policing and crowd control measures.

   In 1989 Liverpool were again involved in a major tragedy involving spectators, this time at Sheffield Wednesday's Hillsborough Stadium. Ninety-six Liverpool fans were crushed to death after too many spectators were allowed to enter an area already dangerously overcrowded. On this occasion it was the failure of ground officials and police to control a reasonably well-behaved crowd that resulted in yet another traumatic mishap. Once again the effects are still reverberating around

British football. Premier League clubs for example, are being forced to make their grounds all-seater stadiums under controversial new legislation designed to enhance crowd safety.

Write the introduction for a new set of guidelines intended for all venues attracting large crowds of spectators. Your report should address the following questions:
- Do you think crowd safety is possible without crowd control?
- Who is responsible for crowd safety at football grounds: the government, the clubs, their employees or spectators?

16.3 Other health and safety legislation

The Health and Safety at Work Act 1974 was introduced to link together numerous other pieces of industrial legislation. These had some health and safety implications, but they were broad acts covering many issues or aimed at specific industries. None the less, it is important for tourism and leisure industry managers and employees to be aware of the wide range of legislation which may affect their operations. The list in Table 16.2 below is meant to be a brief guide and is by no means exhaustive:

Table 16.2 Health and safety laws

1956	Hotel Proprietors Act
1957	Occupier's Liability Act
1961	Factories Act
1963	Office, Shops and Railway Premises Act
1964	Licensing Act
1968	Gaming Act
1968	Trades Descriptions Act
1969	Employers' Liability Acts
1969	Theatres Act
1971	Fire Precautions Act
1972	Road Traffic Act
1975	Safety at Sports Grounds Act
1979	Sale of Goods Act
1982	Local Government (Miscellaneous Provisions) Act
1985	Cinema Act
1987	Consumer Protection Act
1987	Fire Safety and Safety at Place of Sport Act
1989	Children Act
1990	Food Safety Act

The above are examples of Acts of Parliament defined by statutory law. Acts are passed either to:
- regulate or control society;
- raise taxes;
- repeal, amend or update previous Acts.

This explains why some Acts have more than one date. Although Acts of Parliament are often about broad issues and principles, many give the government powers to write specific and detailed rules. These are called regulations and are equally enforceable by law.

275

Activity

1 Select **one** of the Acts of Parliament listed above and research its major health and safety provisions.
2 List what you think are the **five** most common accidents at work. What do you think are the most frequent causes of these accidents? Research an official source to discover the real statistics on accidents in the workplace.

EC legislation

EC involvement has had a profound effect on health and safety legislation over the past few years. For example, in early 1993 the Health and Safety at Work Act was revised and expanded to take account of European Community directives. In addition to placing duties on employers to follow health and safety instructions, and report any danger, the Act now requires employers to consult more closely with employees' safety representatives. The revised Act also brought in several complex pieces of regulation including:

- work equipment regulations placing general duties on employers such as ensuring equipment is suitable for the use that is made of it and conforms with EC product safety directives;
- minimum requirements for work equipment are listed, including every type of tool or plant in all types of installation, operation or maintenance;
- new workplace regulations to include location, size, ventilation, cleanliness, comfort and suitability;
- specific regulations dealing with manual handling procedures, personal protective equipment and display screen equipment.

16.4 Enforcement of health and safety legislation

One of the main terms of the Health and Safety at Work Act 1974 was the creation of monitoring and enforcement agencies. The Health and Safety Commission consists of representatives from local authorities, employers and employees. Their main task is to liaise between industry and the Department of Employment over health and safety issues and regulations. Enforcement of the Act is the duty of the Health and Safety Executive whose inspectors have the power to:

- give verbal or written advice;
- issue improvement notices requiring problems to be rectified within a given time;
- issue prohibition notices requiring immediate action before an activity (or even the entire business) can be resumed;
- prosecute for failure to observe the above. A successful prosecution could result in a fine or imprisonment or both.

The Health and Safety Executive has offices based throughout the UK. In addition there are other locally based organizations responsible for enforcing health and safety legislation. Regional fire authorities have fire safety officers who assist local authority licensing officers in enforcing fire precautions legislation. Local authorities also employ environmental health officers and trading standards officers to enforce much of the wide range of legislation identified above. Each of these has enforcement powers similar to Health and Safety Executive inspectors.

Fire-fighting equipment at Luton Airport

Activity

Contact your local authority and ask for any written information on the work of their Public Protection Department (the department with responsibility for health and safety matters may have a number of different titles in different local authorities).

Analyse this information and discuss any activity which is of relevance to the tourism and leisure industry. For example, environmental health officers inspect premises where food is manufactured, cooked, stored or sold. How is this relevant to the tourism and leisure industry?

16.5 Regulations

In addition to health and safety laws, the government also has the power to write detailed regulations which may elaborate on an Act of Parliament. Since regulations are derived from these Acts, they too are binding on the population and are enforceable by law.

The Health and Safety at Work Act is a very broad piece of legislation designed to protect the safety of staff and customers in almost all occupations (domestic or household staff are the only exceptions). It is obvious that such a document could not deal specifically with every hazard or risk likely to occur at work. The real value of the Act is that it forces employers to address safety issues, and thus consult and abide by the detailed regulations that apply. Compliance with a specific regulation thus guarantees compliance with the more general Act.

Consider the issue of noise at work. The Health and Safety at Work Act places a general duty on employers to protect staff and users, which clearly includes protection from excess noise. The Noise at Work Regulations 1989 are much more explicit and actually quantify noise levels at which protective action must be taken. Employers are thus forced to reduce or eliminate high noise levels or, if this is insufficient, to provide ear protection. For example, most staff and users at airports are protected from aircraft noise by noise reduction measures, i.e. the thick walls and windows of the terminal buildings. Ground maintenance staff on the actual aprons need to be closer to the aircraft and thus must use ear protectors.

As with the large number of parliamentary Acts affecting health and safety at work, there are also numerous regulations to be consulted. Full information can be obtained from enforcing agencies such as Health and Safety Executives or local authorities. Table 16.3 lists some health and safety regulations which affect the tourism and leisure industry.

Table 16.3 Health and safety regulations

1992	Management of Health and Safety at Work Regs
1992	Personal Protective Equipment Regs (PPE)
1989	Noise at Work Regs
1980	Safety Signs Regs
1988	Control of Substances Hazardous to Health Regs
1961	Construction (Lifting Operations) Regs
1972	Highly Flammable and Liquified Petroleum Gas Regs
1989	Electricity at Work Regs
1989	Reporting of Injuries, Diseases and Dangerous Occurrence Regs (RIDDOR)
1980	Health and Safety at Work (First Aid) Regs
1974	Protection of Eyes Regs
1970	Food Hygiene (General Regulations)
1989	Health and Safety Information for Employees Regs
1964	Washing Facilities Regs
1989	Health and Safety (Enforcing Authority) Regs
1992	Work Equipment Regs
1992	Manual Handling Regs
1992	Workplace Health, Safety and Welfare Regs
1992	Display Screen Equipment Regs.

(The last six regulations implement European Community Directives on health and safety at work)

Activity

1 Select **one** of the health and safety regulations listed above and research its major provisions.
2 Show how the regulations you have researched particularly affect tourism and leisure activities. An example to guide you is: 'The 1974 Protection of Eyes Regulations would have to be consulted by anyone operating a paint-gun wargame centre because of the danger of projectiles deliberately aimed at competitors' bodies.'

16.6 Licensing

Another example of health and safety regulation in the tourism and leisure industry is the licensing of public events. There is a wide variety of licences applicable to an equally wide range of events, but all are aimed at protecting the physical and moral safety of the public. Operators must meet stringent standards both prior to application and throughout the valid life of the licence. These particularly apply to:

- the suitability of the premises being used;
- adequate management of personnel and customers;
- appropriate fire precautions.

The enforcement of these standards helps to safeguard the physical well-being of facility users. Licence applicants must also ensure that a particular event or facility is only accessible to appropriate sections of the community. For example, licensees who are permitted to serve alcohol must ensure that minors do not breach under-age drinking laws. Any entertainment provided must also be appropriate for all categories of customer.

No single Act of Parliament covers all aspects of licensing law. In fact, any one event may require several licences (see Tables 16.4 and 16.5 on pages 280 and 281). The Sports Council, in its Recreation Management Facilities Factfile 1, 1994/5: Licensing, identifies six key licences.

Public Entertainments Licence – required by anyone providing public entertainment, music or dancing.

Private Entertainments Licence – for private functions if conducted for financial gain.

Indoor Sports Licence – for sporting events (competition or display) to which the public are invited as spectators.

Theatre Licence – for any public performance of a play.

Cinema Licence – for the public screening of films and (under some circumstances) videos and satellite broadcasts.

Justices' Licence – for any event which permits the sale of intoxicating liquor.

Licence details over the door of a public house

Table 16.4 Types of licence

Activity	Licence
Disco	PEL
Roller Disco	PEL
Tea Dance	PEL
Pop Concert	PEL
Classical Recital	PEL
Pay Party	PEL
Pool Party (if music included)	PEL
Theme Evening (with music or dancing)	PEL
Club version of above (If Private Licensing Provision adopted)	PEL
Play	Theatre
Pantomime	Theatre
Ballet	Theatre
Mime	Theatre
Film show	Cinema
Videos	Cinema
Video Juke Box	Cinema
Satellite TV – Test Match or Big Fight (To an audience)	Cinema
BBC/ITV	TV Licence
Boxing Match	ISL
Wrestling Match	ISL
Darts Demonstration	ISL
Snooker Match	ISL
BMX/Skateboard Display	ISL
Swimming Gala	ISL
Synchronised Swimming Display	ISL
Gymnastics	ISL
Aerobic Display	ISl
Sale of Alcohol	Justices Licence
Night Club	Justices Licence/PEL
Bingo (cashprizes)	Justices Licence
Bingo (no cash prizes)	Lotteries & Amusements Act
Casino	Gaming Act
Gaming Machines	see note 1
Raffle (depends on size of prize)	see note 2
Performing Animals – not invertebrates	
Dangerous Wild Animals	see note 3
Tatooist/Ear Piercing	
Acupuncture	

NOTE 1: See Section on Amusement with prizes above

NOTE 2: Depending on its size the raffle may need to be registered with the local authority

NOTE 3: The provider of these services will need to be registered, check that they are

KEY: PEL – Public Entertainment Licence, ISL – Indoor Sports Licence

Source: Sports Council Recreation Management Facilities Factfile 1, 1994/5: Licensing

Table 16.5 Licence application procedures: who to apply to

Public Entertainment Licence Local Government
(Miscellaneous Provisions) Act 1982

Apply to: District Council
Copies to: Police and Fire
Notice Required: 28 days
NOTE: In London the relevant legislation is the Greater London Government Act 1963
administered by London Boroughs and the City of London Corporation

Private Entertainment Licence Private Places of Entertainment
(Licensing) Act 1967

Same as Public Entertainment Licence

Indoor Sports Licence Local Government
(Miscellaneous Provisions) Act 1982
as amended by Fire Safety and
Safety at Places of Sports Act 1967

Same as Public Entertainment Licence

Theatre Licence Theatres Act 1968
Apply to: District Council
Copies to: Police (Not to the Fire Brigade)
Notice Required: 21 days (although 28 days notice has to be given for a renewal)

Cinema Licence Cinemas Act 1985
Apply to: District Council
Copies to: Police and Fire
Notice Required: 28 days

Gaming Licence Gaming Act 1968
Apply to: Justices (supported by a formal consent from the Gaming Board)
Copies to: Local Authority, Police, Fire, Customs & Excise and Public Notices in the
Newspaper

Gaming Machines (For premises which hold a Gaming Licence)
Apply to: Justices
Copy to: Police

Amusement with Prizes i.e. small value slot machines, Lotteries & Amusements
Act 1976

• If for premises covered by a liquor licence
Apply to: Licensing Justices
• If not for licensed premises
Apply to: District Council
No specific requirement to give notice to anyone else

Liquor Licence Licensing Act 1964
Apply to: Justices Clerk
Copies to: Local Authority and Police
Notice Required: 21 days

NOTE: The legislation cited is that applying in England and Wales. In Scotland and Northern Ireland
the same provisions apply but under Acts or Regulations applying only in those countries.

Source: Sports Council Recreation Management Facilities Factfile 1, 1994/5: Licensing

Applications for licences are made to local authority licensing officers. These officers will inspect premises in co-operation with representatives from environmental health, building control, the police and the fire service. These officials will give advice and report their findings to the granting authority who will then assess each application in the light of:

- the character of the applicant;
- the suitability of the property to be used;
- objections from official or unofficial sources (neighbours etc.);
- the impact the event will have on the surrounding area.

The acquisition of a licence does not mean other applicable legislation can be ignored. Failure to abide by any of the Acts or regulations detailed previously could result in the licence being revoked or in the event or facility being closed down. Flaunting licensing laws can result in severe penalties, such as any combination of large fines, imprisonment or the confiscation of profits. In addition, licensees must be aware of any local Acts or local by-laws which will affect particular activities. These are specific regulations written and enforced by local authorities such as metropolitan, county, district or town councils. For example, local trading and street entertainment conditions in Preston are relaxed every 20 years to allow for increased street activity associated with the Preston Guild celebrations.

Activity

1 Why do you think licenses are aimed at '. . . protecting the physical and moral safety of the public'? What is the difference between physical and moral in this context? Give examples of both.
2 Give an example of how a single event may require more than one licence.
3 Recent press reports have indicated that even much loved and seemingly innocuous pets such as ponies may have to be licensed in the future. Conservation officers are said to be limiting the number of ponies allowed into some environmentally sensitive areas in order to protect footpaths and foliage. There may also be tighter controls on the location and erection of stables in an effort to control yet another booming leisure pastime.

Prepare a short speech which a member of Parliament representing a rural constituency intends to make on the subject of the increased popularity of pony ownership. The speech should address the following questions:
- How would licensing horses protect the countryside?
- Who would administer a licensing system for horses?
- What do you think are the advantages and disadvantages of such a system?
- Do you think such a system could be practical and cost effective?

16.7 Codes of practice

Even more detailed and specific than regulations, codes of practice are an important aid to the actual implementation of preventative or remedial health and safety measures. They may take the form of approved codes. In other words, they may be approved by an enforcing body such as the Health and Safety Commission. Observance of such a code may be compulsory and would virtually guarantee compliance with the legislation it is designed to implement. Alternatively, a code of practice could be written voluntarily by organizations or employers to reflect their own interpretation of regulations. This would probably be done where no approved code existed.

A good example of an approved code is the First Aid at Work Approved Code of Practice (**ACOP**) published by the Health and Safety Commission in 1990. This was designed as an aid to the implementation of the Health and Safety (First Aid) Regulations 1981. It contains very explicit instructions for first aid preparedness.

Level of first aid provision – adequate for the numbers of staff and users at any given time. This is particularly important in the tourism and leisure industry because of usage patterns and seasonality.

First aid boxes and kits – explicit contents lists, again dependent on the numbers of people occupying a facility at any given time.

Supplementary equipment – not included in first aid kits but either required or recommended such as stretchers, wheelchairs etc.

First aid room and equipment – the code of practice gives guidelines on room location and layout.

Qualification and number of first aiders – the need for a certain percentage of staff to have the First Aid at Work Certificate, again depending on numbers of staff and users.

Special training for first aiders – relevant to the particular circumstances of an organization such as treatment of drowning victims at pools.

First aid skills – recommendations for basic first aid skills which should be known to all staff such as action to be taken to stop bleeding and mouth to mouth resuscitation.

Recording first aid treatment – by law all accidents or injuries at work must be recorded in an accident book and, in the event of a fatality or a specified major injury, to the appropriate enforcing authority.

Source: Sports Council Recreation Management Facilities Factfile 1, 1994/5: First Aid and Accident/Incident Reporting

Activity

1 Why do you think the level of first aid provision in the tourism and leisure industry is particularly affected by seasonality and usage patterns?
2 Choose any specific tourism or leisure facility and comment on how it would be affected by each of the Sports Council's first aid categories. Here is an example to guide you: 'A theme park in a warm climate may require its first aiders to be particularly aware of treatment for heat exhaustion'.

16.8 British Standards

The British Standards Institute (BSI) is the national standards body in Great Britain, providing minimum standards for materials, equipment and procedures. It is financed by government grants, contributions from industry, and from the sale of testing and quality assurance services. The BSI also represents Britain in Joint European Standards Institution discussions over common European Standards to which Britain is committed.

There are over 12,000 British Standard publications, dealing with minimum standards, testing, quality assurance and export guidance. In addition to quality assurance, these standards have an important safety role, and health and safety enforcement officers expect British Standard criteria to be met wherever they are applicable. In the tourism and leisure industry there are prescribed standards ranging from aquatic sports equipment to tents and toys. Equipment meeting these standards will bear the BS Kitemark or Safety Mark.

BS 5969, for example, concerns outdoor play equipment intended for permanent installation and was registered in 1986. It comes in three parts:

1 **methods of test** – describes testing and acceptance criteria;
2 **specification for construction and performance** – lays down requirements for the construction and use of playground equipment;
3 **codes of practice for installation and maintenance** – includes explicit guidance for siting, installing and maintaining equipment.

BS 5969 applies to equipment used by the public. Thus, any tourism or leisure facility installing such equipment would have to satisfy the local enforcement officer that the BS criteria were being met before, during and after installation.

Permanent play equipment

The advent of the Single European Market has also led to attempts to harmonize standards between member states. Prior to the introduction of the Single European Act, standards varied from country to country causing confusion and restricting trade throughout the Community. A new EC body, the Comité Européenne de Normalization (CEN), was created to overcome this problem. The CEN uses its own mark, the CE, to show that products have met standardized EC requirements. This will gradually replace individual marks, such as the British Standards kitemark, in all member countries.

Activity ————————————————————————————————

1 Visit your local or college library and inspect a copy of the British Standards catalogue. List five British Standards that you think are applicable to the tourism and leisure industry.
2 Compare your list with your colleagues and discuss why you made your choice.

16.9 Further information

Due to the wide range and complexity of health and safety legislation and regulation, obtaining information is clearly a major concern. Employees of enforcement bodies are prime sources of information. The role of an enforcement officer often includes advice and instruction, as well as regulating workplace practices. In addition, the major enforcement bodies also supply numerous publications on both general and specific topics.

The Health and Safety Executive issues a large number of useful documents ranging from free descriptive or advisory leaflets to detailed guidance notes. The Home Office has published the 'Guide to Fire Precautions in Existing Places of Entertainment and Like Premises', essential reading for any facility manager. Many industrial bodies also publish documents relating to health and safety. The Hotel and Catering Training Company booklet 'Health and Safety in Hotels and Catering' is a good example.

In concluding this section, it is important to stress the need to keep up to date on health and safety issues. Government legislation is continually being amended or updated. This in turn means alterations to regulations, codes of practice and other important publications. Great Britain's membership of the EC will also mean changes to domestic laws and practices. Awareness of continually changing legislation and regulation is a major task for management and staff. The implementation of appropriate codes and guidelines is also essential to ensure the safety of all – management, staff and customers.

Activity

You are an environmental health officer from a local authority. The landlord of a large pub in your area has recently written to your department seeking advice. He plans to extend his premises and change the image of his pub. The pub's upstairs accommodation is rarely used by the public so the landlord wants to convert it into a late night club. He plans to extend his opening hours and provide live, loud, heavy metal music. In addition he wants to encourage competitions downstairs in the main bar area and plans to introduce a 'bar-fly' game. He knows he will need planning permission but wants information on any other rules or regulations he must address.

Provide the landlord with an answering letter and an information pack detailing the following:
- any specific regulations he must be aware of;
- other statutory enforcement agencies he must approach;
- details of licensing laws which will affect his plans;
- how he should proceed with his application;
- any further sources of information he should consult;
- your personal recommendations or comments on his plans.

Ensure your reply is business-like and includes copies of any leaflets or other written information that you think may be helpful.

16.10 Practical health, safety and security measures

So far this chapter has concentrated on the legal aspects of health and safety in the tourism and leisure industry. Of course awareness of key legislation and resultant rights and responsibilities is of fundamental importance. However it is also important that managers act on this knowledge on a day-to-day basis. It is not enough for managers to be aware of their responsibilities under the Health and Safety at Work Act. They must make assessments, draw plans and take action to ensure the working environment under their control is as safe as possible.

16.11 Preventative and remedial measures

The first step in understanding safety in a working environment is being able to differentiate between hazards and risks.

A **hazard** is anything with the potential to inflict harm.

A **risk** is the likelihood that the hazard will actually cause harm.

Hazards must be identified after which risks can be assessed and minimized or eliminated. For example fire in a restaurant kitchen is a hazard. The risks to staff and customers can be reduced through the provision and use of fire extinguishers, doors, signs and escapes. They can be further minimized by ensuring adequate staff training in emergency or evacuation procedures.

To identify hazards and minimize risks, management must conduct **safety audits**.

A safety audit is intended to be a systematic and critical examination of a centre, establishment or location. The aim is to reduce the risk potential and at the same time minimize the subsequent loss.

Source: Sports Council Recreation Management Facilities Factfile 1, 1994/5: Safety Audits

Safety audits are major examinations of all physical and operational aspects of a facility. The results would be written in detailed reports followed by monitored action plans. These reports would include recommendations on all safety issues from communication and training to equipment and procedures. So the owners of a restaurant would be required to analyse methodically all safety aspects of their business.

Activity

1 Choose any one leisure and tourism facility, and identify three hazards associated with it. Describe how measures have been taken to minimize risks. For example, water surrounding a swimming pool is a hazard. The risk of injury by slipping is reduced by provision of a non-slip surface around the water's edge.
2 List the main areas you think would be included in a restaurant safety audit. For example, fire precautions have already been mentioned and could be the first item on your list.

16.12 Communication and training

No matter how thorough a safety audit may be, it will only be effective if its findings are properly communicated to staff. Thus, once an action plan has been drawn up, staff must be given instructions in what to do. This could be by means of:

- manuals;
- seminars;

- standing orders on notice-boards;
- communicating through staff representatives.

It is important to remember that communication should be both ways. The action plan can only be monitored, and adjusted if necessary, if information is fed back to management. Communication must also be clear where the public is concerned. Signs, symbols and public-address systems must all be adequate and properly maintained.

Staff training should begin with an appropriate induction period. As with on-going training, health and safety issues should be integrated with other, job-related instruction. Drills and emergency procedures must be practised on a regular basis. Certain qualifications, such as first aid certificates, need to be updated regularly. Often, specific training needs to be conducted to comply with certain Acts or regulations. Staff preparing food for example, need to be trained in proper hygiene procedures to fulfil the conditions of the Food Hygiene Act.

Activity

1 Devise an induction programme designed to introduce a new employee to relevant health and safety issues in a specialized leisure or tourism workplace such as a zoo, caves open to the public, a climbing wall in a leisure centre or a surfing beach.
2 Explain how you would deliver the induction programme and give reasons for the particular methods you have chosen.

16.13 The working environment

Perhaps a simpler way to describe the working environment is to call it 'housekeeping'. A safety audit must take into account the physical and environmental conditions under which staff and customers work or operate. The main areas that need constant attention are listed below.

Cleanliness – the frequency and standard of cleaning will obviously vary from facility to facility but even outdoor areas need to be regularly brushed and cleaned.

Atmosphere – temperatures must be appropriate for the activities being conducted; rooms must be properly ventilated; machines or equipment creating exhaust gases must be properly vented.

Lighting – working areas must be adequately lit for both short and long term safety reasons.

Disturbance – noise must be kept below recommended levels wherever possible. Failing this, insulation or protective equipment must be available. Staff doing particular jobs, such as bus drivers or ride operators, must be protected from distractions.

Personal hygiene – toilet and washing facilities must be adequate for both staff and customer use, regardless of usage patterns. Washing facilities (and training staff to use them) are particularly important for facilities handling food.

Clothing/footwear – including uniforms, must be suitable for the tasks performed. Comfort, temperature, durability, hygiene and protection are all important considerations.

Personal protective equipment – must be supplied where appropriate. Ear protectors, safety goggles, helmets, gloves etc. must be available to staff and customers if necessary.

Activity

1 Draw up your own safety audit checklist or form. Ensure that you include all the areas listed on page 287 and any others that you think may be important.

2 Visit two different types of leisure or tourism facility, for example a sports centre and a library. Investigate how each addresses the main areas listed above. Compare and contrast the two. Use your own safety audit form for note-taking as you tour each facility.

16.14 Plant and substances

The safety audit will also include an examination of the maintenance, storage and safe handling of plant, machinery and equipment. Put simply this means that any item used in the running of a facility must be properly used and looked after. Ensuring that changing room lockers are properly secured can be just as important as regular and thorough inspections of theme park rides. A faulty plug on a till can be just as dangerous as a more obvious hazard such as a broken chair or broken stair rails.

The handling of equipment or substances also needs to be properly assessed. Ensuring that staff lift heavy loads in a safe manner or operate machinery correctly are examples of this. Similarly, the handling and storage of hazardous substances such as cleaning fluid, pesticides, and lubricants, must be done in accordance with **COSHH** (Control of Substances Hazardous to Health) regulations. Ground staff using toxic weed-killers without protection may be at risk. If they have done so because no protective equipment was available then the employer is at fault. If they have neglected to use equipment supplied to them, then both employer and employee may be to blame.

Activity

Contact your local environmental health office or Health and Safety Executive. Ask for a copy of the HSC's COSHH leaflet. Briefly summarize the leaflet in your own words and provide examples of COSHH in action.

16.15 Building operations

Management must also be aware of any building work being carried out within a facility. This includes both major and minor work such as extensions, alterations, or even simple repairs or renovations. Work should only be conducted by qualified personnel with appropriate authorization or supervision. Care must also be taken to protect other staff, facility users or passers-by during such work. Warning signs should be used where appropriate as well as screens or barriers to contain debris, dust and paint. The use of warning signs is important where conditions have changed for whatever reason or for any length of time. For example, a sign indicating routinely wet or polished floors is just as important as signs warning of falling debris.

Most building work will be sub-contracted to professional builders or tradespeople. Yet facility managers will have a responsibility to ensure that work carried out by contracted staff does not contravene the Health and Safety at Work Act. Contractors themselves may also be liable but overall responsibility for health and safety remains with the facility manager. This is particularly important for public sector facility managers who are now compelled, by compulsory competitive tendering (CCT), to use contracted work wherever possible. The same principle, shared responsibility, applies to any form of contracted work including cleaners, service engineers and drivers.

Activity

1 Give three examples of how failing to maintain plant and equipment in a theme park can be hazardous to health.
2 Apart from ground staff, name three other tourism and leisure occupations where dangerous substances may be handled. Suggest basic advice for their safe handling.
3 List five ways in which contracted workers could cause hazards to health and safety in a theatre.

16.16 Accidents and emergencies

The Health and Safety at Work Act stresses the need for preventative measures and 'risk assessment' in order to safeguard the welfare of employees and customers alike. An important part of this process is the analysis of actions taken before, during and after an accident or emergency. Such an analysis would clearly include:

- the provision of signs for guidance or instruction;
- staff preparedness and response;
- accident and emergency procedures;
- equipment for use during and after the emergency;
- reports on the incident to enable remedial action to be identified and implemented.

All guidance or instruction signs must be easily seen, identified, read and be suitable for the task for which they are intended. Thus many signs now include graphic illustrations of emergency procedures to assist those who have difficulty reading or foreign visitors. Although there are many emergency signs, signs for use in case of fire or accidents are of particular importance.

First aid signs must be provided in a statutory form, namely a green background with white cross and writing. These must include information on how to summon assistance and the names of qualified first aiders. Fire safety signs include fire instruction notices, emergency exit signs, fire fighting equipment points and assembly locations. Other emergency signs are often red and illustrated with symbols as well as written instructions. Emergency exit instructions on passenger vehicles and stop buttons on escalators are two examples of emergency signs that are often taken for granted or ignored.

The importance of properly trained staff cannot be over-stressed in an emergency situation. All staff should be trained and drilled in their own particular roles and responsibilities. Given that accidents and emergencies inevitably occur when least expected, this training is essential if action is to be taken effectively and efficiently. Such training should be included in any basic induction exercises and repeated continuously on a random but organized and structured basis.

Training should include the use of emergency equipment such as fire extinguishers and first aid kits. Clearly staff must be aware of the location of such equipment, and have a duty to ensure that it is stored and maintained in a suitable condition. A properly trained staff member should be able to locate and use an appropriate type of fire extinguisher. It needs to be remembered that if this piece of equipment is moved, misused or neglected, the consequences could be tragic. The same principle applies to the treatment of victims after the emergency has been contained or resolved. Failure to maintain or restock a first aid kit for example, could lead to unnecessary suffering or even loss of life, in spite of the efforts of trained first aiders.

Activity

1 List as many warning, emergency or safety signs as you can find. Can you think of any ways in which they could be improved?

2 Find a fire extinguisher information chart and identify which types of extinguisher (colour and contents) are used for:

(a) paper fires;

(b) electrical fires;

(c) chemical fires.

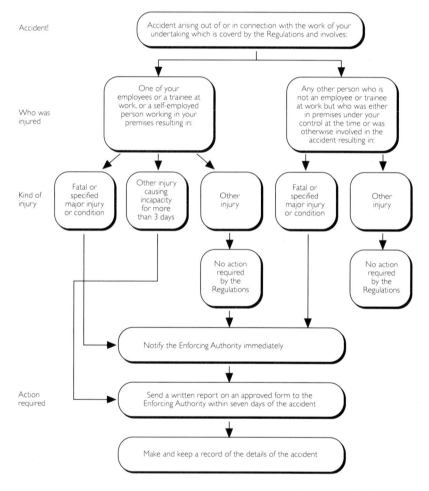

Source: Sports Council Recreation Management Facilities Factfile 1, 1994/5:
First Aid and Accident Reporting Factfile

Figure 16.1 Summary of HSE accident reporting flow-chart under RIDDOR

RIDDOR

Analysis of accidents and incidents is a key step in maintaining health and safety. Much procedural guidance is based on lessons learned from previous events which have been analysed for cause, effect and corrective measures. In fact, this procedure is so important that it has been the subject of legislation to ensure that employers keep appropriate statutory bodies informed. The most important piece of legislation dealing with accident reporting is detailed below.

The Reporting of Injuries, Diseases and Dangerous Occurrences Regulations (RIDDOR) were passed in 1985. They were designed to monitor any incidents named in the title which occur in the workplace. Any such incidents must be notified to an enforcing authority on a pre-printed form, F2508. These authorities, for example the Health and Safety Executive or the local council, then have the right to investigate the incident and take any appropriate action to prevent recurrences. This action could range from advice or cautions to the issue of formal Notices or even prosecution. Figure 16.1 summarizes the application of RIDDOR and is taken from the Sports Council's Recreation Management Facilities Factfile 1, 1994/5: First Aid and Accident/Incident Reporting.

Assignment 16
Health and safety legislation

This assignment develops knowledge and understanding of the following elements:
2.1 Report on the health, safety and security arrangements in a facility
2.2 Propose ways of enhancing the health and safety of customers and staff

It supports development of the following core skills:
Communication 3.2, 3.3, 3.4
Information Technology 3.3

Health and Safety at Work – Staff Briefing

You are the manager of a high street multi-screen cinema with four auditoria, each having its own access to the main foyer and a separate emergency exit. The facility is open 7 days per week, employs up to 12 staff per session and holds a maximum of 500 customers. The cinema caters for a wide range of audiences with Saturday afternoon children's matinees being especially popular. As part of your organization's health and safety policy, you are required to brief your staff on the importance of health and safety in the workplace.

Your tasks

Prepare a ten-minute presentation on health and safety legislation which gives consideration to:

- the importance of health and safety awareness in your cinema;
- the main points behind the Health and Safety at Work Act and their meaning;
- how they are applicable to your organization;
- other relevant safety legislation;
- responsibility for ensuring health and safety at the cinema;
- the consequences of failure to attend to health and safety practices both to the organization and to individuals within the facility.

Remember that this is a presentation so you must use any audio-visual aids you think appropriate to reinforce your message. As your presentation is only of a short duration, supplement it with a fact sheet providing more detailed information on the main points.

17 Rights and responsibilities of employers, employees and consumers

What is covered in this chapter

This chapter opens with a definition of a 'consumer' and a discussion of the nature and background of consumer protection. It examines consumer protection legislation including codes of practice, the main regulatory bodies governing consumer legislation and enforcement procedures, and the role of the EC in protecting consumer rights. It discusses the meaning of rights and responsibilities for employers, employees and customers, and introduces the topic of industrial relations, describing the main groups supporting employers and employees – trade associations, trade unions and professional bodies. It analyses major employment and industrial legislation, and comments on the importance of universal responsibility in organizations.

- Consumers
- Consumer protection
- Regulatory and enforcement bodies
- Roles of the EC
- Rights and responsibilities
- Representative groups
- Industrial legislation
- Universal responsibility

17.1 Consumers

Before discussing consumer protection, it is first useful to clarify the meaning of the word 'consumer'. Consumers are people who purchase goods or services for their own consumption or needs. These purchases are made from individuals or organizations who trade for commercial reasons. It is thus important to note that consumer goods are for personal use only and not goods used as components in a manufacturing or production process. So it is the use to which goods or services are put which determines whether or not they can be classified as consumer items. An individual who buys and eats an ice-cream has purchased a consumer good. A restaurant which buys a drum of ice-cream to make nut sundaes for its customers has not purchased consumer goods. It has bought a component in a manufacturing process. Only consumers are protected by the growing range of consumer legislation.

Consumer goods are tangible items that can be purchased outright or rented for a hire charge, such as a squash racquet or a canoe. Consumer services, on the other hand, are acts of assistance performed by commercial organizations and paid for by the consu-

Table 17.1 Buyers and consumers

Goods (an ice-cream)	Services (a holiday)
Raw materials (milk, sugar etc.) ↓	
Manufacturers (Walls, Mars etc.) ↓	Manufacturers (hotels, airlines etc.) ↓
Wholesalers (cash and carry etc.) ↓	Tour operators (Thomsons, Airtours etc.) ↓
Retailers (shops, vans, caterers etc.) ↓	Travel agents (Lunn Poly, Trading Places etc.) ↓
Customers (the consumer)	Customers (the consumer)

mer. A holiday package is a good example of a service. The tour operator will pre-book and pre-pay for many of the various components which make up the holiday. Ideally the consumer will make only one payment to the operator who will then make all necessary arrangements on his or her behalf. Naturally the operator will charge the consumer for these arrangements by adding a profit margin to the sum of the component costs. The packaging of these various components by the operator constitutes a service.

Any consumer who purchases goods or services is making a contract with the individuals or organizations doing the selling. Many people think of contracts as formal documents, legally binding only if both parties sign in the presence of witnesses. This is a form of contract but by no means the only one. Thus verbal agreements such as ordering meals or buying soft drinks can be just as legally valid as written documents like booking forms or consumer credit agreements. The very act of buying a consumer good or service implies a contract and so invokes the range of consumer protection legislation.

Activity

1. List five organizations in the tourism and leisure industry that provide a service to their customers and five that sell goods.
2. Using Table 17.1 as a guide, trace the distribution chain of one good, and one service relevant to the tourism and leisure industry. At what point does the buyer become the consumer?

17.2 Consumer protection

Chapter 15 briefly defined the different types of laws which apply in Britain (note that Scotland has a different legal structure), namely common, civil, criminal and statute laws. Most of Britain's consumer protection laws come from statute law, that is those laws derived from Acts of Parliament. Successive governments have sought to provide the consumer with protection from commercial organizations whose drive for profits may have led them to deal in an unfair or unsafe manner. Consumers are in particular need of legal assistance where they come into confrontation with rich, powerful or well-organized traders.

Tourists are important customers

For example, a tourist purchasing water resistant sun-tan lotion would expect this product to stay on in the water for a reasonable length of time. If it could be proved that the lotion was not water resistant, then the supplier would have committed a trade description violation. Although the tourist could seek compensation through a civil court, such an action may not be easy against the possible financial might of an established manufacturing company. However, because the supplier would have violated the terms of the Trade Descriptions Act 1969, a prosecution could be launched by a statutory enforcement body such as the Office of Fair Trading.

Consumer legislation has developed considerably over the past few decades and falls into numerous categories. There are Acts of Parliament covering diverse but connected areas ranging from the supply of faulty goods and services to consumer credit regulation. Table 17.2 lists and describes the main pieces of consumer legislation appropriate to the tourism and leisure industry.

Table 17.2 Main legislation protecting consumer rights

Name of legislation	Description	Example
1955 Food and Drugs Act	Sets out rules relating to the quality of food and drugs, and hygiene regulations during preparation and storage.	A hot dog kiosk selling meat that had not been stored at an appropriate temperature is selling food unfit for human consumption.
1963 and 1985 Weights and Measures Acts	Deals with the technicalities of packaging goods, including the testing and inspection of equipment and machinery. The Act also makes it a criminal offence to give short measure, weight or number of goods, either intentionally or accidentally.	'Optics' are the chambers connected to alcoholic spirit bottles in pubs and restaurants, and ensure that each measure of liquid is the same. These can be inspected by trading standards officers and, if found to be faulty, the pub owner can be prosecuted for providing short measures.

Table 17.2 *Continued*

Name of legislation	Description	Example
1967 Misrepresentation Act	Enables consumers to seek compensation in a civil court for any misrepresentation on the part of the seller.	Salespeople cannot make statements of fact about their products which are untrue. If a customer buys a travel kettle because a salesperson states that the element will last over 12 months and this is proved untrue, the Act has been breached.
1968 and 1972 Trade Descriptions Acts	It is a criminal offence for suppliers to falsely describe goods and services, either verbally or in written form.	If a holiday brochure describes a hotel as being 200 yards from the beach, this description must be accurate.
1974 Prices Act	This Act gives the government powers to regulate the display of prices.	Restaurants must display price lists which include VAT and clearly describe any other additional charge such as service fees or corkage.
1974 Consumer Credit Act	Provides a framework for the control of all forms of personal credit dealings.	Credit cards are frequently used for overseas holidays and card users are charged for these credit services. All terms and conditions of use must be clearly and unambiguously stated. In addition credit providers must now calculate interest amounts using the same formula and inclusive of any other charges (Visa and Access charge an annual fee in addition to interest on all balances not paid within a month of the statement date). This all-inclusive formula is called the annualized percentage rate (APR) and allows consumers to compare credit terms regardless of differences in presentation or calculation.
1977 Unfair Contract Terms Act	This Act seeks to protect the consumer from terms imposed by suppliers or manufacturers. In particular the consumer is protected where a supplier seeks to limit its liability through the publication of their own terms and conditions of use.	A warning sign on a white knuckle ride would not necessarily absolve the operator from liability in the event of injury or mishap to a customer. Regardless of warnings or disclaimers, the operator is still liable for personal injury caused by negligence.
1979 Sale of Goods Act	All goods sold or hired must be 'fit for the purpose' for which they were acquired, be of 'merchantable quality' and match their description whether verbal or written.	A tourist who pre-books a hire car from a brochure would expect to receive the category of vehicle chosen. If this category described family estate cars and the tourist was given a 'mini' which breaks down within an hour of delivery, the Act has been violated in all three of its aspects.
1982 Supply of Goods and Services Act	Provides the consumer with similar rights to the Sale of Goods Act but includes the supply of services.	In addition to selling golf supplies at a 'Pro-shop' golf club staff also repair damaged equipment. This is a service and as such must be performed within a reasonable time, and with reasonable care and skill.

Table 17.2 *Continued*

Name of legislation	Description	Example
1987 Consumer Protection Act	A major piece of legislation which seeks to close loopholes by addressing three main areas.	
	1 Product liability attempts to ensure that producers are liable to consumers for their products regardless of the length of the distribution chain.	Even if a major hotel chain purchases and repackages soap with its own wrappers, the original manufacturer is liable for the quality of the product.
	2 Consumer safety is regulated by the Act in areas of product composition, design and manufacture. It is also illegal to sell goods which are known to be unsafe.	The same hotel chain would be liable if it purchased and wrapped a batch of soap knowing that the soap had been rejected on safety grounds
	3 Prices of goods and services must be clearly and fairly displayed so as not to mislead the public.	Retailers must display prices which include VAT or any other charges (such as delivery).

Activity

Each of the above listed Acts cites an example to show the Act's relevance to the tourism and leisure industry. Give at least one more example for each Act.

17.3 Regulatory and enforcement bodies

Public sector

The principal statutory body responsible for monitoring and controlling consumer affairs is the **Office of Fair Trading** (OFT). Established in 1973 from the terms of the Fair Trading Act, it is headed by the Director General of Fair Trading who is responsible to the Secretary of State for Trade. The Office of Fair Trading is divided into three divisions: Consumer Affairs Division; Competition Policy Division; Legal Division.

These combine to perform a variety of consumer protection activities ranging from information collection, analysis and distribution to control of the credit industry. The OFT is also active in encouraging trading organizations to self-regulate through industry-specific codes of practice. For example the ABTA (Association of British Travel Agents) Code of Conduct recommends that sales information should be screened to highlight any examples of false or misleading information. Theoretically this should reduce the number of customer complaints but any problems that still arise should be dealt with in accordance with the Code's published complaints procedure. In cases where these codes prove ineffective or insufficient, the OFT Legal Division is instrumental in bringing legal action against offenders or in recommending new legislation to forestall future violations.

As well as liaising with industry over consumer protection affairs, the OFT deals closely with other statutory and non-statutory bodies. The Monopolies and Mergers Commission (MMC) and the National Consumer Council are two independent public bodies set up by the government to monitor trading activity. The MMC scrutinizes potential company mergers or takeovers and decides whether or not these are in the public's interest. For example, British Airways' recent takeover of Dan-Air was investigated by the MMC to consider whether or not such a takeover would reduce competition and thus adversely affect the consumer.

The National Consumer Council, on the other hand, has no direct say in business dealings. It was established in 1975 to research and campaign on many aspects of consumer affairs. The Council is not directly accessible to the consumer but it does lobby public and private sector organizations to affect policy decision on the consumer's behalf.

Local government also plays an important part in regulating consumer affairs through public protection departments. These offices employ a variety of inspectors such as environmental health officers and trading standards officers. For example, any consumer served sub-standard food in a restaurant could contact their local environmental health office (EHO). An EHO would then investigate the premises and decide if any breach of food safety regulations had taken place. Similarly, any instances of unfair trading practice, such as false advertising or sale of unsuitable goods, could be reported to a local trading standards office.

Private sector

There are numerous private or voluntary organizations concerned with consumer issues. The network of Citizens' Advice Bureaux is staffed largely by volunteers who offer a wide range of initial advice to the public. The Consumers' Association is the trading arm of a registered charity, the Association for Consumer Research. This organization offers totally independent advice and information through its *Which?* guides. The media also represent a forum through which consumer issues can be aired.

Many newspapers and magazines have consumer columns which provide publicity or access to wider sources of advice or information. In addition, popular television programmes such as *Watchdog* and *That's Life* have carried consumer issues to a mass audience and provide the high profile sometimes needed to address safety concerns. Consumers who have specific problems or interests can join or contact one of numerous associations such as the Football Supporters' Association or the Rail Commuters' Association. These provide an on-going forum for exchange of information or advice as well as lobbying industry or government for particular issues. The Football Supporters' Association, for example, is active in attempts to ensure better conditions and value for money for football supporters in England. It was also understandably very active during the enquiry and Royal Commission into the Hillsborough Stadium disaster and represented consumers' views on ground maintenance and supervision.

17.4 The European Community

The advent of the Single European Market at the end of 1992 has united the EC's 12 member states into a single trading block. The removal of trade restrictions and border controls within the Community is designed to ease trade and movement throughout the continent. Naturally this will lead to movement of goods across a wide geographic area and thus may lead to problems where consumer dissatisfaction is concerned. To offset this potential problem, the EC is also active in attempting to guarantee consumer protection.

EC regulations on package travel, holidays and tours are good examples of EC legislation to protect the consumer. Designed to protect tourists travelling on packaged trips, these regulations apply to organizers of trips which include at least two components, such as transport, accommodation or ancillary tourist services. Thus packages are not only 7 or 14-night holidays booked from brochures. Any inclusive arrangements, whether from a tour operator or tailor-made by an organizer, may be subject to these regulations. These regulations provide improved consumer rights for several reasons:

- travellers are entitled to know who is responsible for organizing their travel arrangements. They must be given easily readable contract terms, emergency contact numbers and proof of the organizer's financial security;
- price increases after booking are only allowed under certain strictly defined circumstances;
- if prices are increased or the arrangements are cancelled, customers are entitled to alternate arrangements of equal or higher value, reimbursement where this is not possible or desirable, repayment in full of monies already paid, compensation if the terms of the contract are broken;
- compensation or suitable alternative arrangements must be provided if the services agreed are not supplied;
- any literature used to describe or advertise the arrangements must be easily read and must clearly state price, destination, itinerary, transport type, meal arrangements, deposits, cancellation deadlines and minimum numbers of passengers.

Activity

1 The Department of the Environment is considering a change to current legislation which regulates safety standards in bedsitters. The government is being pressured into changing these protective laws by business interests, keen to reduce paper work and restrictions.

At present, local authorities are responsible for the registering and monitoring of bedsits, to ensure the safety of residents. Local government officers fear that many multiple-occupier buildings are safety hazards and the risk of serious injury or death is considered many times higher than in a family home.

Clearly there may be ramifications for the tourism and leisure industry if these changes take place. If registration schemes for bedsitters are cancelled, it is possible that safety standards in tourist accommodation may also be affected. Hoteliers may also seek a reduction in their 'red-tape' burden in an effort to seek savings in time and money. This may well result in increased profitability but at what cost?

Suppose that these safety standards also applied to bed and breakfast establishments in tourist destinations.

(a) What advantage would business gain from re-examining the registration schemes?

(b) Which consumers are likely to be affected by these proposals?

(c) Compose a letter expressing your concern at these proposals and explaining your reasons for opposing them.

(d) To whom would you send this letter and why?

2 Get hold of a current package tour brochure and examine its contents. Identify where the brochure complies with the EC regulations on package tours. Are there any omissions or ambiguous areas?

17.5 Rights and responsibilities

The rest of this chapter examines more closely the way employees and employers treat each other. This area – industrial relations – is extremely complex and concerns both legislation and regulation. The manner in which management and labour relate to each other is critical to the smooth working of a free enterprise economy such as that of the UK.

Employees are generally concerned with:
- personal job security;
- pay rates;
- promotion prospects;
- hours and conditions of work.

However, many organizations in the leisure and tourism industry face particularly difficult trading conditions such as:
- long opening hours;
- low profit margins;
- seasonality;
- fierce competition.

Owners can therefore be faced with high risks and low returns on their investments. The rights and responsibilities of employers and employees in this industry are thus particularly delicate issues. Clearly, in attempting to achieve their differing aims, some degree of conflict between these groups is probably inevitable. Minimizing or controlling this conflict, either through legislation or through co-operation, is the essence of industrial relations.

Activity

1 Using the last paragraph as a guide, list three rights and three responsibilities which should be available to all employees in the leisure and tourism industry.
2 List three rights and responsibilities which you think should be available to all employers and customers in the leisure and tourism industry.

17.6 Representative groups

There are three main types of groups representing the different interests of employers and employees. These are: employers' or trade associations; trade unions; professional associations.

Employers' or trade associations

These are groups of employers, usually from the same or allied industries, who have joined together to protect their interests. They have several aims and functions including:
- collective negotiation with trade unions over pay and conditions;
- providing other information and advice such as marketing services, legal advice, technical updates;
- acting as a forum for members to meet and discuss relevant issues;
- maintaining a professional image to the public;
- representing the views and needs of the industry to the government.

It is important to understand that membership of these associations is only open to organizations involved in an appropriate industry. Individuals wishing to protect their interests or join together for professional advancement must join either a trade union or a professional body.

The Sports and Allied Industries Federation is a good example of a trade association. Membership of the federation is only open to manufacturers and wholesalers of sports equipment. Members are expected to abide by regulations and maintain standards laid down by the organization. They must conduct their businesses in a professional manner to enhance both their own image and that of the industry as a whole. In addition, members benefit from the exchange of ideas and information, as well as the increased power or influence that collective **lobbying** can bring. This may be particularly important where, for example, proposed government legislation on new safety standards for sports equipment threatens the industry.

Activity

1 List five trade associations connected with the tourism and leisure industry.
2 Choose one of these and investigate the organization more thoroughly. Compile a portfolio and compare your organization's activities with those investigated by other students in your group.
3 Describe possible ways in which proposed government legislation on new safety standards for sports equipment might affect the industry. What actions do you think the Sports and Allied Industries Federation might take if it felt new legislation posed a threat to its future success?

Trade unions

These are made up of groups of workers, usually from allied occupations or industries, who have joined together to protect their interests. Throughout the UK there are over 350 trade unions with a total membership of well over 10 million. Some unions are quite small with fewer than 50 members. Others, such as the largest, UNISON with over 1.5 million members, are very powerful and influential organizations. (UNISON is actually an amalgamation of three large public sector unions – COHSE, NALGO and NUPE.)

The main aim of any trade union is to attempt to ensure that its members are treated fairly by their employers. They do this by involving themselves in almost every area of industrial relations. These include:

wage negotiations – ensuring that wages rise at least in line with inflation and that parity is maintained with other occupations;

working conditions – ensuring that physical and even psychological working environments are safe and suitable;

workers' rights – ensuring employers abide by employment legislation relating to racial and sexual harassment or discrimination, unfair dismissal, equal pay and opportunities, sick leave, holiday entitlement, redundancy pay and maternity rights;

ensuring that correct procedures are carried out regarding discipline, grievance, appraisal, dismissal;

lobbying government and industrial bodies over any major strategic issues which concern their members.

Some would argue that trade unions are not as prominent in the tourism and leisure industry as in others. There may be several reasons for this. Mass tourism, for example, only became recognized as a major industry in the 1970s. The importance of leisure as a specialist area has only really been appreciated since the 1980s. During this time, periods of mass unemployment have somewhat diluted the influence of the unions and have allowed the government to pass legislation limiting union power. This would have particularly influenced new, growth industries in which unions would not have had any historical involvement.

Staff in many tourism and leisure occupations tend to change jobs quite frequently. This may well be because of relatively poor working conditions and hours, but it is also possible that even career-minded staff change jobs regularly because of the breadth of experience such movement gives them. Tourism and leisure organizations also tend to employ large numbers of part-time or temporary staff due to the seasonality of the industry. An industry with such high levels of staff turnover would provide frequent vacancies and opportunities. This in itself would encourage a flexible and mobile workforce – not an ideal climate or breeding ground for trade union activity.

So with such apparent drawbacks as limited union protection; long and unsociable hours; comparatively low wages; split shifts; and seasonal employment, why do people actually work in these industries? There may be several answers. Certainly the mass unemployment mentioned earlier would be a major contributing factor. Married couples with children may find it useful for one parent to work unusual hours. Young, single people may also find they are not too inconvenienced by working conditions associated with the tourism and leisure industries. These conditions may be particularly offset by job satisfaction, promotion prospects, employment 'perks' or even the glamour of being employed in certain occupations. All of these factors may contribute to leisure and tourism employees placing a lower emphasis on trade union membership than is the case in some other industries.

Activity

1 Give three reasons why trade unions are not prominent in the tourism and leisure industries.
2 If wages and conditions can be relatively poor in these industries, why are people still attracted to them?
3 Table 17.3 on page 303 is a list of trade unions connected with the tourism and leisure industry. Contact one of these unions and ask for further information.
4 Discuss how each of these unions is connected to the leisure and tourism industry.

Professional associations

The comparative lack of union activity in the tourism and leisure industry may be offset by the large number of professional associations that serve and support the industry. These are groups of people who combine to support a common interest, occupation or industrial sector. As with employers' associations and trade unions they have several aims and functions, including:
- establishing and monitoring educational standards within the sector;
- using these standards to control entry to both the industry and the association;
- framing codes of conduct and standards of behaviour for members;
- acting as a forum for the exchange of ideas between members;
- acting as a lobby group to further the interests of the association's members.

Table 17.3 Trade unions connected to tourism and leisure

Trade Union	Membership
Association Society of Locomotive Engineers and Firemen	18,685
Association of Cinematograph, Television and Allied Technicians	29,976
Bakers, Food and Allied Workers Union	34,379
British Actors' Equity Association	44,269
British Airline Pilots Association	4,722
Broadcasting and Entertainment Trades Alliance	31,719
Civil and Public Services Association	127,976
Film Artistes Association	2,114
General, Municipal and Boilermakers Union	823,176
National and Local Government Officers' Association	750,562
National Association of Licensed House Managers	11,539
National Union of Civil and Public Servants	115,606
National Union of Marine, Aviation and Shipping Transport Officers	18,459
National Union of Public Employees	604,912
National Union of Railwaymen	103,000
National Union of Seamen	20,308
Transport and General Workers' Union	1,270,776
Transport Salaried Staffs' Association	36,052
United Road Transport Union	20,370
Union of Shop, Distributive and Allied Workers	375,891

Source: Trade Union Handbook, 1992

Another reason why the tourism and leisure industry is so well supported by such associations is the very diverse nature of the industry itself. There are too many associations to list all of them here but the point can be illustrated by naming just a few:

 the Institute of Travel and Tourism (ITT);
 the Tourism Society;
 the Hotel, Catering and Institutional Management Association (HCIMA);
 the Chartered Institute of Transport (CIT);
 the Guild of Guide Lecturers (GGL);
 the Institute of Leisure and Amenity Management (ILAM);
 the Institute of Baths and Recreation Management (IBRM);
 the Institute of Entertainments and Arts Management (IEAM).

Membership of these organizations provides access to information and contacts of value to individuals and industries alike. It is also an indication of an individual's commitment to his or her profession. In addition, most of these associations have provision for low cost student membership. This enables students or trainees to capitalize on an association's services very early in their careers. Figure 17.1 graphically illustrates the relationship between the different types of organizations in the tourism and leisure industry representing employers', employees' and consumers' interests.

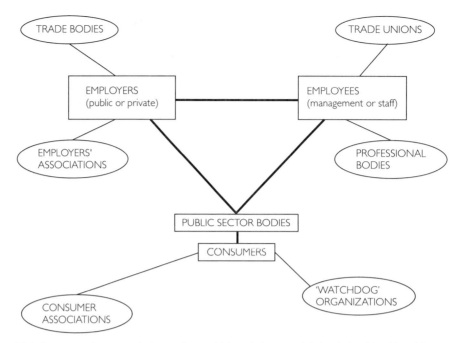

Figure 17.1 *Representative groups in the tourism and leisure industry and their relationship with public sector organizations*

Activity

1 Identify the professional association which serves a sector of the leisure and tourism industry that interests you. Contact the membership secretary of this association and ask for an information pack. (If you are stuck, visit your library and ask for a copy of *Trade Associations and Professional Bodies of the UK*. This contains details of more than 3,600 such bodies throughout the UK.)
2 Give a brief presentation to your class detailing the activities of your chosen body. Include structure, objectives, membership requirements, fees and any other relevant information.

17.7 Industrial legislation

Today the rights and responsibilities of employers and employees are largely regulated by government legislation. Some of this legislation has been brought about by pressure and lobbying from some of the groups already mentioned. Other Acts of Parliament have been influenced by the EC as Britain becomes more reliant on, and integrated with, her European neighbours.

Whatever the cause of these changes, the effects have been to raise working standards and levels of protection afforded to our workforce. Statutory bodies have also been created to ensure that this legislation is enforced and problems or disputes can be resolved. If, as discussed, union influence in the tourism and leisure industry is not as strong as elsewhere, this legislation is of vital importance to the welfare of staff employed in this industry. There are more than 30 Acts of Parliament that affect employers and employees, half of which have been introduced or updated in the last 25 years. Table 17.4 summarizes the most important Acts.

Table 7.14 Industrial legislation – principal Acts

Act of Parliament	Main terms
1963 and 1972 Contracts of Employment Act	All employees must be given a contract of employment within 13 weeks of starting a new job. This document is a primary statement of rights and responsibilites and must include: job title; date of commencement; rate of pay; hours of work; holiday entitlement; sickness entitlement and benefits; dates of payment; pension scheme provisions (if applicable); grievance and discipline procedures; trade union rights; and minimum notice for termination of employment due from either party.
1965 Redundancy Payments Act	All employees who have completed 2 years' service over the age of 18 years are entitled to compensation if they are made redundant. Redundancy means there is no longer any work for the employee, i.e. he or she has been dismissed through no fault of their own. Particularly important in the tourism and leisure industry which has a high number of casual or temporary workers.
1969 Employers Liability (Compulsory Insurance) Act	This Act states that a certificate must be permanently displayed to prove that all employees are insured, by the employers, against industrial injury or disease.
1969 Employers Liability (Defective Equipment) Act	Employers are at fault if any injury or illness is inflicted on employees through defective equipment.
1970 Equal Pay Act, 1984 Equal Pay (Amendment) Regs	Men and women are to be paid the same for doing the same or similar work. These Acts were designed to eliminate sexual discrimination over pay, overtime, bonuses, sickness benefit and holiday entitlement.
1975 and 1978 Employment Protection Acts	Provided the framework for better industrial relations. Employee rights were enhanced to include: short-time or lay-off pay entitlements; improved maternity rights; time off allowed for certain legitimate reasons (e.g. public service); itemized pay-slips; written contracts of employment; an appeals procedure for unfair dismissal. The Act also enabled the formation of ACAS (the Advisory, Conciliation and Arbitration Service). This independent body attempts to improve general industrial relations and to settle industrial disputes. It is used and consulted by collective groups and individuals alike.
1975 and 1986 Sex Discrimination Acts	Following this Act it is now illegal to discriminate on grounds of sex in education, training or employment. This applies equally to job applications and promotion opportunities during service. The Act is enforced by the Equal Opportunities Commission and was updated in 1986 in line with European Community directives
1976 Race Relations Act	It is unlawful to discriminate against anybody because of their ethnic origin, colour, race or nationality. The Commission for Racial Equality was established to enforce this legislation but victims of racial discrimination also have the right of appeal to industrial tribunals and civil courts.
1974 and 1993 Health and Safety at Work Acts	This is a major piece of industrial legislation aimed at protecting the health and safety of employees and public alike.

Activity

Give examples of how each of the above Acts may affect organizations in the tourism and leisure industry. Remember that some of this legislation applies to customers as well as employees. For example, a hotelier was recently fined for refusing to rent a room to a customer because of his race.

17.8 Universal responsibility

This section has been about the rights and responsibilities of employers and employees. Most of the legislation discussed here would appear to be aimed at protecting employees from exploitation by employers. It is important to remember that rights and responsibilities apply to everybody – employers, employees and customers. Customer rights and responsibilities have been dealt with previously. This last section concentrates on how both employers and employees must work together to achieve an organization's goals.

Employers may have invested time, money and hard work to build their businesses. They have a right to expect a reasonable return on these different types of investment. This is particularly so when considering the risks taken to keep the entrepreneurial spirit alive. Without these risk-takers and investors, economies stagnate, industries decline and, most pertinent to employees, unemployment increases. So what should employers fairly expect from their staff ?

Aside from specific skills or aptitudes applicable to specific jobs, an employer would at least expect the right attitude from staff. Without this attitude, productivity, the key to almost any business organization's success, would be poor. Alongside attitude an employer would probably expect commitment and loyalty from the workforce. These in turn would probably encourage good working practices, timekeeping and attendance. Honesty, initiative and co-operation would also contribute greatly to the smooth running and profitability of any organization. Of course these will only be encouraged and achieved by the mutual recognition of each other's motivations and needs.

Assignment 17
Rights and responsibilities of employers, employees and consumers

This assignment develops knowledge and understanding of the following elements:
2.2 Propose ways of enhancing the health and safety of customers and staff
2.3 Propose ways of enhancing security in leisure and tourism
4.3 Plan promotional activities
4.4 Evaluate promotional activities

It supports development of the following core skills:
Communication 3.1, 3.2, 3.3, 3.4
Information Technology 3.3

You work in the legal division of the Office of Fair Trading (OFT). The OFT is planning to launch a new information and education campaign aimed at pre-empting conflict in industry. A range of information leaflets and advisory seminars are to be included in the plan. To ensure that information is relevant and concise, teams have been assigned to produce information for specific industries. You are in charge of the team producing this 'proactive' information for the tourism and leisure industry. The aim of the campaign is to produce information which will reduce the incidence of conflict:

1 between organizations and regulatory bodies;
2 between management and staff;
3 between organizations and consumers.

The department has decided that the best way to achieve these objectives is to produce and deliver information to management and staff working in the tourism and leisure industry. If management and staff in these organizations are aware of their rights and responsibilities, and abide by employment regulations, then conflict should be reduced. Clearly, this policy must include the relationship between the organization and the consumer. If staff treat their customers within the framework of consumer legislation, then cause for complaint from these consumers should also be reduced.

Your tasks

1 Design a leaflet, using layperson's language, outlining the current OFT strategy. Explain what it means and what it hopes to achieve. Your leaflet should include examples from industry to illustrate your point.
2 Produce a series of factsheets aimed at tourism and leisure industry personnel. These should address each of the three aims listed in the assignment scenario. They should include descriptive summaries of:
   (a) consumer rights and responsibilities;
   (b) employee rights and responsibilities;
   (c) employer rights and responsibilities;
   (d) organizations which support these different groups and their activities – these should be both statutory and non-statutory bodies;
   (e) key legislation enforcing these rights.
3 Present your information package to your colleagues, taking the role of an OFT adviser delivering a training seminar to a tourism or leisure organization. Use appropriate material to make your presentation as informative and interesting as possible.

Recommended additional reading

Anderton, D. *Looking at Leisure* (Hodder and Stoughton)
Bull, A. *The Economics of Travel and Tourism* (Pitman)
Burkhart and Medlik *Tourism – Past, Present and Future* (Heinemann)
Burton, R. *Travel Geography* (Pitman)
Cheers and Sampson *The Leisure Environment* (MacMillan)
Colquhoun, M. *The Leisure Environment* (Pitman)
Davidson, R. *Business Tourism* (Pitman)
Davidson, R. *Tourism* (Pitman)
Davidson, R. *Tourism in Europe* (Pitman)
Doggett and O'Mahony *The Leisure Environment* (Stanley Thornes)
Foster, D. *Travel and Tourism Management* (Macmillan)
Holloway and Plant *Marketing for Tourism* (Pitman)
Holloway, C. *The Business of Tourism* (Pitman)
Horner, P. *The Travel Industry in Britain* (Stanley Thornes)
Lavery, P. *Travel and Tourism* (Elm Publications)
Lea, J. *Tourism and Development in the Third World* (Routledge)
Mason, P. *Tourism – Environment and Development Perspectives* (World Wide Fund for Nature)
Medlik, S. *The Dictionary of Travel, Tourism and Hospitality* (Butterworth Heinemann)
Middleton, V. *Marketing in Travel and Tourism* (Heinemann)
Pearce, D. *Tourist Development* (Longman)
Pearce, D. *Tourism Organisations* (Longman)
Ryan, C. *Recreational Tourism* (Routledge)
Sports Council Recreation Management Facilities Factfile 1, 1994/5 (£35)
Tancred, W. & G. *Leisure Management* (Hodder and Stoughton)
Urry, J. *The Tourist Gaze* (Sage Publications)
Ward, J. *Tourism in Action* (Stanley Thornes)

Videos

'Working in Tourism' Department of Employment Training Agency

'Working in Hotels & Catering' c/o Careers and Occupational Information Centre (COIC) Moorfoot, Sheffield S1 4PQ (Tel: 0742 753275)

'Opportunities in Hotels & Catering – A job worth having' Hotel & Catering Training Company, International House, High St, Ealing, London W5 5DB

'Airline and Travel Operations – an insight' TTP, 3 Redman Court, Bell St, Princes Risborough, Bucks HP27 0AA (Tel: 0844 344208)

'The Independent Travellers Guides' (series of tourist destination videos) Video House, 32 Ash St, Fleetwood, Lancs FY7 6TH (Tel: 0253 770510)

Periodicals

Annals of Tourism Research Pergamon Press, quarterly (academic journal)

Caterer and Hotelkeeper weekly from: Reed Business Publishing Group, Oakfield House, Perrymont Rd, Haywards Heath, West Sussex RH16 3DH (Tel: 0622 721666)

Sports and Leisure Sports Council, six per year

Tourism Intelligence Quarterly BTA, London, quarterly

Tourism six per year from The Tourism Society, 26 Chapter St, London SW1P 4ND (Tel: 071 834 0461)

Travel Weekly weekly from: Reed Group/Travel Weekly, 6 Chesterfield Gardens, London W1Y 8DN (Tel: 071 355 1600)

Travel Trade Gazette weekly from: EBIS Ltd, Riverbank House, Angel Lane, Tonbridge, Kent TN9 1SE (Tel: 0732 362666)

Tourism Enterprise monthly from: ETB Publications, 37, St Barnabus St, London SW1 8QB (Tel: 071 730 8253)

Tourism Marketplace ETB, London, monthly

Leisure Management monthly from: Dicestar Ltd, 40 Bancroft Buildings, Hitchin, Herts SG5 1LA (Tel: 0462 431385)

Leisure Opportunities Dicestar Ltd, Hitchin, monthly

Glossary

acculturation the impact of different cultures on each other when they come into contact, either by direct meeting of peoples or through the influence of the media, and the changes which result

à la carte **menu** one where customers pay separately for each item they choose

branding using a name or trade mark to make individual products easy to distinguish from their competitors, and to establish them in the minds of existing and potential customers

break even point the position where a company's sales just cover the total costs of providing a product or service

bonding a financial guarantee, protecting clients and creditors if a company ceases trading

cash flow the flow of actual cash in and out of a business, regardless of how much remains owed or owing

charter flights flights booked, most commonly by tour operators, for a special purpose, such as transporting a group of holidaymakers to a specific destination

commission a percentage payment received from a supplier of goods or services in return for selling these, generally rising as the volume of sales increase, e.g. payment by a tour operator to a travel agent based on the number of the operator's holidays sold by the agent

compulsory competitive tendering (CCT) a requirement of the Local Government Act 1988 setting up a process by which some local authority services, such as leisure provision, have to be defined in a contract for which private companies wishing to manage these services can compete

computer reservations system (CRS) a means of using computer links to read information about, and make bookings of holidays, accommodation, vehicle hire and entertainments

consolidation the practice of combining separate holiday bookings or flight departures into a single trip in order to increase numbers

consumers people who purchase goods or services for their own consumption or needs

consumer audit a survey of the purchasing habits of a representative sample of consumers

Crown classification scheme a voluntary scheme indicating the services and facilities available in hotels

customer service audit a check, carried out by an independent group, which analyses in detail the quality of the service which a specific company is providing to customers

demonstration effect imitation of the behaviour and customs of others, especially the tendency of host communities to copy dress and consumption patterns of tourists

depreciation the falling cash value of equipment over a period of time

direct mail sending promotional material through the post to selected names and addresses

diversification the practice of broadening the range of products or services which a business depends on, or of introducing products into new markets, usually to protect a company in the event of a single product or service running into financial difficulties

domestic tourism residents taking holidays within their own country

economy of scale the ability of large purchasers to save money by negotiating better rates than those placing small orders

excursionist a person spending less than 24 hours in the location which they are visiting

fast food outlet offering inexpensive food in informal circumstances and aiming to serve a high volume of customers, either as a takeaway service or encouraging relatively quick consumption times on the premises

fixed costs items such as rent, rates, heat and light, and administrative expenses - sometimes called **overheads**

fly-drive a holiday arrangement whereby flights and a hire car are provided, with clients able either to follow a set itinerary or to choose their own

franchise a relationship between two companies in which one pays to sell products or services designed by the other, or to use a brand name developed by the other and obtain the marketing benefits associated with using it

incentive schemes schemes offering rewards to successful employees, e.g. gifts, discounts, subsidised travel

induction training training given to new employees, introducing them to a company's policies and practices

industrial heritage sites associated with past industrial development, e.g. mills, mines, factories, many of which are being refurbished as visitor attractions

inflation a progressive increase in the general level of prices, leading to a reduction in buying power and increases in estimated costs of unfinished projects

in-flight catering the preparation, transportation and serving of meals to airline passengers

infrastructure developments needed to support economic expansion, e.g. roads, public transport, telecommunications links, water and power supplies

kitemark a mark placed on goods, indicating that they conform to standards of quality specified by the British Standards Institution

labour intensive business activity which requires a much higher level of expenditure on staff than on materials or equipment, e.g. catering services

leakages revenue derived from tourism which is not retained in the host country but returns to foreign producers, owners and investors

leasing the practice, widely used by airlines to reduce the cost of acquiring new planes or to make fuller use of their existing fleet, of paying to use equipment which remains the property of another company

leisure time available to people after they have completed duties and necessities, like working, going to school or sleeping

lobbying seeking to influence officials of politicians on behalf of an industry or a campaign

long haul requiring a long aeroplane flight, usually in excess of five hours or more than 3000 kilometres away from the point of origin. Shorter journeys may be referred to as **short haul**

marketing the process of finding out what customers want and then developing, promoting and distributing goods and services to them which meet their needs, and which make a profit for the company involved.

marketing mix the factors which a company can vary in trying to achieve its desired level of sales, including the product itself, its price, where it can be obtained and how it is promoted

market research collecting and making use of information to assist in decisions relating to the marketing process

market segmentation a method of dividing potential customers into groups with distinctive characteristics, using criteria like age, gender, income or area of residence

market share the volume of business a company has, expressed as a percentage of the total amount of business conducted in the sector in which it operates

mission statement a brief description of a company's present position and future objectives, intended to create a united purpose among employees

multiples a term often applied to travel agency companies with many separate branches around the country, e.g. Thomas Cook, Lunn Poly

multiplex a leisure facility in which a number of films can be transmitted simultaneously in different auditoriums, sometimes with other leisure facilities incorporated into the complex

multiplier effect the principle that expenditure on one economic activity, such as tourism, has an effect on the turnover of other businesses in the same location

niche market a potential group of customers with very specific characteristics or interests in common

occupancy rates a means of measuring how successfully hotels are performing by calculating the percentage of rooms occupied and whether each of these is a single or double occupancy

package holiday (sometimes referred to as **ITC** or **inclusive tour by charter**) a holiday booking which includes the cost of more than one part of the basic elements of the holiday, i.e. travel, accommodation, food, services, activities

park and ride schemes encouraging visitors to park on the outskirts of cities and continue their journeys into the centre by bus services aimed at reducing traffic congestion

payroll the gross pay of all employees of a company, including all contributions by employer and employee to National Insurance and superannuation schemes

performance targets standards drawn up by a company against which each employee can measure how effectively they are doing their job

portfolio (of products) a range of products, usually at different stages of development

primary data information derived from research commissioned in response to a particular set of questions a company wants answering

product life cycle the process which goods and services go through, generally including their conception, their launch, their establishment in the market and their decline

profit and loss account a statement showing a company's financial performance over a specified period of time

profit margin the percentage of the selling cost not accounted for by any costs

quango a government-funded body appointed to administer or develop areas of public interest or service (Quasi-Autonomous Non-Governmental Organization)

recreation the activities which people take part in during their leisure time

resort representative a person employed by a tour operator to ensure that their clients are given good on-the-spot advice and service in their chosen holiday destination

retail audit a survey measuring the sales volume and price of goods and services in a number of retail outlets

roster a list which assigns named employees to specific duties at particular dates and times

scheduled flight flights which run according to an airline's regular timetable

safety audit an examination of the physical and operational aspects of a facility in order to identify hazards and minimize risks

safety margin the difference between the value of land or property offered as security and the amount of a loan offered on the basis of this security

secondary data information derived from existing sources such as reports, statistics and general market surveys

self-catering accommodation accommodation, such as holiday apartments, where visitors make their own arrangements for providing meals

serviced accommodation accommodation, such as a hotel, where food and service are provided

shuttle service one which runs frequently and in both directions between two locations, generally not too far distant from each other

SWOT analysis a means of assessing a company or a project's overall position by analysing its Strengths, Weaknesses, Opportunities and Threats

table d'hote menu one where a single set price is charged for a combination of courses

timeshares accommodation, usually furnished and serviced, sold to clients for their exclusive use for a specified period each year

travellers' cheque a cheque issued to an individual in one country which can be exchanged by the cheque-holder for local currency in another

variable costs items like materials and labour which change as the volume of business the company is transacting varies

vertical integration where a company seeks to extend its business activities by taking control of other companies in the same line but involved at a different stage of creating or distributing the product

virtual reality recreation facilities which use audio and video technology to create an impression of real, dramatic events

white knuckle ride rides, like the larger roller-coasters, intended to provide thrills by their changes of speed, direction and height

Index